The Jewish Divide Over Israel

The
Jewish Divide
Over Israel

Accusers and Defenders

Edward Alexander
Paul Bogdanor
editors

Transaction Publishers
New Brunswick (U.S.A.) and London (U.K.)

Library of Congress Catalog Number: 2006040366
ISBN: 0-7658-0327-5
Printed in the United States of America

Library of Congress Cataloging-in-Publication Data

The Jewish divide over Israel : accusers and defenders / Edward Alexander, Paul
    Bogdanor, editors.
        p. cm.
    ISBN 0-7658-0327-5
        1. Israel and the diaspora. 2. Jews—United States—Attitudes toward
    Israel. 3. Jews—United States—Intellectual life. 4. Arab-Israeli conflict—
    Foreign public opinion, American. I. Alexander, Edward. II. Bogdanor,
    Paul.

DS132.J49   2006   2006040366

This book is dedicated to the memory of
Lilly Beckett
And the future of
Philip Alexander

Contents

Acknowledgements

For help and suggestions of various kinds we are indebted to: Rebecca Alexander, Adam Bogdanor, Judy Bogdanor, Bruce Borrus, Werner Cohn, Sam Cramer, Gabriel Schoenfeld, Martin Jaffee, Steve Plaut, and Steve Rittenberg,

We gratefully acknowledge the following publications and publishers for permission to use, in whole or in part, previously published material:

Commentary: "Group Memory," by David Roskies. Copyright *Commentary*, reprinted from the September 1999 *Commentary* with permission, all rights reserved.

Judaism: "'No, It's Not Antisemitic': Judith Butler vs. Lawrence Summers," by Edward Alexander. August 2004 American Jewish Congress.

Middle East Quarterly: "Benny Morris' Reign of Error, Revisited," by Efraim Karsh. Spring 2005.

Encounter Books: "Chomsky's War Against Israel," by Paul Bogdanor, from *The Anti-Chomsky Reader*, ed. Peter Collier and David Horowitz.

World Affairs: "Israeli Intellectuals and Israeli Politics," by Edward Alexander. Winter 1997. Copyright World Affairs/The American Peace Society.

Random House: "Afterword by Cynthia Ozick," by Cynthia Ozick, copyright © 2004 by Cynthia Ozick, from *Those Who Forget the Past*, ed. Ron Rosenbaum. Abridgment used by permission of Random House Trade Paperbacks, a division of Random House Inc.

Azure: "George Steiner's Jewish Problem," by Assaf Sagiv. Reprinted with permission from volume 15, Summer 2003.

Society: "Academics Against Israel," by Edward Alexander. November/December 2003.

Introduction

I

"Jewish boys and girls, children of the generation that saw Auschwitz, hate democratic Israel and celebrate as 'revolutionary' the Egyptian dictatorship. Some of them pretend to be indifferent to the anti-Jewish insinuations of the Black Panthers; a few go so far as to collect money for Al Fatah, which pledges to take Tel Aviv. About this, I cannot say more; it is simply too painful."
                                                            —*Irving Howe, 1970.*[1]

Those "Jewish boys and girls" who made Howe's heart sink in 1970 are now, many of them, well-established figures in the academic and journalistic worlds, tigers of wrath who became tenured insurrectionaries or established editors or columnists for the *New Yorker* and *New York Times*. To Howe, who (it should be remembered) was himself not only a lifelong socialist but also a lifelong non-(but not anti-) Zionist, there was something indecent about young Jews, a mere quarter century after the Holocaust, not only acquiescing in but actively supporting a program of politicide against the Jewish state. Three decades later, those same Jews would deride anyone who dared to mention the Holocaust in relation to Israel's constant burden of peril—Thomas Friedman's glib vulgarities about Israel as "Yad Vashem with an Air Force" being the best-known example. Indeed, they would cast Israel itself as the aggressor, pretending (as Friedman himself invariably did) that it was the "occupation" that led to Arab hatred and violence and not Arab hatred and aggression that led to occupation.

Take the case of Professor Joel Beinin. In the late sixties he was an undergraduate at Princeton University, where—so he later claimed—he was "repressed" by the established professoriat, prevented from doing his senior thesis on the post-1948 Palestinian national movement, officially because it was too "modern" a topic, but actually because of his passionately anti-Israel views. "Professors in Princeton's Department of Near Eastern Studies who were critical of Israel," he has alleged, "rarely expressed their views to students." In 1970 he moved from Princeton to Harvard, where he completed an MA, but was rejected for its doctoral program in Middle East Studies—rejected, so he claims, for his expression of pro-Arab views during the Yom Kippur War. And so he moved west to Michigan. There too he was forced to write his thesis about Egypt rather than the Palestinian working class because of his "fear that those who held the then dominant views in the field of Middle Eastern Studies would use their power to... impede the advancement of those with unorthodox views."[2] Not that he was bashful about expressing his anti-Israel and Marxist views. One student of the then young instructor at Ann Arbor recalls the following scene from the early eighties: "One day, at a particular forum, [Beinin] gave what I can only describe as a kind of beer-hall speech. Shouting and pumping his fist, he admonished the Arabs to forget any negotiating with Israel and to stay true to pure radicalism."[3]

Two decades later, Beinin, now a professor of history at Stanford, would become president of the Middle East Studies Association (MESA). He took office in November 2001, a few weeks after the massacres of 9/11. But MESA's official statement about 9/11 avoided using the words "terror," "terrorism," and "terrorists"; it reluctantly admitted that crimes had been committed but opposed the use of force—"misguided retaliation"—against the "criminals." The organization of 2,600 academics now presided over by the once "repressed" Beinin had not planned a single panel on terrorism until after the World Trade Center and Pentagon massacres, which they proceeded—with the full blessing of Beinin himself—to blame on America and Israel.[4]

In his presidential address, Beinin made the obligatory allusion to his childhood study of the Mishnah to establish his Jewish credentials. This—or so he thought—permitted him to allege that all critics of MESA were "neo-conservative true believers with links to the Israeli right" and to attack the president of Harvard University, Lawrence Summers, for posing a "grave threat to academic freedom" by describing the campaign to boycott Israel as antisemitic. He also complained that perpetrators of the killings at Sabra and Shatilla had never been brought to justice, and implied that Ariel Sharon had arranged for the murder of Elie Hobeika, a potential witness against him in the (aborted) show trial of Sharon planned in Belgium. Journalists covering the conference at which Beinin was crowned head of the whole Middle Eastern Studies establishment observed that the professors of Middle East Studies called "terrorism" a racist term, but that if the typical MESA member were forced at gunpoint to offer a definition of terrorism, he would likely reply: "Whatever Israel does."[5]

By December 2004 Beinin, addressing another cadre of academic leftists, declared that "In my view, the state of Israel has already lost any moral justification for its existence." For his uneasiness about sharing the planet with a Jewish state, he gave two reasons, apparently of equal weight. The first was that "Israel oppresses the Palestinians"; the second was that "its claim to represent all Jews throughout the world endangers even Jews who totally reject Zionism or are severe critics of Israeli policies" (i.e., Joel Beinin).[6]

Another of those "Jewish boys and girls" whose hostility to Israel shocked Howe in 1970 was Michael Lerner. In the fall of 1969 Lerner commenced his open battle with what he called "the Jewish establishment" of "fat cats and conformists" in an article entitled "Jewish New Leftism at Berkeley" in *Juda-*

ism magazine. It followed the ancient pattern of blaming Jews for the violence unleashed against them. "Black anti-Semitism," wrote Lerner, "is a tremendous disgrace to Jews; for this is not an anti-Semitism rooted in... hatred of the Christ-killers but rather one rooted in the concrete fact of oppression by Jews of blacks in the ghetto... in part an earned anti-Semitism." Lest antisemites (Jewish as well as gentile) be confused about the location of their rightful targets, he added that "The synagogue as currently established will have to be smashed." As for the anti-Zionism of many young Jews (again, those "boys and girls"), it was "irrational in its conclusions [that Israel should be destroyed]," but "I know it to be correct in its fundamental impulses."[7]

After a short-lived (indeed disastrous) academic career, Lerner turned to left-wing journalism and founded *Tikkun* magazine, which had two declared purposes: one was to pull down *Commentary* magazine, the other "to mend, repair, and transform the world." But what brought him to national prominence was the zeal with which he argued the Palestinian cause within the Jewish community. When the (first) intifada was well on its bloody course it was hard to watch American television or read the American press for very long without becoming aware that Lerner himself had become, if not quite the Jewish establishment, then the omnipresent, gentile-appointed voice of the Jewish community. Nevertheless his anti-establishment rhetoric remained very much what it had been in 1969-70. On February 24, 1989 the *New York Times* afforded him space to hold forth on the way in which the voice of progressive Jews like himself, "the silenced majority" who were "appalled by Israel's brutal repression of the Palestinian uprising," had been "stifled" by the "establishment leadership." Rarely had a stifled voice been heard by so many millions. As he had done in 1969, but now far more absurdly, he adopted the pose of a lonely knight, a sensitive soul sallying forth to confront a mob of thick-skinned conformist louts who would eat him alive if only they could. Here was a rotund beard-plucker of vaguely rabbinic appearance (in later years he would actually become a "rabbi" of sorts) who could always be relied on to blame Israel rather than the Arabs for the absence of peace, and to liken Israeli defense against Palestinian Arab violence in the intifada to "medieval Christian mobs... organizing pogroms against the whole Jewish community."[8]

When the second intifada (otherwise known as "the Oslo War") commenced in 2000, Lerner, long since dislodged from his role as the Clintons' White House Rasputin, again donned the antique robes of biblical prophet and defined his moral purity in opposition to the State of Israel. Yes, he wrote in the *Nation* in May 2002, Palestinian suicide bombings and lynchings and pogroms were "immoral," but Israel was not justified in protecting itself against them because it too was ethically impure: "Israeli treatment of Palestinians has been immoral and outrageous." Besides, Israeli military response to Arab terror was bad for the Jews, in Berkeley and other centers of prophetic morality: it had caused "a frightening upsurge in anti-Semitism."

During the Iraq war he behaved true to form. In October 2005 he invited Cindy Sheehan, the professional grieving mother, to address his congregation in San Francisco on Yom Kippur. Sheehan had for weeks been haranguing President Bush with the antisemitic slogans of the day; "You get Israel out of Palestine"; "my son was killed for a neoconservative agenda to benefit Israel." Once again, Lerner showed how nothing antisemitic is entirely alien to him.

II

Where, one asks, did the Joel Beinins and Michael Lerners and scores just like them come from?

Jewish intellectuals, to an even greater extent than Jews at large, have long assumed that Judaism follows an arrow-straight course from Sinai to liberal and leftist politics. So long as the existence of the State of Israel was in harmony with liberal ideals, it could be supported or at least accepted by the majority of Jewish liberals, especially in the wake of the Holocaust. Prior to the Holocaust, Jewish liberals were deeply divided about Zionism. Lionel Trilling, for example, recalled that he and the other editors of *Menorah Journal*, a precursor of *Commentary*, "were inclined to be skeptical about Zionism and even opposed to it, and during the violence that flared up in 1929 some of us were on principle pro-Arab."[9] But the June 1967 war, or rather its aftermath, required them to choose between liberal pieties and defense of the beleaguered Jewish state. Prior to the war, there were no "occupied territories"; for nineteen years the so-called West Bank had been entirely in the hands of the Arabs, theirs to do with whatever they liked (and what they liked did *not* include an independent Palestinian Arab state). Nevertheless, in the months leading up to the war, the Arabs had vowed to "turn the Mediterranean red with Jewish blood" and Egypt's Nasser had declared that "Israel's existence is itself an aggression." The Arab nations appeared to be, as indeed they were, imperialist and racist aggressors bent on conquering the .02 of the Middle East that they did not control.

But, after suffering a catastrophic defeat, the Arabs showed that their inferiority to the Jews on the battlefield could be overcome by their superiority in the war of ideas. They ceased speaking in English of their desire to reduce Israel to sandy wastes and instead redefined their struggle as the search for a haven for homeless Palestinian Arabs. Ruth Wisse has argued that this transformation of their rhetoric of opposition to Israel from the Right to the Left was a calculated appeal to liberals, not least to Jewish liberals. It shrewdly recognized that Israel's attractiveness to liberals—as a tiny, besieged, socialist country with (very aggressive) labor unions and women's rights—ended with its victory in the Six Day War.[10]

If ideological liberals became unsympathetic to the fate of the Jews in the Middle East because it contradicted their sanguine view of the world, the tenacity of the Arabs' rejection of Israel and their campaign—aggressively and adroitly pursued in the schools and universities, in the churches, in the news media, in the publishing houses, in the professional organizations—to destroy Israel's moral image was bound to cause the mass defection of Jewish liberals too from Israel. For Jewish liberals had the additional motive of seeking to escape from the negative role in which they were being cast by the alleged misdeeds of Israel.

Careful readers of broadsides against Israel by Jewish intellectuals will note the frequency with which they mention the shame and embarrassment endured at cocktail parties or faculty lounges, so much so that they help one to understand the frequency with which Jewish prayer begs that "we shall not be shamed, nor humiliated."[11] Thus Berkeley professor (of history) Martin Jay's notorious essay blaming Ariel Sharon for the rise of the new antisemitism begins as follows: "'No one since Hitler,' my dinner partner [another Jewish academic "proudly identified with his Jewish heritage"] heatedly contended, 'has done as much damage to the Jews as Ariel Sharon.'... This stunning accusation [was] made during a gracious faculty soiree in Princeton... "[12]

One hears from countless Jewish accusers and prosecutors of Israel about how grievously they suffer from—embarrassment. The executive director of a group called Jews for Peace in Palestine and Israel complains that "there are many American Jews who are flat-out embarrassed" by Israeli actions. Jacqueline Rose, "appalled at what the Israeli nation perpetrated in my name" and wishing to live "in a world in which we did not have to be ashamed of shame," hopes to cure her shame-sickness by destroying its cause: Israel. Professor Tony Judt, the subject of Benjamin Balint's essay in this book, is perhaps the most famous victim of this newest entry in the nosology of social diseases. "Today," he writes in his highly publicized essay (in the *New York Review of Books*) calling for an end to Israel, "non-Israeli Jews feel themselves once again exposed to criticism and vulnerable to attack for things they didn't do.... The behavior of a self-described Jewish state affects the way everyone else looks at Jews.... The depressing truth is that Israel today is bad for the Jews."[13] About this astonishing passage (very similar to the aforementioned cry of self-pity from Beinin) Leon Wieseltier has written: "Bad for the Jews! This is the parodic formula for a ludicrous degree of Jewish insecurity, an almost comic infirmity... The behavior of the self-described Jewish state seems to have affected the way everyone else looks at *him*. I detect the scars of dinners and conferences."[14]

In a later essay in the *Nation* (January 2005), Judt expatiated further on the embarrassment factor, especially the great question of how people look or are looked *at*. He exhorted Germans, French, and "others" to "comfortably condemn Israel without an uneasy conscience" so that they "can look their Muslim fellow citizens in the face." While the Jews in Israel worry about suicide bombers, Tony Judt worries about how to conciliate (or perhaps join) their apologists. While the Jews in Israel have for over half a century been forced daily to defend their lives, Jewish intellectuals who have never been called on to defend anything more than a dissertation find sustained exertion on behalf of

Israel too great a burden to bear. And so, by a cruel irony, the Jews who try desperately to evade the (supposed) moral taint of defending harsh Israeli measures of self-defense have found themselves, in this age of suicide bombers, playing the role of accessories to murder, advocates of what David Frum has called "genocidal liberalism,"[15] accomplices of Iran's president Ahmadinejad exhorting the mob to remove "this disgraceful blot [Israel] from the Islamic world."

III

Howe, speculating on the spiritual ancestry of those "Jewish boys and girls" mentioned above, thought that he saw in the anti-Israel vehemence of the Jewish branch of the New Left the pampered suburban descendants of the Jewish anarchists of the 1880s who had ostentatiously eaten ham sandwiches at their Yom Kippur balls; Alvin Rosenfeld's essay in this volume provides a detailed account of the cold indifference of American Jewish intellectuals to the plight of their European brethren during the Holocaust. But both those *fin de siècle* exhibitionists and the "New York (Jewish) Intellectuals" of the thirties and forties were themselves the latest representatives of a long-standing tradition of violent dissociation, brazenly assuming postures of hatred and contempt for their fathers. Such Jewish intellectuals have long played a crucial role in the Jewish world, especially during periods of persecution. Indeed, they have made such large contributions to the theology of religious Jew-hatred and the politics of modern antisemitism that both might fairly be called offspring of the Judeo-Christian tradition, a hideous progeny elaborately traced in Sander Gilman's book, *Jewish Self-Hatred*. At the very end of his book, Gilman suggested the need for a sequel: "One of the most recent forms of Jewish self-hatred is the virulent opposition to the existence of the State of Israel.... The older European form seems no longer to have validity."[16]

Of all the Jewish self-haters portrayed by Gilman, the one most relevant to consideration of the current bumper crop of Jewish enemies of Israel is Karl Marx. Although only a minority of the Jewish prosecutors of Israel discussed in this book are orthodox, unrepentant Marxists, almost all of them identify with the political left and take Karl Marx as an exemplar of wisdom on a large range of issues, including the Jewish one. For that reason alone, Marx's relation to both Judaism and Jewishness is worth recalling. Marx was converted to Lutheranism at age six, a year after his father had joined the Lutheran church. For his mother's tardiness in converting (she did not do so until age 38, when her father, a rabbi, died) as well as for other "despised remnants of [her] Judaic practice," Marx never forgave her. Throughout his career he mocked the "Jewish" character of his various rivals for revolutionary leadership in the Communist and working-class movements. Moses Hess was "Moysi the communist rabbi," Eduard Bernstein, "the little Jew Bernstein." The choicest epithets were reserved for Ferdinand Lassalle (himself a Jewish antisemite of formidable derangement): "It is now completely clear to me," wrote Marx to Engels, "that, as his cranial formation and hair show, he is a descendant of the Negroes who attached themselves to the march of Moses out of Egypt (assuming his mother or grandmother on the paternal side had not crossed with a nigger).… The pushiness of this fellow is also nigger-like." Nor did one have to be a socialist rival to arouse Marx's anti-Jewish spleen: Moses Mendelssohn, he wrote to Engels, was a "shit-windbag"; Polish Jews, the "filthiest of all races."[17] None of which has kept Marx from being drafted (along with the even more vituperative Jewish antisemite Karl Kraus) into the pantheon of Diaspora Jewish all-stars by such accusers of Israel as George Steiner, whose high-minded (and high-mandarin) anti-Israelism is analyzed in Assaf Sagiv's essay.

These accusers play a crucial role in the current upsurge of antisemitism, which is tersely described in Cynthia Ozick's "The Modern Hep! Hep! Hep!" We have not seen the likes of it since the Hitler era. Although most of the antisemitic physical violence in Europe today is the work of cadres drawn from the fifteen to twenty million Muslims now living there, the verbal violence there and in North America is the work primarily of leftists and liberals, of strugglers against racism, of the learned classes. Because such people usually pride themselves on their rejection of anything smacking of racism and prejudice, they must cast the Israelis themselves as the new Nazis in order to make antisemitism, which had (so to speak) been given a bad name by the Holocaust, again "respectable," but under the new name of anti-Zionism. This explains their ubiquitous exploitation of the Israeli-Nazi equation (which originated in British circles in the Middle East as far back as 1941).

The disproportionate influence of Jewish accusers depends in large part on the fact that they demonize Israel precisely as Jews; indeed, since religion and tradition count for little in most of them, it is the demonization of Israel that *makes* them Jews. For them the old wisecrack (first used in a short story by the Israeli writer Haim Hazaz in 1942) that "When a man can no longer be a Jew, he becomes a Zionist" no longer applies; rather they embody a new reality: "When a man can no longer be a Jew, he becomes an anti-Zionist." By declaring themselves in favor of Jewish powerlessness—which according to Steiner, for example, "made us [Jews] the princes of life" as opposed to the Israelis, who torture and humiliate Palestinian Arabs[18]—they announce, with a vanity at once personal and ethnic, both their virtue and their "Jewishness." They have apparently forgotten what the powerlessness of virtue (and the supposed virtue of powerlessness) ended in for European Jewry. The existence of Israel also affords them the opportunity to formulate policy—from the safety of Maryland or Manhattan—for a country in which most of them do not live and whose burdens they do not bear. Martin Krossel's essay shows how Thomas Friedman, that self-appointed diplomat from Chelm, planted in James Baker's brain the idea of publicly asking Prime Minister Shamir to phone him when he really wanted to pursue peace, and later found himself magically in harmony (and collusion) with the potentates of Saudi Arabia over how to solve the Israel problem; and Jacob Neusner's contribution explores the mindset of Jerome Segal and other Jewish "advisers" to the PLO. Moreover, by a colossal irony, the policy formulations of those Jews who themselves contend that Israel should not exist at all invariably rest on the premise that Israel can afford unlimited concessions of territory and easing of security because the Palestinian Arabs recognize Israel's "right to exist."

IV

But what then shall we say of the *Israeli* intellectuals who have turned against their own country? Most of them do not live in Maryland or Manhattan, and it was to them, or at least to their parents and grandparents, that Hazaz's quip applied. *They* do not want to be identified either as Zionists or as Jews, and their fierce diatribes against their own country express a double emptiness. It has been well described by the Israeli novelist Aharon Appelfeld, condescendingly referred to, because of his preoccupation with the Holocaust, as "the Jew" by many of his trendier Israeli literary colleagues:

> Today the Jewish people [in Israel] are waging two existential wars simultaneously. One for the body, against the Arabs, and a second for the soul, against itself. The identification of Judaism with a religion from which people are trying to dissociate themselves is creating a very serious vacuum here. The result is a black hole of identity. That is why there is a deep recoil from everything Jewish. But without some sort of Jewish identity, we will not be able to exist... A society without true roots is a society without a future.[19]

The mindset of Israelis who often outdo their Diaspora counterparts in venomous attacks on Israel, is explored in this book's essay on "Israelis Against Themselves," in part of Alvin Rosenfeld's essay on modern Jewish intellectual failure, and in Efraim Karsh's discussion of Benny Morris, the best-known of the Israeli "new historians." The special contribution of Israeli accusers of Israel to the larger campaign against their country has been their compulsive promotion, with countless variations on the theme, of the Israeli-Nazi equation. The Israeli novelist Aharon Megged observed in an explosive essay of 1994 that this uniquely spiteful (and obscenely licentious) equation was already, *in Israel itself*, the dominant idea of "*thousands* [emphasis added] of articles and reports in the press, hundreds of poems... dozens of documentary and feature films, exhibitions and paintings and photos."[20] Indeed, even Noam Chomsky, in a rare fit of (needless) modesty, in 2003 expressed his indebtedness to the late Israeli philosopher Yeshayahu Leibowitz for this "insight."[21] Megged went still farther in his severe judgment of his fellow writers and thinkers: "Since the Six Day War, and at an increasing pace, we have witnessed a phenomenon which probably has no parallel in history: an emotional and moral identification by the majority of Israel's intelligentsia with people openly committed to our annihilation."

Once the academic boycott of Israel, an attempt by (mostly British) haters of Israel to translate the fifty-seven-year-old Arab economic boycott of Israel into intellectual form, got under way in April 2002, it produced tragicomic episodes of staggering dimensions: Israelis like Oren Yiftachel of Ben-Gurion University, who had for years castigated his own country as blacker than Gehenna and the pit of hell, now hoist on his own petard, or like Ilan Pappe of Haifa University calling for a British boycott of his own university—and himself.[22]

V

To the new antisemitism Jewish progressives are indispensable because they are ever at the ready to declare that what might seem antisemitic to untutored minds is really nothing more than "criticism of Israeli policy." After all, who should know better than Jews whether something is antisemitic or not? Antisemitism-denial (a term coined by Gabriel Schoenfeld)[23] has become the predictable response of Jewish haters of Israel to all of the following: demonization of Israel as the center of the world's evil; calls for its abolition or destruction; economic or academic warfare against it; burning of synagogues or murder of Jews in Istanbul or Buenos Aires; allegations of Jewish control of American foreign policy.

Jewish experts in antisemitism-denial are now omnipresent. A Jewish (also Israeli) Dr. Pangloss named Amitai Etzioni assures the readers of the *Chronicle of Higher Education* that "calls to destroy Israel, or to throw it into the Mediterranean Sea... are not evidence of hatred of Jews" but merely "reflect a quarrel with the State of Israel"; moreover, apart from "the troubling exception of Iran's trial in 2000 of thirteen Jews who supposedly spied for Israel," Jews in Iran have as much religious freedom as Muslims.[24] Another Jewish academic named Andrew Bush breaks new ground in the field of euphemism (at Vassar College) by defining Intifada II, in the course of which Palestinian Arab suicide bombers, pogromists, and lynch mobs slaughtered a thousand people (most of them Israeli Jews) and maimed 10,000 more, as "a critique of Zionism."[25] The most fully articulated example of recent antisemitism-denial—analyzed in detail in this book—is the August 2003 essay in the Israelophobic *London Review of Books* by University of California feminist Judith Butler entitled "No, it's not anti-semitic," a broadside against Harvard University president Lawrence H. Summers for his speech of September 20, 2002 deploring the upsurge of antisemitism in many parts of the globe.

But the gold standard in Jewish antisemitism-denial has been established by Noam Chomsky, not a surprising achievement for the person who previously earned laurels for his collaboration with and support for neo-Nazi Holocaust deniers. "Anti-Semitism," he declared in 2002, "is no longer a problem, fortunately. It's raised, but it's raised because privileged people want to make sure they have total control, not just 98% control. That's why anti-Semitism is becoming an issue."[26] Is it, one wonders, because of such delicate perceptions about the Jews or because of his seething hatred of America that, according to Larissa MacFarquhar of the *New Yorker*, "Wherever he goes, [Chomsky] is sought after by mainstream politicians and the mainstream press, and when he speaks it is to audiences of thousands, sometimes tens of thousands."[27]

As Chomsky's charming observation suggests, the line between antisemitism-denial and antisemitism—the thing itself—is a fine one. Many Jewish prosecutors of Israel resemble medieval apostates who confided to their new Christian co-religionists that Jews made Passover matzohs out of Christian blood, or desecrated the Host, or that the males among them menstruated. They compete successfully with the Alexander Cockburns and Ward Churchills in the extravagance of their accusations. Writers in Lerner's journal *Tikkun* warn of Jewish "conspirators" who run the U.S. government on behalf of "Jewish interests" and—as if this were not explicit enough—refer to "the industrial sized grain of truth" in the *Protocols of the Learned Elders of Zion*, the early twentieth-century tsarist police forgery purporting to describe a meeting held at the founding of the Zionist movement in 1897.[28] The *Protocols* have fueled antisemitic violence for a century. But Jewish endorsement of them is something new. So too is explicit endorsement of violence against Jews by other Jews, exemplified by the *ne plus ultra* of unabashed Jewish antisemitism, Professor Michael Neumann of Trent University in Canada. Speculating, in a 2003 interview, on the best strategy "to help the Palestinians," Neumann proposes the following:

> If an effective strategy means that some truths about the Jews don't have to come to light, I don't care. If an effective strategy means encouraging reasonable anti-Semitism, or reasonable hostility to Jews, I also don't care. If it means encouraging vicious, racist anti-Semitism, or the destruction of the state of Israel, I still don't care.... To regard any shedding of Jewish blood as a world-shattering calamity... is racism, pure and simple; the valuing of one race's blood over all others.[29]

Earlier, in Cockburn's *Counterpunch* of June 4, 2002, he had announced that "we should almost never take anti-Semitism seriously, and maybe we should have some fun with it." Lower than the fun-loving Neumann in this sea of bloodlust it might seem impossible to sink. But wait: there is still Chomsky's acolyte Norman Finkelstein, who thinks "the honorable thing now [December 2001] is to show solidarity with Hezbollah";[30] there is also Jacqueline Rose, who not only regurgitates the standard cliches about Palestinian mass murderers as "people driven to extremes," but rhapsodizes about bonding with Islamist fanatics, lashes out against "those wishing to denigrate suicide bombers and their culture," and declares that "culture" superior to the Jewish culture of a butchered Israeli teenager—Malki Roth—who had addressed a Rosh Hashanah letter to God expressing the hope she would live another year and that the Messiah would arrive.[31] "In the lowest deep," as Milton's Satan observes, "a lower deep."

VI

The solution to their predicament which most of the Jewish "self-haters" studied by Gilman chose was conversion to Christianity. In the modern world, however, the contradiction between liberal pieties and the intellectual defense of Israel is very rarely resolved by apostasy. Two possible (potential) exceptions to this generalization might be the "theological" Israel-haters discussed in this volume: Daniel Boyarin, the Berkeley professor (of Talmud!) treated by Menachem Kellner, and the wandering "liberation theologian," Marc Ellis, whose works are dissected by Alan Mittleman. Boyarin, once an Israeli, now identifies himself as a Jew "destined by fate, psychology, personal history, or whatever, to be drawn to Christianity." Second to nobody in his hatred and denunciation of Israel, Boyarin adds his very own complaint to the endless list of accusations against the Jewish state: "My Judaism may be dying at Nablus, Daheishe, Beteen"—i.e., places that the Israeli army has entered to pursue Muslim fanatics who have massacred Jews. Boyarin seems to threaten to turn Christian if the Israeli government refuses to dance to his tune and return Jews to the subordinate position that he, like Saint Augustine, believes to be their special destiny.[32] Ellis spends Yom Kippur publicly confessing the sins of (other) Jews against Palestinian Arabs in front of a Christian audience at the (Protestant) Union Theological Seminary.

But if conversion to Christianity is no longer, as in Europe it almost always was, required of Jews eager to play a special role as accusers of Jews (as they did in the forced debates of the Middle Ages, for example) the supersessionist Christian worldview nevertheless lurks in the recesses of their brains. The mental universe of Israel's fiercest Jewish accusers is permeated by a messianic utopianism that depicts Israel as the Devil's very own experiment station, the one stumbling block impeding the arrival of a post-national new heaven and new earth, the one nation in the world whose "right to exist" is considered a legitimate subject of debate.[33]

Carlyle used to observe that people can live without heaven, but not without hell or the Devil. For such Jewish demonizers of Israel as the Chomskys, the Finkelsteins, the Ellises, the Butlers, the three Roses of England (Steven and Hilary, originators of the academic boycott of Israeli teachers and researchers, who publicly renounced their "right of return" to a Jewish country, and Jacqueline, author of yet another pseudo-scholarly tract elucidating reasons why Israel ought not to exist)[34] Israel is hell on earth, the lair of Satan. What Paul Berman said in *Terror and Liberalism* about the failure of liberalism's angelic sociology in the face of suicide bombers has been still truer of the prodigious "explainers" in the ranks of Jewish liberals:

> Each new act of murder and suicide testified to how oppressive were the Israelis. Palestinian terror, in this view, was the measure of Israeli guilt. The more grotesque the terror, the deeper the guilt... And even Nazism struck many of Israel's critics as much

too pale an explanation for the horrific nature of Israeli action. For the pathos of suicide terror is limitless, and if Palestinian teenagers were blowing themselves up in acts of random murder, a rational explanation was going to require ever more extreme tropes, beyond even Nazism.[35]

The desperate search for these "extreme tropes" is everywhere evident in the way that Jews who hate Israel exhaust themselves in the attempt to find language adequate to express their visceral loathing. Jacqueline Rose calls Zionism itself "defiled," "demonic," "deadly," "corrupt," responsible for the ruin of Judaism's moral mission to the world (a subject about which she knows and cares exactly nothing) and for much of the misery of the world itself. Butler promotes a petition ("Stop the Wall Immediately") that calls all the citizens of Israel "a people of [concentration] camp wardens." Chomsky would be rendered virtually speechless if deprived of the epithet "Nazi" for Israel; but he is outdone by his late collaborator Israel Shahak and by his chief disciple Norman Finkelstein, the dream-Jews of the world's antisemites. For Finkelstein (like most of Edward Said's Jewish acolytes) not only are the Israelis *worse* than the Nazis,[36] but Jews who do not stand against Israel are morally worse than Germans who did not oppose Hitler: "The Germans could point in extenuation to the severity of penalties for speaking out against the crimes of state. What excuse do *we* have?"[37]

This frenzied rhetoric expresses a utopian messianism (ostensibly secular) that plays an enormous role in Jewish intellectuals' disparagements of Israel. Perhaps its earliest exponent was George Steiner, that distinctly British citizen of the world. Starting in the late sixties, this self-proclaimed wanderer, outsider, *luftmensch*, and exile, offered himself as the embodiment of what a Jew should be—especially if, while constantly discoursing on the fate of the Jews, that Jew refused to learn Hebrew or to read (even in translation) anything written by Yiddish and Hebrew writers on the subject in question. Writing with his characteristic mixture of innocence and corruption, Steiner constantly asked: "Might the Christian West and Islam live more humanely, more at ease with themselves, if the Jewish problem were indeed 'resolved' (that *endlösung* or 'final solution')? Would the sum of obsessive hatred, of pain, in Europe, in the Middle East, tomorrow, it may be, in Argentina, in South Africa, be diminished?"[38] If only Israel and indeed the Jews themselves would disappear, everyone from China to Peru might inhabit Eldorado. In his lucubrations on "the redefinition of culture," Steiner always found it more convenient to locate the cause of Nazism in the psychic damage mankind had inherited from Moses than in certain easily identifiable German and Christian traditions, and more safe to blame the helpless Jewish victims than such formidable institutions as the Vatican and Stalinism, to say nothing of National Socialism itself.

Professor Peter Novick, the subject of David Roskies' essay, became wildly popular (if not quite as much so as Finkelstein) in Germany because he published a book in 1999 deploring American Jews' supposed "obsession" with the

Holocaust, an obsession he blamed—naturally—on Israel and Zionism. The very word "Holocaust," he argued, was an alien import from Israel at the time of the Eichmann trial. The campaign to "vilify" Hannah Arendt for her Eichmann book was also, he says (still more absurdly), orchestrated from Israel.[39] At no point does it occur to Novick, who knows about as much of the inner life of Jews as Jacqueline Rose does, that a European Jewish survivor of the camps might have *wanted* to emigrate to Palestine, or that American Jews might have *instinctively* responded to the trauma of the Yom Kippur War by remembering the Holocaust unless the tentacles of the Zionist propaganda machine had taken possession of their brains. If not for their Zionist-induced Holocaust memories, Novick argues, the American Jewish community would be hard at work feeding the hungry, and so the millions of innocent children round the world would not today be dying of starvation.

Judt, yet another utopian enemy of Israel, does not pretend to worry about the demise of American Jewish liberalism; he is too obsessed with the need to eliminate Israel altogether to bother with such parochial concerns. He merely argues that the problems of the Middle East and by extension of the whole world would be solved by demolishing the Jewish state, which he presents as the sole "anachronism" of "a world that has moved on, a world of individual rights, open frontiers, and international law."[40] Judt is untroubled by anachronism in the strenuous attempt of Israel's Muslim neighbors to restore the world of the eighth century: clitorectomy, jihad, beheadings, murder, torture, dismemberment. It is much easier for him to envision the realization of utopia by the elimination of Israel than by the arduous business of bringing democracy to Arab countries and throwing back the tide of militant Islam.

If, after the Stalin and Hitler revolutions (and *1984* and *Animal Farm*), one needed additional demonstrations that utopianism expresses not love but hatred, the febrile lucubrations of the Steiners, the Judts, and the Novicks about Israel provide them in abundance. And just where does this notion that Jewish collective existence is an obsolete anachronism originate but in Christianity? John Henry Newman, the great figure of Anglo- and then, from 1845, Roman Catholicism, inherited from the first and second century Alexandrian theologians Clement and Origen his assumption that "In the fullness of time... Judaism had come to nought." Newman wrote this in his *Apologia Pro Vita Sua* in 1864, over three thousand years after Judaism was born; Steiner, Judt, and Novick have consigned Israel to the dustheap of history less than sixty years after it was created.

VII

We have selected our subjects not because they are "critics of Israel" or of Israeli policies, but because they either explicitly advocate Israel's removal from the family of nations or else seek to besmirch, vilify, blacken, and delegitimize it so as to render it both morally and politically vulnerable to the onslaught of its (numerous) enemies. Our writers (who range in political allegiance from left to right), so far from insisting that Israel should be immune from criticism for what it does or does not do, argue that even if it did *everything* wrong it would not deserve to be made a pariah nation whose "right to exist" is open to debate, any more than the Jews of Europe deserved to be made a pariah people whose "right to live" was contingent upon the willingness of Germans to share the earth with them.

And just what is this Israel whose erasure promises—to the Steiners and Judts and Chomskys and Finkelsteins and Roses—the best of all possible worlds? Even less extreme figures like Jay take it for granted that Israel is a society that falls far short of the prophetic standards they have established for it, indeed a "failed" society. Of this smug, spiteful, and by now almost fixed epithet, Edward Luttwak wrote in spring of 2004:

> That is an interesting way of describing a state that from 1948 till the present has advanced from poverty to a GDP per capita in the European range, even while its population increased tenfold. Very few states have done better (Ireland, Singapore) and for all their virtues, they would not pretend to compete with Israel in scientific research or overall cultural achievement, however that may be judged. But of course Israel's greatest achievement has been to restore the broken morale of Jews worldwide by winning its wars and battles against all comers—although I do understand that some are repelled by that very thing, seemingly viewing an incapacity to fight, if only to protect oneself from violence, as a positive moral attribute in itself. Such people see great virtue even in plain cowardice. They would no doubt find a weak and defeated and thus nonexistent Israel altogether more attractive.[41]

"Cowardice" is the word that springs to mind most often as the suitable epithet for Israel's Jewish enemies. This is not only because coming to the defense of this tiny and beleaguered nation (or of the Jews themselves) has never been an exercise for the timid, but also because of the abundant accolades these accusatory Jews have received for their *courage* from persons not exactly famous as discerning judges of character. "I deeply sympathize with you," said the late Yasser Arafat to the Jewish "critics" of Israel in 1975, "and with the numerous other Jewish dissenters who have raised their voice with courage and dedication to save the adherents of the Jewish faith from the pitfalls and dangers of Zionism. The heavy price you are all paying for your courageous positions sets you apart as symbols of courage and moral integrity, in a troubled world... "[42] Vying with Arafat in admiration for the "courage" of Jewish enemies of Israel is the American Nazi leader David Duke:

> Unexpectedly, I found that there are a number of Jews who dare to expose the truth about Zionism and Jewish supremacism. A much-persecuted and slandered group, they are just as appalled as I was about the intolerant and hateful strains of Judaism that had arisen in the Jewish community and the Zionist state. They have included Americans such as Alfred Lilienthal, Noam Chomsky, Norman Finkelstein, and a courageous Jew in Israel, the late Dr. Israel Shahak. These scholars have dared to stand up against Jewish intolerance.[43]

We began these reflections with Irving Howe's cry of pain at the spectacle of young Jews wallowing in hatred of Israel. Although a non-Zionist, Howe understood the difference between debating the desirability of a Jewish state a hundred years ago and doing so half a century after the destruction of European Jewry—"the six million"—and the establishment, at tremendous human cost, of a living society of (now) nearly six million people. He was also a man of great moral intelligence and decency, able to recognize, despite deep-seated ideological prejudices, that the foundation of the state of Israel was one of the few redeeming acts of a century of blood and shame, "perhaps the most remarkable assertion a martyred people has ever made."[44]

Notes

1.   "Political Terrorism: Hysteria on the Left," *New York Times Magazine*, April 12, 1970.
2.   Joel Beinin, MESA Presidential Address, November 24, 2001.
3.   Jay Nordlinger, "Impromptus," *National Review Online*, November 20, 2001.
4.   Martin Kramer, "Terrorism? What Terrorism?!" *Wall Street Journal*, November 15, 2001.
5.   See Franklin Foer, "San Francisco Dispatch: Disoriented," *New Republic*, December 3, 2001.
6.   Message sent December 2, 2004 by Joel Beinin to the "alef" (academic left) list (alef@list.haifa.ac.il).
7.   Michael Lerner, "Jewish New Leftism at Berkeley," *Judaism*, Fall 1969, 474-76.
8.   *Moment*, June 1990, 33.
9.   *The Last Decade: Essays and Reviews: 1965-75* (New York: Harcourt Brace Jovanovich, 1979), 11.
10. Ruth R. Wisse, *If I Am Not for Myself... The Liberal Betrayal of the Jews* (New York: Free Press, 1992). On this topic, see also Fiamma Nirenstein's book, *The Liberal Anti-Semites* (Milan: Rizzoli, 1994).
11. Second blessing in the daily prayer book before the morning Shema.
12. Martin Jay, "Ariel Sharon and the Rise of the New Anti-Semitism," *Salmagundi*, Winter-Spring 2003, 12.
13. Jaccqueline Rose, *The Question of Zion* (Princeton, NJ: Princeton University Press, 2005), xvi, 144; Tony Judt, "Israel: The Alternative," *New York Review of Books*, October 23, 2003.
14. "Israel, Palestine, and the Return of the Bi-National Fantasy: What Is Not to be Done," *New Republic*, October 27, 2003.
15. David Frum, "The Alternative," *National Review Online*, October 14, 2003. *Black's Law Dictionary* defines "accessory" as it is used in criminal law:

     Contributing to or aiding in the commission of a crime. One who, without being present at the commission of a felonious offense, becomes guilty of such offense, not as a chief actor, but as a participator, as by command, advice, instigation... either before or after the fact of commission.

16. *Jewish Self-Hatred: Anti-Semitism and the Hidden Language of the Jews* (Baltimore: Johns Hopkins University Press, 1986), 391.
17. Frank E. Manuel, *A Requiem for Karl Marx* (Cambridge, MA: Harvard University Press, 1995), 15.
18. Quoted in Stuart Schoffman, "Mental Borders," *Jerusalem Report*, February 21, 2005.

19. Interview with Ari Shavit, "A Jewish Soul," *Ha'aretz*, February 13, 2004.
20. Aharon Megged, "The Israeli Suicide Drive," *Jerusalem Post International Edition*, July 2, 1994.
21. Quoted in Larissa MacFarquhar, "The Devil's Accountant," *New Yorker*, March 31, 2003, 74.
22. See the discussion of the case of Yiftachel in Edward Alexander, "Hitler's Professors, Arafat's Professors," *Judaism*, Winter/Spring 2003, and Pappe's letter in the *Guardian* of April 20, 2005.
23. *The Return of Anti-Semitism* (San Francisco: Encounter Books, 2004).
24. Amitai Etzioni, "Harsh Lessons in Incivility," *Chronicle of Higher Education*, November 1, 2002.
25. Andrew Bush, "Postzionism and Its Neighbors," *Judaism*, Winter/Spring 2003, 111.
26. Noam Chomsky, Speech to the Scottish Palestine Solidarity Campaign (delivered by live video from MIT), October 11, 2002; published as "Anti-Semitism, Zionism and the Palestinians," *Variant* (a Scottish arts magazine), Winter 2002.
27. "The Devil's Accountant," *New Yorker*, 67.
28. Paul Buhle, "The Civil Liberties Crisis and the Threat of 'Too Much Democracy,'" *Tikkun*, May 2003.
29. See Jonathan Kay, "Trent University's Problem Professor," *National Post*, August 9, 2003.
30. Letter to (Beirut) *Daily Star*, December 2001, posted at http://www.normanfinkelstein.com.
31. "Deadly Embrace," *London Review of Books*, November 4, 2004.
32. "Interrogate My Love," in *Wrestling With Zion*, ed. Tony Kushner and Alisa Solomon (New York: Grove Press, 2003), 198, 202. See also Jay M. Harris, "A Radical Jew," *Commentary*, June 1995.
33. As an example of the perfect ease with which "progressive" Jewish minds take up the question of whether the Jewish state should exist at all, as if it were the most natural question in the world, take Scott Simon, long-time host of National Public Radio, in June 2004, interviewing a strident "critic of Israel" named Richard Ben Cramer: "Is there," asked Simon, "still a need for the state of Israel?" Cramer, author of a book excoriating Israel, thought not.
34. See the discussion of Rose's *The Question of Zion* in Alvin Rosenfeld, "A Poisonous Perspective," *New Leader* (May/June 2005) and Benjamin Balint, "What Zion is Not," *Weekly Standard*, November 14, 2005.
35. *Terror and Liberalism* (New York: W. W. Norton, 2003), 134, 137.
36. "I can't imagine," Finkelstein has said, "why Israel's apologists would be offended by a comparison with the Gestapo. I would think that, for them, it is like Lee Iacocca being told that Chrysler is using Toyota tactics." Quoted in John Dirlik, "Canadian Jewish Organizations Charged with Stifling Campus Debate," *Washington Report on Middle East Affairs*, May/June 1992.
37. *Image and Reality of the Israel-Palestine Conflict* (London: Verso, 1995), 4.
38. *Errata: An Examined Life* (London: Weidenfeld and Nicolson, 1997), 52.
39. *The Holocaust in American Life* (Boston: Houghton Mifflin, 1999), 207.
40. Tony Judt, "Israel: The Alternative," *New York Review of Books,* October 23, 2003. The most thorough demolition of the utopian fantasy that not just the Middle East but the whole world would be at peace if Israel disappeared is Josef Joffe's "A World Without Israel," *Foreign Affairs*, January/February 2005.
41. Letters, *London Review of Books*, March/April 2004.

42.   Public statement of January 31, 1975. See Ruth R. Wisse, "Israel and the Intellectu-
      als: A Failure of Nerve?" *Commentary*, May 1988, 19.
43.   http://www.davidduke.com/index.php?p=148.
44.   *A Margin of Hope* (New York: Harcourt Brace Jovanovich, 1982), 276.

1

The Modern "Hep! Hep! Hep!"

Cynthia Ozick

I

We thought it was finished. The ovens are long cooled, the anti-vermin gas dissipated into purifying clouds, cleansed air, nightmarish fable. The cries of the naked, decades gone, are mute; the bullets splitting throats and breasts and skulls, the human waterfall of bodies tipping over into the wooded ravine at Babi Yar, are no more than tedious footnotes on aging paper. The deportation ledgers, with their scrupulous lists of names of the doomed, what are they now? Museum artifacts. The heaps of eyeglasses and children's shoes, the hills of human hair, lie disintegrating in their display cases, while only a little distance away the visitors' cafeteria bustles and buzzes: sandwiches, Cokes, the waiting tour buses.

We thought it was finished. In the middle of the twentieth century, and surely by the end of it, we thought it was finished, genuinely finished, the bloodlust finally slaked. We thought it was finished, that heads were hanging—the heads of the leaders and schemers on gallows, the heads of the bystanders and onlookers in shame. The Topf company, manufacturer of the ovens, went belatedly out of business, belatedly disgraced and shamed. Out of shame German publishers of Nazi materials concealed and falsified the past. Out of shame Paul de Man, lauded and eminent Yale intellectual, concealed his early Nazi lucubrations. Out of shame Mircea Eliade, lauded and eminent Chicago intellectual, concealed his membership in Romania's Nazi-linked Iron Guard. Out of shame memorials to the murdered rose up. Out of shame synagogues were rebuilt in the ruins of November 9, 1938, the night of fire and pogrom and the smashing of windows. Out of shame those who were hounded like prey and fled for their lives were invited back to their native villages and towns and cities, to be celebrated as successful escapees from the murderous houndings of their native villages and towns and cities. Shame is salubrious: it acknowledges inhumanity, it admits to complicity, it induces remorse. Naïvely,

1

foolishly, stupidly, hopefully, ahistorically, we thought that shame and remorse—worldwide shame, worldwide remorse—would endure. Naïvely, foolishly, stupidly, hopefully, ahistorically, we thought that the cannibal hatred, once quenched, would not soon wake again.

It has awakened.

In "The Modern Hep! Hep! Hep!"—an 1878 essay reflecting on the condition of the Jews—George Eliot noted that it would be "difficult to find a form of bad reasoning about [Jews] which had not been heard in conversation or been admitted to the dignity of print." She was writing in a period politically not unlike our own, Disraeli ascendant in England, Jews prominent in liberal parties both in Germany and France. Yet her title points to something far deadlier than mere "bad reasoning." Hep! was the cry of the Crusaders as they swept through Europe, annihilating one Jewish community after another; it stood for *Hierosolyma est perdita* (Jerusalem is destroyed), and was taken up again by anti-Jewish rioters in Germany in 1819. In this single raging syllable, past and future met, and in her blunt bold enunciation of it, George Eliot was joining bad reasoning— i.e., canard and vilification—to its consequences: violence and murder. The Jews, she wrote, have been "regarded and treated very much as beasts hunted for their skins," and the curse on them, the charge of deicide, "was counted a justification for hindering them from pursuing agriculture and handicrafts; for marking them out as execrable figures by a peculiar dress; for torturing them, spitting at them and pelting them; for taking it as certain that they killed and ate babies, poisoned the wells, and took pains to spread the plague; for putting it to them whether they would be baptized or burned, and not failing to burn and massacre them when they were obstinate; but also for suspecting them of disliking their baptism when they had got it, and then burning them in punishment of their insincerity; finally, for hounding them by tens on tens of thousands from their homes where they had found shelter for centuries, and inflicting on them the horrors of a new exile and a new dispersion. All this to avenge the Savior of mankind, or else to compel these stiff-necked people to acknowledge a Master whose servants showed such beneficent effects of His teaching."

As an antisemitic yelp, Hep! is long out of fashion. In the eleventh century it was already a substitution and a metaphor: Jerusalem meant Jews, and "Jerusalem is destroyed" was, when knighthood was in flower, an incitement to pogrom. Today, the modern Hep! appears in the form of Zionism, Israel, Sharon. And the connection between vilification and the will to undermine and endanger Jewish lives is as vigorous as when the howl of Hep! was new. European and British scholars and academicians, their Latin gone dry, will never cry Hep!; instead they call for the boycott of Israeli scholars and academicians.

II

Current antisemitism, accelerating throughout advanced and sophisticated Europe—albeit under the rubric of anti-Zionism, and masked by the deceptive lingo of human rights—purports to eschew such primitivism. After all, Nazism and Stalinism are universally condemned; anti-Judaism is seen as obscurantist medievalism; the Vatican's theology of deicide was nullified four decades ago; Lutherans, at least in America, vigorously dissociate themselves from their founder's execrations; and whatever the vestiges of Europe's unregenerate (and often Holocaust-denying) Right may think, its vociferous Left would no more depart from deploring the Holocaust than it would be willing to be deprived of its zeal in calumniating the Jewish state. It is easy enough to shed a tear or two for the shed and slandered blood of the Jews of the past; no one will praise Torquemada, or honor Goebbels. But to stand up for truth-telling in the present, in a mythologizing atmosphere of pervasive defamation and fabrication, is not a job for cowards.

In the time of Goebbels, the Big Lie about the Jews was mainly confined to Germany alone; much of the rest of the world saw through it with honest clarity. In our time, the Big Lie (or Big Lies, there are so many) is disseminated everywhere, and not merely by the ignorant, but with malice aforethought by the intellectual classes, the governing elites, the most prestigious elements of the press in all the capitals of Europe, and by the university professors and the diplomats.

The contemporary Big Lie, of course, concerns the Jews of Israel: they are oppressors in the style of the Nazis; they ruthlessly pursue, and perpetuate, "occupation" solely for the sake of domination and humiliation; they purposefully kill children; their military have committed massacres; their government "violates international law"; their nationhood and their sovereignty have no legitimacy; they are intruders and usurpers inhabiting an illicit "entity," and not a people entitled as other peoples are entitled; and so on and so on. Reviving both blood libel and deicide, respectable European journals publish political cartoons showing Prime Minister Sharon devouring babies, and Israeli soldiers bayoneting the infant Jesus.

III

Among the sophists and intellectuals, the tone is subtler. Here it is not Jewish lives that are put in jeopardy so much as it is Jewish sensibility and memory that are humbled and mocked. Pressing political analogies, however apt, are dismissed as "confused" or "odious." When history is invoked, it is said to be for purposes of coarse extortion: Israel is charged, for instance, with "using" the Holocaust as sympathetic coinage to be spent on victimizing others. In a *New York Times Magazine* piece called "How to Talk About Israel," Ian Buruma, alluding to Israel's 1981 bombing of Iraq's nuclear installation, contends that "it might have been justified in many legitimate ways"—but he derides Menachem Begin's appeal to the memory of the one and a half million Jewish children who were annihilated by the applied technology of an earlier barbarous regime.

Is the imagination's capacity to connect worthy of such scorn, or is this how human beings ought to think and feel? Saddam Hussein's nuclear bomb was plainly a present danger to living Israeli children; and conscious of the loss of so many children within the lifetime of a generation, Jewish memory declines to be untender. Nor is the denigration of tenderness a pretty trait in itself, or a sign of rational objectivity. "The politics of the Middle East may be murderous," Buruma comments, "but it is not helpful to see them as an existential battle between good and evil." This suggests a popular contemporary form of liberal zealotry, very nearly the mirror-image of religious fanaticism—a great wash of devotedly obstinate indifference to the moral realities of human behavior and motivation, a willed inability to distinguish one thing from another thing. A switchblade is not a dinner knife; the difference between them is "existential." And "not helpful" is one of those doggedly bland (yet contemptuous) jargonlike therapeutic phrases that reveal a mind in need of a dose of Dostoyevsky. Or of Mark Twain, who understood the real nature of what he dubbed "evil joy."

I would not wish to equate, in any manner or degree, the disparagement of Jewish memory and sensibility with antisemitism, a term that must be reserved for deadlier intentions. Disparagement is that much lighter species of dismissal that is sometimes designated as "social antisemitism," and is essentially a type of snobbery. Snobbery falls well short of lethal hatred—but it conveys more than a touch of insolence, and insolence in a political context can begin to be worrisome; it is, one might say, not helpful.

Judith Butler, identifying herself as a Jew in the *London Review of Books*, makes the claim that linking "Zionism with Jewishness… is adopting the very tactic favored by antisemites." A skilled sophist (one might dare to say solipsist), she tosses those who meticulously chart and expose antisemitism's disguises into the same bin as the antisemites themselves. Having accused Israel of the "dehumanization of Palestinians"; having acknowledged that she was a signatory to a petition opposing "the Israeli occupation, though in my mind it is not nearly strong enough: it did not call for the end of Zionism"; and having acknowledged also that (explicitly) as a Jew she seeks "to widen the rift between the state of Israel and the Jewish people," she writes:

> It will not do to equate Jews with Zionists or Jewishness with Zionism…. It is one thing to oppose Israel in its current form and practices or, indeed, to have critical questions about Zionism itself, but it is quite another to oppose "Jews" or assume that all "Jews" have the same view; that they are all in favor of Israel, identified with Israel, or represented by Israel….

To say that all Jews hold a given view on Israel or are adequately represented by Israel, or, conversely, that the acts of Israel, the state, adequately stand for the acts of all Jews, is to conflate Jews with Israel and, thereby, to commit an antisemitic reduction of Jewishness.

One can surely agree with Butler that not all Jews are "in favor of Israel": she is a dazzling model of one who is not, and she cites, by name, a handful of "post-Zionists" in Israel proper, whom she praises. But her misunderstanding of antisemitism is profound; she theorizes rifts and demarcations, borders and dikes; she is sunk in self-deception. The "good" anti-Zionists, she believes, the ones who speak and write in splendidly cultivated English, will never do her or her fellow Jews any harm; they are not like the guttersnipe antisemites who behave so badly. It is true that she appears to have everything in common with those Western literary intellectuals (e.g., Tom Paulin and the late Edward Said) whose aspirations are indistinguishable from her own: that Israel "in its current form" ought to disappear. Or, as Paulin puts it, "I never believed that Israel had the right to exist at all." Tony Judt, a professor of European history, confirms this baleful view; writing in the *New York Review of Books*, he dismisses the Jewish state as—alone among the nations–"an anachronism."

Yet Butler's unspoken assumption is that consonance, or collusion, with those who would wish away the Jewish state will earn one a standing in the European, if not the global, anti-Zionist world club. To a degree she may be right: the congenial welcome she received in a prestigious British journal confirms it, and she is safe enough, for the nonce, in those rarefied places where, as George Eliot has it (with a word altered), it would be "difficult to find a form of bad reasoning about [Zionism] which had not been heard in conversation or been admitted to the dignity of print." In that company she is at home. There she is among friends.

But George Eliot's Zionist views are notorious; she is partial to Jewish national liberation. A moment, then, for the inventor of the pound of flesh. Here is Cinna, the poet, on his way to Caesar's funeral:

> Citizen: As a friend or an enemy?
> Cinna: As a friend.
> Citizen: Your name, sir, truly.
> Cinna: Truly, my name is Cinna.
> Citizen: Tear him to pieces; he's a conspirator.
> Cinna: I am Cinna the poet, I am Cinna the poet! I am not Cinna the conspirator!
> Citizen: It is no matter, his name's Cinna…. Tear him, tear him! Come, brands, ho! firebrands! Burn all!

And here is Butler, the theorist, on her way to widen the rift between the state of Israel and the Jewish people:

> Citizen: As a friend, or as a Zionist?

Butler: As an anti-Zionist Jew.
Citizen: Tear her to pieces, she's a Jew.
Butler: I am Butler the anti-Zionist, I am Butler the anti-Zionist! I am not Butler the Zionist!

What's in a name? Ah, the curse of mistaken identity. How many politically conforming Jews will suffer from it, even as they toil to distance themselves from the others, those benighted Jews who admit to being "in favor of Israel"? As for that nobly desired rift, one can rely on Hep! to close it. To comprehend this is to comprehend antisemitism at its root. And to assert, as Butler does, that in the heart of this understanding lurks "the very tactic favored by antisemites" is not merely sophistry; not merely illusion; but simple stupidity, of a kind only the most subtle intellectuals are capable of.

The melancholy encounter with antisemitism is not, after all, coequal with Jewish history; the history of oppression belongs to the culture of the oppressors. The long, long Jewish narrative is in reality a procession of ideas and ideals, of ethical legislation and ethical striving, of the study of books and the making of books. It is not a chronicle of victimhood, despite the centuries of travail, and despite the corruptions of the hour, when the vocabulary of human rights is too often turned ubiquitously on its head. So contaminated have the most treasured humanist words become, that when one happens on a mass of placards emblazoned with "peace," "justice," and the like, one can see almost at once what is afoot—a collection of so-called anti-globalization rioters declaiming defamation of Israel, or an anti-Zionist campus demonstration (not always peaceful), or any anti-Zionist herd of lockstep radicals, such as ANSWER, or the self-proclaimed International Parliament of Writers, or the International Solidarity Movement, which (in the name of human rights) shields terrorists. Or even persons who are distinguished and upright. Rabbi Abraham Joshua Heschel, who marched at Selma, and who was impassioned in protesting the Vietnam War, appealed to his peace-and-justice colleagues to sign a declaration condemning the massacre of Israeli athletes by Palestinian terrorists at the 1972 Olympics. Too many refused.

It is long past time (pace Buruma, pace Butler) when the duplicitous "rift" between anti-Zionism and antisemitism can be logically sustained. Whether in its secular or religious expression, Zionism is, in essence, the modern flowering of a vast series of diverse intellectual and pietistic movements, all of them steeped in the yearning for human dignity—symbolized by the Exodus from slavery—that has characterized Jewish civilization for millennia. Contempt and defamation from without have sometimes infiltrated the abject psyches of defeatist Jews, who then begin to judge themselves according to the prevailing canards. Such Jews certainly are not what is commonly called self-haters, since they are motivated by the preening self-love that congratulates itself on always "seeing the other side." Not self-haters, no; low moral cowards, rather, often trailing uplifting slogans.

2

Modern Jewish Intellectual Failure:
A Brief History

Alvin Rosenfeld

"It snows history, which means what happens to somebody starts in a web of events outside the personal.... We're all in history, that's sure, but some are more than others, Jews more than some. If it snows not everybody is out in it getting wet. He had been doused. He had to his painful surprise stepped into history more deeply than others.... Why he would never know.... It was, you could say, history's doing."
—*Bernard Malamud,* The Fixer

In the twentieth century, "history's doings" with the Jews were massive and radically and permanently redefined the nature of Jewish life. The Nazi campaign of persecutions and mass murder of the 1930s and 1940s destroyed a third of the Jewish people and decimated the biological, cultural, and religious centers of European Jewish civilization. Then, with the creation of the state of Israel a mere three years after the end of this catastrophe, Jews reclaimed an independent national existence for the first time in millennia and reassumed political sovereignty in their ancestral homeland. We live in the aftermath of these transforming developments, whose consequences continue to reverberate decades later and significantly influence how Jews think and conduct their individual and communal lives.

Both events, the Shoah and the founding of Israel, took place in areas geographically distant from the United States, yet Jews in America were aware of them and responded, or failed to respond, in ways that are telling. What Jews did then and do or keep from doing today, at a time when antisemitism has reasserted itself and the state of Israel remains embattled and far from secure, says a lot about who American Jews are and what is most important to them in a collective, as well as a personal, sense.

This essay examines some of these responses, especially among American Jewish intellectuals and others with a prominent voice in the public sphere (as an extension of these reflections, some contemporary Israeli voices will also be presented). Of necessity, it does so selectively and without any claim to being

7

a systematic or comprehensive study of its subject. The chief focus will be on how some prominent figures in American cultural and intellectual life reacted to what was happening to the Jews of Europe and Palestine in the 1930s and 1940s and how some of their successors regard the present moment in Jewish life, which is a complex and, in some ways, sharply polarizing one, marked by a high degree of individual comfort, prosperity, and success, on the one hand, and, on the other, by more than a healthy dose of collective anxiety and perceived peril.

While I happily acknowledge the enormous accomplishments of American Jews and see their current place in this country as stable and secure, the emphasis in the pages that follow will be on failure rather than success—on historical misperceptions, political miscalculations, intellectual compromises, weak and often faulty moral judgments. I stress the negative not because I believe there have been no Jews in America who have responded to moments of critical historical importance in exemplary ways—fortunately there have been and still are such people—but because when the stakes are so high, it may be more important to recognize why some people are more able than others to read events accurately and respond appropriately. In the 1930s and 1940s, the stakes were exceptionally high and, in retrospect, it is evident that too many Jews did not measure up to them well. History never quite duplicates itself, and today's circumstances do not, in fact, closely resemble those of several decades ago. And yet serious challenges once again face the Jews, and they need to be responded to in clear-headed and resolute ways. Because it is imperative that we try to avoid the errors of the past, I offer some limited exposure to them here in the hope that we can learn from them rather than repeat them.

I

In November 2003, the famed Greek composer, Mikis Theodorakis, used the occasion of a public address in Athens about the accomplishments of Greek culture to denounce the Jews and deride Judaism. Among other extravagantly abusive charges, he leveled this one: "Today it is possible to say that this small nation is at the root of evil. It is full of self-importance and evil stubbornness." Needless to say, there were Jews who did not appreciate his words and were quick to condemn them. Theodorakis was surprised by their reaction (why is anybody's guess) and upset that his characterizations of the Jews as implicated in evil were "misunderstood" as being antisemitic. After all, as he stated in his defense, he is the composer of the "Ballad of Mauthausen," a moving elegiac tribute to the Jewish victims of Hitler. In Theodorakis's view, this strongly felt work should demonstrate once and for all that he is a friend and not an enemy of the Jews. He knows of their pain during World War II and wants it known that his solidarity with them over their suffering is sincere. Yet, like numerous others, Theodorakis has a harder time relating to Jews who are not on the receiving end of history's blows but have become independent shapers of their own fate. Such Jews, and especially those who exercise military power to support the interests of a nation-state, do not fit his moral paradigm. And so he denounced them; and, when they took him to task for his reckless charges, he complained angrily of being maligned by the very people he professes to admire.

The incident evidently remained with Theodorakis, and a year later, when much of the world's press was focused on the 2004 Olympic games in Athens, he invited Ari Shavit, a prominent writer with the Israeli newspaper *Ha'aretz*, for four days of discussion about the Jews and his complex relationship with them. Shavit's report of his lengthy interview, published under the title "The Jewish Problem, According to Theodorakis" (*Ha'aretz*, August 27, 2004), is a remarkable document for many reasons. Like almost no other public testament by a contemporary cultural figure of any significance, the interview encapsulates in a short space virtually the entire history of antisemitism. Ostensibly speaking to clarify, if not make amends for, his earlier outrageous remarks about the Jews, Theodorakis ends up extending and amplifying his noxious views and, in so doing, very likely carries his already strained relationship with them beyond the point of repair.

The Jews, says Theodorakis, are "masochistic" and "want to feel [like] victims." Moreover, they are "sly," and by turning their sense of victimhood to advantage they feel entitled, "psychologically but also politically," to "do whatever they want." And what is it they want? To dominate and control. They achieve these ends by sticking together and "pulling strings to help one another progress." They are also "fanatic" and employ their fanaticism as part of "their self-defense." Self-defense against what? "Antisemitism," they say, but Theodorakis assures them, "There is no Jewish problem in Europe today. There is no antisemitism"—this at a time when Jews and Jewish institutions have been repeatedly attacked in countries across Europe. A gifted people, they are nevertheless untrustworthy and unloyal to the nations in which they reside. Thus, while large numbers of the Jews who live in France can "speak the French language perfectly" and "succeed in their work," "they are not French. They always think of going back to Jerusalem." Jews are also "arrogant and aggressive" and "hold world finance in their hands... This gives them a feeling of superiority." They dominate in the cultural sphere as well and "control most of the big symphonic orchestras in the world." That is why, Theodorakis indignantly insists, "I cannot work with any great orchestras. They refuse me." Nor does their power stop there: "The international Jewish community... appears to control the big banks. And often the governments... And certainly the mass media." George Bush is beholden to them, and "the war in Iraq and the aggressive attitude toward Iran is greatly influenced by the Israeli secret services." Israel itself, controlled by a leader who "is going to lead the Jews just as Hitler led the Germans," "is very much connected with Nazism," and Israeli behavior is "similar to Nazi behavior."

The interview continues in this extreme accusatory mode, touching on the "superiority complex" that Judaism's notion of chosenness fosters among the Jews: "The whole Bible wants to prove that God loves only one people, and that is the Jewish people." Theodorakis then alludes to the fact that "Christ was Jewish. But the Jewish people for some reason are against a Jew that all the others love... I don't know why you are against the love of Jesus." Continuing in this vein, he acknowledges a family line of suspicion of and revulsion towards the Jews, mentioning his pious grandmother, who told him as a young boy that the Jews "were the ones that crucified Christ" and warned him not to go to the Jewish quarter during Easter because, during that holiday period, "the Jews put Christian boys in a barrel with knives inside. Afterward they drink their blood."

As these wild indictments of the Jews demonstrate—and many more like them could be cited—Theodorakis employs virtually the whole repertoire of antisemitic clichés; and, let us recall, he does so in a conversation with an Israeli, whom he evidently takes to be a representative of the Jews at large. He begins his interview with Shavit by declaring he was hurt by the Jewish reaction to his earlier words—"It was not a civilized reaction"— and concludes by stating he would now like a reconciliation with the Jews: "It would be tragic for me to remain an enemy of your people. It is unjust. It is very, very unjust. I am a true friend of the Jewish people."

It is an astonishing performance—as revelatory of the personal and ideological passions that fuel much of present-day antisemitism among European intellectuals as anything that has been published to date. And the response evoked in Ari Shavit by the confessions of this "true friend of the Jewish people" is itself revealing. Time and again, Theodorakis's Israeli interlocutor seems stunned by what he is hearing; and, no doubt sensing that his conversation partner is effectively exposing himself through his own words, Shavit feels no need to comment critically on his outlandish pronouncements.

However, once the interview is over, Shavit adds some remarks of his own about Theodorakis. Among other things, he notes that the Greek composer is sometimes mentioned as a possible candidate for the presidency of his country, that his status as Greece's most important musician is unquestioned, and that throughout Western Europe, "Theodorakis is a cultural figure of the first rank. Some consider him a person whose work and life embody the spirit of the contemporary European left." Shavit is correct on all of these points. But he also adds the following: "From the point of view of the Israeli peace camp, Mikis Theodorakis' practical political views are at least reasonable. He recognizes the right of the State of Israel to exist as a Jewish state. He believes in a two-state solution... [But] he's afraid of the rise of a new Nazism, [and] he thinks the role of the Jews is to come out against the new Nazism. And that, therefore, Israel stands at a critical crossroads. It must choose Europe rather than America. Peace rather than war. It must be faithful to its historic destiny."

In this view, the "new Nazism" is being advanced by America, and Theodorakis is dismayed at the Jewish state's support for it, which "darkens the image of Israel." As former victims of Nazism, the Jews should not lend credibility to "this fascist policy" but rather loosen their ties to America and return to their true destiny.

Historical destinies are always tricky to define, but it's hard to believe that someone with the views of Theodorakis, who personally led massive anti-Israel rallies in Athens and Thessaloniki in 2002, could possibly contribute anything positive to help Israel define its future. Most Israelis, after all, are Jews, and people who think and feel about the Jews as Theodorakis clearly does are not likely to be friends of a Jewish people or a Jewish state, whatever their protestations to the contrary. After cornering his man and "outing" him as an impassioned antisemite, though, Shavit nonetheless concludes that Theodorakis's political views are "reasonable" and in line with those of Israel's "peace camp." That is like regarding Yasir Arafat's political views as "reasonable," for the PLO leader stated repeatedly in recent years that he, too, was for "peace" and wanted a "two-state solution"— even as he did whatever he could to undermine the Jewish state whose existence he supposedly affirmed. Antisemitism and reason simply do not square, and Shavit's attempt to bring them into alignment in Theodorakis's case, after effectively exposing the celebrated Greek composer's reprehensible views, moves one to ponder what it is that brings some Jews to mistake their enemies for friends or even to disbelieve that they have enemies at all.

II

The failure of Jews to recognize hostility toward them and, in some cases, the willingness of Jews to collude with the agents of such hostility is an old story. While no one is immune to blindness of this sort, over the past century it has been especially endemic among Jews under the sway of Marxist or other utopian and universalist ideologies. The consequences for Jewish communal well-being and, in the case of Israel, for national existence are more than just disheartening, for Jewish intellectual myopia is often a forerunner to and determinant of Jewish political miscalculation, sometimes of a very costly kind.

Consider the following as a case in point. In a study of reactions to the rise of Nazism in left-wing American Yiddish newspapers of the 1930s, Abraham Brumberg finds a general misperception of the menace developing in Germany and, consequently, a relative passivity before it. In early editorials in the socialist *Forverts* (*Forward)* and the Communist *Frayhayt* (*Freedom*) about Hitler's ascent to power, Brumberg uncovers almost no insights into the real threat that the Nazi leader would pose to Germany's Jews or the world at large. Here, from an editorial in the *Forward*, published just after the *Reichstag* election in September 1930 that gave the Nazi party a huge electoral success, is but one example of such shortsightedness:

Hitler's recent speech demonstrates that he is no more than a windbag, stupid, filled with *khutspe*, yet not one to be worried about. No doubt his followers will realize that they are dealing with a shallow, impotent demagogue, a man who presents no danger whatever, given to excitable verbal out-pourings rather than reasonable talk, a man with a forked tongue—all told, not a serious figure.

The socialists, continued the editorial, are the

one guarantee for the future of the republic. Their outstandingly calm demeanor, their wonderful discipline, all offer a guarantee that the Nazi victory is but a spasm from which the German people will soon recover.[1]

The *Forward*'s editors were hardly alone in registering such a response, for others, too, seriously underestimated Hitler, especially in the early years of his party's ascendancy. Could they have seen him otherwise as early as 1930? Hitler was not a subtle politician, and while his militarism and expansionism would surface only later, he declared his hostility to the Jews openly and vociferously right from the start. Far from being a mere "windbag," he was, indeed, a figure "to be worried about." The *Forward's* views of Hitler and the threats he posed evolved over time, and the editorial quoted above does not represent a fixed position. Yet, as Brumberg notes, the "stubborn optimism of the *Forward* did not waver" even in the face of mounting evidence that the Nazi leader and his supporters were a growing danger; and, after looking at countless stories and editorials over several years, he concludes that "it is extraordinary that experienced political observers could be so misled" (28).

What misled them? Brumberg attributes the shortcomings of the Jewish socialists at the *Forward* chiefly to romantic notions many of them held about German culture and also to the kinship and enthusiasm they felt for the German Social Democrats. There may indeed have been qualities to admire in each, but when admiration clouds political judgment to the point that one no longer recognizes a sizable threat unfolding before one's eyes, the result is bound to be a gravely distorted reading of reality.

In the case of the Jewish Communists, the distortion was even greater. Here again is Brumberg's report on his findings: "I have gone through three years of the *Frayhayt* and found not a single piece of writing that attempts to come to grips with the nature of the Nazi menace, with the historical and social roots of Nazism, or with the reasons for the Nazis' maniacal antisemitism. Nor did any contributor to the *Frayhayt* attempt to analyze the similarities and differences between Italian fascism and Hitlerism" (32). The question, of course, is why? The Jewish Communists were not oblivious to the sufferings of the Jews in Germany. "The rise of the Nazis, the Stormtroopers' brutality, and its anti-Jewish component were all duly noted by the *Frayhayt*. But all this was secondary to the reports about putative Communist 'successes' and the 'crimes' committed by the 'social fascists'" (32). The Jewish Communists in America were, in fact, horrified by what was happening to the Jews, but for many of them, including, as Brumberg notes, "many of the *Frayhayt* editors and writers, loyalty to the Communist cause and ardent belief that Moscow was *by definition* always right... were stronger than their commitments to Jewish values" (34).

Brumberg concludes his analysis with a brief but sobering statement about the consequences of the story he has reported:

> Did the reaction of, on the one hand, the Jewish Socialists, and, on the other, the Jewish Communists, affect their subsequent response to the Final Solution? The answer is that it did. The failure to appreciate the full dimension of the Hitler catastrophe was still perceptible in 1940-41. The failure of the Jewish community to put their differences over a Jewish Homeland aside in order to at least *try* to save as many Jews as possible from the maws of Germany, or to persuade the Allies to bomb Auschwitz, or demand that the United States open its doors to Jewish refugees—all this had a beginning, it seems to me, in the inadequate perception of the Hitler menace in the 1930s.
>
> The Socialists contributed to this misperception with their myths, though... some of those myths began to wane as time went on. The Communists were so mired in *their* myths that they hardly realized that civilization as a whole was on the verge of extinction. Thus it was that as the Nazis were marching to power, few (including the Jews) could see the writing on the wall (36).

The circulation of the American Yiddish newspapers was fairly sizable in those days, and a readership made more alert to the true nature of what was happening to their kinsmen in Europe might have rallied to public protests for earlier and more active American intervention. There were stories in the *Forward* and *Frayhayt* about events in Nazi Germany, yet the failure of the newspapers' writers to assess these events clearly must have facilitated a certain misperception in their readers about the full gravity of the dangers unfolding in Europe. When one turns from the left-wing Yiddish newspapers of the prewar period to the *New York Times* of the war years, an even more egregious failure becomes evident. And not just a failure of perception but of moral understanding and commitment. The story of the *Times'* journalistic irresponsibility during the years of the Nazi Holocaust has been studied and commented on by others—none more thoroughly and perceptively than Laurel Leff. She deserves to be quoted at length:

> ...in 2,077 days of war in Europe, what was happening to the Jews was never the lead story in the *New York Times*... Even when the Holocaust made the *Times* front page, the stories obscured the fact that most of the victims were Jews. So newspaper-reading Americans may have been aware that millions of civilians had been murdered during the war without connecting those deaths to the distinctly Jewish Holocaust. In addition, the *Times* only intermittently and timidly editorialized about the extermination of the Jews, and the paper rarely highlighted it in either the *Week in Review* or the magazine section. It is not surprising, therefore, that the Holocaust did not penetrate America's wartime consciousness.[2]

The situation that Leff describes here goes well beyond a newspaper's unwitting neglect of important stories and, in the words of Max Frankel, himself a former executive editor of the *Times*, amounts to a failure of "staggering, staining" proportions—indeed, "the century's bitterest journalistic failure."[3] I will return to Frankel's assessment of his newspaper's pathetic coverage of Jewish fate in Europe during the war years, but no one sums it up as cogently as Leff :

> You could have read the front page of the *New York Times* in 1939 and 1940 without knowing that millions of Jews were being sent to Poland, imprisoned in ghettos, and dying of disease and starvation by the tens of thousands. You could have read the front page in 1941 without knowing that the Nazis were machine-gunning hundreds of thousands of Jews in the Soviet Union. You could have read the front page in 1942 and not have known, until the last month, that the Germans were carrying out a plan to annihilate European Jewry. In 1943, you would have been told that Jews from France, Belgium, and the Netherlands were being sent to slaughterhouses in Poland and that more than half of the Jews in Europe were dead, but only in the context of a single story on a rally by Jewish groups that devoted more space to who had spoken than to who had died. In 1944, you would have learned from the front page of the existence of horrible places such as Maidanek and Auschwitz, but only inside the paper could you find that the victims were Jews. In 1945, Dachau and Buchenwald were on the front page, but the Jews were buried inside (70).

Many other American newspapers were similarly remiss in their coverage of the Nazi persecutions and mass murder of Europe's Jews (the Hearst newspapers being a notable and praiseworthy exception), but as the country's paper of record and the one others looked to especially for foreign news reporting, the role of the *Times* in this regard is lamentable. The absence of attention is made painfully graphic in a postwar in-house account, *The Story of the New York Times* (1951), by staff writer Meyer Berger, who devoted ninety-two pages of his 565-page book to the *Times'* coverage of World War II and, as Leff points out, "never once mentioned the extermination of the Jews" (73).

While Leff's study has great descriptive value, she never inquires into motive, whereas Frankel does. What, after all, explains his newspaper's "turning away from the Holocaust?" No doubt there were more reasons than one, but it is to Frankel's credit that he does not flinch from examining the most sensitive of these:

> There is no surviving record of how the paper's coverage of the subject was discussed by *Times* editors during the war years of 1939-45. But within that coverage is recurring evidence of a guiding principle: do not feature the plight of Jews, and take care, when reporting it, to link their suffering to that of many other Europeans (80).

The *Times*, like the *Washington Post* of that period, which was similarly reluctant to give prominent coverage to the mass killings of the Jews, did not want to be seen as "a Jewish-owned paper" and was wary of being denounced by antisemites as overly partisan or parochial in its views. Almost certainly, some of its timidity derives from such concerns. But Frankel correctly looks beyond these and focuses squarely on the newspaper's publisher, who played a major role in determining what news was fit to print and how it should be shaped and commented on:

> The reluctance to highlight the systematic slaughter of Jews was also undoubtedly influenced by the views of the publisher, Arthur Hays Sulzberger. He believed strongly

and publicly that Judaism was a religion, not a race or nationality—that Jews should be separate only in the way they worshiped. He thought they needed no state or public institutions of their own. He went to great lengths to avoid having the *Times* branded a "Jewish newspaper." He resented other publications for emphasizing the Jewishness of people in the news (81).

Sulzberger was hardly alone among influential Jews of his generation who fit this profile. Walter Lippmann, arguably the most prominent news commentator and political analyst of his day, never wrote a word about the Nazi genocide, also no doubt out of a personal reluctance to be publicly linked to the Jews. As his biographer, Ronald Steel, remarks, although Lippmann had grown up in a Jewish world, "he resisted identifying with it. He dealt with his Jewish identity largely by choosing to ignore it."[4] For Lippmann to ignore his connection to the Jews meant disconnecting from them at the time of their greatest need for sympathetic public attention. Whatever the liberating or debilitating consequences of such detachment may be personally, in certain historical circumstances, the effects on others are often harmful. In the case of the *New York Times*, it is apparent, for instance, that Sulzberger's unease with his own Jewish identity dictated a subdued approach to the dangers facing European Jewry. Operationally, the negative implications of such self-imposed restraints were serious; as Frankel puts it, ordinary readers of the *Times*, denied prominent news coverage and forceful editorial commentary about the Third Reich's campaign of genocide against the Jews, "could hardly be faulted for failing to comprehend the enormity of the Nazis' crime" (81).

Among people who wield substantial influence in the public sphere, the tie between personal repression and cultural suppression can be an intimate one, and its effects are potentially broadly detrimental. It is probably the case that Jews who do not want to be seen as Jews will do what they can to keep others from seeing and understanding Jews. Nowhere was this desire to become invisible more prominent than in Hollywood. As is well known, many of those who established America's film industry were Jews, but in the period of open and increasingly brutal antisemitism leading up to World War II and during the war years as well, Jewish film moguls avoided sponsoring works that explicitly dealt with the escalating violence directed against the Jews of Europe. The Israeli film scholar, Ilan Avisar, accurately describes the situation:

> In the years 1940-1945, Hollywood produced five hundred narrative movies on the war and war-related themes, out of a total of seventeen hundred feature films. In examining this harvest, we find striking avoidance of any explicit presentation of the Jewish catastrophe during the course of the war. Chaplin's movie *The Great Dictator* (1940) was a remarkable exception. Hollywood (which the Nazis had claimed was dominated by Jewish interests) paid abundant tribute to the sufferings of other peoples during the war... while it completely ignored the contemporaneous, systematic extermination of European Jews.[5]

Avisar attributes the Jewish movie producers' avoidance of Jewish themes to several factors, ranging from a desire to protect valuable business interests to a wariness of American antisemitism, which at the time was intimidating for many. The Jewish filmmakers also did not want to be seen as working at cross-purposes with the Roosevelt administration, which itself was reluctant to focus prominently on the plight of European Jewry. And so they accommodated themselves to the public mood of the time, which they understood to be largely indifferent to the fate of the Jews, and consequently did nothing to focus on the crimes of the Holocaust. Hollywood's Jews simply turned their eyes away from the Jewish catastrophe abroad, for they believed that attention to it would only bring unwanted attention to themselves at home. The producer David Selznick probably spoke for more than just himself when he remarked, "I am not interested in Jewish political problems. I'm an American and not a Jew."[6] When Hollywood finally did bring to the screen a major film about antisemitism—such as *Gentlemen's Agreement*, produced by Darryl Zanuck, a non-Jew—it focused on the "softer" American strain of social exclusion. That was in 1947, by which time millions of Jews had already been turned to ash.

At the time when it most counted, the response of American Jewish artists, writers, intellectuals, and religious and community leaders was mixed. Some accurately perceived the dangers that Europe's Jews were facing and worked strenuously to rally public protests against the Nazi persecutions and killings. Mass demonstrations were organized by several American Jewish organizations soon after Hitler came to power and continued intermittently during the 1930s and into the war years. One of the most energetic of these efforts was spearheaded by a small group of Jewish writers, actors, and musicians—among them Ben Hecht, Moss Hart, Kurt Weill, Edward G. Robinson, Paul Muni, and Billy Rose—who put on a wartime pageant entitled *We Will Never Die* that brought tens of thousands of people to Madison Square Garden and afterwards played to sizable audiences in other American cities. For reasons that have been described by David Wyman and others,[7] though, this group, which worked with the political activist Peter Bergson, was out of favor with major Jewish organizations, which actively opposed Bergson, Hecht, and their colleagues and effectively limited the impact of their activities. Their success in this regard brought no honor to the wartime leadership of American Jewry, much of whose own efforts to move the Roosevelt administration to aid the endangered Jews of Europe too often came to little. Resolutions were signed, petitions presented, and funds raised, but in the view of most historians who have studied this issue, the result of American Jewish activities on behalf of Jews in Nazi-occupied Europe did not begin to match the need. Given the political realities of the time, what more could have been done by a less fractious and more unified Jewish community remains an open question to this day.[8]

III

When one considers the work of the so-called "New York intellectuals" during this same period from the standpoint of the issues under review here, it is hard to grant them much honor either. Most of the writers loosely gathered under this rubric were Jews, but Judaism as such hardly figured in their writing, and their major work is notable for its reluctance to acknowledge, let alone to evaluate, the Nazi destruction of European Jewry and the establishment of an independent Jewish state in Palestine. In a sardonic but well-founded judgment, Ruth Wisse has written that "the New York intellectuals... spent the 1940s as a Jewish *arrière-garde*, sheltered by the conviction that they were serving a higher purpose."[9]

In most cases, this "higher purpose" took the names of socialism or cosmopolitanism—the promised land of a classless, internationalist society. Ideologically committed to an abstract and largely utopian view of the world, many of the New York Jewish intellectuals seemed all but oblivious to events unfolding in their own lifetimes that were to have such a massive impact on Jewish life. European antisemitism, culminating in the Nazi crimes, seems barely to have registered on their thinking at all. Looking back years later on the absence of any real response to this catastrophe on his part and that of others, Irving Howe commented,

> Some of us continued to think more or less in Marxist categories—loosened and liberalized, but Marxist still... [And] Marxism, by remaining fixed upon class analysis and social categories appropriate only to the bourgeois-democratic epoch, kept us from seeing the radically novel particulars of the Nazi regime... It could [not] begin to explain what had happened at Auschwitz.[10]

Leslie Fiedler, whose "holy books," by his own admission, "were not the Torah and Talmud, but the collected works of Marx, Engels, and Lenin," said more or less the same thing, confessing that it was only in middle age that he came "begrudgingly and at long last to recognize the full scope and horror of the Holocaust, of which I had for so long remained at least half-deliberately unaware." During the war years themselves, he was convinced that the real enemy "was the ruling class of one's country." He actively opposed America's entry into World War II—he saw it as an "imperialist" adventure—and discounted the veracity of news accounts of the Nazi persecution and slaughter of European Jewry.[11]

The failures here not only of perception but of historical and political judgment are hardly unique to Howe and Fiedler but are repeated in the work of most of the New York Jewish intellectuals. One searches their writings in vain for any sustained, contemporaneous commentary on the Nazi assault against European Jewry or on the efforts to establish a Jewish homeland in Palestine. Given the fact that, as public intellectuals, most of these writers were passionately engaged with other major issues of their day, this absence is astonishing.

Alexander Bloom, author of a well-informed book on the New York intellectuals, notes that the pages of *Partisan Review* and other journals that carried the work of these writers contained almost no references in the late 1930s to the persecution of the Jews. One of the few exceptions was Sidney Hook's "Tragedy of German Jewry," which appeared in the *New Leader* in November 1938; but, as Bloom observes, Hook's article was not about Hitler nearly so much as it was about Stalin. Moreover, lest his concern for the Jews be considered too narrowly parochial, Hook felt the need to add a broad-based disclaimer: "Let us bear in mind that in protesting against Hitler's anti-Jewish brutalities we are also protesting against the hounding of other religious and political minorities."[12] "Tragedy of German Jewry" was published on the heels of Kristallnacht— the bloodiest pogrom in Central Europe in modern times, whose *only* target was Jews, not other "minorities." Yet the thrust of Hook's thinking was conspicuously "cosmopolitan" and reflected his anti-Stalinism more passionately than it did his concern with the victims of violent antisemitism. He was not cold to Jewish suffering, but he was reluctant to single it out—this at a time when Hitler himself was focusing his wrath specifically on the Jews. "Let's face it," Alfred Kazin acknowledged many years later, "If these intellectuals had gone on a great deal... about Jews and the war... they would have seemed a good deal less 'American,' less assimilated."[13]

Looking back, Irving Howe, in many ways the most seriously self-reflective and admirably forthright of the New York Jewish writers, summed up his own position in terms that readily apply to others of his generation:

> In the years before the war people like me tended to subordinate our sense of Jewishness to cosmopolitan culture and socialist politics. We did not think well or deeply on the matter of Jewishness—you might say we avoided thinking about it... Jewishness did not form part of a conscious commitment, it was not regarded as a major component of the culture I wanted to make my own, and I felt no particular responsibility for its survival or renewal.[14]

Howe admitted that it took years for him to acknowledge the full horror of the Nazi killings and that his true awakening to the ramifications of these crimes developed as he became "less ideological and more responsive morally."[15] As for his response to the creation of the Jewish state, it was notably tepid: "I would be lying if I said I was tremendously excited by the formation of Israel in 1948. It didn't, at first, touch me very much per se... I was for the state; it was okay. But I wasn't so deeply stirred emotionally."[16] On another occasion Howe wrote, "I wasn't one of those who danced in the streets when Ben-Gurion made his famous pronouncement that the Jews, like other peoples, now had a state of their own... My biases kept me from open joy."[17]

These biases were widespread among the New York Jewish intellectuals and distanced most of them from any positive attachment to Israel, as from most other things that were publicly linked to Jewishness. In thinking about himself, his friend and fellow writer Philip Rahv, and others in these terms, Howe invoked Isaac Deutscher's well-known coinage of the "non-Jewish Jew" and believed that he and his fellow intellectuals proudly embraced "the tradition of the estranged Jew."[18] But whatever the satisfactions of affirming oneself as an alienated Jew, there was an emotional price to pay for keeping aloof, which Howe later admitted and even came to feel a bit ashamed of. "One's first response to the Holocaust," he acknowledged, "had to be a cry of Jewish grief."[19] But he did not cry at the time of the most profound Jewish sorrow, just as he did not feel joy at the creation of the Jewish state.

Nor did many others in his circle. Lionel Trilling and Sidney Hook never once visited Israel. Leslie Fiedler did, more than once, but as he wrote, "never have I felt less like a Jew... I have gone back... five or six times over the years, only to leave each time further confused and dismayed."[20] In Fiedler's case, confusion regarding the Jewish state seemed to be a permanent condition. From the start, he was not keen to see such a country established—"the last thing an already atomized world needed was one more nation state"—and, for a while, he admitted, "I was tempted—following the Communist and Trotskyist line—to side in that struggle with the Arabs." In keeping with his cultural and political biases, he identified the Arabs with the American Indians and the Jews with exploitative colonizers, a formula that Fiedler subsequently recognized as simplistic and abandoned as he retreated from the convictions of his earlier Marxist loyalties. But since he also wanted no part of Zionism and had no real connections to Judaism, he was basically at a loss when it came to thinking about the Israelis and the Arabs; ultimately, he threw up his hands and confessed, "I have ended by crying out... a curse on both your houses; though, of course, I would prefer to wish on both the blessing of universal brotherhood."[21]

On the way to seeing such a blessing realized, some Jews have observed events more clearly than others and have worked effectively in the world of practical politics for positive change. By any historical measure, one of the most dramatically transforming of these changes in the last century was the establishment of Israel, which Irving Howe, in a bold revision of his earlier thinking, came to hail as "perhaps the most remarkable assertion that a martyred people has ever made."[22] Howe did not arrive at such an affirmation easily, though, for, as he put it, his ideological orientation encouraged in him and countless other Jewish intellectuals of his generation "a deep, blind hostility to the Zionist movement" and the state it created.[23] While most Jews in America probably harbor no such hostility today, it is alive among others, and for many of the same reasons already described in these pages.

We will consider the views of some of these people shortly and see that, in many cases, they are little more than a reiteration of the "blind hostility" to the Jewish state to which Howe belatedly and rather ashamedly confessed. One difference between present-day Jewish opponents of Israel and their predecessors, though, is that no shame whatsoever is to be detected among them. Another is their active engagement as often bitter adversaries of Zionism and the country it created. The Jews of Howe's intellectual and political circle, like the Jews of Hollywood and some of the newspapers cited above, can properly be faulted for their silences—for what they failed to say and omitted to do during critical moments of Jewish history. In some cases, they are culpable of complacency; in others, of willful self-deception; and in still others, of the compromises that accompanied a strong desire for social assimilation. In addition, a common, if not necessarily conscious, element among many was the understandable anxiety, in an age of less than full acceptance of their "kind," not to be singled out as Jews. As the sociologist Daniel Bell put it years later, "There was a great awareness of anti-Semitism, but a great fear of open discussion."[24] Just how many Jewish intellectuals were intimidated by such fear is impossible to say today, but an uncharacteristic reticence on the part of otherwise highly voluble figures seems to attest to the silencing effects of a low-key but palpable antisemitism.

From the very different vantage point of today, one can say that it would have been commendable for Jewish intellectuals then to stand up to such hostility and face it down, but for a variety of motives, most chose not to. If, with respect to this matter, therefore, one looks back in time and finds them wanting, it is not because they acted out of malice or spoke with disdain about their fellow Jews but chiefly because they failed to act or speak meaningfully at all.

IV

This picture changes, and not for the better, when the focus shifts to today and the words and actions of some of this generation's Jewish intellectuals. To Jews who are "unreconstructed assimilationists," as Leslie Fiedler described himself, the idea of a predominantly Jewish nation state defies the dream of a world without national borders, flags, or ethnic and religious divisions. By virtue of its very being, therefore, Israel is bound to be problematic for such people, for it calls the world's attention to the persistence of Jewish particularity and, ipso facto, to themselves as Jews; hence, it is objectionable as such. To the progeny of the Sulzbergers and Lippmanns of an earlier generation of assimilationist Jews, many of whom protested vociferously against the establishment of a Jewish state, Israel stands as an ethnic embarrassment and is a source of continuing personal resentment.

There are also Jews who object to the state on ideological grounds of another kind and regard Zionism as retrograde and out of sync with their preferred version of political reality. While they will support Palestinian Arab nationalism, they have little stomach for Jewish nationalism, especially as embodied in a Jewish state that does not hesitate to use its military power to defend itself. Their criticisms of particular Israeli policies and actions may be perfectly legitimate, but the passions that fuel their arguments often reveal differences with Israel that lie deeper than those that belong to politics alone.

For some, these arguments express their own drive for broader social acceptance. In a reprise of the anti-establishment behavior of the 1960s, public dissent from Israel is a way to certify their bona fides in "progressive" circles and gain entrance into today's version of an adversary culture, which may include Jews but is thought to be free of Jewish "chauvinism," "nationalism," and other unwanted "tribal" attributes. As one can detect in the bravura sometimes displayed in the actions of newly radicalized Jews, the heady feelings that accompanied the old "revolutionary struggle" are being revived in the new struggle against Zionism and Israel. In a much-publicized incident, for example, when Israeli cabinet minister Natan Sharansky spoke on the campus of Rutgers University, a Jewish student of this stripe shoved a cream pie in his face. The political drama that he was acting out finds its inspiration in many of the new progressive movements, in which anti-Zionism has succeeded socialism as a core ideological and political value. As Andrei Markovits has convincingly argued, anti-Zionism, together with anti-Americanism, is "a new litmus test of progressive politics... If one is not at least a serious doubter of the legitimacy of the state of Israel (never mind the policies of its government)... one runs the risk of being excluded from the entity called 'the left.'"[25] The fact that anti-Zionism—the negation of the long-established Jewish right to a secure national homeland in Israel—is essentially nothing more than a version of antisemitism either eludes or fails to trouble Jews in these movements.

For still other Jews, public dissent from Israel, far from being an expression of assimilationist yearnings, is affirmed as a privileged form of Jewish identity. Jews who embrace this position are convinced that the Jewish state compromises and corrupts the Jewish religion, and, in the name of Judaism, they are quick to denounce the state as "unholy." Within Israel, the adherents of Neturei Karta are the best-known representatives of this view. While they reside in the country, they see its establishment as blasphemy—the unwarranted preemption of the Messiah's exclusive right to restore the nation in Zion—and withhold allegiance to it. In America, the motives that lead some religious Jews to condemn Israel for the sake of a purer, deterritorialized form of Judaism are different. They are rooted in an idealized version of prophetic Judaism whose vision of justice is so lofty that no state on earth could possibly fulfil it. Israel, though, is not just any state but the Jewish state, and if it fails to live up to the most exacting standards of morality prescribed in Judaism's ethical tradition, Jews of the prophetic persuasion are quick to condemn it. The most impassioned articulation of this view was made by Henry Schwarzchild in 1982 at the time of the war in Lebanon:

> The resumption of political power by the Jewish people after two thousand years of diaspora has been a tragedy of historical dimensions. The State of Israel has demanded recognition as the modern political incarnation of the Jewish people. To grant that is to betray the Jewish tradition... I now conclude and avow that the price of a Jewish state is, to me, Jewishly unacceptable and that the existence of this (or any similar) ethnic-

religious nation state is a Jewish, i.e. a human and moral disaster and violates every remaining value for which Judaism and Jews might exist in history... I now renounce the State of Israel, disavow any political connection or emotional obligation to it, and declare myself its enemy.[26]

Schwarzchild's denunciation of Israel and rejection of any personal loyalty to it were so extreme that few of his successors have been able to match it. Nevertheless, even if not at this intense level of vituperation, a range of other angry dissenters have no reservations in denouncing the Jewish state in the name of Judaism. To such Jews, prophetic Judaism knows no middle ground. If Israel cannot fulfil its national destiny to be "a light unto the nations," it does not deserve to be at all.

V

Then there are Jews whose anger at Israel and public denunciations of the Jewish state seem simply hateful or pathological.

Sadly, some of the deepest of these pathologies are to be found in Israel itself, where the public rhetoric of self-incrimination often surpasses the bounds of the reasonable, with consequences that reach well beyond the borders of the state and can only cause it serious harm. If, as was noted at the beginning of this essay, Mikis Theodorakis reviles Israel's current prime minister as a leader on the model of Adolf Hitler and condemns the country itself for exhibiting "Nazi-like" behavior, his comments, reprehensible as they are, merely repeat the vicious slurs that Israel's most prominent philosopher Yeshayahu Leibowitz made years ago when he vilified his country as a "Judeo-Nazi" state and said that it would soon be setting up "concentration camps" for the Arabs. Unfortunately, Leibowitz's vilifications are by no means idiosyncratic, for Israelis on both the left and the right of the political spectrum regularly take recourse to the words and images of the Third Reich to malign fellow Jews whose actions or opinions they dislike.

In a rhetorical move that changes the register slightly but hardly softens it, the vocabulary of denunciation is sometimes drawn not from the lexicon of Nazi obscenities but from that of South African racism. For instance, it is a common feature of present-day antisemitism worldwide to condemn Israel as a racist and apartheid state, but while such a charge has no basis in fact, to some Israelis it does not go nearly far enough.[27] Thus, at a recent conference on "Resisting Israeli Apartheid," held at the University of London (December 2004), Haim Bresheeth, an Israeli academic currently teaching in England, declared, "There is no valid comparison between South Africa and Israel; Israel is much worse. South Africa exploited its native population while Israel expelled and committed genocide against its native population."[28] Lev Grinberg, a professor of political science at Ben Gurion University, modifies Bresheeth's extreme judgment only slightly in writing about Israel's "symbolic genocide": "Unable to rehabilitate from the Holocaust trauma,...the Jewish people, the latest victims of a genocide, carry out a genocide against the Palestinians at the moment. The world will not allow complete genocide, and [so] instead of this, it is symbolic genocide."[29] Grinberg's indictment was triggered by the killing of Ahmed Yassin, the leader of Hamas, an organization sworn by its charter to the destruction of Israel. Most Israelis would probably regard the removal of Yassin as a reasonable act of national self-defense and, even if they thought its timing unwise or its methods objectionable, would not see it as in any way genocidal; but within the hyperbolic climate of Israeli political feuding, reason tends to evaporate, often with common sense itself.

Otherwise, it is difficult to explain such an unfounded allegation as this one, recently made by the Israeli journalist Uri Avnery: "The pro-Israel lobby... pushed the American administration to start a war." Those who wonder why American troops are dying in Iraq now have an answer: the Jews sent them there. For Patrick Buchanan and others who promote Jewish conspiracy theories, Israelis like Uri Avnery are a godsend. From them, the very source of truth itself, it must seem, comes proof that the real power decisions in Washington are determined by the interests of Jerusalem and Tel Aviv. And if one dares to cross such power, as Avnery further elaborates, one pays the ultimate price; for the same crowd that pushed America into Iraq on behalf of Israel is quick to "eliminate... American politicians who do not support the Israeli government unconditionally," as they demonstrated vividly with the "'public execution' [of]... the black congresswoman Cynthia McKinney... [who] dared to criticize the Sharon government."[30] McKinney, as is well known, was defeated in the 2002 Democratic primary in Georgia (she has since been reelected to Congress) in part because of the incendiary rhetoric of her campaign, which included, among other irresponsible charges, the allegation that President Bush may have known in advance about the 9/11 terror attacks and for reasons of personal profit did nothing to stop them. Her father and others in her campaign also made ugly charges about undue "Jewish influence." Yet all that Uri Avnery can say about her is that "this young, active, intelligent, and very sympathetic woman" fell victim to "the Jewish establishment." He adds, surely to the delight of antisemites everywhere, that if one wants to understand what fuels suspicion of Jews today and is likely to provoke even greater hostility towards them tomorrow, one should consider "the conspicuousness of the Jews in the United States, especially in the media, and their disproportionate influence over the Congress and the White House."[31] Jews, in other words, as those who detest them never tire of repeating, control and manipulate power to their own advantage. Although anyone familiar with the standard antisemitic repertoire will instantly recognize this libel for what it is, Uri Avnery is evidently oblivious to its poisonous character and seems to confirm it.

Avnery is well known in Israel as a cranky, contentious figure, whose accusations are meant to cause outrage, geared as they typically are to identifying the Jews themselves as the cause of the enmity directed against them. He charges not only American Jews but those of his own country, for instance, with "causing the resurrection of antisemitism.... The Sharon government is a giant laboratory for growing the anti-Semitism virus. It exports it to the whole world."[32] Unfortunately, statements of this kind have become almost normative within Israeli public discourse, and they can be heard from mainstream public figures as well as more maverick types, with all of the negative consequences that inevitably follow in their wake. If, after all, an Israeli as prominent as Avraham Burg, former speaker of the Israeli Knesset and former chairman of the Jewish Agency for Israel, can write that "the end of the Zionist enterprise is already on our doorstep," that his country today, growing "strange and ugly," "rests on a scaffold of corruption and on foundations of oppression and injustice,"[33] who abroad will be apt to gainsay him—especially among those who believe that the whole Zionist project was a mistake to begin with and should come to an end sooner rather than later?

Burg's hyperbolic charges about the imminent collapse of Israeli society originally appeared in an article in *Yediot Aharonot*, but they were not intended only for local consumption. Before long they were also available to readers of the *Forward*, the *International Herald-Tribune*, *Le Monde,* the *Guardian*, *Süddeutsche Zeitung*, and other newspapers. Avnery's denunciations of his countrymen are also regularly quoted abroad, as are similar accusations by other Israelis about the failures and corruptions of their society. If ever evidence were needed to confirm the robustness of Israel's democracy and the freedom of its press, in fact, it could be gathered in liberal quantities from the presence of such Israeli voices in the foreign press. With respect to its general view of the Israeli-Palestinian conflict, however, the latter is hardly neutral, as any reader of the *Guardian*, *Le Monde*, and other left-leaning media outlets will see. When one adds to the frequently slanted news coverage of Israel in much of the European media the incendiary character of Israeli self-denunciations, one should not be surprised to learn from a recent poll in Great Britain that Israel is judged to be the "the country least deserving of international respect."[34] Nor should one wonder at the findings of a new survey of German public opinion, which finds that more than half of Germans believe Israeli policies towards Palestinians are similar to the Nazi treatment of the Jews during the Holocaust or that over two-thirds of Germans believe that Israelis are waging a "war of extermination" against Palestinians.[35] While the British and Germans may have their own reasons for holding such damning views, they can only find support for them in the pronouncements of Israelis who themselves condemn the Jewish state in the harshest of terms.

To quote Avraham Burg once again: "A state lacking justice cannot survive." In the most sweeping, and unfounded, of terms, Burg argues that Israel has become such a state in a fundamental sense. He even goes so far as to seem to justify the terrorist outrages of Palestinian suicide bombers: "Israel, having ceased to care about the children of the Palestinians, should not be surprised when they come washed in hatred and blow themselves up in the centers of Israeli escapism." Although it has been shown that many of those who carry out these vicious attacks come from relatively well-educated and even middle class backgrounds, Burg insists that the Palestinian murderers who target diners in Israeli restaurants "are hungry and humiliated." The record indicates otherwise, but in Burg's view a country grown so morally callous as Israel gets what it deserves. And so, he darkly concludes, "the countdown to the end of Israeli society has begun." There are many outside of his country and more than a few inside it who want him to be right, cheer him on, and even do what they can to bring about the end he foresees. As a former French diplomat memorably put it, why does the world need "this shitty little country" anyway?

Whatever its shortcomings and errors, to entertain such a vision of Israel as that presented by Burg, Avnery, Bresheeth, Grinberg, and numerous other Israeli writers, scholars, and intellectuals is to betray a failure of reason, judgment, and simple good sense so extreme as to elude ready understanding. Some are given to explaining such behavior as a recognizable part of Israeli politics—notoriously not an arena for measured debate and reasonable compromise but more akin to a bloodsport. Within Israel's overheated and badly polarized political culture, choices are defined as "black or white," "right or wrong"—these are Avraham Burg's own terms—and, in this zero-sum game, no mercy is to be shown to one's opponents and no credibility granted to alternative political visions of the country's future. And so, those now on the other side of political power take recourse to rhetorical power and proclaim, as Burg does, that the country may not even *have* a future: "the Zionist revolution is dead."

Among other things, these hyperbolic accusations seem to reveal a species of moral hysteria, according to which some arrogate to themselves special and superior moral insight lacking in their opponents. It excuses them from any need to regard counter-arguments as worthy of their attention and instead dismisses these out of hand as ignorant or immoral or both. From this perspective, Israel's fate will be determined by their way or no way at all.[36]

Others try to explain the extremity of Israeli political rhetoric in psychological terms. Kenneth Levin, a historian and psychiatrist, for instance, finds parallels to certain kinds of Israeli behavior in the delusional thinking of those who have lived under siege and been subjected to long-term abuse. According to Levin, such people tend to develop a psychological defense mechanism whereby they come to "embrace the indictments of their abusers."[37] Thus, if Israelis are accused often enough of being as cruel as the Nazis, some will accept the charge as valid, "control" or "master" the indictment by adopting it as their own self-criticism, and then project it onto those of their fellow countrymen whom they see as the source of such pain. Following this logic, the abused becomes an abuser and locates the primary fault of his victimization not, for example, with Palestinian suicide bombers and those who brainwash and dispatch them to do their bloody work but with Ariel Sharon and a "corrupt Israeli society." Such a move, Levin argues, has been taking place within the pressure-cooker of Israeli public life for a number of years, with effects that are both debilitating and dangerous.

These matters are obviously complex and require more sustained study, but one thing about them is already clear: the strong indictments of their country by the Israelis cited in these pages and others like them are so total and so fierce as to render Israel's true face today almost unrecognizable. The image that emerges is one of a morally polluted and physically infirm nation. "The disease eating away at the body of Zionism has already attacked the head," Burg insists. He envisions the entire edifice as close to "collapse" and predicts it may soon "come crashing down"—with catastrophic results for Jews outside of Israel as well as within. However Israelis themselves may understand such apocalyptic projections, their effects on the country's standing abroad have been steadily corrosive.

VI

Like all states, the Israeli state has its flaws and makes mistakes. The present policy of large-scale settlement and long-term military occupation of the West Bank and (until recently) Gaza is fraught with problems, which have grown dramatically in recent years. To safeguard its presence in these territories and also to defend its major population centers within the country's pre-1967 borders, Israel has taken some harsh measures and, on occasion, transgressed its own laws and standards of morality. To point out these errors, as many of Israel's critics do, is not necessarily to act with ill intent. Many Jews who dissent from Israel's settlement or occupation policies remain within a general consensus of support for the country and its Zionist credo. Other Jews, however, have gone well beyond such critique and express attitudes to the Jewish state, and sometimes also to Jews, that resemble those of Israel's most outspoken enemies.

The hostility that such Jews express is usually linked to the question of Israeli settlements, and there is no doubt that the expansion of these into areas that Israel conquered in the Six Day War of June, 1967 has brought Israel plenty of sharp criticism. For some, however, the settlements may be only the latest pretext for an adversarial stance toward the Jewish state that long predates the Israeli presence in the West Bank and Gaza. There are continuities between today's anti-Zionism and that of the 1960s, which originate in the opposition of the Marxist left to Zionism as such. Just as Jewish universalists and internationalists then looked upon Zionism as an unacceptably bourgeois and nationalist movement, so "progressive" Jews today are apt to view the Zionist state as an outmoded expression of Jewish particularism and nationalism. As Seymour Martin Lipset wrote as far back as 1969, "the support which the intellectual left once gave to Israel is gone, and it is not likely to be revived... Israel must expect to be criticized by the extreme left for the foreseeable future."[38] At the time when Lipset wrote these lines, Israel's settlement policy was not very ambitious and its military presence on the West Bank and Gaza hardly provoked the kind of criticism it was later to draw. Nevertheless, as Lipset correctly concluded almost four decades ago, the Jewish state could expect nothing but opposition from the ideological left, whose ranks then were filled with Jews and remain so today.

This matter would be troubling at any time, but in a period of renewed antisemitism, much of which takes the form of anti-Zionism, it is particularly disheartening to observe the contributions of Jews themselves to some of the most extreme forms of anti-Israel and even antisemitic invective. In addition to those already cited, I refer to a diverse array of oppositional figures, ranging from old-line anti-Zionists of a leftist persuasion, like Noam Chomsky and Norman Finkelstein, to self-proclaimed "Jews of conscience," who feel a newly inspired call to redeem the Zionist state from its supposed "moral bankruptcy." Readers interested in the first type will find them liberally represented in the pages of the *Nation*. For the second, they can consult the pages of *Tikkun*. Israel's harshest Jewish critics also include an assortment of ideological diasporists, who have no particular affinity with or use for a Jewish state and may see it, in the words of the historian Tony Judt, as an "anachronism" that no longer deserves to exist. Moreover, according to Judt, "Israel today is bad for the Jews." In this view—and it is gaining acceptance among Jews on the far left—Israel itself has brought on much of today's antisemitism, and without it, Jews elsewhere would be better off. As Judt puts it, "Today, non-Israeli Jews feel... exposed to criticism and vulnerable to attack for things they didn't do... [The] Jewish state is holding them hostage for its own actions."[39]

This is lopsided reasoning, for if Jews are held responsible for "things they didn't do," let alone are made "vulnerable to attack" as a result of false accusations against them, the blame surely lies not with the Jewish state but with those who find it abhorrent and turn aggressively against those Jews they identify as its surrogates and supporters. In a sharp critique of Judt's charges, Leon Wieseltier pointed out that to confuse the object of antisemitic hostility with its cause, as Judt does, is not to understand antisemitism but to reproduce it.[40] Wieseltier is right, but such confusions are common today, and there are Jews who say and do things that are hardly distinguishable from what is said and done by the fiercest anti-Zionists.

Consider the reflections on Israel and present-day antisemitism by Michael Neumann, a professor of philosophy at Trent University in Canada and the author of *What's Left: Radical Politics and the Radical Psyche*. Neumann accuses Israel of committing "Zionist atrocities" and of waging "race war" whose purpose is nothing less than "the extinction of a people." Towards this end, it is embarked on "genocide"—"a kinder, gentler genocide that portrays its perpetrators as victims." The Palestinians "are being shot because Israel thinks all Palestinians should vanish or die... This is not the bloody mistake of a blundering super-power but an emerging evil." Moreover, the guilt belongs not only to the Israelis but to Jews in general, "most of whom support a state that commits war crimes." Such support implicates all Jews, Neumann contends, so much so that "the case for Jewish complicity seems much stronger than the case for German complicity" in the Holocaust. He is aware there are those who will resent an assessment that paints Jews in such black colors, but he will run the risk of their ire. Indeed, "if saying these things is anti-Semitic, then it can be reasonable to be anti-Semitic." Moreover, "some anti-Semitism is acceptable." What would he say, one wonders, if an "acceptable" level of anti-Semitism were to lead to outright aggression against Jews? He answers: "Who cares?... To regard any shedding of Jewish blood as a world-shattering calamity... is racism, pure and simple; the valuing of one race's blood over all others."[41]

The thinking here is so breathtakingly awry that one hardly knows where to begin in addressing it. For one, Jews do not typically define themselves in racial terms or value other people's lives according to their "blood." To claim that they do shows either gross ignorance or outright malice. The Jews in Israel, far from wishing each and every Palestinian Arab dead, as Neumann declares, are looking for ways to either make peace with them or live apart from them. By no reasonable standard of historical comparison or legal judgment can one show that Israel is intent on genocide; nor are the Israelis engaged in a "race war." Indeed, if there is "racism" to be perceived in this conflict, it is far more likely to appear in Arab teachings and preachings about the Jews than the other way around. Israel's aim is to free itself finally from the state of siege that has been the country's fate since its inception and enjoy something like a normal life. Short of that, it does what it believes it needs to do to protect its citizens from being blown apart as they sit in cafes and on city buses by suicide bombers intent on their own campaign of "extinction." Given what they know first-hand of the lethal character of antisemitism, the Jews of Israel will not endorse any form of antisemitism as "reasonable" or "acceptable." Professor Neumann believes otherwise and even proposes that "we should almost never take anti-Semitism seriously, and maybe we should have some fun with it." How many other Jews, one wonders, will want to join him in pursuing such fun?

In fact, there are lots of others, as anyone who surfs the Internet will see merely by clicking on "Jews against Israel." Hundreds of entries that sound like Neumann's article instantly appear, many of them representing anti-Zionism at its most aggressive. For an exposure to the full range of such sentiment within a single volume, one can consult the recently published collection, *Wrestling with Zion: Progressive Jewish-American Responses to the Israeli-Palestinian Conflict*, edited by Tony Kushner and Alisa Solomon (New York: Grove Press, 2003). Liberally sprinkled through the pages of this book are references to Israeli "apartheid," "racism," "colonialism," and "ethnic cleansing." These descriptives have become part of normative discourse among "progressive" American Jews, who seem to take for granted that the historical record shows Israel to be an aggressor state guilty of sins comparable to those of Verwoerd's

South Africa and Hitler's Germany. As for "Zionism," gone are the days when it was praised by those on the left as a movement of Jewish national liberation. One contributor, Joel Kovel, who is writing a book on a post-Zionist Israel, suggests that Zionism "is equivalent to a form of racism" and is unforgiving that it brought about "the Jewish homeland at the expense of another people" (357). The prominent poet Adrienne Rich proposes that the very word "Zionism"—"so incendiary, so drenched in idealism, dissension, ideas of blood and soil, in memories of victimization and pursuant claims of the right to victimize"— "needs to dissolve before twenty-first century realities" (164). She neglects to say precisely what these "realities" are, but inasmuch as she affirms the extraterritorial ideal of "a Jew without borders" (165), it is evident that for her the word "Zionism" along with the whole Zionist project have served their purposes and should be retired. Still another contributor, Sara Roy, who identifies herself as the daughter of Holocaust survivors, notes that "within the Jewish community it has always been considered a form of heresy to compare Israeli actions or policies with those of the Nazis" (176). Then she proceeds to draw just such a comparison by accusing Israel of replicating Nazi occupation policies. In more condensed form, Irena Klepfisz, a poet and Holocaust survivor, declares that "you can be a victim and also a victimizer," (367) a charge routinely made by those who want to tar Israel with the Nazi brush.

Some of Israel's Jewish critics are irate at the country for still other reasons: in their eyes, Judaism itself has fallen casualty to Israel's sins, and the cost to their religious principles is so high as to render questionable the value of the state's existence. "I'm not against Israel," writes the author Douglas Rushkoff, but the Jewish state, which he refers to as "this nationalized refugee camp," is "a compromise of Jewish ideals, and not their realization... We get a claim on some land, but we lose our religion in the process" (181, 182). Daniel Boyarin, a professor of Talmud at the University of California at Berkeley, joins Rushkoff in this critique but goes him one better. Just as Christianity may have died at Auschwitz, Treblinka, and Sobibor, laments Boyarin, so "I fear... that my Judaism may be dying at Nablus, Deheishe, Beteen (Beth-El), and al-Khalil (Hebron)" (202). As always, the recourse to Holocaust references is a sure sign that lucid thinking has been distorted by bias. In this case, as in others, Jewish identity is affirmed in opposition to the Jewish state.

Some Jews devise novel changes in the practice of Judaism to reflect the ways in which, it is claimed, Israel has damaged the religion. Jews who are members of JATO ("Jews Against the Occupation"), for instance, build what they call "an anti-occupation *sukkah* with pictures of destroyed Palestinian buildings," adorning its walls. Marc Ellis, a professor of Jewish Studies at Baylor University, proposes that the synagogue Torah scrolls be replaced in the Ark of the Covenant by replicas of Israeli helicopter gunships, which he argues are the true symbol of Israeli reality today (155). Anti-Zionist Jews have introduced other rituals as well, such as an oath against the Right of Return—a privilege of citizenship in Israel that every Jew in the world currently enjoys. "Far from being protected by Israel, I feel exposed to danger by the actions of the Israeli state," writes Melanie Kaye/Kantrowitz. "I am declaring another way to be Jewish... I renounce my right to return" (256). At the ritual circumcision of their son, Meg Barnett and Brad Lander issued a similar declaration: "We are thrilled to pronounce you a Jew without the Right of Return. Your name contains our deep hope that you will explore and celebrate your Jewish identity without confusing it with nationalism" (293).

As these gestures of Jewish dissent indicate, there is a tendency among American Jews who identify themselves as "progressive" to embrace positions on Zionism and Israel that are as negative, and sometimes even as damning, as any to be found among the most fervent anti-Zionists. One recognizes in their writings passions of anger and indignation, bitterness and repudiation that transcend those of mere politics. Israel in their eyes is guilty of a great betrayal and should be punished. Never mind that more than a thousand of its citizens have been murdered in the last few years and that thousands more have been maimed for life. Never mind that Israelis are regularly condemned as the new Nazis and reviled as the children of monkeys and pigs. Never mind as well that their country is singled out more than any on the globe for inaccurate and one-sided condemnations of human rights abuses and targeted for boycotts and divestment campaigns. And never mind that, alone among the world's countries, Israel's very existence is considered an aggression, its legitimacy put in doubt, and its right to a future openly questioned. No historical or political explanations of Israel's current predicament are acceptable to some of the country's Jewish critics, nor can it be easily redeemed from its perceived wrongdoings. "History is screwing us totally up... forget the history," suggests Irena Klepfisz (358-359). She is for less explanation and more action—and *now*. Like other "oppressive" regimes before it, Israel is judged to be guilty of the worst and must be brought to heel. The journalist Esther Kaplan, commenting on the charge by a young Rutgers University activist that "Israel is a racist state, an imperialist state—it is and should be a pariah state," remarks: "[I]f that's what it takes to bring down the occupation... Israel should absolutely become a pariah state... The time has come when Israel must be totally isolated by world opinion and forced, simply forced, to concede" (87).

While their numbers are still relatively small, activists in groups like Jews Against the Occupation, A Jewish Voice for Peace, Jews for Peace in Palestine and Israel, Students for Justice in Palestine, the Labor Committee for Peace and Justice, and other "communities of the principled and disobedient"—the term is Susan Sontag's (348)—are organizing to bring about these political ends, whatever their costs. With others who condemn Israel as a "racist state, an imperialist state," they will do what they can to make it a pariah state. The full effects of their efforts may or may not be clear to these Jews, for they couch their ambitions in the high-sounding terms of "peace," "justice," and "reconciliation" and may not realize how reckless they really are. Should they ever succeed in reducing Israel's already embattled status to that of a rogue state "totally isolated by world opinion," once again, as in 1948, there will be dancing in the streets. But this time it will be in the streets of Nablus, Cairo, Damascus, and Tehran—and also, no doubt, Berkeley, Cambridge, New York, and Tel Aviv.

Notes

1. Abraham Brumberg, "Towards the Final Solution: Perceptions of Hitler and Nazism in the US Left-of-Center Yiddish Press, 1930-1939," in *Why Didn't the Press Shout? American & International Journalism during the Holocaust*, ed. Robert M. Shapiro (New York: Yeshiva University Press/KTAV, 2003), 23-24.
2. Laurel Leff, "When Facts Didn't Speak for Themselves: The Holocaust in the *New York Times*, 1939-1945," in *Why Didn't the Press Shout?*, 54, 55. See also Laurel Leff, *Buried by the Times: The Holocaust and America's Most Important Newspaper* (Cambridge, UK: Cambridge University Press, 2005).
3. Max Frankel, "Turning away from the Holocaust: The *New York Times*," in *Why Didn't the Press Shout?*, 79-80. Frankel's article originally appeared in the *Times* on November 14, 2001 as part of the newspaper's 150th year retrospective.
4. Ronald Steel, *Walter Lippmann and the American Century*. New Edition. (New Brunswick, NJ: Transaction Publishers, 1999), 186.
5. Ilan Avisar, *Screening the Holocaust* (Bloomington: Indiana University Press, 1988), 96-97.
6. Cited in Barry Rubin, *Assimilation and Its Discontents* (New York: New York Times Books, 1995), 79.
7. See David Wyman, *The Abandonment of the Jews* (New York: Pantheon, 1984) and David Wyman and Raphael Medoff, *A Race against Death: Peter Bergson, America, and the Holocaust* (New York: New Press, 1992).
8. In addition to the work of David Wyman, see Henry Feingold, *The Politics of Rescue: The Roosevelt Administration and the Holocaust, 1938-1945* (New Brunswick, NJ: Rutgers University Press, 1970) and, by the same author, *Bearing Witness: How America and Its Jews Responded to the Holocaust* (Syracuse, NY: Syracuse University Press, 1995); and also, Gulie N. Arad, *America, Its Jews, and the Rise of the Nazis* (Bloomington: Indiana University Press, 2000).
9. Ruth Wisse, "The New York (Jewish) Intellectuals," *Commentary* (November 1987), 36.
10. Irving Howe, *A Margin of Hope: An Intellectual Autobiography* (New York: Harcourt Brace Jovanovich, 1982), 249-250.
11. Leslie Fiedler, *Fiedler on the Roof: Essays on Literature and Jewish Identity* (Boston: David R. Godine, 1991), 163, 166, 167.
12. Alexander Bloom, *Prodigal Sons: The New York Intellectuals and Their World* (New York: Oxford University Press, 1986), 138.
13. Ibid.
14. *A Margin of Hope*, 251.
15. Irving Howe, "The Range of the New York Intellectuals," in *Creators and Disturbers: Reminiscences of Jewish Intellectuals in New York,* ed. Bernard Rosenberg and Ernest Goldstein (New York: Columbia University Press, 1982), 285.
16. Ibid., 286.
17. *A Margin of Hope*, 276.
18. Ibid., 252.
19. Ibid., 251.

20.   *Fiedler on the Roof,* 176.
21.   Ibid., 168, 169.
22.   *A Margin of Hope,* 276.
23.   "The Range of the New York Intellectuals," 276.
24.   *Prodigal Sons,* 138.
25.   Andrei Markovits, "The European and American Left Since 1945," *Dissent,* Winter 2005.
26.   Schwarzchild's denunciation of Israel was delivered as he withdrew from the Editorial Advisory Board of the journal *Sh 'ma.* The text is reprinted in *Wrestling with Zion,* 35-36.
27.   For a brief but clarifying article that exposes the falsity of these charges, see Benjamin Pogrund, "Is Israel the New Apartheid?" Yakar's Center for Social Concern, Jerusalem. September 7, 2004.
28.   See Atarah Haber, "'Genocide' big word at London anti-Israel academic conference," *Jerusalem Post,* December 7, 2004. See also Philologos, "Horror Is as Horror Speaks," *Forward,* September 14, 2001.
29.   See Susanne Urban, "Friend or Foe? Jewish Self-Degradation and Its Misuse by Anti-Semites in Contemporary Germany," *NATIV Online,* April 2004; http://www.acpr.org.il/ENGLISH-NATIV/03-issue/urban-3.htm; Joel Fishman, "Lev Grinberg and the Meaning of 'Symbolic Genocide,'" *NATIV Online,* June 2004; http://www.acpr.org.il/ENGLISH-NATIV/04-issue/fishman-4.htm.
30.   Uri Avnery, "Manufacturing Anti-Semites," in *The Politics of Anti-Semitism,* ed. A. Cockburn and J. St. Clair (Oakland, California: AK Press/CounterPunch, 2003), 45.
31.   Ibid, 46.
32.   Ibid, 43.
33.   Avraham Burg, "A Failed Israeli Society Collapses While Its Leaders Remain Silent," *Forward* August 29, 2003.
34.   Anthony Kind, "The Countries That We Love and Hate," *Daily Telegraph,* January 3, 2005.
35.   See Etgar Lefkovits, "Over 50% of Germans Equate IDF With Nazi Army," *Jerusalem Post* December 7, 2004.
36.   I am indebted to Professor Bernard Harrison for some of the insights formulated here.
37.   Kenneth Levin, *The Oslo Syndrome: Delusions of a People Under Siege* (Hanover, New Hampshire: Smith and Kraus Global, 2005), xix.
38.   Seymour Martin Lipset, "'The Socialism of Fools': The Left, the Jews, and Israel," in *The New Left and the Jews,* ed. Mordecai Chertoff (New York: Pitman Publishing Corporation, 1971), 128.
39.   Tony Judt, "Israel: The Alternative," *New York Review of Books,* October 23, 2003.
40.   Leon Wieseltier, "What Is Not to Be Done," *New Republic,* October 27, 2003, 23.
41.   Michael Neumann, "What Is Anti-Semitism?" in *The Politics of Anti-Semitism,* 3, 4, 5, 6, 10.

3

Israelis Against Themselves

Edward Alexander

"Antisemitism directed at oneself was an original Jewish creation. I don't know of any other nation so flooded with self-criticism. Even after the Holocaust…harsh comments were made by prominent Jews against the victims…. The Jewish ability to internalize any critical and condemnatory remark and castigate themselves is one of the marvels of human nature…. Day and night…that feeling produces dread, sensitivity, self-criticism and sometimes self-destruction."
—*Aharon Appelfeld (*New York Times Book Review, February 28, 1988)

I

In his essay of 1838 on Jeremy Bentham, J. S. Mill wrote that "speculative philosophy, which to the superficial appears a thing so remote from the business of life and the outward interests of men, is in reality the thing on earth which most influences them, and in the long run overbears every other influence save those which it must itself obey." Of course Mill was not always willing to wait for the long run and was often tempted by shortcuts whereby speculative philosophers and other intellectuals could make their influence felt upon government. Frightened by Tocqueville's observations of American democracy, Mill sought to prevent the "tyranny of the majority" by an elaborate scheme of plural voting which would give everybody one vote but intellectuals a larger number; when he awoke to the folly and danger of such a scheme he switched his allegiance to proportional representation as a means of allowing what he calls in *On Liberty* the wise and noble few to exercise their due influence over the mindless majority.

By now we have had enough experience of the influence of intellectuals in politics to be skeptical of Mill's schemes. To look back over the major intellectual journals of America in the years prior to and during the Second World War—not only Trotskyist publications like *New International* or Dwight Macdonald's *Politics*, but the highbrow modernist and Marxist *Partisan Review*—is to be appalled by the spectacle of the finest minds of America vociferous in opposition to prosecuting the war against Hitler, which in their view was just a parochial struggle between two dying capitalist forces. The pacifism of English intellectuals in the late thirties led George Orwell to declare that some ideas are so stupid that only intellectuals could believe them; and in one of his *Tribune* columns of 1943 he said of the left-wing rumor in London that America had entered the war only in order to crush a budding English socialist revolution that "one has to belong to the intelligentsia to believe something like that. No ordinary man could be such a fool."

If we look at the influence of Israeli intellectuals upon Israeli policy in recent decades, and especially during the Yitzhak Rabin/Shimon Peres and Ehud Barak governments that prepared the Oslo Accords (and Intifada II), we may conclude that Mill and Orwell were both right, Mill in stressing the remarkable power of ideas, Orwell in insisting that such power often works evil, not good.

Among the numerous misfortunes that have beset the Zionist enterprise from its inception—the unyielding hardness of the land allegedly flowing with milk and honey, the failure of the Jews of the Diaspora to move to Zion except under duress, the constant burden of peril arising from Arab racism and imperialism—was the premature birth of an intellectual class, especially a literary intelligentsia. The quality of Israel's intelligentsia may be a matter of dispute. Gershom Scholem once remarked, mischievously, that talent goes where it is needed, and in Israel it was needed far more urgently in the military than in the universities, the literary community, the arts, and journalism. But the influence of this intelligentsia is less open to dispute than its quality. When Shimon Peres (who views himself as an intellectual) launched his ill-fated election campaign of spring 1996 he surrounded himself with artists and intellectuals on the stage of Tel Aviv's Mann Auditorium.[1] Three months earlier, he had listed as one of the three future stars of the Labor Party the internationally famous novelist Amos Oz, the same Amos Oz who was notorious among religiously observant Jewish "settlers" for having referred to their organization Gush Emunim (Block of the Faithful) in a speech of June 1989 in language generally reserved for thieves and murderers: they were, he told a Peace Now gathering of about 20,000 people in Tel Aviv's Malchei Yisrael Square, "a small sect, a messianic sect, obtuse and cruel, [who] emerged a few years ago from a dark corner of Judaism, and [are] threatening to... impose on us a wild and insane blood ritual... They are guilty of crimes against humanity." [2]

Intellectuals in many countries have adopted the motto: "the *other* country, right or wrong," and worked mightily to undermine national confidence in their country's heritage, founding principles, *raison d'être*. But such intellectuals do not usually arise within fifty years of their country's founding, and in no case except Israel have intellectuals cultivated their "alienation" in a country whose "right to exist" is considered an acceptable subject of discussion among otherwise respectable people and nations. As Midge Decter shrewdly put it in May 1996, "A country only half a century old is not supposed to have a full fledged accomplished literary intelligentsia... This is an extravagance only an old and stable country should be allowed to indulge in."[2]

The seeds of trouble amongst intellectuals in Zion antedated the state itself. On May Day 1936 the Labor Zionist leader Berl Katznelson asked, angrily:

> Is there another people on earth whose sons are so emotionally and mentally twisted that they consider everything their nation does despicable and hateful, while every murder, rape and robbery committed by their enemies fills their hearts with admiration and awe? As long as a Jewish child... can come to the Land of Israel, and here catch the virus of self-hate... let not our conscience be still.[3]

But what for Katznelson was a sick aberration would later become the normal condition among a substantial segment of Israeli intellectuals. A major turning point came in 1967, when the doctors of Israel's soul, a numerous fraternity, concluded that in winning a defensive war which, if lost, would have brought its destruction, Israel had bartered its soul for a piece of land. The Arab nations, shrewdly sensing that Jews were far less capable of waging the war of ideas than the war of planes and tanks, quickly transformed the rhetoric of their opposition to Israel's existence from the Right to the Left, from the aspiration to "turn the Mediterranean red with Jewish blood" (the battle cry of the months preceding the Six Day War) to the pretended search for a haven for the homeless. This deliberate appeal to liberals, as Ruth Wisse has amply demonstrated,[4] created legions of critics of the Jewish state, especially among devout believers in the progressive improvement and increasing enlightenment of the human race. Israeli intellectuals who were willing to express, especially in dramatic hyperbole, criticism of their own country's alleged racism, imperialism, and religious fanaticism quickly became celebrities in the American press. They were exalted by people like Anthony Lewis as courageous voices of dissent, even though what they had joined was, of course, a community of *con*sent.

But it was not until a decade later that the Israeli intelligentsia turned massively against the state, against Zionism, against Judaism itself. For in 1977 the Labor Party lost its twenty-nine-year-old ownership of government to people it considered its cultural inferiors, people Meron Benvenisti described as follows: "I remember traveling on a Haifa bus and looking around at my fellow passengers with contempt and indifference—almost as lower forms of human life."[5] Such hysteria (which burst forth again in May 1996 when Benjamin Netanyahu won the election) now became the standard pose of the alienated Israeli intellectual, and it was aggressively disseminated by American publications such as the *New York Times*, ever eager for Israeli-accented confirmation of its own views. Amos Oz, for example, took to the pages of the *New York Times Magazine* during the Lebanon War to deplore the imminent demise of Israel's "soul": "Israel could have become an exemplary state... a small-scale laboratory for democratic socialism." But that great hope, Oz lamented, was dashed by the arrival of Holocaust refugees, various "anti-socialist" Zionists, "chauvinistic, militaristic, and xenophobic" North African Jews, and so forth.[6] (These are essentially the reasons why it was not until Menachem Begin became prime minister that the Ethiopian Jews could come to Israel.) By 1995 Oz was telling

New York Times readers that supporters of the Likud party were accomplices of Hamas.[7] Even after spiritual brethren of Hamas massacred three thousand people in the United States on September 11, 2001, Oz declared that the enemy was not in any sense the radical Islamist or Arabic mentality but simply "fanaticism," and that in any case the most pressing matter he could think of was to give "Palestinians their natural right to self-determination." For good measure he added the patently false assertion that "almost all [Muslims] are as shocked and aggrieved [by the suicide bombings of America] as the rest of mankind."[8] Apparently Oz had missed all those photos of Muslims round the world handing out candy, ululating, dancing, and jubilating over dead Jews and dead Americans. It was a remarkable performance, which made one wonder whether Oz gets to write about politics because he is a novelist or gets his reputation as a novelist because of his political views.

People like Benvenisti—sociologist, deputy mayor of Jerusalem until fired by Teddy Kollek, and favorite authority on Israel for many years of the *New York Times* and *New York Review of Books*—foreshadowed the boasting of the intellectual spokesmen of later Labor governments that they were not only post-Zionist but also post-Jewish in their thinking. Benvenisti, writing in 1987, recalled proudly how "We would observe Yom Kippur by loading quantities of food onto a raft and swimming out with it to an offshore islet in the Mediterranean, and there we would while away the whole day feasting. It was a flagrant demonstration of our rejection of religious and Diaspora values."[9]

Anecdotal evidence of the increasingly shrill anti-Israelism (or worse) of Israeli intellectuals is only too easy to amass. Some years ago the sculptor Yigal Tumarkin stated that "When I see the black-coated *haredim* with the children they spawn, I can understand the Holocaust."[10] Ze'ev Sternhell, Hebrew University expert on fascism, proposed destroying the Jewish settlements with IDF tanks as a means of boosting national morale.[11] In 1969 the guru of Labor Party intellectuals, the late Professor Yeshayahu Leibowitz, as Alvin Rosenfeld observes elsewhere in this book, began to talk of the inevitable "Nazification" of the Israeli nation and society. By the time of the Lebanon War he had become an international celebrity because of his use of the epithet "Judeo-Nazi" to describe the Israeli army. When Iraq invaded Kuwait in 1990, he outdid even himself by declaring (in words redolent of what Katznelson had deplored in 1936): "Everything Israel has done, and I emphasize *everything*, in the past 23 years is either evil stupidity or stupidly evil."[12] And in 1993 Leibowitz would be honored by the government of Yitzhak Rabin with the Israel Prize.

In third place after Oz and Benvenisti among the resources of intellectual insight into Israel's soul frequently mined by Anthony Lewis, Thomas Friedman, and like-minded journalists is David Grossman, the novelist. Grossman established his credentials as an alienated intellectual commentator on the state of his country's mind in a book of 1988 called *The Yellow Wind*, an account of his seven-week journey through the "West Bank," a journey under-taken in order to understand "how an entire nation like mine, an enlightened nation by all accounts, is able to train itself to live as a conqueror without making its own life wretched."[13] This is a complicated book, not without occa-sional patches of honesty. But its true flavor can be suggested by two succes-sive chapters dealing with culture and books, especially religious ones. Grossman first visits the Jewish settlement of Ofra, at which he arrives fully armed with suspicion, hostility, and partisanship, a "wary stranger" among people who remind him, he says, of nothing human, especially when they are "in the season of their messianic heat" (52). In Ofra, Grossman does not want "to let down his guard" and be "seduced" by the Sabbath "warmth" and "festivity" of these wily Jews (34). Although most of his remarks to Arabs in conversation recounted in *The Yellow Wind* are the perfunctory gestures of a straight man to whom his interlocutors pay no serious attention, he angrily complains that the Jewish settlers don't listen to or "display a real interest" in him. He asks them to "imagine themselves in their Arab neighbors' places" (37) and is very much the angry schoolmaster when they don't act like compliant puppets or accept his pretense that this act of sympathetic imagination is devoid of political mean-ing. Neither are the settlers intellectually nimble enough to make the appropri-ate reply to Grossman: "My dear fellow, we will imagine ourselves as Arabs if you will imagine yourself as a Jew." But Grossman has no intention of suspend-ing his own rhythms of existence long enough to penetrate the inner life of these alien people: "What have I to do with them?" (48) His resentment is as much cultural as political. He complains that the settlers have "little use for culture," speak bad Hebrew, indulge in "Old Diaspora type" humor, and own no books, "with the exception of religious texts" (46). And these, far from mitigat-ing the barbarity of their owners, aggravate it. The final image of the Jews in this long chapter is of "potential [!] terrorists now rocking over their books." (51) For Grossman, the conjectural terrorism of Jews is a far more grievous matter than the actual terrorism of Arabs.

The following chapter also treats of culture and books, including religious ones. Grossman has come to Bethlehem University, one of several universities in the territories that have been punningly described as branches of PLO State. Here Grossman, though he admits the school to be "a stronghold of the Demo-cratic Front for the Liberation of Palestine," sees no terrorists rocking over books, but rather idyllic scenes that remind him of "the pictures of Plato's school in Athens" (57). Bubbling with affection, eager to ascribe only the high-est motives, Grossman is now willing to forgive even readers of religious books. He has not so much as a snort or a sneer for the Bethlehem English professor who ascribes Arabs' supreme sensitivity to lyric rhythm in English poetry to the "rhythm of the Koran flow[ing] through their blood" (59). The author's ability to spot racism at a distance of twenty miles when he is among Jews slackens when timeless racial categories are invoked in Bethlehem.

When the Labor Party returned to power in 1992, so too did the Israeli intellectuals and their disciples. People once (rather naively) casually referred to as extremists moved to the centers of power in Israeli government and policy formation. Dedi Zucker, who used to accuse Jewish "settlers" of drinking blood on Passover, and Yossi Sarid, who once shocked Israelis by declaring that Holocaust Memorial Day meant nothing to him, and Shulamit Aloni, whose statements about religious Jews would probably have landed her in jail in European countries that have laws against antisemitic provocation, all became cabinet ministers or prominent spokesmen in the government of Rabin. Two previously obscure professors laid the foundations for the embrace of Yasser Arafat, one of the major war criminals of the twentieth century, responsible for the murder of more Jews than anyone since Hitler and Stalin. The Oslo process put the PLO well on the way to an independent Palestinian state, had Arafat desired one (a conjectural state, it should be added, that probably commands the allegiance of more Israeli intellectuals than does the actual Jewish one). Amos Oz and A. B. Yehoshua and David Grossman were delighted. Oz announced in 1993 that "death shall be no more," and Grossman assured Anthony Lewis that Israel had finally given up its "instinctive suspicion," and that although "we have the worst terrorism," "we are making peace."[14] Benvenisti proved harder to satisfy: in 1995, he published a book called *Intimate Enemies*, the ads for which carried glowing endorsements from Thomas Friedman and Professor Ian Lustick, in which he proposed dissolution of the State of Israel.

Only a few figures within Israel's cultural establishment expressed dismay at what was happening. The philosopher Eliezer Schweid warned that a nation which starts by abandoning its cultural memories ends by abandoning its physical existence.[15] Amos Perlmutter analyzed the "post-Zionism" of Israeli academics as an all-out attack on the validity of the state.[16] A still more notable exception to the general euphoria of this class was Aharon Megged. In his *Ha'aretz* essay of June 1994 called "The Israeli Suicide Drive" this long-time supporter of the Labor Party connected the Rabin government's record of endless unreciprocated concessions (to a PLO that had not even cancelled its Charter calling for Israel's destruction) to the self-destructiveness that had long before infected Israel's intellectual classes. Megged argued that since 1967 the Israeli intelligentsia had more and more come "to regard religious, cultural, and emotional affinity to the land... with sheer contempt"; and he observed that the equation of Israelis with Nazis had become an article of faith for the otherwise faithless learned classes. He also shrewdly remarked on the methods by which anti-Zionist Israeli intellectuals disseminated their message and reputations. Writers like Benny Morris, Ilan Pappe, and Baruch Kimmerling "mostly publish first in English to gain the praise of the West's 'justice seekers.' Their works are then quickly translated into Arabic and displayed in Damascus, Cairo and Tunis. Their conclusion is almost uniform: that in practice Zionism amounts to an evil, colonialist conspiracy... "[17]

The minds of the majority of those who carried on the Oslo Process of the Israeli government from 1993 to 1996 were formed by the writers, artists, and publicists whom Megged excoriated. Although Shimon Peres' utterances about the endless war for independence which his country has been forced to wage often seemed to come from a man who had taken leave of the actual world, they were rooted in the "post-Zionist," post-Jewish, and universalist assumptions of the Israeli intelligentsia. Just as they were contemptuous of any tie with the Land of Israel, so he repeatedly alleged that land plays no part in Judaism or even in the Jewish political philosophy that names itself after a specific mountain called Zion. Like the Israeli intelligentsia, he accused Israel's religious Jews of an atavistic attachment to territory over "spirit," claiming that Judaism is "ethical/moral and spiritual, and not an idolatry of soil-worship."[18] Just as Israeli intellectuals nimbly pursued and imitated the latest cultural fads of America and Europe, hoping to be assimilated by the great world outside Israel, so did Peres hope that Israel would one day be admitted into the Arab League.[19]

Despite the enlistment of then President William Clinton as his campaign manager, and the nearly unanimous support he received from the Israeli and world news media, to say nothing of the herd of independent thinkers from the universities, and the rented academics of the think tanks, Shimon Peres and his Oslo process were decisively rejected by the Jewish voters of Israel. Predictably, the Israeli intellectuals (not guessing that Labor's successors would blindly continue the process) reacted with melodramatic hysteria. David Grossman, in the *New York Times* of May 31, wailed sanctimoniously that "Israel has moved toward the extreme right... more militant, more religious, more fundamentalist, more tribal and more racist."[20]

Among the American liberal supporters of Israel's intellectual elite, only the *New Republic* appeared somewhat chastened by the election result. Having for years, perhaps decades, celebrated the ineffable genius of Shimon Peres and his coterie, the magazine turned angrily upon the Israeli intellectuals for failing to grasp that "their association with Peres was one of the causes of his defeat."

> Disdainful of [Jews] from traditional communities, they thought of and called such people "stupid Sephardim." This contempt for Arab Jews expresses itself in a cruel paradox, for it coexists with a credulity about, and esteem for, the Middle East's Christians and Muslims—Arab Arabs. Such esteem, coupled with a derisive attitude toward Jewish symbols and texts, rituals, remembrances and anxieties, sent tens of thousands to Netanyahu.[21]

II

The most ambitious attempt to trace the history and analyze the causes of the maladies of Israeli intellectuals is Yoram Hazony's book *The Jewish State*, which appeared early in the year 2000. Within months of its publication the dire consequences of the Oslo accords, post-Zionism's major political achievement, became visible to everybody in Israel in the form of Intifada II, otherwise known as the Oslo War, a campaign of unremitting atrocities—pogroms, lynchings, suicide bombings—launched by Yasser Arafat after 97 percent of his demands, including an independent Palestinian state, had been conceded by the government of the hapless Ehud Barak.

The Jewish State is a broadside aimed at those Israelis who, in what its author calls "a carnival of self-loathing,"[22] are busily eating away at the Jewish foundations of that state. The book's very title is a conscious affront to Israel's *branja*, a slang term for the "progressive" and "enlightened" experts whose views, according to Supreme Court Chief Justice Aharon Barak, should determine the court's decisions on crucial matters. For these *illuminati* have sought to enlist no less a figure than Theodor Herzl in their campaign to de-Judaize the state of Israel. Nearly all the "post-Zionists" discussed in *The Jewish State* claim that Herzl did not intend the title of his famous book to be *The Jewish State* at all, that the state he proposed was in no significant sense intrinsically Jewish, and that he believed in a total separation of religion from the state. Hazony argues (and massively demonstrates) that Herzl believed a Jewish state was essential to rescue the Jewish people from both antisemitism and assimilation, the forces that were destroying Jewish life throughout the Diaspora. (Most of Herzl's rabbinic opponents argued that Zionism was itself but a thinly veiled form of assimilation.)

Hazony's *Jewish State* has two purposes. The first is to show that "the idea of the Jewish state is under systematic attack from its own cultural and intellectual establishment" (xxvii). These "culture makers" have renounced the idea of a Jewish state—"A state," claims Amos Oz, "cannot be Jewish, just as a chair or a bus cannot be Jewish" (338). The writers who dominate Israeli culture, Hazony argues, are adept at imagining what it is like to be an Arab; they have, like the aforementioned David Grossman, much more trouble imagining what it is like to be a Jew.

If Israeli intellectuals were merely supplying their own illustration of Orwell's quip about the unique susceptibility of intellectuals to stupid ideas, their hostility to Israel's Jewish traditions and Zionist character would not merit much concern. But Hazony shows that they have had spectacular success, amounting to a virtual coup d'etat, in their political struggle for a post-Jewish state. "What is perhaps most remarkable about the advance of the new ideas in Israeli government policy is the way in which even the most sweeping changes in Israel's character as a Jewish state can be effected by a handful of intellectuals, with only the most minimal of opposition from the country's political leaders or the public" (52).

The post-Zionists imposed their views in the public-school curriculum, in the Basic Laws of the country, and in the IDF (Israel Defense Force), whose code of ethics now excluded any allusion to Jewish or Zionist principles. The author of the new code was Asa Kasher, one of Israel's most enterprising post-Zionists, who modestly described his composition as "the most profound code of ethics in the world of military ethics, in particular, and in the world of professional ethics, in general"—so terminally profound, in fact, that an Israeli soldier "doesn't need to think or philosophize anymore. Someone else already... did the thinking and decided. There are no dilemmas" (53, 56).

The ultimate triumph of post-Zionism, Hazony argues, came in its conquest of the Foreign Ministry and the mind of Shimon Peres. Both came to the conclusion that Israel must retreat from the idea of an independent Jewish state. In the accord reached with Egypt in 1978 and even in the 1994 accord with Jordan, Israeli governments had insisted that the Arab signatories recognize the Jewish state's "sovereignty, territorial integrity, and political independence" (58). But the Oslo accords with the fanatically anti-Zionist PLO conceded on every one of these issues; and if the agreement with the PLO was partly an effect of post-Zionism, it was an effect that became in turn a cause—giving respectability and wide exposure to post-Zionist political prejudices formerly confined to coteries in Rehavia and Ramat-Aviv.

Thereafter, Peres and his Foreign Office routinely promoted the interests not of a sovereign Jewish state but of the (largely Arab) Middle East. In a reversal of policy akin to that of the Soviet Foreign Ministry in the wake of Stalin's pact with Hitler, Uri Savir and other Foreign Ministry officials exhorted American Jews who had for decades resisted the Arab campaign to blacken Israel's reputation to support U.S. foreign aid to the two chief blackeners, the PLO and Syria. They—it was alleged—needed dollars much more than Israel. Peres himself, as we observed earlier, carried the post-Zionist campaign for assimilation and universalism to the global level, grandly announcing in December 1994 that "Israel's next goal should be to become a member of the Arab League" (67).

The second part of Hazony's book has a twofold purpose. The first is to write the history of the ideological and political struggle within the Jewish world itself over the idea of the Jewish state, paying particular attention to how that ideal, which a few decades ago had been axiomatic among virtually all Jews the world over, had so quickly "been brought to ruin among the cultural leadership of the Jewish state itself" (78). Hazony's second aim as historian is to demonstrate the power of ideas, especially the truth of John Stuart Mill's axiom about the practical potency, in the long run, of (apparently useless) speculative philosophy. It was the power of ideas that enabled philosopher Martin Buber and other opponents of the Jewish state to break Ben-Gurion and to undermine the practical-minded stalwarts of Labor Zionism. (Likud hardly figures in this book. The quarrels between Ben-Gurion and Begin have from Hazony's perspective "the character of a squabble between the captain and the first mate of a sinking ship" [79].)

Hazony is a masterful political and cultural historian, and his fascinating account of the long struggle of Buber (and his Hebrew University acolytes) against Herzl and Ben-Gurion's conception of a genuinely Jewish state is told with tremendous verve and insight. Buber is at once the villain and the hero of this book. He is the villain in his relentless opposition to a Jewish state; in his licentious equations between Labor Zionists and Nazis; in his fierce anti-(Jewish) immigration stance (announced the day after he himself had immigrated from Germany in 1938). But he is the hero because his posthumous ideological victory over Labor Zionism—most of today's leading post-Zionists claim that their minds were formed by Buber and his binationalist Brit Shalom/Ihud allies at Hebrew University—is in Hazony's view the most stunning example of how ideas and myths are in the long run of more political importance than kibbutzim and settlements. Because Buber understood the way in which culture eventually determines politics and grasped the potency of books and journals and (most of all) universities, his (to Hazony) malignant influence now carries the day in Israel's political as well as its cultural wars.

Hazony argues that since the fall of Ben-Gurion, Israel has had no prime minister—not Golda Meir, not Menachem Begin—who was an "idea-maker." Even the very shrewd Ben-Gurion and Berl Katznelson (who presciently warned of the dangers lurking in the "intellectual famine" (299) of Labor Israel) were slow to recognize the potentially disastrous consequences of entrusting the higher education of their children to a university largely controlled (for twenty-four years) by the anti-Zionist Judah Magnes and largely staffed by faculty he recruited. Magnes, in language foreshadowing the cliches of today's post-Zionists, charged that the Jewish settlement in Palestine had been "born in sin"(203); moreover, he believed that seeing history from the Arabs' historical perspective was one of the main reasons for establishing the Hebrew University.

Hazony's book is written backwards, something like a murder mystery. He begins with a dismaying, indeed terrifying picture of a nearly moribund people, exhausted, confused, aimless—their traditional Labor Zionist assumptions declared "effectively dead" by their formerly Labor Zionist leaders, most crucially Shimon Peres. He then moves backward to seek the reasons why the Zionist enterprise is in danger of being dismantled, not by Israel's Arab enemies (who gleefully watch the spectacle unfold), but by its own heavily petted intellectual, artistic, and political elite—professors, writers, luminaries in the visual arts.

The material in the early chapters is shocking, and I speak as one who thought he had seen it all: the visiting sociologist from Hebrew University who adorned his office at my university with a PLO recruiting poster; the Tel-Aviv University philosophy professor who supplied Noam Chomsky's supporters with a letter of kashrut certifying the "lifelong dedication to Israel" of their (Israel-hating) idol; the Haifa University sociologist active in the American-Arab Anti-Discrimination League (a PLO front group); the contingent of Israeli professors taking up arms on behalf of the great prevaricator Edward Said. But the material Hazony has collected (and dissected) from Israel's post-Zionist and post-Jewish intellectuals shocks me nevertheless. Compared with the Baruch Kimmerlings, the Asa Kashers, the Ilan Pappes, and other protagonists in Hazony's tragedy,

Austria's Jorge Haider, the right-wing demagogue about whom the Israeli government kicked up such a fuss some years ago, is a Judeophile and Lover of Zion.

Hazony carefully refrains from applying the term "antisemitic" to even the most extreme defamations of Jewish tradition and of the Jewish state by post-Zionists and their epigones. But surely such reticence is unnecessary when the secret has long been out. As far back as May 1987 the Israeli humorist and cartoonist Dosh, in a column in *Ma'ariv*, drew a picture of a shopper in a store that specialized in antisemitic merchandise reaching for the top shelf—on which lay the most expensive item, adorned by a *Stürmer*-like caricature of a Jew and prominently labeled "Made in Israel." The article this cartoon illustrated spoke of Israel's need to increase exports by embellishing products available elsewhere in the world with unique local characteristics. Israel had done this with certain fruits and vegetables in the past, and now she was doing it with defamations of Israel, produced in Israel. Customers were getting more selective, no longer willing to make do with grade B merchandise produced by British leftists or French neo-Nazis. No, they wanted authentic material, from local sources; and Israeli intellectuals, artists, playwrights, were responding with alacrity to the opportunity.

But Dosh had spoken merely of a specialty shop. To accommodate the abundant production of Hazony's gallery of post-Zionist/post-Jewish defamers of Israel (both the people and the Land) would require a department store twice the size of Macy's or Harrod's. On bargain day, one imagines the following recitation by the elevator operator: "First floor, Moshe Zimmermann, Yeshayahu Leibowitz, and 68 other members of the progressive and universalist community on Israelis as Nazis; second floor, A. B. Yehoshua on how Israeli Jews might become "normal" by converting to Christianity or Islam; third floor, Boaz Evron in justification of Vichy France's anti-Jewish measures; fourth floor, Idith Zertal on Zionist absorption of Holocaust refugees as a form of rape; fifth floor, Benny Morris on Zionism as ethnic cleansing; attic, Shulamit Aloni on Zionism (also Judaism) as racism; basement, Ya'akov Yovel justifying the medieval blood libel; sub-basement, Yigal Tumarkin justifying Nazi murder of (religious) Jews. Watch your step, please."

Although Hazony's argument for the large role played by Israel's professoriat in dismantling Labor Zionism is convincing, it cannot be a sufficient cause of current post-Zionism and post-Judaism. The habitual language of post-Zionists, and most especially their hammering insistence on the contradiction between being Jewish and being human, is exactly the language of European Jewish ideologues of assimilation over a century ago. Gidon Samet, one of the numerous resident ideologues of post-Judaism and post-Zionism at *Ha'aretz*, is not far from the truth when he likens their attractions to those of American junk food and junk-music: "Madonna and Big Macs," Samet says," are only the most peripheral of examples" of the wonderful blessings of Israel's new "normalness" (71-72). Of course, whatever we may think of those who in 1900 urged fellow-Jews to cease being Jewish in order to join universal humanity, they at least were not promoting this sinister distinction in full knowledge of how it would be used by Hitler; the same cannot be said of contemporary Israeli ideologues of assimilation and universalism.

Most readers of post-Zionist outpourings have little to fall back on except their native mistrust of intellectuals. Thus, when Hebrew University professor Moshe Zimmermann declares that Zionism "imported" antisemitism into the Middle East (11), it requires knowledge (not much, to be sure) of history to recognize the statement as preposterous. But sometimes the post-Zionists are tripped up by overconfidence into lies that even the uninstructed can easily detect. Thus Avishai Margalit, a Hebrew University philosophy professor spiritually close to, if not quite a card-carrying member of, the post-Zionists, in a *New York Review of Books* essay of 1988 called "The Kitsch of Israel," heaped scorn upon the "children's room" at Yad Vashem with its "tape-recorded voices of children crying out in Yiddish, 'Mame, Tate [Mother, Father].'" Yad Vashem is a favorite target of the post-Zionists because they believe it encourages Jews to think not only that they were singled out for annihilation by the Nazis but also—how unreasonable of them!—to want to make sure they do not get singled out for destruction again. But, as any Jerusalemite or tourist who can get over to Mount Herzl will quickly discover, there is no "children's room" and there are no taped voices at Yad Vashem. There is a memorial to the murdered children and a tape-recorded voice that reads their names.[23] Margalit's skullduggery is by no means the worst of its kind among those Israelis involved in derogating the memory and history of the country's Jewish population. But it comes as no surprise to learn from Hazony that Margalit believes Israel is morally obligated to offer Arabs "special rights" for the protection of their culture and to be "neutral" toward the Jews (13). With such neutrality as Margalit's, who needs belligerence?

In Hazony Israel has perhaps found its latter-day Jeremiah, but given the widespread tone-deafness of the country's enlightened classes to their Jewish heritage, perhaps what is needed at the moment is an Israeli Jonathan Swift, especially the Swift who in his versified will "gave the little wealth he had/To build a house for fools and mad;/And showed by one satiric touch,/No nation wanted it so much."

I began this essay with statements by J. S. Mill and George Orwell about the role of intellectuals and their ideas in politics, and I shall conclude in the same way. The first statement, by Mill, might usefully be recommended as an aid to reflection by the intellectuals of Israel: "The collective mind," wrote Mill in 1838, "does not penetrate below the surface, but it sees all the surface; which profound thinkers, even by reason of their profundity, often fail to do..." The second statement, by Orwell, seems particularly relevant as the Arab siege of Israel rages on: "if the radical intellectuals in England had had their way in the

20's and 30's," said Orwell, "the Gestapo would have been walking the streets of London in 1940."[24]

Notes

1. *Jerusalem Post*, April 6, 1996.
2. Midge Decter, "The Treason of the Intellectuals," *Outpost*, May 1996, 7.
3. *Kitvei B. Katznelson* (Tel Aviv: Workers' Party of Israel, 1961), Vol. 8, p. 18.
4. Ruth R. Wisse, *If I Am Not for Myself... The Liberal Betrayal of the Jews* (New York: Free Press, 1992).
5. Meron Benvenisti, *Conflicts and Contradictions* (New York: Villard, 1986), 70.
6. *New York Times Magazine*, July 11, 1982.
7. *New York Times*, April 11, 1995.
8. "Struggling Against Fanaticism," *New York Times*, September 14, 2001.
9. *Conflicts and Contradictions*, 34.
10. *Jerusalem Post*, December 1, 1990.
11. Ibid.
12. *Jerusalem Post*, January 16, 1993.
13. *The Yellow Wind*, trans. Haim Watzman (New York: Farrar, Straus & Giroux, 1988), 212. Subsequent references to this work will be cited in text.
14. *New York Times*, May 17, 1996. The most detailed account of the influence of Israeli intellectuals specifically on the Oslo accords is Kenneth Levin, *The Oslo Syndrome: Delusions of a People Under Siege* (Hanover, NH: Smith and Kraus Global, 2005).
15. *Jerusalem Post International Edition*, April 15, 1995.
16. "Egalitarians Gone Mad," *Jerusalem Post International Edition*, October 28, 1995.
17. Aharon Megged, "The Israeli Suicide Drive," *Jerusalem Post International Edition*, July 2, 1994.
18. Quoted in Moshe Kohn, "Check Your Quotes," *Jerusalem Post International Edition*, October 16, 1993.
19. The Arab League contemptuously replied that Israel could become a member only "after the complete collapse of the Zionist national myth, and the complete conversion of historical Palestine into one democratic state to which all the Palestinians will return."
20. "The Fortress Within," *New York Times*, May 31, 1996.
21. "Revolt of the Masses," *New Republic*, June 24, 1996.
22. *The Jewish State* (New York: Basic Books, 2000), 339. Subsequent references to this work will be cited in parentheses in the text.
23. Ten years later, Margalit reprinted this piece in a collection of his essays called *Views in Review*. There he says he has omitted a sentence from the original essay that "had wrong information in it about the children's memorial room at Yad Vashem." But he blames this on "an employee" who misled him. Margalit's sleight of hand here reveals two things: (1) When he says in his introduction to the book that "I am not even an eyewitness to much of what I write about," we can believe him. (2) The Yiddish writer Shmuel Niger was correct to say that "we suffer not only from Jews who are too coarse, but also from Jews who are too sensitive."
24. In *The Lion and the Unicorn* (1941) Orwell also wrote: "The really important fact about the English intelligentsia is their severance from the common culture of the country... In the general patriotism, they form an island of dissident thought. England is the only great nation whose intellectuals are ashamed of their country." This, not to put too fine a point upon it, no longer seems true.

4

George Steiner's Jewish Problem

Assaf Sagiv

In a lecture delivered in 1966, noted Hebrew University scholar Gershom Scholem offered his impressions of the widespread assimilation that German Jewry had undergone over the course of two centuries of emancipation. Though many Jews took great pains to obscure their origins, Scholem argued, they never were able to earn full acceptance in German society. Cut off from both their own religious heritage and the culture of Christian Europe, assimilated Jews came to be seen by many Germans as the embodiment of alienation:

> The German Jew was held to blame for his own estrangement or alienation from the Jewish ground that had nourished him, from his own history and tradition, and was blamed even more for his alienation from the bourgeois society that was then in the process of consolidating itself. The fact that he was not really at home, however much and emphatically he might proclaim himself to be…, constituted, at a time when alienation was still a term of abuse, a powerful accusation.[1]

After the Holocaust, however, intellectual circles in Central and Western Europe came to appreciate and even admire the alienation of the exiled Jew. The same sense of estrangement and rootlessness that once inspired contempt now represented the antithesis of that chauvinist romanticism of blood and land that had dominated Europe; the Jew in exile now wore a tragic, heroic mantle. The traditional image of the Jew as perpetual stranger became an ideal, extolled by intellectuals such as Hannah Arendt, Edmond Jabès, Jean-François Lyotard, and Zygmunt Bauman.[2] For them, the "otherness" of the Jew was nothing less than a badge of honor.

Today, such a positive view of Jewish alienation still has many adherents, of whom perhaps the most prominent is George Steiner, a professor of comparative literature at Oxford and Cambridge and one of the more original intellectuals in the contemporary cultural landscape. Since the publication of his first book, *Tolstoy or Dostoevsky* (1959), Steiner has gained renown for his remarkable erudition and his willingness to tackle the most difficult questions facing modern Western culture. Through twenty books and numerous essays, he has explored the mystery of human creativity, the power of language and its limits, the connections between art and theology, and the moral condition of modern civilization. In Britain, Steiner has become a cultural mandarin, a high priest of good taste and spiritual refinement. His most important mission has been to promote, for the English-speaking world, the ideas emanating from the intellectual centers of Central Europe—Vienna, Berlin, Budapest, and Frankfurt—and to draw attention to the achievements of German art and culture. Bryan Cheyette, a comparative literature professor at the University of Southampton, credits Steiner with being "the first telling those who would listen in Britain about Heidegger, Benjamin, and Paul Celan.... Now work on those figures is an industry, but he was a lone voice in the 1960s."[3] Lisa Jardine, a Renaissance scholar at the University of London, describes Steiner as "a rebel who made us aspire to be European; he helped move British culture from utter provincialism to cosmopolitanism."[4] A similar account of Steiner's influence was described by the Irish author and critic John Banville: "A door was flung open on what had been there all the time, at our backs, namely, our European heritage. He told us not to be cowed by insularity or hidebound by small minds, but to look beyond the border."[5]

Although not as influential in the United States, Steiner has certainly left his mark there as well. In 1966, he was asked by the *New Yorker* to pen a regular column on culture and literature, filling the post left by the celebrated critic Edmund Wilson. In that capacity he published more than 150 columns and articles, giving his American readers a taste of the European spirit and redefining the position of cultural critic in the American landscape. In 2000 he was awarded the coveted position of Norton Professor of Poetry at Harvard University, previously held by T.S. Eliot, Robert Frost, and Jorge Luis Borges. *World Literature Today* has called him "the most influential cultural mediator writing in English today"; *L.A. Weekly* has dubbed him "the prime minister of culture."[6]

Steiner's writings reflect an unflagging commitment to the cosmopolitan ideal, a belief in forging a common human consciousness that dissolves barriers of language, ethnicity, and territory. This view is most vividly expressed in his discussion of his own Jewish identity, the focal point of some of his most important essays. Steiner has no sympathy for the more isolationist elements of Jewish tradition, contending that such tendencies—and particularly their manifestation in Zionism and the State of Israel—"debase" Judaism and undermine its most important qualities. According to Steiner, the true mission of the Jews is to be found in exile: It is to be "guests" among the nations, aliens who live as refugees, restless and dispossessed. Only when they are outside of their homeland, Steiner argues, have the Jews served as the cultural vanguard and moral conscience of the nations, as prophets of a lofty and profound human ideal.

Steiner's opinions on Jews and Judaism may be impassioned, but they nonetheless reflect a surprising degree of alienation from the Jewish tradition itself.

His views, rather, seem to have been inspired mainly by the depictions appearing in Christian theology and German philosophy—traditions whose approach to Judaism has tended to be anything but sympathetic. As a result, Steiner's observations on Judaism approach their subject from a distance, and bring to bear far less knowledge than one would expect from a thinker of his caliber.

This is evident not only in the fact that Steiner is one of the most prominent contemporary Jewish thinkers willing to cast doubt on the moral justification for the Zionist enterprise. It also comes through in his willingness to question whether even the continued survival of the Jewish people is itself desirable. Steiner sees in the existence of the Jews not only a blessing but also a moral and psychological burden on humanity, one that is perhaps too heavy to bear. If so, he suggests, the only relief for the human race may consist in the complete assimilation of the Jews, and the disappearance of the Jewish people as such. Such thoughts are a difficult pill for most Jews to swallow, and it is hard to imagine any non-Jewish thinker daring to voice them openly today. Nevertheless, when adorned with the impressive moral rhetoric of a man of Steiner's stature, they resonate in a way that is difficult to ignore.

It should be stated from the outset that Steiner's opposition to Zionism and his challenge to Jewish collective existence contain no hint of what is often called Jewish self-hatred. On the contrary, Steiner is proud of his origins, of belonging to a people that has played such a decisive role in the development of civilization. He lauds the moral vision of the Jews, which has set them apart from other peoples. But despite his appreciation of Jewish uniqueness in history, Steiner's approach is emphatically universalistic. The Jews' achievement, he argues, consists solely in their contribution to the rest of humanity—a contribution that was made possible by the unique conditions of exile that shaped the Jewish genius over the centuries. Indeed, Steiner's cosmopolitan view of Jewish existence leaves little room for national or communal concerns. Rather, the Jews must remain true to their vocation in exile, scattered and wandering among the nations.

Steiner's attitude reflects, in part, his own life story. The child of Viennese parents who moved to Paris in 1924, and then to the United States in 1940, Steiner has described himself as a perpetual migrant, everywhere a guest and nowhere at home. His childhood fashioned in him a kind of refugee consciousness, which would form the core of his identification as a Jew: Steiner not only lives in exile, he lives the exile. For him, exile is an emotional, spiritual, and cultural condition from which one must never—indeed, can never—sever oneself. The anomaly of Jewish rootlessness, which most Jews over the generations have perceived as a divine punishment, is depicted by Steiner as a great virtue: "Instead of protesting his visitor-status in gentile lands, or, more precisely, in the military camps of the diaspora," he writes, "the Jew should welcome it."[7] For Steiner, exile is no punishment; it is, rather, a liberating state of detachment which enables the Jew to undertake his authentic mission on earth:

> Stalin and Hitler made of the glorious noun "cosmopolitan," with its promise of the inalienable, a murderous sneer. But did not Rashi himself, acutest of talmudic readers, tell of the everlasting need for Abraham to abandon his tent and rejoin the road? Did Rashi not instruct us that, when asking the way, a Jew should prove deaf to the right answer, that his mission lay with being errant, which is to say, in error and wandering?[8]

The Jews' status as guests among the nations has far-reaching moral implications. The Jew's wandering in the gentile world enables him to act as "moral irritant and insomniac among men," a role that Steiner calls an "honor beyond honors."[9] Among the nations, the Jew represents the uncompromising demand for universal morality, that man overcome his selfish impulses and tear down the walls dividing him from his fellow. This vision is Judaism's great contribution to humanity, writes Steiner, an exalted message that revealed itself in three historical moments: At the revelation at Mount Sinai, the defining event of Israelite monotheism, which bequeathed to the world a belief in the existence of a single, omnipotent, and incorporeal God from whose judgment no one is immune; in Jesus' Sermon on the Mount, in which he called upon human beings to "turn the other cheek," forgive their enemies and oppressors, and share all their belongings with one another; and, finally, in the utopian socialism of Karl Marx the Jew, which preached a just and egalitarian social order, devoid of commerce and property, in which "love shall be exchanged for love, trust for trust." The establishment of an inescapable divine Conscience, of an uncompromising demand for moral elevation, for unconditional love, and for total altruism—this is the great legacy of the Jewish people, through which it has irrevocably changed the moral face of mankind.[10]

Beyond this moral mission, however, life in exile also offers an unexpected cultural dividend: Rejection by and separation from the gentile community, and the sense of not belonging, served, in Steiner's view, as catalysts for the creative impulse in the Jewish character. Steiner points to the genius of figures such as Marx, Sigmund Freud, and Albert Einstein as evidence of the advantages conferred by a perpetual "otherness," which lacks any clear sense of "home." Unable to put down roots in foreign lands, the Jews developed a talent for abstraction and a facility in the international languages of music, mathematics, and the hard sciences. Since the tribal and national particularisms of the gentiles were alien to them, Jews began exploring the universal aspects of humanity. "Admittedly, I am a wanderer, a *luftmensch*, liberated from all foundations," writes Steiner. "Yet I have transformed the persecutions and the irony, the tension and the sophistry these arouse in the Jewish sensitivity, into a creative impulse which is so powerful that through its power it reshapes large sections of politics, art, and the intellectual structures of our generation."[11]

The analogy between the detachment of the exiled Jew and the alienation that fuels the work of the modern artist has frequently been invoked by modern thinkers to explain the unique contribution of the Jews to Western civilization. Steiner, obviously, is attracted by this idea. As a literary scholar, he takes a particular interest in the textual skills of writing, reading, and interpreting in which Jewish creativity found expression. The "text," in his view, is the true homeland of the People of the Book. More than any other people, he argues, the Jewish people "read, reread without cease, learnt by heart or by rote, and expounded without end the texts which spell out its mission."[12] A total and ongoing immersion in Jewish texts turned the Jew into the quintessential bibliophile, for whom "the text is home; each commentary a return."[13] The Jews therefore became the "librarians" of civilization: "The Mystery and the practices of clerisy are fundamental to Judaism. No other tradition or culture has ascribed a comparable aura to the conservation and transcription of texts."[14]

This commitment to a textual "homeland" contrasts sharply with nationalism centered on a physical homeland, which Steiner sees as the blight of modernity. "Nationalism, and with it tribalism, its primordial shade, is the nightmare of our age. Despite the fact that these are devoid of content, humans bring mad destruction down upon one another in their name."[15] By contrast, the "man of the book" is not misled by tribal, ethnic, or nationalist fantasies. He lives in a different world altogether, removed from the violence of the masses. For Steiner, the life of the spirit fosters a critical moral perspective that rejects collective bravado and subverts the oppressive authority of the national state:

> The man or woman at home in the text is, by definition, a conscientious objector: To the vulgar mystique of the flag and the anthem, to the sleep of reason which proclaims, "My country, right or wrong," to the pathos and eloquence of collective mendacities on which the nation state—be it a mass-consumer mercantile technocracy or a totalitarian oligarchy—builds its power and aggressions.[16]

The contradiction Steiner perceives between life "in the text" and political life is most clearly evident in the modern rupture of Jewish life, and in particular in the cultural and moral recklessness embodied in Zionism. By settling in the physical homeland of Palestine, the Jews have effectively turned their backs on their textual homeland, exchanging the spiritual riches of exile for a piece of Middle Eastern real estate. "Where it has traded its homeland in the text for one of the Golan Heights or in Gaza," he writes, "Judaism has become homeless to itself."[17]

At times, Steiner couches his antipathy for Zionism in more ambivalent terms. "Israel is an *indispensable miracle*," he writes at one point. "Its coming into being, its persistence against military, geopolitical odds, its civic achievements, defy reasoned expectations."[18] But generally, Steiner is vehemently opposed to the very idea of a Jewish state: Seduced by vulgar national sentiments, he argues, Israeli Jews have shed the tragic glory of their forefathers. Their attempt to refashion the Chosen People in the image of other nations constitutes a low point in their great history of sublime torment:

> It would, I sense, be somehow scandalous... if the millennia of revelation, of summons to suffering, if the agony of Abraham and of Isaac, from Mount Moria to Auschwitz,

had as its last consequence the establishment of a nation state, armed to the teeth, a land for the bourse and of the mafiosi, as are all other lands. "Normalcy" would, for the Jew, be just another mode of disappearance.[19]

Steiner's opposition to Zionism, then, stems not merely from his rejection of nationalism in general, but primarily from his belief that the Zionist enterprise amounts to nothing less than a rejection of the Jews' universal calling. Jews should abandon the boring dream of security and normalcy, and instead pursue the anomaly of exile, however painful it may be. Only through estrangement may the Jews learn to serve humanity as moral standard-bearers and creative geniuses. When the Jews betray their historic role, warns Steiner, they undermine the only possible justification for the suffering that has been their fate from time immemorial.

Steiner is, of course, not the first Jewish thinker to praise the exilic condition. In the early part of the twentieth century, philosophers such as Hermann Cohen and Franz Rosenzweig viewed the exile as a necessary condition for the advancement of Judaism's moral and cultural message. For this reason, they opposed the emerging Zionist movement, arguing that by submitting themselves to the laws of history and the corrupting influence of power politics, the Jews would betray their noble destiny. "To the eternal people," wrote Rosenzweig, "home never is home in the sense of land, as it is to the peoples of the world who plow the land and live and thrive on it, until they have all but forgotten that being a people means something besides being rooted in a land. The eternal people has not been permitted to while away time in any home. It never loses the untrammeled freedom of a wanderer, who is more faithful a knight to his country when he roams abroad...."[20]

Steiner, however, follows a different path. For while Cohen and Rosenzweig were inspired by, and in some sense responding to, the currents of contemporary German philosophy, their ultimate goal was always to delineate what they understood to be the true spirit of Judaism. Cohen's *Religion of Reason Out of the Sources of Judaism* (1919) and Rosenzweig's *Star of Redemption* (1921) are both theological works, efforts to express a religious consciousness formed primarily from within the sources of Jewish tradition. Steiner, on the other hand, makes no serious attempt to understand the Jewish experience from within. Rather, his writings on Judaism are grounded almost exclusively in external views. Now, this need not be problematic in and of itself: Jewish self-identity developed to a large extent through an intensive dialogue with surrounding cultures, and it bears the imprint of non-Jewish beliefs and ideas. The problem is that many of the ideas and images that have clearly inspired Steiner's beliefs are not merely non-Jewish in origin; some of them are the product of theological and philosophical sources that are clearly anti-Jewish in nature. Their impact on his thought can be seen in the alienated and critical positions that Steiner often adopts towards Judaism.

Indeed, Steiner himself acknowledges his deep estrangement from traditional Jewish culture. Though a celebrated polyglot, he never took the time to learn Hebrew or Aramaic, the languages in which the principal Jewish texts were written. And in fact, his familiarity with those sources is quite superficial. Moreover, his attitude towards the Jewish religion, so far as can be gleaned from his writings, is aloof. If Jewishness is to be understood as having some level of commitment to the faith of the Patriarchs, Steiner writes, then he should be considered Jewish "outwardly, in name only."[21]

It is hardly surprising, then, that Steiner identifies deeply with the assimilated Jewish intellectuals of the late nineteenth and early twentieth centuries in Central Europe. It is precisely this period, in which a great many Jewish thinkers and artists were publicly rejecting the traditions of their forefathers, that Steiner depicts as a kind of golden age of Jewish modernity. He looks back nostalgically on the role played by eminent Jewish thinkers and artists in the vanguard of the philosophical, scientific, and artistic development of the period. The list of names is breathtaking: Sigmund Freud, Albert Einstein, Ludwig Wittgenstein, Franz Kafka, Arnold Schoenberg, Edmund Husserl, Karl Kraus, Theodor Adorno, Gustav Mahler, George Cantor, Hermann Broch, Walter Benjamin, Ernst Bloch, Hannah Arendt, and numerous others. Rarely has civilization known such a concentrated burst of creativity as that which seemed to flow directly from the Jewish genius that had been liberated from the ghetto. In Steiner's view, these—and not the texts and traditions of Judaism that developed over thousands of years—are the crowning achievement of the Jewish historical enterprise.[22]

Steiner views himself as a scion of this assimilated intellectual dynasty. Like many of its outstanding representatives, he cut himself off from all elements of the traditional Jewish experience and embraced a worldview rooted in German thought. His conception of Jewish identity manifests this clearly. For example, the depiction of the Jew as having "chosen" the fate of alienation and detachment (rather than having it imposed upon him, as the Jewish tradition has always held) is openly influenced by G.W.F. Hegel's essay "The Spirit of Christianity and Its Fate" (1798). In this essay, which Yirmiyahu Yovel of the Hebrew University characterized as "the fiercest anti-Jewish text ever written by Hegel,"[23] the German philosopher charges the spirit of Judaism with negating the fundamental unity of man and nature which had been the sublime achievement of Greek civilization, and choosing instead to deepen the rift between man and the world. The patriarch Abraham appears as the archetypal alienated figure: Abraham, writes Hegel, chose to cut himself off from his homeland and his dearest relations, from his ties to people and nature, in order to reinforce within himself the spirit of "self-maintenance in strict opposition to everything."[24] As a result of this deliberate choice, Abraham became a rootless person, "a stranger on earth, a stranger to the soil and to men alike."[25] Hegel regards Abraham's divorce from normal existence as the route chosen by Abraham's descendants, the Jews, a people whose fate destines them to live a life of willful detachment.

Steiner is captivated by this Hegelian reading of Judaism, and quotes it admiringly and at length. He inverts the point, however, taking what Hegel saw as an impeachment of the Jews to be a cause for enthusiasm: "What is to Hegel an awesome pathology, a tragic, arrested stage in the advance of human consciousness towards a liberated homecoming from alienation, is, to others, the open secret of the Jewish genius and of its survival."[26] Like Hegel before him, Steiner ignores the fact that the divine imperative instructing Abraham to leave the land of his birth and his family does not send him to a life of eternal vagrancy, but to a specific destination, a designated land. The divine promise to Abraham, whereby "I give all the land that you see to you and your offspring forever,"[27] is grasped by Steiner as a "theological-scriptural mystique," which contravenes the Jew's true mission—to be a restless wanderer on earth, an eternal "guest."[28]

This depiction of the Jew as "guest," as one who is forever living in the lands of others, is also influenced to a large extent by German thought. Here Steiner is clearly following in the footsteps of Martin Heidegger, whose works he studied extensively.[29] In his greatest work, *Being and Time* (1927), Heidegger describes human existence as being "thrown" into the world. Man is hurled into existence; his very birth and death are not determined through his own free choice. Therefore, man must regard his place in the world as one who is "dwelling in a house of which he is, at his rare best, a custodian, but never architect or proprietor."[30] Steiner, "utterly persuaded" by these words of Heidegger, embraces this view of man, and amplifies it with respect to the Jews.[31] "All of us are guests of life," he writes. "No human being knows the meaning of its creation, except in the most primitive, biological regard. No man or woman knows the purpose, if any, the possible significance of their 'being thrown' into the mystery of existence."[32] The unique circumstances of the Jew's existence, therefore, epitomize the rootlessness to which all human beings are in truth condemned, and allow the Jew to embody the idea of human moral responsibility in the world, a position that relies on no claims of sovereignty or possession: "It may be that the Jew in the diaspora survives in order to be a guest—still so terribly unwelcome at so many shut doors. Intrusion may be our calling, so as to suggest to our fellow men and women at large that all human beings must learn how to live as each other's 'guests-in-life.'"[33]

But beyond Steiner's acceptance of German philosophical notions of Jews and Judaism, many of his thoughts have a more ancient provenance: Early Christian theology. Indeed, Steiner is far more knowledgeable on Christian than on Jewish sources; he cites them frequently and at length, and is in constant dialogue with them. He himself candidly acknowledges the "Christianizing" tendency of his thought, underscoring the significance of "Augustinian, Thomist, and Pascalian semantics" in his theological statements, such as are found in his *Real Presence* (1986)—the title of which refers to the Catholic doctrine that consecrated bread and wine taken at mass are in fact the flesh and blood of Christ—as well as in his *Grammars of Creation* (2001).[34]

The mark left by Christian thought on Steiner's understanding of the Jews' role on earth is unmistakable. Christian motifs appear throughout Steiner's conceptual world, as has been elaborated by the historian of religion Hyam Maccoby, who points to the striking similarity between Steiner's ideal figure of the exilic Jew and the Christian archetype of the "wandering Jew."[35] This legend, which appears in a number of Christian sources starting in the thirteenth century, relates that Jesus, bearing the cross through the streets of Jerusalem on the way to his crucifixion at Golgotha, encountered a Jewish spectator, who pushed and taunted him. As punishment from heaven, this Jew was condemned to an eternity of restless wandering upon earth—a dramatic symbol of his people's fate.

An even more direct Christian source for Steiner's beliefs, however, is the theology of Augustine. In particular, it is Augustine's notion of "the eternal witness," which had a dramatic impact on the way the Church related to Jews in Europe, that reappears in Steiner's writings. Augustine held that the Jews' continuing survival and dispersion are ongoing proof of the punishment decreed upon them for rejecting Jesus, and of the truth of Christian supersession. Like the biblical figure Ham, the Jew is condemned to live a life of service: His mission is to preserve the texts of the Old Testament wherever he goes, to offer proof to the world that Christianity has not fabricated the biblical prophecies regarding the coming of the Messiah. In Augustine's view, the Jews are to be understood primarily as the "guardians of their books" and "librarians"—in other words, a people that lives around the text and for the text, and whose home is the text.[36]

This image of the Jews as living under a canopy of text made a profound impression on Christianity. In Christian polemics, the Jews were depicted as clinging to a simplistic and superficial reading of the Old Testament, refusing to accept the allegorical, spiritual meaning that the Christians found in it. But though the Jews' allegiance to the literal reading blinded them to the Christian truth, they nevertheless enjoyed a special status in the Church's view of the world. Precisely because they refused to abandon the Written Law, they became "eternal witnesses," who bore the Book of Books with them everywhere they went. In this spirit, wrote Bernard of Clairvaux, a preeminent twelfth-century religious leader, Jews constitute for Christians the "living letters" of Scripture.[37]

It is hard to deny the influence that this doctrine has had on Steiner, who argues that the authentic "homeland" of the People of the Book is textual—a view that is far more difficult to find in the Jewish sources themselves. Jonathan Sacks, chief rabbi of Great Britain and a professor of philosophy at the University of London and the Hebrew University, notes the difficulty: "If Jews in exile found a homeland in the text, it was because it was not *a*, but *the* text, the Tora, the written record of the divine covenant, locating Jews in time and space… and making them a people, despite their dispersion, who shared a constitution and a culture."[38] The Jews were dedicated not primarily to texts as such, but to the covenant, which was their founding constitutional source. While Steiner insists that a special Jewish intimacy with texts in general is inherent in the Jews' commitment to the Torah, the Jews generally had little interest in any texts other than their own.[39]

Steiner's views, therefore, are in many ways a product of his sources: By filtering his understanding of Jewish identity through the prism of Christian theology and German philosophy, he has produced a view of Judaism which, while far more sympathetic in practice to the Jews than were Hegel and Augustine, nonetheless preserves the core of their arguments about Judaism. As a result, Steiner is not undertaking anything that can be called a "Jewish" discussion; he has placed himself outside the pale of internal Jewish discourse. The result is a picture of Jewish history painted in dramatic strokes but lacking depth and empathy. Like the Christian and German sources themselves, it is hard to read this view of Judaism today, for its moral implications can be disturbing. For Steiner, these emerge most fully when he comes to address the larger question of what role Judaism should play in the future of mankind.

Given his enthusiasm for the Jews' mission as prophets of a universal morality, it may come as a surprise that Steiner ends up casting serious doubt on the moral validity of the entire Jewish effort. Since his uncompromising cosmopolitanism leads him to weigh all questions solely according to their implications for the moral fate of mankind as a whole, he allows himself to come to the conclusion that humanity not only has benefited, but has also suffered greatly, from the Jews' existence. Astonishingly, Steiner judges the Jews unfavorably for filling the very role in history that he has assigned them.

In Steiner's view, the presence of the Jew is eternally bound up in that of evil: Not only as its archetypal victim, but also as an unwitting catalyst and interlocutor for the darkest impulses of man. One example of this is found in Steiner's charge against the Jews—for which he has coined the jarring phrase "innocent guilt"—to the effect that they are responsible for the appearance of antisemitism. In addition to the spiritual heritage which the Jews have given humanity, he writes, one must never forget the heavy price they have exacted: The monstrous hatred they aroused in their neighbors, the antisemitism that reached its climax in the death camps of Germany, which dragged man down into the abyss of evil. "Jews are compelled to envisage, if not to allow, if not to rationalize, the hideous paradox of *their innocent guilt*, of the fact that it is they who have, in Western history, been the occasion, the recurrent opportunity, for the gentile to become less than a man."[40]

Steiner traces the origins of antisemitism to the Jewish rejection of Jesus. In his mind, this case of Jewish restlessness and endemic dissatisfaction had an enduring impact on the way Christendom related to the Jews. Echoing his friend and colleague, the antisemitic Catholic philosopher Pierre Boutang, Steiner contends that "the Jews, by virtue of their rejection of the Messiah-Jesus, hold mankind to ransom."[41] Since the embrace of the Christian faith by the entire human race is a condition for the appearance of the Messiah, the kingdom of grace and compassion on earth cannot be built so long as the Jew insists on remaining outside the Church.[42] The result of this historic choice was a bitter antisemitism that charted a course of hatred from Golgotha to Auschwitz. "We are that which has shown mankind to be ultimately bestial," Steiner asserted in an interview with journalist Ron Rosenbaum, for a book the latter wrote on Adolf Hitler. "We refused Jesus, who died hideously on the cross. And then mankind turns on us in a vulgar kind of counter-Golgotha, which is Auschwitz. And when somebody tortures a child, he does it to the child, he does it to himself, too."[43]

The idea that the Jews are somehow to blame for their own persecution finds expression in a number of Steiner's essays, but its most vivid development is found in *The Portage to San Cristobal of A.H.* (1981), a novel that Steiner composed over the course of three feverish days and nights. Its central theme is one that has occupied Steiner's writings incessantly over the years: The riddle of National Socialism and the singular evil manifested in the Final Solution. Yet as the story progresses, the narrative, which Steiner calls "a parable about… the abyss of pain endured by the victims of Nazism," develops into a harsh indictment of these same victims, the Jewish people—not only for debasing humanity by bringing about antisemitism, but for actually developing the ideas that brought about Nazism and for causing untold suffering to mankind.

The plot is simple and provocative. An Israeli commando unit snares the ninety-year-old Adolf Hitler (the "A.H." named in the title), who has been hiding since the war deep in the South American jungle. On their way back to San Cristobal, where he is to be tried, the soldiers succumb to illness and exhaustion. Fearing they may not reach their destination alive, the Israelis decide to try their captive in a field tribunal. Over the objections of their commander, who has warned them against Hitler's hypnotic rhetoric, they allow the defendant to speak in his own defense. The speech, which appears in the novel's last chapter, has made *The Portage to San Cristobal of A.H.* one of Steiner's most controversial works.[44]

Hitler's defense is indeed spellbinding. It has an almost demonic quality, yet within the torrent of words there is also an inner logic. The defendant makes three claims as to why his war against the Jews should not be considered a simple tale of aggressor and victim.

First, he argues, it was not the Germans but the Jews themselves who invented the ideology of the master race. His views, after all, are only a shadow of the great biblical idea of the Chosen People—"the only race on earth chosen, exalted, made singular among mankind."[45] Furthermore, it was not Germans but Jews who thought up the monstrous tool of genocide, of annihilating races for ideological reasons. Hitler cites the account in the book of Joshua of the systematic destruction visited by Israel upon the Canaanites: "And they utterly destroyed all that was in the city, both man and woman, young and old, and ox, and sheep, and ass, with the edge of the sword."[46] At this point, Hitler takes pains to honor his spiritual precursors:

> From you. Everything. To set a race apart. To keep it from defilement. To hold before it a promised land. To scour that land of its inhabitants or place them in servitude. Your beliefs. Your arrogance... The pillar of fire. That shall lead you to Canaan. And woe unto the Amorites, the Jebusites, the Kenites, the half-men outside God's pact. My "Superman"? Second-hand stuff. Rosenberg's philosophic garbage. They whispered to me that *he* too. The Name. My racism was a parody of yours, a hungry imitation. What is a thousand-year *reich* compared with the eternity of Zion? Perhaps I was a false Messiah sent before. Judge me and you must judge yourselves. *Übermenschen*, chosen ones![47]

The idea of Hitler as a messianic figure in Jewish history is developed further on in the speech, when he presents his second argument: That just as Moses is in some sense the true father of Nazism, so is Hitler the true founder of the Jewish state. "That strange book *Der Judenstaat*. I read it carefully. Straight out of Bismarck. The language, the ideas, the tone of it. A clever book, I agree. Shaping Zionism in the image of the new German nation. But did Herzl create Israel, or did I?"[48] Were it not for the Holocaust, Steiner's protagonist argues, the Jews would never have taken their fate into their own hands and established a sovereign state, becoming sufficiently emboldened in the process to dispossess the Arab inhabitants of the land: "That made you endure knowing that those whom you had driven out were rotting in refugee camps not ten miles away, buried alive in despair..."[49] Perhaps, muses the defendant, he himself is the Messiah, who has been charged with spurring the Jews to return to their homeland? Turning to his captors, he beseeches them: "Should you not honor me, who has made you into men of war, who has made of the long vacuous daydream of Zion a reality?"[50]

Steiner's Hitler, however, is not content to acknowledge the debt he owes to Judaism, and the debt owed him, in turn, by the State of Israel. Most of his address is dedicated to a third claim, one that casts him as defender of the world's peoples from the worst aggression of all, that perpetrated by Jewish morality. The Jews, harbingers of a universal humanism, prophets of absolute justice, have encumbered humanity with an unbearable moral burden. This "blackmail of the ideal," the exacting demand for perfection, is the cruelest oppression of all—the oppression of the ego, of desire, of human nature:

> You call me a tyrant, an enslaver. What tyranny, what enslavement has been more oppressive, has branded the skin and soul of man more deeply than the sick fantasies of the Jew? You are not God-killers, but *God-makers*. And that is infinitely worse. The Jew invented conscience and left man a guilty serf.[51]

Most stunning is the fact that this speech marks the end of *The Portage to San Cristobal of A.H.* In Steiner's fantasy, Hitler remains unanswered. One of the witnesses, Teko the Indian, who has watched the entire drama from the side, wants to shout, "Proven!" but is silenced by the roar of landing helicopters. With this, the novel closes, as does the play that was later based on it. A reporter from the *Observer* who attended the play's London performance in 1982 recounted that it was received with raucous applause, and wondered whether that applause was not also intended for Hitler's monologue of self-justification.[52] In a later interview, Steiner frankly acknowledged that "I don't think that *I* even know how to answer what I say in the last speech."[53]

This is an understatement. In fact, it is difficult to find any clear distinction between Steiner's own professed views and those he puts in the mouth of A.H. Of course, Steiner does not endorse the historical Hitler's monstrous crimes. On the contrary, Hitler stands in Steiner's eyes as the incarnation of unprecedented and unparalleled evil; Nazism is for him a tortuous riddle, a dark cloud that influenced his entire life and work. And yet, it seems very much as though this speech in A.H.'s defense, this casting of the Jews as archetypal twin to the Nazis—part rival, part partner in crime—is meant to serve as a platform on which Steiner the Jew permits himself to enunciate his most vexing thoughts. And in fact, every one of the arguments raised by A.H. finds voice elsewhere in Steiner's writings on the Jewish problem: He points out the biblical sources of the idea of the master race, for instance, in his article "The Wandering Jew" (1969); the idea of the "blackmail of the ideal" of Jewish universal morality is presented in the books *Errata* (1997) and *In Bluebeard's Castle* (1971);[54] the connection between Herzl's Zionism and the German national state of Bismarck is mentioned in "A Kind of Survivor" (1965);[55] and the claim that Hitler made a valuable contribution to the establishment of a Jewish state is repeated in Steiner's interview with Rosenbaum.[56]

In *The Portage to San Cristobal of A.H.*, particularly in its concluding chapter, we find one of the central insights in the discourse Steiner has developed on the Jewish question: The claim that there is an inextricable link between the singularity of absolute evil perpetrated by the Nazis and the singularity of Jewish existence. The appearance of Nazism, the satanic climax of Jew-hatred, was possible only as a reaction to the moral, theological, and cultural uniqueness of Jewish identity.

Steiner does not shrink from the implications of such a claim. By his own testimony, he has found himself increasingly disturbed by a question first posed by the philosopher Sidney Hook, in an interview he gave on his deathbed to Norman Podhoretz in 1989.[57] Would not the world be a better place, mused Hook, if the Jews would stop being Jews, if they would just assimilate altogether or disappear from the face of the earth? "I've found myself thinking about the crazy Zealots...," he told Podhoretz. "What if the whole Palestinian Jewish population of that time had gone down fighting? Just think what we would have been spared, two thousand years of antisemitic excesses... Under some circumstances I think it's better not to be than to be."[58]

Steiner, too, seems to be troubled by a similar question:

> What I am asking is this: Might the Christian West and Islam live more humanely, more at ease with themselves, if the Jewish problem were indeed "resolved" (that *endlösung* or "final solution")? Would the sum of obsessive hatred, of pain, in Europe, in the Middle East, tomorrow, it may be, in Argentina or South Africa, be diminished? Is liberal erosion, is intermarriage the true road? I do not think the question can simply be shrugged aside.[59]

There is a certain moral impudence in the asking of such questions. In effect, Steiner has entered Jewish existence in an accountant's ledger, and seems to be asking whether the Jews have not been more of a liability to mankind than an asset. "Has the survival of the Jew been worth the appalling cost?" he asks starkly. "Would it not be preferable, on the balance sheet of human mercies, if he was to ebb into assimilation and the common seas?"[60]

Through such questions, Steiner's pristine logic leads us to the brink of the abyss. In the name of a universal morality, he manages to lead his reader from a well-intentioned cosmopolitanism to a direct challenge to the Jewish people's right to exist. Steiner's willingness to entertain the idea of the disappearance of the Jewish people would surely have been met with disdain, if not outright disgust, had it come from anyone other than a prominent Jewish intellectual of Steiner's caliber. Yet it raises serious questions about the quality of Steiner's moral judgment.

In reading Steiner's writings, it becomes clear that he regards himself as possessing an acute moral sensibility that sets him apart from the masses. Whereas most people are primarily concerned about the well-being of their closest relations—family, community, and nation—Steiner is guided by a conscience that seeks the benefit of all mankind. But it is just this higher concern which propels Steiner along a trajectory that leads from affirmation of the exile to negation of Jewish existence. Just as he demands that the Jews serve as the prophets of a universal and altruistic humanity, so he also assails their particular existence as an obstacle to fulfilling this promise.

Such beliefs have always had a powerful appeal to idealists. On paper, the fulfillment of the cosmopolitan dream will ineluctably relieve humanity of the impossible burdens of prejudice and bigotry. But when taken to their logical conclusions and applied in practice, good intentions can make hell on earth. One does not have to delve too deeply into recent historical memory to recognize this. It is ironic that one of Steiner's articles on the fate and role of the Jews closes with a quotation from Leon Trotsky concerning his vision of the moral elevation of man. "The average human type," wrote Trotsky, "will rise to the heights of an Aristotle, a Goethe, or a Marx. And above this ridge new peaks will rise."[61] Trotsky, a Jew, fervently believed in cosmopolitan ideals, and in the obligation of Jews like himself to submit to them without qualification. The

regime Trotsky helped establish sought to "redeem" the Jews from their persecuted isolation by integrating them into Soviet society. The results are known:
In the name of an ultimate universal dogma, the Soviet state made the decision
to eradicate Jewish identity. The Jewish religion was criminalized, synagogues
were closed, communities dissolved, and the use of Yiddish and Hebrew pro-
hibited. Jews in the Soviet Union suffered under a regime of brutal cultural
oppression.

Steiner, of course, abhors violence, and cannot be suspected of promoting
any kind of aggressive solution to the Jewish problem. Nevertheless, the web of
arguments he weaves relies on many of the same images and ideas that have fed
antisemitism over the generations, beginning with Augustine's notion of the
"eternal witness." Too reminiscent of classical antisemitic apologetics, Steiner's
argument portrays the Jews as rootless creatures and embraces a moral reasoning that puts the blame for persecution on its victims. In the end, his formidable
intellect falls prey to what appears to be a tentative, yet unmistakable, rap-
prochement with what is essentially an antisemitic position.

"He who thinks greatly must err greatly," Steiner quotes Heidegger.[62] True
enough. But one wonders whether some errors are not too great to be so easily
written off.

Notes

1. Gershom Scholem, "Jews and Germans," in Gershom Scholem, *On Jews and Judaism in Crisis: Selected Essays*, ed. Werner J. Dannhauser (New York: Schocken Books, 1976), 82-83.
2. Hannah Arendt, *The Jew as Pariah: Jewish Identity and Politics in the Modern Age* (New York: Grove, 1978); Edmond Jabès, "The One Who Says a Thing Doesn't Strike Roots," interview with Bracha Lichtenberg-Ettinger, in *Paths of Nomadism: Migration, Journeys, and Passages in Current Israeli Art,* ed. Sarit Shapira (Jerusalem: Israel Museum, 1991); Zygmunt Bauman, "Allosemitism: Premodern, Modern, Postmodern," in *Modernity, Culture and "the Jew,"* ed. Bryan Cheyette and Laura Marcus (Cambridge, UK: Polity, 1998), 143-56; Jean-Francois Lyotard, *Heidegger and "the Jews,"* trans. Andreas Michael (Minneapolis: University of Minnesota Press, 1990).
3. Maya Jaggi, "George and His Dragons," *Guardian,* March 17, 2001.
4. Ibid.
5. Ibid.
6. The citation from *World Literature Today* is quoted on the back cover of George Steiner, *A Reader* (New York: Oxford University Press, 1984). The citation from *L.A. Weekly* is taken from George Schialabba, "The Prime Minister of Culture," *L.A. Weekly,* March 20-26, 1998.
7. George Steiner, "The Wandering Jew," *Petahim*, Vol. 1, No. 6, 1968, 21.
8. George Steiner, *Errata: An Examined Life* (London: Weidenfeld and Nicolson, 1997), 57.
9. Ibid., 62.
10. Ibid., 56-61.
11. Steiner, "The Wandering Jew," 21.
12. George Steiner, "Our Homeland, the Text," in *No Passion Spent: Essays 1978-1996* (London: Faber and Faber, 1996), 312.

13. Ibid., 307.
14. Ibid., 318.
15. Steiner, "The Wandering Jew," 20.
16. Steiner, "Our Homeland," 322.
17. Ibid., 324.
18. Steiner, *Errata*, 54. [emphasis in the original]
19. Ibid., 54.
20. Franz Rosenzweig, *The Star of Redemption*, trans. William W. Hallo (South Bend, IN: University of Notre Dame Press, 1985), 299-300.
21. George Steiner, "A Kind of Survivor," in Steiner, *A Reader*, 222.
22. Steiner, "A Kind of Survivor."
23. Yirmiyahu Yovel, *Dark Riddle: Hegel, Nietzsche, and the Jews* (Cambridge, UK: Polity, 1998), 35.
24. G.W.F. Hegel, "The Spirit of Christianity and Its Fate," in G.W.F. Hegel, *Early Theological Writings,* trans. T.M. Knox (Chicago: University of Chicago Press, 1948), 186.
25. Hegel, "The Spirit of Christianity and Its Fate," 186.
26. Steiner, "Our Homeland," 307.
27. Genesis 13:15.
28. Steiner, *Errata,* 54.
29. See, for example, Steiner's brilliant monograph *Heidegger* (Glasgow: Fontana, 1978).
30. Ibid., 124.
31. George Steiner, "A Responsion," in *Reading George Steiner,* ed. Nathan A. Scott, Jr. and Ronald A. Sharp (Baltimore, MD: Johns Hopkins University Press, 1994), 277.
32. Steiner, *Errata,* 54.
33. Ibid., 56.
34. Steiner, "A Responsion," 280; see also George Steiner, *Real Presence* (Cambridge, UK: Cambridge University Press, 1986); George Steiner, *The Grammars of Creation* (New Haven, CT: Yale University Press, 2001).
35. Cited in Ron Rosenbaum, *Explaining Hitler: The Search for the Origins of His Evil* (London: Macmillan, 1998), 332.
36. Jeremy Cohen, *Living Letters of the Law: Ideas of the Jew in Medieval Christianity* (Berkeley: University of California Press, 1999), 36.
37. Ibid., 2.
38. As Sacks points out, "the texts of the Greeks were not to be studied. At best, they were *bitul tora*, a distraction from Tora-learning."— Jonathan Sacks, "A Challenge to Jewish Secularism," *Jewish Spectator,* Summer 1990, 28.
39. Ibid.
40. George Steiner, "Through That Glass Darkly," in *No Passion Spent,* 334. [emphasis in the original]
41. Steiner, *Errata*, 137.
42. Steiner, "Through That Glass Darkly," 338; *Errata,* 137-138.
43. Rosenbaum, *Explaining Hitler,* 314.
44. It should come as no surprise that when the book was adapted for the stage (by Christopher Hampton) and performed at the Mermaid Theater in London in February 1982, the response was stormy - as illustrated, for example, by the protesters demonstrating outside the theater during show times. Both the provocative arguments and the dramatic platform chosen by Steiner to present them drew much attention and earned the public's scorn. By his own report, Steiner himself was

alarmed by the reception accorded his work. *The Portage to San Cristobal of A.H.*, according to Ron Rosenbaum, turned into a "Frankenstein story: About a frightening creature that escaped from its creator."— Rosenbaum, *Explaining Hitler*, 300.

45.   George Steiner, *The Portage to San Cristobal of A.H.* (Chicago: University of Chicago Press, 1999), 161.
46.   Ibid., 162. See also Joshua 6:21.
47.   Ibid., 163-64.
48.   Ibid., 169.
49.   Ibid.,
50.   Ibid., 170.
51.   Ibid., 165. [emphasis in the original]
52.   Victoria Radin, "Finding the Führer," *Observer,* February 21, 1982.
53.   Rosenbaum, *Explaining Hitler*, 312.
54.   Steiner, *Errata,* 56-61; George Steiner, *In Bluebeard's Castle: Some Notes Toward the Redefinition of Culture* (New Haven: Yale University Press, 1971).
55.   Steiner, "A Kind of Survivor."
56.   Rosenbaum, *Explaining Hitler*, 312.
57.   Steiner, "Through That Glass Darkly," 346; Rosenbaum, *Explaining Hitler*, 314.
58.   Sidney Hook, "On Being a Jew," *Commentary,* October 1989, 36.
59.   Steiner, *Errata*, 52.
60.   Ibid., 51.
61.   Ibid., 62.
62.   Ibid., 171.

5

Future Imperfect:
Tony Judt Blushes for the Jewish State

Benjamin Balint

I

Spurred by the Intifada of the last four years, another generation of anti-Israel intellectuals is just now coming into its own. To understand what this portends, we would do well to listen to recent pronouncements of Tony Judt, historian *première classe* and outstanding representative of a new group that dangerously restyles old ideas.

Born in 1948 and raised in London's East End, Judt studied at Cambridge University and volunteered on a kibbutz in the mid-1960s. He is now an accomplished professor of history at New York University who brings both impressive lucidity and considerable learning to his uncommonly readable studies of French nineteenth- and twentieth- century social history. He has also long since adopted the orthodoxies of the liberal academic class in his adopted country, favoring intervention in Kosovo, for instance, but opposing it in Iraq.

Yet Judt is never more emphatic than when he addresses the subject of Israel, as his recent contributions to the *New Republic,* the *Nation* and the *New York Review of Books* show. Two months after 9/11, for example, he was claiming: "The Israel-Palestine conflict and America's association with Israel are the greatest single source of contemporary anti-U.S. sentiment."[1] The war on terrorism, he later said, "has put U.S. foreign policy into Ariel Sharon's back pocket." Or, using a slightly more vivid metaphor, the U.S. has "voluntarily attached itself to a leash marked 'terrorism' with which Sharon can jerk it to and fro at will."[2]

Not only does the Jewish state bring unpleasantness to Americans; by Judt's lights "Israel today is bad for the Jews."[3] Just over a hundred years after Herzl expressed the hope that antisemitism would ebb with the establishment of a Jewish state, Judt declares without irony that in fact the Jewish state exacerbates antisemitism. As he put it this January:

> It is the policies of Israeli governments, especially in the past two decades, that have
> provoked widespread anti-Jewish feelings in Europe and elsewhere... Israel is not the

state of all its citizens, much less all its residents; it is the state of (all) Jews. Its leaders purport to speak for Jews everywhere. They can hardly be surprised when their own behavior provokes a backlash against... Jews.[4]

The Jewish state, he says, is dysfunctional and morally corrupt, so much so that "even if I felt threatened as a Jew," as he told the *Forward*, "I would never want to go to Israel."[5] He writes that after 1967, Israelis yielded to "a self-satisfied arrogance" and an "overweening superiority" in which "their aggressive nationalism was paired with a sort of born-again, messianic Judaism."[6] "An anachronistic Israeli conflation of land with security," he says, has burdened the country with "a post-'67 irredentist eschatology" and has turned it into

a place where sneering 18-year-olds with M-16s taunt helpless old men ("security measures"); where bulldozers regularly flatten whole apartment blocks ("rooting out terrorists"); where helicopters fire rockets into residential streets ("targeted killings"); where subsidized settlers frolic in grass-fringed swimming pools, oblivious of Arab children a few meters away who fester and rot in the worst slums on the planet... [Israel] has lost everything in domestic civility and international respectability, and has forfeited the moral high ground forever.[7]

Israel's new security fence, Judt adds, like the late Berlin Wall, merely "confirms the moral and institutional bankruptcy of the regime it is intended to protect."[8]

In a widely reprinted and much cited piece in the *New York Review of Books* entitled "Israel: The Alternative,"[9] Judt goes still farther and calls into question not this or that Israeli policy, but the very idea of the Jewish state *tout court*. Judt faults Israel with artificially importing "a characteristically late-19th-century separatist project into a world that has moved on, a world of individual rights, open frontiers and international law." But unlike European states that evolved from *fin de siècle* nationalisms into a multinational European Union, Israel has not moved on. An "ethno-religious" state that privileges its Jewish citizens and seeks to preserve its Jewish character is henceforth an anachronism "in an age when that sort of state has no place." Judt has a specific, if not very detailed "alternative" in mind. "The time has come to think the unthinkable," he says: the replacement of the Jewish state with "a single, integrated, binational state of Jews and Arabs."

II

Yet if anything is passé it is binationalism itself—and the old Marxist equation of Zionism with reactionary bourgeois nationalism on which it depends. (One thinks here of Lionel Trilling's line that Marxism combined "a kind of disgust for humanity as it is and a perfect faith in humanity as it is to be.") Judt's critics – the best thus far are Ran Halévi in *Policy Review*, Alain Finkielkraut in *L'Arche*, and Leon Wieseltier in the *New Republic*[10] – point out that far from the new and "unthinkable" idea Judt apparently takes it to be, binationalism has been thought, and then rethought. It was espoused by the tiny organizations

Brit Shalom and Ihud (founded respectively in 1925 and 1940),[11] by early notables like Judah L. Magnes,[12] Ernst Simon,[13] Martin Buber, Gershom Scholem, Henrietta Szold, Hugo Bergmann, and Joseph Horowitz,[14] and later by Hannah Arendt.[15] But in the face of Arab terrorism, rioting, and adamant opposition to Jewish immigration, not to mention its rejection by Arab nationalists, the "one state, two peoples" idea passed into disrepute.

Today, binationalism is almost universally rejected by both sides (with exceptions like Jewish maverick Haim Hanegbi and Arab Knesset member Azmi Beshara).[16] Salim Tamari, director of the Institute for Jerusalem Studies, offers one explanation: "All the major Islamic groups find [binationalism] an anathema, since they reject the idea that the Israelis (or the Jews for that matter) constitute a nationality."

Those who *did* favor binationalism, on the other hand, did so precisely because it would bring about the defeat of the Zionist project: Yasir Arafat (who in his 1974 "olive branch" speech to the UN dreamt of "one democratic state where Christian, Jew, and Muslim live in justice, equality, fraternity, and progress"); Noam Chomsky from 1967 until he jettisoned the idea in the mid-70s;[17] and Edward Said.[18] Each knew that binationalism would flood Israel with millions of Palestinian "returnees," whose addition to the 3.5 to 3.8 million Palestinians in the West Bank and Gaza and 1.2 million Palestinian Israelis inside the pre-1967 borders would swiftly create a Palestinian majority and hence a Palestinian state.

For this reason, Judt's exercise in wishful thinking, as Michael Walzer notes, would serve merely to replace one nation-state with another.[19] In the new state, the survival of the Jewish minority, like the Lebanese Christians, would depend upon the not exactly proven tolerance of its Arab governors. If the past record of how governments treat Jews in states with Arab majorities is any indication (nearly 900,000 Jews have been uprooted from Arab countries since the 1940s), Judt's performance as an engaged intellectual issues in a dangerously naive social idealism.

The performance is also less than intellectually graceful on the question of nationalism and democracy. Judt mistakenly assumes an inherent contradiction between the Jewish identity of the state and its democratic character. Hebrew University professor Ruth Gavison, among others, understands democracies as legitimately reflecting the preferences of the majority (in this case by maintaining the Jewish character of Israel), so long as they do not thereby infringe on the rights of the minority.[20] Uniquely among its neighbors, Israel's Declaration of Independence promises that the state will foster the development of the country for the benefit of all its inhabitants; it will be based on freedom, justice, and peace as envisaged by the prophets of Israel; it will ensure complete equality of social and political rights to all its inhabitants irrespective of religion, race or sex; it will guarantee freedom of religion, conscience, language, education and culture; it will safeguard the Holy Places of all religions.[21]

One can legitimately argue that Israel ought better to protect the rights of its non-Jewish minority by, for example, reducing the gap in per-capita investment in education that currently separates Arab and Jewish students. But one cannot reasonably assert that the state's Jewish character precludes possibility of equal treatment. Many democracies retain a strong national character, and Israel's Jewish character need not thwart its democratic nature.[22]

Indeed, there are good reasons to consider a pronounced national identity necessary to foster the mutual commitment a democracy needs to function, an idea that stretches from J.S. Mill's *Considerations on Representative Government* (1861) to the contemporary Georgian political philosopher Ghia Nodia. Democracy never exists without nationalism, the latter argued in an important 1992 essay, because "the political cohesion necessary for democracy cannot be achieved without the people determining themselves to be 'the nation.'"[23]

III

But what has hitherto been crucially missed is the degree to which Judt's arguments founder on inconsistency. This inconsistency not only shows us why his arguments are wrong but also reveals them to be animated by something deeper than run-of-the-mill, binationalist post-Zionism.

Outside of the Israeli context, to begin with, Judt himself clearly recognizes the peril—and the futility—of trying to put nationalism behind us. In a slim book called *A Grand Illusion? An Essay on Europe*,[24] Judt acknowledges the return of nationalisms and admits that the nation-state is "the only remaining, as well as the best-adapted, source of collective and communal identification." A "truly united Europe," he says with some skepticism, is so unlikely that it would be "unwise and self-defeating to insist upon it." And in an article entitled "The Past is Another Country: Myth and Memory in Postwar Europe," he writes:

> From Spain to Lithuania the transition from past to present is being recalibrated in the name of a 'European' idea that is itself a historical and illusory product... But what will not necessarily follow is anything remotely resembling continental political homogeneity and supranational stability—note the pertinent counterexample of the last years of the Habsburg Monarchy, where economic modernization, a common market, and the free movement of peoples was accompanied by a steady increase in mutual suspicion and regional and ethnic particularism.[25]

All of this brings us closer to Judt's naked double standards. First, this supranationalism, which Judt considers illusory and unwise in Europe, is precisely what he demands from Israel.[26] But as he later clarified: "it is not the state that is anachronistic ... but the Zionist version of it."[27] If European unity by means of "supranational stability," despite a common cultural heritage and despite a common commitment to democratic values, is a "grand illusion," how much more so a comity imposed upon Israelis and Palestinians, who do not share these? Second, of the many countries that employ legal and social means to preserve national character, why is Israel's Jewish character singularly offensive?[28] The answers, it happens, turn on another question: why might a first-rate intellectual indulge in such double standards? Fortunately, Judt himself indirectly tells us, and thereby reveals yet another layer of telling inconsistency.

IV

In his impressive book, *Past Imperfect: French Intellectuals, 1944-1956*,[29] Judt paints a devastating portrait of what he calls "the opinions and silences of a generation of Left intellectuals in the era of high Stalinism." He recounts in unsparing detail the failure of postwar French writers adequately to respond to Soviet totalitarianism, repression, tyranny, state antisemitism, antisemitic purges, labor camps, and the East European show trials of 1947-53 (especially when the accused were accused of "nationalism," as they often were). He depicts their insouciance, cowardice, conformism, disingenuousness, and ethical incoherence, their "insufferably superior moral tone." He offers fascinating examples— in men like Sartre and Merleau-Ponty and Emmanuel Mounier—of a community "distinguished by its unique mix of political urgency and moral airiness," an entire generation sunk in *bien-pensant* progressivism, in "self-imposed moral anesthesia," and in alienation from its own culture. These otherwise incisive philosophers emptied their energies into passionate polemics characterized by "a hidden and half-admitted fury," and "immodest and immoderate language." But most of all, these anti-anti-Communists engaged in what Judt calls "double-entry moral book-keeping" and cultivated an "epistemological double vision, which made it possible to explain Soviet behavior in terms not invoked for any other system."

"What is at issue here," Judt says by way of trying to account for these failures, "is not *understanding*, the cognitive faculty usually associated with intellectuals, but faith." These leading lights of the fellow-traveling intelligentsia signed away their critical faculties, Judt suggests, "to give some meaning to their 'little private histories.'" "Their engagements and affiliations," he says, "smack less of a sense of collective moral responsibility or a desire to influence public sentiment than of the need to give themselves a clean social and political conscience."

The fascinating part of all this, to return to our question, is that Tony Judt, who has made a career of identifying the moral irresponsibility of intellectuals past, when it comes to the case of Israel plainly exhibits much the same species of irresponsibility, as if the historian-cum *intellectuel engagé* has stepped into one of his own historical studies. (Whatever his personal history or political conscience may include, he might have done better to inhabit another of his books. In *The Burden of Responsibility*, he admires Albert Camus for refusing to indulge in the search for "speculative musings upon ideal solutions... the search for ultimate resolution in exotic locales, or hyperrational abstractions from metahistorical premises.")[30] The faith in Judt's case, however, is a counter-faith, and it takes its nourishment from that oldest of counter-faiths: classical Christian anti-Judaism.

V

It goes without saying that criticisms, even very harsh criticisms, of Israeli policies are not *ipso facto* antisemitic, and that vigorous dissent ought to be welcomed. But in Judt's strident call for what amounts to politicide we have something else altogether, of which the ugly caricature of Israeli society and the double standards are but initial symptoms. Harvard professor Ruth R. Wisse has made the point that anti-Zionism absorbs many of the themes of conventional antisemitism, reworking the old critique of the Jew into a new critique of Israel. Indeed, what is most striking about Judt's views is the way they echo some old antisemitic canards. As mentioned, he depicts a sinister Ariel Sharon, whom he calls "Israel's dark Id,"[31] yanking around the U.S. on a leash and manipulating President Bush like a "ventriloquist's dummy." He criticizes Senator Hillary Clinton for "ostentatiously prostrating herself before the assembled ranks of AIPAC." He considers the claim that "Israel and its lobbyists have an excessive and disastrous influence on the policies of the world's superpower" a "statement of fact," as if the cunning Jewish mind is coercing the world to do its will."[32]

More deeply, however, Judt's insistence on the Jewish state's "anachronism" seems to edge close to a secular version of Christian supersessionism. Where once Christians wanted Jews to acknowledge the obsolescence of Judaism, Judt wants them to recognize the obsolescence of the Jewish state ("an oddity among modern nations"). Where Christianity considered the Jewish faith refuted by theological history, Judt deems the Jewish state revoked by political history.[33] Where once Christians accused Jews of stubbornly refusing the inexorable advance of Religion toward messianic fulfillment, Judt charges Israel with declining to yield to the inexorable progress of History toward enlightened universalism.[34] Europe, the new "spiritual Israel," has, in its own eyes, surpassed and superseded the Jewish state, the new "carnal Israel."

In either case, Jews are resented for atavistically refusing to "conform to the times." "In a world where nations and peoples increasingly intermingle and intermarry at will..." Judt writes in "Israel: The Alternative," "where more and more of us have multiple elective identities and would feel falsely constrained if we had to answer to just one of them; in such a world Israel is truly an anachronism." Both Christian and Judtian catholicism call into question Jewish "difference" and exceptionalism by calling upon Jews to shed particularism. Israel is merely the new ground upon which the old battle over Jewish distinctiveness is currently being waged.

VI

In the end, Judt's selective anti-nationalism amounts to a specially applied endorsement of a sentiment the French critic Julien Benda voiced in 1932:

"Intellectuals of all countries, you must be the ones to tell your nations that they are always in the wrong by the single fact that they are nations... [The Roman philosopher] Plotinus blushed at having a body. You should blush at having a nation."[35] Judt, in short, blushes for the Jews.

But modern Zionism emerged precisely from disappointment with nationlessness. Count Clermont-Tonnere, among the chief advocates for Jewish emancipation in the French National Assembly, famously summed up the promise of emancipation in 1791: "To the Jews as individuals, everything; to the Jews as a nation, nothing"—and ever since, many Jews have rushed to shed their distinctive identities.[36] They yearned to join themselves, if not to another nationalist identity, then to an emancipated "supranational" human society. Political Zionism – as it was first advanced by Leon Pinsker in *Auto-Emancipation* and then by Theodor Herzl in *The Jewish State*—began in the painful recognition that no such society exists, or is ever likely to exist.

The United States, Judt writes, "had no direct experience of the worst of the twentieth century—and is thus regrettably immune to its lessons."[37] From the twentieth century, many in Europe absorbed a mistaken lesson concerning the dangers of unbridled nationalism: national belonging, it was deduced, begets violence. ("The Second World War," John O'Sullivan remarks in a recent number of the *National Interest*, "was caused by the colliding ambitions of the two great transnational ideologies hostile to nationalism: Nazism, with its belief in a racial hierarchy transcending nations, and communism, with its belief in a class hierarchy transcending nations.")[38]

Jews, however, who *did* directly suffer the worst of the twentieth century, derived the opposite conclusion: had they possessed a state with which to defend themselves, had they not been thrown on the benevolence of other nations, the Holocaust would not have raged nearly so destructively. Jews learned that supposedly universal human rights are meaningless unless rooted in a state that enforces them; that national belonging offers not only physical survival, but also cultural regeneration; that the national Jewish mission, far from denying the universal human mission, can do much to encourage it—and since the days of the biblical prophets already has.[39] They learned—and are now proving—that not every exercise of national self-determination is imperial expansion, nor is every nationalism a chauvinism, any more than every religion is fanaticism.[40] They learned, finally, that Diaspora statelessness is historically anomalous—and that they need no longer blush in overcoming it.

To unlearn these lessons, as more and more intellectuals in these days of high anti-Zionism urge, would be the true anachronism.

Notes

1. Tony Judt, "America and the War," *New York Review of Books*, November 15, 2001.
2. Tony Judt "The Road to Nowhere," *New York Review of Books*, May 9, 2002.

3.   Tony Judt "Israel: The Alternative," *New York Review of Books*, October 23, 2003. This increasingly fashionable sentiment, of course, is hardly Judt's alone. This January, for instance, Avi Shlaim, Amira Hass, and Jacqueline Rose argued in a public debate for the proposition: "Zionism today is the real enemy of the Jews." In the post-debate vote, the London audience, by a margin of 355 to 320, agreed.— "Is Zionism Today the Real Enemy of the Jews?" *International Herald Tribune*, February 4, 2005.

4.   Tony Judt, "Goodbye to All That?" *Nation*, January 3, 2005 (parentheses and second ellipses in the original).

5.   Nathaniel Popper, "Embattled Academic," *Forward*, December 26, 2003.

6.   "After Victory," *New Republic*, July 29, 2002. For a list of the many factual errors Judt makes in this piece, see Michael Oren, Letters, *New Republic*, September 30, 2002.

7.   Tony Judt, "The Rootless Cosmopolitan," *Nation*, July 19, 2004.

8.   Tony Judt, "Israel: The Alternative," *New York Review of Books*, October 23, 2003.

9.   October 23, 2003. Reprinted, for example, as an op-ed in the *Los Angeles Times*, October 10, 2003 ('Jewish State' has become an anachronism); as "Israël: l'alternative," *Le Débat*, January/February 2004, republished on Al-Awda.org, the website of the Palestine Right to Return Coalition (http://www.al-awda.org/judtonbinationalstate), and discussed in "Die Alternative," *Frankfurter Allgemeine Zeitung*, November 12, 2003. Amos Elon, writing from his home in Buggiano, Italy, found the essay "refreshingly free from the usual cant about Israel's allegedly robust democracy." ("An Alternative Future: An Exchange," *New York Review of Books*, December 4, 2003).

10.   Ran Halévi, "Israel and the Question of the National State," *Policy Review*, April 2004; Alain Finkielkraut, "Juifs, donc anachroniques," *l'Arche*, April 2004 [French]; Leon Wieseltier, "Israel, Palestine, and the Return of the Bi-National Fantasy: What is Not to be Done," *New Republic*, October 27, 2003.

11.   At no point could either organization count more than 100 members.

12.   In a long letter to the editor of *Commentary,* October 1948, for instance, Magnes called for a federated, binational "United States of Palestine."

13.   In "The Costs of Arab-Jewish Cold War," *Commentary*, September 1950, Simon described Ihud as an organization of "intellectuals who in their political thinking had gone beyond the notion of the state, believing that the social and political conditions of modern life required broader and more comprehensive forms of national and social organization."

14.   For an account of how these figures' binationalist ideology influenced Israel's founding generation, see *From Brit Shalom to the Ihud: Judah Leib Magnes and the Struggle for a Binational State in Palestine* by Joseph Heller (Jerusalem: Magnes Press, 2004 [Hebrew]).

15.   In *The Jew as Pariah*, Arendt (before the establishment of Israel) called Zionism a "sectarian ideology" that borrowed "categories and methods of the nineteenth century," and that asked for a state "only when the whole concept of national sovereignty had become a mockery." More consistently—and subtly—than Judt, she based her opposition to nationalism on a kind of universalism, and thus sought to drive a wedge between the state and the nation. As she put in an essay entitled "The Nation":

      The state, far from being identical with the nation, is the supreme protector of a law which guarantees man his rights as man, his rights as citizen, and his rights as national... Of these rights, only the rights of man and citizen are primary rights, whereas the rights of nationals are derived and implied in them.

She recommended instead a binational state that incorporated a "federated structure [based on] Jewish-Arab community councils."

16.	Another defense of binationalism comes from Georgetown law professor Lama Abu-Odeh: "Palestinians would be far better off economically, in my view, if they attached their legal claims directly to the resources of the state of Israel as national budget (to be distributed, after a struggle, equally and justly among its national subjects, Jews and non-Jews alike), rather than hoping to benefit from the pursuit of national economic development within the boundaries of a nominally independent Palestinian state" ("The Case for Binationalism," *Boston Review*, December 2001/ January 2002). See also Michael Tarazi, "Two Peoples, One State," *New York Times*, October 4, 2004.

17.	See, for example, his *Peace in the Middle East? Reflections on Justice and Nationhood* (New York: Pantheon Books, 1974). Bernard Avishai (no right-winger himself) dismissed Chomsky's socialist binationalism as "misleading and contradictory," which goes to show that the *NYRB* itself wasn't always warm to the idea. ("The Jewish State in Question", *New York Review of Books*, January 23, 1975) These days, Chomsky advocates a "no-state" solution,

> based on the recognition that the nation-state system has been one of the most brutal and destructive creations of Europe and its offshoots, imposed by force on much of the rest of the world, with horrendous consequences for centuries in Europe, and elsewhere until the present. For the [Middle East], it would mean reinstating some of the more sensible elements of the Ottoman system (though, obviously, without its intolerable features)

("Advocacy and Realism," *ZNet*, August 26, 2004, http://www.zmag.org/content/showarticle.cfm?ItemID=6110).

18.	In Said's words:

> [Theodor] Adorno says that in the twentieth century the idea of home has been superseded. I suppose part of my critique of Zionism is that it attaches too much importance to home. Saying, we need a home. And we'll do anything to get a home, even if it means making others homeless. Why do you think I'm so interested in the binational state? Because I want a rich fabric of some sort, which no one can fully comprehend, and no one can fully own. I never understood the idea of this is my place, and you are out.

("My Right of Return: An Interview with Edward Said," *Ha'aretz Magazine*, August 18, 2000). See also Said's "The One-State Solution," *New York Times Magazine*, January 10, 1999.

19.	Michael Walzer, "An Alternative Future: An Exchange," *New York Review of Books*, December 4, 2003.

20.	According to Gavison:

> The principles of democracy, individual rights, and equality before the law do not necessitate a rejection of the Jewish character of the state. On the contrary: The fact of Israel's democratic nature means that it must also be Jewish in character, since a stable and sizable majority of its citizens wants the state to be a Jewish one.

("The Jews' Right to Statehood: A Defense," *Azure*, Summer 2003). See also Roger Scruton's "In Defense of the Nation," in *The Philosopher on Dover Beach* (Manchester, UK: Carcanet Press, 1990).

21.	Israel's Declaration of Independence.

22.   See Amnon Rubinstein and Alex Yakobson, *Israel and the Family of Nations: The Nation State and Human Rights in Israel and Around the World* (Tel Aviv: Schocken, 2003).

23.   Ghia Nodia, "Nationalism and Democracy," in *Nationalism, Ethnic Conflict, and Democracy,* ed. Larry Diamond and Marc Plattner (Baltimore, MD: Johns Hopkins University Press, 1994), 8. Francis Fukuyama, on p. 23 of that volume, agrees that nationalism and democracy "are in fact two sides of the same coin."

24.   Tony Judt, *A Grand Ilusion? An Essay on Europe* (New York: Hill and Wang, 1996).

25.   István Deák, Jan T. Gross, Tony Judt, eds., *The Politics of Retribution in Europe* (Princeton, NJ: Princeton University Press, 2000), 317.

26.   Amos Oz notices the hypocrisy here: "It took [the Europeans] a thousand years to make peace," he recently told the *New Yorker*. "Even as they wag their fingers at us like a Victorian governess, they have a history of rivers of blood."

27.   "An Alternative Future: An Exchange," *NYRB*, December 4, 2003.

28.   As the historian Omer Bartov notes,

> Judt neglects to mention that Germany, the most populous and important European country, still bases its citizenship on a law dating back to 1913, which defines Germans by blood and heritage, and that a majority of Germans today support the idea of minorities accepting the Leitkultur (primary culture) of the land.

(Letters, *NYRB*, December 4, 2003). Paul Bogdanor gives many other examples in his essay on Noam Chomsky in this volume.

29.   Tony Judt, *Past Imperfect. French Intellectuals, 1944-1956* (Berkeley: University of California Press, 1992). Originally published as *Passé imparfait: Les Intellectuels en France, 1944-1956* (Librairie Arthème Fayard, 1992).

30.   Tony Judt, *The Burden Of Responsibility* (Chicago: University of Chicago Press, 1998), p. 26.

31.   Tony Judt, "The Road to Nowhere."

32.   Tony Judt, "The New World Order," *NYRB*, July 14, 2005.

33.   It is no coincidence, if we are right, that Berkeley professor Daniel Boyarin's book-length study of Paul culminates in his fiercest critique of Zionism (chapter 10 of *A Radical Jew: Paul and the Politics of Identity* [Berkeley: University of California Press, 1994]). Paul's theological project, Boyarin says, aimed primarily at overcoming human difference. "There are no more distinctions between Jew and Greek, slave and free, male and female, but all of you are one in Jesus Christ," Paul declares in Galatians 3:28. Paul's view, in Boyarin's reading, comes as a reaction to the Judaic ethnocentric "tendency towards contemptuous neglect for human solidarity." From this Boyarin develops his anti-Zionism: "modern Jewish statist nationalism has been...very violent and exclusionary." Jews ought rather practice "self-deterritorialization" and embrace a "subaltern" status, advice one reviewer observed "resembles nothing so much as Augustine's prescription for Jewish subordination" (Jay M. Harris, *Commentary*, June 1995). I am indebted to Shai Held for this point.

34.   "In the nineteenth century History replaces God as the all powerful force in the destiny of men," remarks François Furet, "but only in the twentieth century do we see the political madness caused by this substitution." *Le Passé d'une illusion: Essai sur l'idée communiste au XXe siècle* (Laffont/Calmann-Lévy, 1995), 45. Cited in Alain Finkielkraut, *In the Name of Humanity* (New York: Columbia University Press, 2000), 63.

35.   *Discours à la nation européenne* (Gallimard, 1992), 71. Cited in Finkielkraut, 98.

36.   Arthur Hertzberg, in his book *The French Enlightenment and the Jews* (New York: Columbia University Press, 1990), finds a deep and pervasive hostility to the Jews even among their self-declared emancipators. On the same subject, see also Ronald Schechter, *Obstinate Hebrews: Representations of Jews in France, 1715-1815* (Berkeley: University of California Press, 2003).

37.   "Europe vs. America," *New York Review of Books*, February 10, 2005.

38.   John O'Sullivan, "In Defense of Nationalism," *National Interest*, Winter 2004-5, 33-40.

39.   In the last sentence of *The Jewish State*, Herzl writes, "Whatever we attempt there for our own welfare will spread and redound mightily and blessedly to the good of all mankind."

40.   As University of Chicago professor Mark Lilla remarks, "the legitimacy of the nation-state should not be confused with the idolatry of the nation-state"("The End of Politics," *New Republic*, June 23, 2003).

6

The Devil State:
Chomsky's War Against Israel

Paul Bogdanor

"I'm not a maniac."— *Noam Chomsky*[1]

In Noam Chomsky's political campaigns stretching back for decades, one theme is constant: his portrayal of Israel as the devil state in the Middle East, a malevolent institutional psychopath whose only redeeming feature is the readiness of its own left-wing intelligentsia to expose its uniquely horrifying depravity. Although he is the son of Hebrew teachers and a former kibbutz resident, for much of his adult life Chomsky has been in the grip of an obsessive hatred of the Jewish homeland. It began in the 1970s, when he demanded the extinction of Zionism in the name of the socialist revolution; it escalated in the 1980s, with his discovery that Israel was an imperialist terror state incubating a genocidal "final solution" for the human race; and it continues in the new century with an avalanche of increasingly hysterical books, essays, speeches, and interviews.[2] But Chomsky's diatribes on the Arab-Israeli conflict are not only the product of his uniquely paranoid and vituperative mind; they also bear the hallmarks of his intellectual repertoire—massive falsification of facts, evidence, sources, and statistics, conducted in the pursuit of a fanatical and totalitarian ideological agenda.

Those who wish to sample Chomsky's lucubrations on the wickedness of the Zionists will find that they have much to discover. From Chomsky they will learn that the establishment of Israel was "wrong and disastrous.... There is not now and never will be democracy in Israel."[3] From Chomsky they will learn that the Jewish state—a country one-tenth the size of Ecuador—is "a Middle East Sparta in the service of American power." From Chomsky they will learn that "Israel aided the US in penetrating Black Africa with substantial secret CIA subsidies." From Chomsky they will learn that Israel's reach extended "beyond the Middle East, Africa and Latin America, to Asia as well" and that "Israel showed how to treat Third World upstarts properly." From Chomsky they will learn that no nation is safe from the Zionist peril, which includes "direct involvement in terrorism in Europe," as well as "Mossad efforts to aid the Red Brigades in an apparent effort to destabilize Italy."[4] From Chomsky they will learn that the Jewish state has been "part of an international terror network that also included Taiwan, Britain, Argentine neo-Nazis, and others, often with Saudi funding."[5] From Chomsky they will learn all of these "facts"—unless they are prepared to question his sanity.

No allegation is so horrible, no libel so scurrilous, that Chomsky will not put it to use against the Zionist devil. Mass killings are routine: in parts of Lebanon, "All teen-age and adult males were blindfolded and bound, and taken to camps, where little has been heard about them since."[6] Weapons of mass destruction are merely par for the course: "Israel is in effect using chemical warfare with our support right now," causing "a substantial number of abortions, infant deaths, and so on."[7] Quite generally, Israelis can be divided into two categories of evil: "If you are a beautiful Israeli, you cry when you shoot. If you are not a beautiful Israeli, you just shoot."[8] Indeed, the "greatest danger" posed by Israel is "the 'collective version' of Samson's revenge against the Philistines... pressures on Israel to accept a political settlement could lead to an international conflagration."[9] Fortunately, the oracle of MIT is at hand to expose the Jewish state's nefarious plans to re-enact Samson's revenge against the Philistines with the aid of Saudi money, the Italian Red Brigades and chemically induced abortions.

In Chomsky's mental universe, there are few questions about Israel and the Middle East that cannot be resolved by equating Jews with Nazis. Does Israel have a right to pre-emptive self-defense? Such arguments recall "Hitler's moves to blunt the Czech dagger pointed at the heart of Germany... Hitler's conceptions have struck a responsive chord in current Zionist commentary."[10] Does Israel face threats to its security? "Hitler and Goebbels... gave a similar justification for their resort to force."[11] Does Israel conduct military operations against terrorists? "Gestapo operations in occupied Europe also 'were justified in the name of combating "terrorism"'..."[12] Has Israel shown a commitment to the peace process? "Does it deserve to be described as a 'peace process'? Hitler's campaign to conquer Europe was also dubbed a 'peace process.'"[13] How much time and effort Chomsky would save if he simply programmed his computer to spew out "Hitler" and "Goebbels" and "Gestapo" and "Nazi" at every mention of the wicked Zionists!

In parallel with Chomsky's hatred for Israel is an abiding contempt for American Jews, who "get their psychological thrills from seeing Israel, a superman, stomping on people's faces."[14] They are responsible for "a very efficient defamation campaign of the sort that would have made the old Communist Party open-mouthed in awe... you just tell as many lies as you can and hope that some of the mud will stick. It's a standard technique used by the Stalinist parties, by the Nazis and by these guys."[15] The methods employed by their "thought police" include "furious articles and letters to the press, circulation of fabricated defamatory material concerning the heretics," and so on.[16] One can well appreciate the wounded innocence of this sensitive soul, tormented by letters to the press, as he pursues his transcendent vocation in the art of Socratic dialogue.

The Destruction of Israel

> "Embodied in the political institutions of a Jewish state, concepts of purity of nation and race can prove quite ugly."— *Noam Chomsky*[17]

The central theme of Chomsky's anti-Zionist propaganda—the *idée fixe* that underlies all his books, articles, speeches, and interviews on the subject—is that the Jewish state must cease to exist. This desideratum is set out in his earliest writings: "In a Jewish state," he maintains, "there can be no full recognition of basic human rights.... Such limitations are inherent in the concept of a Jewish state that also contains non-Jewish citizens."[18] Blessed with this unique revelation, he will march forth to defend the Gentiles from the Jewish oppressor. Of course, Chomsky gives no reason why a Jewish state must deprive its non-Jewish citizens of the right to vote, form political parties, or hold elective office; nor does he explain why it must deny them freedom of speech, freedom of religion, freedom of association, or other important liberties. Nor does he reveal why Israel is notably deficient in comparison with the many brutal and bloodstained dictatorships to which he has been attracted—for example, Maoist China, which he considered "quite admirable"; or Stalinist Vietnam, where he found "a miracle of reconciliation and restraint"; or Pol Pot's Cambodia, which he compared favorably with the American Revolution, with liberated France, and—to return to our topic—the Israeli kibbutz system.[19]

For Chomsky, the Jewish character of Israel is a hideous mutation, a crippling deformity that turns the entire country into a living abomination. In his view, Israel's Jewishness "resides in discriminatory institutions and practices... expressed in the basic legal structure of the state," which defines it as the home of all Jews, wherever they live.[20] Here is a typical example of the selective morality for which he is infamous. The Armenian constitution seeks "the protection of Armenian historical and cultural values located in other countries" and permits individuals "of Armenian origin" to acquire citizenship through "a simplified procedure." The Lithuanian constitution proclaims: "Everyone who is ethnically Lithuanian has the right to settle in Lithuania." The Polish constitution stipulates: "Anyone whose Polish origin has been confirmed in accordance with statute may settle permanently in Poland." And the Ukrainian constitution promotes "the consolidation and development of the Ukrainian nation" and provides for "the satisfaction of national and cultural and linguistic needs of Ukrainians residing beyond the borders of the State."[21] Yet Chomsky, obsessed with the dread threat of Jewish national independence, does not rail against the existence of these countries. His abhorrence of the democratic nation-state is reserved for Israel.

In Chomsky's eyes, a Jewish state with non-Jewish citizens is no more legitimate than "a White State with Black citizens" or "a Christian State with Jewish citizens." Here, yet again, his arguments are riddled with ignorance and incompetence. He compares the principle that Israel is a Jewish state, "a democracy dominated by Jews," to the suggestion that "England is a Christian state, a democracy dominated by Christians," which he apparently regards as a *reductio ad absurdum*.[22] In fact, as every high school student knows, there is no state called England; but there is a country called Britain, which is indeed a Christian state, with an official Protestant church, a Protestant head of state, a Protestant state education system, etc.[23] Does Chomsky doubt the legitimacy of Britain, a Christian state with non-Christian citizens? Does he oppose the existence of other democratic Christian states, including Denmark, Finland, Greece, and Norway? Does he campaign against the creation of a Basque state with a Catalan minority, a Tibetan state with a Chinese minority, a Tamil state with a Sinhalese minority, or a Kurdish state with an Arab minority? By the standards he applies to Israel, the list of illegitimate states must be rather long, incorporating not only the examples just mentioned but also every Arab or Muslim society—although it does not seem to include his preferred communist tyrannies in Vietnam, which expelled its Chinese population, drowning up to 250,000 boat people; or in Cambodia, where ethnic and religious minorities were slaughtered by the Khmer Rouge.[24] For Chomsky, the establishment of democratic Israel was "wrong and disastrous," but terrorist revolutions entailing the murder of hundreds of thousands or even millions of people are "constructive achievements" in the finest traditions of socialism.

Not content with sophistical meditations on the immorality of Israel's very existence, Chomsky embarrasses himself still further by venturing into the history of Zionist politics. He refers to "the powerful influence of Bolshevik ideas on the Labor Party, particularly its leader, David Ben-Gurion," adding that "the Revisionists, the precursors of [Menachem] Begin's Herut, were in fact an offshoot of European fascism."[25] Presumably the "Bolshevik ideas" of the Labor Zionists would include Ben-Gurion's insistence that the Jewish state must guarantee "the general voting right of all its adult citizens" as well as "freedom of worship and conscience," along with the principle that "there will be no discrimination among citizens of the Jewish state on the basis of race, religion, sex, or class."[26] As for the "fascism" of the Revisionist Zionists, this was articulated by their leader, Vladimir Jabotinsky, who warned that "where there are no guarantees for freedom of the individual, there can be no democracy," avowing that in a Jewish state, "the minority will not be rendered defenseless," since the "aim of democracy is to guarantee that the minority too has influence on matters of state policy. After all, that minority comprises individuals who were also created in the image of God."[27] Contrast these sentiments with Chomsky's profound admiration for the murderers of millions in China, Vietnam, and Cambodia.

Chomsky's alternative to the Jewish state is "socialist binationalism." And this proves to be far more objectionable than a Jewish state with non-Jewish citizens: in his ideal scheme there would be Jewish cantons with Arab inhabitants, and Arab cantons *with no Jewish inhabitants*. At one point he does stipulate that any individual "will be free to live where he wants." But then he abandons this principle in favor of "the most desirable" binational system, one in which "Palestinian Arabs who wish to return to their former homes within the Jewish-dominated region would have to abandon their hopes," while "Jews who wish to settle in the Arab-dominated region would be unable to do so."[28] In other words, Arabs would not become a *majority* in Jewish areas, while Jews would be forbidden even to live as a *minority* in Arab areas. The founders of apartheid would surely applaud.

The details of Chomsky's plans are even more sinister. His binational socialist state would re-enact the "successful social revolution" in communist Yugoslavia, where 70,000-100,000 people were butchered in the postwar massacres alone.[29] And it would have to be "integrated into a broader federation" even though "support for compromising Israeli independence is virtually non-existent in Israel."[30] So Chomsky demands that Israelis accept a revolutionary socialist state on the model of totalitarian Yugoslavia, which would then be absorbed into the Arab world by force. The suspicion is that this program would require a great deal of killing. Perhaps this explains why Chomsky sponsored a lecture tour by the leader of Israel's Marxist-Leninist Matzpen party, who openly advocated terrorist atrocities against his compatriots and promised that unless they were "split from Zionism," they would suffer "another Holocaust," because "the Arab revolution is going to win."[31] This, apparently, is the true meaning of the "successful social revolution" prescribed by Chomsky's ideology.

With the passage of time, even Chomsky came to understand that there was little immediate hope of establishing a socialist binational state in order to re-enact the horrors of Yugoslavia's communist bloodbath. Rather, an independent Palestine in the West Bank and Gaza was the prerequisite for Israel's demise. Indeed, Chomsky has redefined the term "rejectionism" to include both the Arab aim of conquering Israel and Israel's alleged reluctance to accept a PLO terror state next to its cities. Thus he equates the destruction of a free country and the massacre of its population with the refusal to establish a terrorist dictatorship intent on accomplishing that goal.[32] Is it really too much to ask of the author of *Language and Responsibility* that he refrain from manipulating the meaning of words? Would it not be better if Chomsky unambiguously renounced his dreams of Israel's destruction? Pressed for details, he freely admits that his two-state proposal is a mere ruse. "The first [step] is to implement a two-state settlement," he explains. "The second step is to proceed from there. For reasons that are clear to anyone familiar with the region, two states in cis-Jordan [Palestine] make little sense..."[33] In other words, the Jewish state must cease to exist. Such is Noam Chomsky's considered contribution to the struggle for peace in the Middle East.

Arab "Moderation" in Fact and Fantasy

"… the formation of al-Fatah might prove to be a significant step towards peaceful reconciliation."— *Noam Chomsky*[34]

If Chomsky's desire for the destruction of Israel makes him less than reliable in the definition of words, such peccadilloes are as nothing compared to the mendacity of his misstatements on matters of fact. So extreme is his commitment to the deep structure of ideological falsehood that there is hardly a single event in the entire history of the Arab-Israeli conflict that he fails to twist, embroider, mutilate or falsify.

When the United Nations voted for a two-state solution in 1947, the Jewish community under the British Mandate overwhelmingly accepted the plan, while the Arab world unanimously rejected it. Fighting immediately erupted, with Arab leaders frankly admitting that they were the aggressors.[35] As the Arab armies invaded the new State of Israel, the secretary-general of the Arab League, Azzam Pasha, declared "a war of extermination and a momentous massacre which will be spoken of like the Mongolian massacres and the Crusades."[36] This was the first in a long series of genocidal outbursts displaying Arab attitudes towards Israel—a record that Chomsky (with his unique interpretation of the responsibility of the intellectuals) is determined to suppress.

Thus it should occasion little surprise that in Chomsky's diatribes, we find no mention of the Egyptian military orders in 1956 calling for "the annihilation of Israel and her extermination in the shortest possible time, in the most brutal and cruel battles"; no mention of the Saudi reaction to the capture of Adolf Eichmann, "who had the honor of killing five million Jews"; no mention of the Jordanian demand for "the liquidation of the remaining six million" to avenge Eichmann's memory; no mention of the promise by Egyptian dictator Gamal Abdel Nasser that "we shall not enter Palestine with its soil covered in sand," but "with its soil saturated in blood"; no mention of the pledge by Syrian defense minister Hafez al-Assad to "take the initiative in destroying the Zionist presence in the Arab homeland."[37] All of these expressions of fascist hatred and Nazi fanaticism are simply consigned to oblivion by the mandarin of MIT—even as he insists that the facts are being "reconstructed to serve the desired illusions" of the omnipotent Zionist propaganda machine.[38]

Chomsky's suppression of the crucial historical background is matched by his apologetics for the PLO, a movement built on the premise that "armed struggle" is the only way to liberate Palestine, that the state of Israel is "entirely illegal, regardless of the passage of time," and that "the liberation of Palestine will destroy the Zionist and imperialist presence."[39] In Chomsky's ethical code, "the PLO has the same sort of legitimacy that the Zionist movement had in the pre-state period," an insight that might have been valid if the pre-state Zionist movement had been founded with the goal of destroying a country and murdering its population, or if it had been armed and financed by the surrounding dictatorships in order to facilitate this war of annihilation.[40] But such comparisons are only to be expected from a man who believes (as we have already seen) that modern Zionists are inspired by Hitler, that Israel sponsored the Red Brigades in a plot to destabilize Italy, or that the Jewish state is in league with Argentine neo-Nazis and financed by Saudi Arabia.

The list of absurdities culminates in Chomsky's main argument: there is an "international consensus," embracing "the major Arab states, the population of the occupied territories, and the mainstream of the PLO," in support of "a two-state political settlement," which is being frustrated only by America and Israel.[41] The capitalist propaganda system is guilty of "suppressing the efforts of the Arab states and the PLO to advance a nonrejectionist settlement, depicting the PLO in particular as violent extremists."[42]

Descending into this vortex of fantasy, Chomsky pretends to believe in Nasser's public overtures, a sign that Arab rejectionism "began to erode" after 1967.[43] But Nasser had made his intentions crystal clear: "The real Palestine problem," according to his regime, was "the existence of Israel in Palestine. As long as a Zionist existence remains even in a tiny part of it, that will mean occupation."[44] In fact, Nasser was planning "a far-reaching operation" against Israel. Conscious of the need to "hide our preparations under political activity," he instructed his generals: "You don't need to pay any attention to anything I may say in public about a peaceful solution."[45] And Chomsky's account of the ensuing developments is no less deceitful:

> After Nasser's death, the new President, Anwar Sadat, moved at once to implement two policies: peace with Israel and conversion of Egypt into an American client state. In February 1971, he offered Israel a full peace treaty on the pre-June 1967 borders, with security guarantees, recognized borders and so on… Sadat's offer was in line with the international consensus of the period…[46]

But Egyptian planners were telling a very different story: "There are only two specific Arab goals at present," declared Sadat's official mouthpiece: "elimination of the consequences of the 1967 aggression through Israel's withdrawal from all the lands it occupied that year, and elimination of the consequences of the 1948 aggression through the eradication of Israel… we should learn from the enemy how to move step by step."[47] Chomsky's central thesis is thus directly contradicted by the evidence, which he twists to suit his ideological agenda.

The 1973 war, Chomsky admits, "was a clear case of an Arab attack," but this was directed against "territory occupied by Israel, after diplomatic efforts at settlement had been rebuffed."[48] Unfortunately for his credibility, Arab leaders refuted this argument when they started their assault. Hafez Assad, by this time Syrian dictator, vowed "to strike at enemy forces until we regain our positions in our occupied land *and continue then until we liberate the whole land.*"[49]

Mohammed Heikal, the prominent Egyptian government adviser, was at pains to emphasize that "the issue is not just the liberation of the Arab territories occupied since June 5, 1967... if the Arabs are able to liberate their territories occupied since June 5, 1967 by force, what can prevent them in the next stage from liberating Palestine itself by force?"[50] Zionist propaganda had ensnared the Arab leaders themselves, if we are to believe Chomsky's rhetoric.

Further "diplomatic efforts" occurred in 1974, when the PLO approved its infamous "Phased Plan," advocating "armed struggle" to establish a "combatant national authority" in the West Bank and Gaza before achieving "a union of the confrontation countries" with the aim of "completing the liberation" of Palestine.[51] Chomsky consigns this event to an Orwellian memory hole, pretending that the Arab states and the PLO made "an important effort to bring about a peaceful two-state settlement." As an example of this effort, he repeatedly adduces the draft UN Security Council resolution of January 1976, which he depicts in glowing terms:

> In January 1976, the US was compelled to veto a UN Security Council Resolution calling for a settlement in terms of the international consensus, which now included a Palestinian state alongside Israel... The resolution was backed by the "confrontation states" (Egypt, Syria, Jordan), the PLO, and the USSR... Israel refused to attend the January 1976 Security Council session, which had been called at Syrian initiative.[52]

Entirely suppressed in Chomsky's account of this "important effort" is a rather crucial fact: the resolution endorsed the PLO's "Right of Return" for millions of Palestinian Arabs, which would reduce Israeli Jews to minority status as a prelude to their ultimate disappearance.[53] Heralding the "important effort" were Farouk Kaddoumi, head of the PLO's Political Department, who vowed that "this Zionist ghetto of Israel must be destroyed," and PLO deputy leader Salah Khalaf (Abu Iyad), who exclaimed: "Let us all die, let us all be killed, let us all be assassinated, but we will not recognize Israel." But Chomsky is undeterred: "The Arab states and the PLO continued to press for a two-state settlement," he assures us, "and Israel continued to react with alarm and rejection."[54] Such falsehoods abound in Chomskyan propaganda. How else does he expect to persuade his readers that the Soviets, the Syrians and the PLO were forlornly begging for peace, only to be thwarted by the fanaticism of the State Department and the Israeli Labor Party?

Chomsky's fictitious history of the conflict proceeds in this vein. When Israel surrendered the Sinai Peninsula to Egypt and agreed to Palestinian self-government in the West Bank and Gaza in 1979, PLO leader Yasser Arafat declared that "when the Arabs set off their volcano there will be only Arabs in this part of the world," pledging "to fuel the torch of the revolution with rivers of blood until the whole of the occupied homeland is liberated, the whole of the homeland is liberated, not just a part of it."[55] One year later, Arafat delivered another outburst:

Peace for us means the destruction of Israel. We are preparing for an all-out war, a war which will last for generations... We shall not rest until the day when we return to our home, and until we destroy Israel... The destruction of Israel is the goal of our struggle, and the guidelines of our struggle have remained firm since the establishment of Fatah in 1965.[56]

Shortly afterwards, Arafat's Fatah faction reiterated its founding commitment to "the complete liberation of Palestine" and "the liquidation of the Zionist entity economically, militarily, politically, culturally and intellectually."[57] A prominent PLO representative helpfully explained: "We wish at any price to liquidate the State of Israel."[58] Surveying this record, Chomsky reaches the inevitable conclusion: "it is quite clear" that the PLO "has been far more forthcoming than either Israel or the US with regard to an accommodationist settlement."[59] Would the editors of *Pravda* dare to compete with Chomsky?

While Chomsky offers every conceivable excuse for Arab racism and fascism, he applies very different standards to his fellow Jews. In his version of reality, one of the "constant themes" of Israel's first prime minister, David Ben-Gurion, was conquest of the whole region, "including southern Lebanon, southern Syria, today's Jordan, all of cis-Jordan [Palestine], and the Sinai," thus establishing Zionist hegemony "from the Nile to Iraq" in line with his "long-term vision," which extended "from the Nile to the Euphrates."[60] Indeed, Israel's "long-term goal" may be "a return to something like the system of the Ottoman empire." Israeli missiles are meant to "put US planners on notice" that genuine peace efforts "may lead to a violent reaction" intended to cause a confrontation between the superpowers, "with a high probability of global nuclear war." These threats are manifestations of Israel's "Samson complex," the product of an "Israeli Sparta" which has become the world's "fourth greatest military power," menacing the Saudi oil fields and even the USSR, and inexorably travelling "the road to Armageddon," which will terminate in "a final solution from which few will escape."[61]

That last assertion is a striking innovation in the field of hate literature. After all, *The Protocols of the Elders of Zion*, perhaps the most notorious antisemitic forgery of the twentieth century, merely asserted that Jews were planning to subjugate the world. We are indebted to the unique intellect of the sage of MIT for the revelation that the Jews are actually plotting to annihilate the human race.

Lebanon: Heroes and Criminals

"... it was considered legitimate to round up all teen-age and adult males and ship them off to concentration camps..." — *Noam Chomsky*[62]

Perhaps the most elaborate product of Chomsky's warped perception is his massive coverage of the war in Lebanon. Here, again, the heroes are the terrorists of the PLO, while the criminals are the democratically elected leaders of Israel. Thus Chomsky assigns "unique credibility" to an Arab journalist who discovered "relative peace" in PLO-controlled areas of Lebanon. His source was writing in the midst of the 1982 Israeli invasion,[63] when PLO terrorists could no longer perpetrate acts of slaughter such as this:

> An entire family had been killed, the Can'an family, four children all dead and the mother, the father, and the grandfather. The mother was still hugging one of the children. And she was pregnant. The eyes of the children were gone and their limbs were cut off. No legs and no arms.

After the PLO "fighters" had butchered and raped their way through this defenseless Christian town, they left the survivors to enumerate the corpses: "Many of the bodies had been dismembered, so they had to count the heads to number the dead. Three of the men they found had had their genitals cut off and stuffed into their mouths." The murderers slaughtered 582 people in this massacre, one of numerous examples.[64] In another case, 100 civilians, "mostly women, children and old men," were slaughtered with knives and bayonets, some of them decapitated; in yet another, sixty-five villagers "were locked in a church by PLO fighters and machine-gunned to death."[65]

Many other incidents are omitted from Chomsky's argument in support of the claim that there were "no cases of murder or rape" under PLO rule and that "atrocities were rare." These include the following:

> The PLO men killed Susan's father and her brother, and raped her mother, who suffered a haemorrhage and died. They raped Susan "many times." They cut off her breasts and shot her. Hours later she was found alive, but with all four of her limbs so badly broken and torn with gunshot that they had to be surgically amputated. She now has only the upper part of one arm.

After Israel evicted the PLO from Beirut in 1982, "some Christian women conceived the idea of having Susan's picture on a Lebanese stamp, because, they said, her fate symbolizes what has happened to their country—'rape and dismemberment by the PLO,'" but they were dissuaded.[66] We can also learn of a pregnant mother of eleven children who was murdered "just for the fun of it" along with her infant; small children mutilated and killed when terrorists threw a grenade at them; a man whose limbs were chained to four vehicles which were then driven in opposite directions, tearing him to pieces; a newspaper editor found with his fingers cut off joint by joint, his eyes gouged out and his limbs hacked off; a local religious leader whose family was forced to watch as his daughter was raped and murdered, with her breasts torn away; a dead girl with both hands severed and part of her head missing; men who were castrated during torture sessions; men and women chopped to pieces with axes; and various other manifestations of "relative peace" under the benevolent rule of the PLO.[67]

Chomsky's delusions about the PLO were not shared by its victims. The American Lebanese League stated that the country had been "occupied by PLO terrorists" who "committed an orgy of atrocities and desecration against women and children, churches and gravesites... From 1975 through 1981 the toll among civilians was 100,000 killed, 250,000 wounded, countless thousands made homeless," with 32,000 orphans and the capital city "held hostage by PLO criminals."[68] Many years later, the World Lebanese Organization, the World Maronite Union, and multiple human rights groups concerned with the Middle East issued a public declaration accusing the PLO of genocide in Lebanon and addressing Yasser Arafat in these terms: "You are responsible for the killing of 100,000 Lebanese civilians... The United States government should have asked you to appear at the Hague for the crimes you perpetrated in Lebanon..."[69] But while the victims commemorate the "rape and dismemberment" of their country by the PLO, Chomsky ponders a slightly different question: whether "the PLO will be able to maintain the image of heroism with which it left Beirut."[70]

The "heroism" of the PLO was frequently on display. Lebanese medical staff in Sidon demanded "an international investigating committee to look into the crimes against humanity" of PLO terrorists who turned their hospital into a battleground, sacrificing the lives of patients.[71] Palestinian residents of Ein Hilweh testified that PLO forces trapped them inside the camp: "the militiamen were shooting civilians who tried to escape," and in one case, "three children had been riddled with bullets before their parents' eyes because their father had dared to suggest calling an end to the fighting so at least the children of Ein Hilweh could be saved."[72] Elsewhere, a Palestinian witness recalled that "the PLO would not let anybody out" of his camp, and murdered a neighbor who tried to leave. With respect to casualties from the fighting, he asked, "Who is to blame for their death? Write it down—the PLO."[73] According to *New York Times* Jerusalem bureau chief David Shipler:

> The huge sums of money the PLO received from Saudi Arabia and other Arab countries seem to have been spent primarily on weapons and ammunition, which were placed strategically in densely populated civilian areas in the hope that this would either deter Israeli attacks or exact a price from Israel in world opinion for killing civilians... crates of ammunition were stacked in underground shelters and antiaircraft guns were emplaced in schoolyards, among apartment houses, next to churches and hospitals.

In addition, the "PLO conscription program drafted Palestinian boys as young as 12," but Palestinian children are less eager to die than their foreign admirers would wish: the draft "apparently stirred resentment," and the PLO was obliged to establish checkpoints to catch children who were trying to run away, another sign of its courage and valor.[74]

But Chomsky will not allow facts to get in the way of his totalitarian allegiances. He finds it perfectly obvious that the PLO withdrew from Beirut for humanitarian purposes, "to save the city from total destruction" at the hands of the criminal Israelis—so obvious, in fact, that he regards anyone who disagrees as a disciple of Goebbels and Stalin.[75] Needless to say, this is the exact opposite of the truth. Far from attempting to save the population, the PLO was threatening its annihilation. Arafat made it clear that "if the Israelis attempted to break into West Beirut, the PLO would simultaneously blow up 300 ammunition dumps and bring holocaust down on the city."[76] No doubt Chomsky would regard this as yet another manifestation of "the heroic PLO resistance against overwhelming odds."[77]

Deploring Israel's conduct of the fighting, Chomsky writes that in a comparable case, "few would have hesitated to recall the Nazi monsters."[78] He believes that if Israel "cannot be compared to Nazi Germany," there are nevertheless "points of similarity, to which those who draw the analogies want to draw attention." He constantly refers to Israeli "concentration camps," and, for good measure, he recalls "the genocidal texts of the Bible."[79] He is even prepared to equate Israeli tactics with the barbarism of Pol Pot (having previously argued that the brutality of the Khmer Rouge "may actually have saved many lives.")[80] By contrast, military historian Richard Gabriel observes that "concern for civilian casualties marked almost all IDF [Israel Defense Forces] operations throughout the war," to the extent that it "reduced the speed with which the Israelis were able to overcome enemy opposition."[81] After witnessing the combat first-hand, Trevor Dupuy and Paul Martell concluded:

> As military historians we can think of no war in which greater military advantages were gained in combat in densely populated areas at such a small cost in civilian lives lost and property damaged. And this despite the PLO's deliberate emplacement of weapons in civilian communities, and in and around hospitals...[82]

A specialist in the international law of war recorded that military experts he had consulted were "unanimous" in their confirmation of Israel's "exercise of care for the civilian population in light of the PLO's efforts at using that population as a shield from attack," noting the PLO practice of placing "artillery and aircraft weapons on top of or immediately adjacent to hospitals, churches and mosques."[83] Perhaps we should see all of this as just another sign of the insidious power of the capitalist propaganda system, in which "Israel has been granted a unique immunity from criticism," such that expert observers simply cannot perceive the truths that are so obvious from the seminar rooms in Cambridge, Massachusetts.[84]

Chomsky's evidence that Israel was running "concentration camps" and generally acting in accord with "the genocidal texts of the Bible" leaves much to be desired. A typical source is the "Canadian surgeon" Chris Giannou, who testified before Congress that he had witnessed "the blind, savage indiscriminate destruction of refugee camps"; the shelling of hospitals, with one shell killing 40-50 people; the use of cluster bombs and phosphorus bombs; 300 corpses during the evacuation of a government hospital; "savage and indiscriminate beatings" of prisoners; and so on. Chomsky dismisses the Israeli charge that Giannou was "a liar suspected of working for the PLO," ignoring Giannou's own testimony that he was an employee of the Palestine Red Crescent Society, an official PLO institution; Giannou's sponsors subsequently admitted that he had been in contact with Arafat "on a daily basis."[85] Chomsky, however, insists that Giannou's tales were "confirmed" by a "Norwegian doctor and social worker" who reported "extensive violence" against prisoners, including lethal beatings, although readers who take the trouble to check his source—it is, of course, the PLO's *Journal of Palestine Studies*—will discover that the pair were working "in accordance with an agreement between the Norwegian Palestine Front and the Palestine Red Crescent Society."[86] Chomsky's remaining "evidence" is equally trustworthy.

Manipulation of statistics is a classic propaganda technique, and Chomsky is an expert in the field. Consider the subject of casualty figures. In the first week of the Israeli invasion, the PLO concocted an estimate of 10,000 dead in south Lebanon, with 600,000 homeless, more than the total population of the area. The PLO fabrications, adopted by the Red Cross and the Lebanese authorities, rapidly circulated around the world. "It is clear to anyone who has traveled in southern Lebanon" that these numbers were "extreme exaggerations," wrote David Shipler.[87] Nevertheless, the PLO news agency soon became the "primary source of information both for Western reporters and for the Lebanese state radio and television."[88] As a result, official Lebanese casualty estimates came to mirror the PLO inventions, recording 19,085 dead, 57 percent combatants and 43 percent civilians.[89] Chomsky, in turn, recycles the Lebanese official statistics derived from PLO propaganda, and then edits the numbers to suggest that nearly all of the dead were civilians.[90] Thus he maintains that "there seems little reason to doubt the final estimates of close to 20,000 killed, *overwhelmingly civilian*."[91] Entirely absent from his mathematical manipulations is a rather pertinent fact: in 1984 these inflated estimates were publicly repudiated by the Lebanese authorities, who announced that "about 1,000 Lebanese were killed as a result of the Israeli invasion."[92]

This is only the beginning of Chomsky's statistical legerdemain. "Since the end of Israel's invasion of Lebanon in 1982," he writes, "some 25,000 Lebanese and Palestinians have been killed, according to Lebanese officials and international relief agencies, along with 900 Israeli soldiers." As evidence, he relies on a single sentence in a newspaper report citing an anonymous estimate that plainly applies to the period *including* the Israeli invasion.[93] Thus Chomsky, having falsified statistics which were themselves based on PLO disinformation and later repudiated by the Lebanese authorities, refers the reader to a single unsourced comment in a newspaper article and then distorts its meaning so that he can count the same set of figures twice. This further deception allows him to deduce that "during the 22 years that Israel illegally occupied southern Lebanon... they killed about maybe [sic] 45,000 or 50,000 Lebanese and Palestinians."[94] Elsewhere he writes with pretended indignation:

> The 1982 invasion and its immediate aftermath left some 20,000 dead; according to Lebanese sources, the toll in the following years was about 25,000. The topic is of little concern in the West, on the principle that crimes for which we are responsible require no inquiry, let alone punishment or reparations.[95]

He contends that "Israeli terrorist acts" have "undoubtedly claimed far more victims than those of the PLO."[96] Recall that the actual death toll from the Israeli invasion was 1,000, according to the Lebanese. These examples call to mind Walter Laqueur's observation that "even on the rare occasions when Mr. Chomsky is dealing with facts and not with fantasies, he exaggerates by a factor of, plus or minus, four or five"—or, in this case, forty or fifty.[97]

Discussing the Phalangist massacre of hundreds of people in the Sabra and Shatila refugee camps, Chomsky refers to "high-level planning and complicity" by the Israelis.[98] The Kahan Commission, by contrast, found that Israeli commanders first attempted to persuade the Lebanese army to search the camps; only when these efforts failed did they turn to the Phalangists, repeatedly warning them "not to harm the civilian population."[99] American courts judged as "false and defamatory" the claim that Ariel Sharon had intended the deaths of civilians.[100] Robert Hatem, security chief to the Phalangist commander Elie Hobeika, recently published a book, *From Beirut to Damascus*, which was promptly banned in Syrian-occupied Lebanon; there he related that "Sharon had given strict orders to Hobeika... to guard against any desperate move," and that Hobeika perpetrated the massacre "to tarnish Israel's reputation worldwide" for the benefit of Syria.[101] Hobeika subsequently joined the Syrian occupation government and lived as a prosperous businessman under Syrian protection; further massacres in Sabra and Shatila occurred under the Syrian aegis in 1985, initiating the slaughter of 3,781 people by Syrian-backed Amal terrorists and their PLO opponents—a bloodbath which evoked no reaction from Chomsky.[102]

Chomsky's determination to convict Israel for the crimes of Lebanese Christians who were retaliating for previous PLO atrocities contrasts rather starkly with his bizarre contention that the Phalangists themselves had no cause to investigate their actions, for to do so "would have destroyed what minimal possibilities may exist for the restoration of a Lebanese state" under Phalangist control.[103] It is remarkable, if not very surprising, that as soon as he has finished exploiting the Sabra and Shatila massacres to blacken the image of the Jewish state, Chomsky hastens to forgive the perpetrators.

The Methods of an Intellectual Crook

"It is the responsibility of intellectuals to speak the truth and to expose lies."
— *Noam Chomsky*[104]

No one should think that Chomsky's propaganda efforts are limited to the mutilation of historical fact. Deliberate misquotation of statements plays a central role in his anti-Zionist polemics. Diligent readers will find many examples to ponder.

Typical of Chomsky's methods is his portrayal of Ben-Gurion as a fanatical imperialist whose devilish designs mandated a Jewish state from the Nile to the

Euphrates. According to Chomsky—citing the Marxist-Leninist "historian" Simha Flapan—Ben-Gurion demanded "expansion into the whole of Palestine by a Jewish-Arab agreement" and promised that the Zionist state would preserve order "not only by preaching morality but by machine guns." Chomsky explains: "The 'agreement' that Ben-Gurion had in mind was to be with King Abdullah of Jordan, who would be induced to cede areas of cis-Jordan under his control, while many of the Arab residents would leave... circumstances would later permit a further expansion of the borders of the Jewish state..."[105] Turning to the original text, we find that Ben-Gurion intended nothing of the kind. His goal was "Arab agreement to *mass Jewish immigration*," and since the Jewish state would be only a stage in the realization of Zionism, "we are obliged to run the state *in such a way that will win us the friendship of the Arabs both within and outside the state.*" He continued:

> The state will of course have to enforce order and security and will do this not only by moralizing and preaching "sermons on the mount" but also by machine guns should the need arise. *But the Arab policy of the Jewish state must be aimed not only at full equality for the Arabs but at their cultural, social and economic equalization, namely, at raising their standard of living to that of the Jews.*[106]

Chomsky's deception is transparent. Contrary to Chomsky, Ben-Gurion's aim was not the expansion of the Jewish state's borders but Arab agreement to Jewish settlement outside its borders; the agreement was not to be made with the King of Jordan but with the Arabs of Palestine; and far from seeking to dispossess the Arabs, he wanted to offer them complete equality. In his own words, "Arab inhabitants of Palestine should enjoy all the rights of citizens and all political rights, *not only as individuals, but as a national community, like the Jews.*"[107] Is it possible to imagine a more extreme falsification of the historical record than Chomsky's rendition of these sentiments?

On a similar level of veracity, Chomsky explains that the "military doctrine of attacking defenseless civilians derives from David Ben-Gurion," who is supposed to have confided in his diary: "If we know the family—strike mercilessly, women and children included. Otherwise the reaction is inefficient. At the place of action there is no need to distinguish between guilty and innocent."[108] This is an interesting illustration of Chomsky's technique: the alleged quotation is not from Ben-Gurion, but an adviser, Gad Machnes. And the latter's comments were very different from Chomsky's version: "These matters necessitate the utmost precision—in terms of time, place, and whom and what to hit... only a direct blow and *no touching of innocent people!*"[109] Moreover, Ben-Gurion's own views were clear and explicit: "There is no other way than by sharp, aggressive reprisal, *without harming women and children*, to prevent Jews from being murdered..."[110] As these examples indicate, any resemblance between Chomsky's quotations and the real world is entirely coincidental.

Falsification and misquotation also play a central role in Chomsky's prolonged and increasingly bizarre campaign to portray the PLO as the epitome of moderation and the Israeli Labor Party as the fountainhead of extremism in the Middle East. Obsessed with vindicating this curious dogma, Chomsky succeeds only in revealing the depths of his own mendacity:

> The Palestinian National Council, the governing body of the PLO, issued a declaration on March 20, 1977 calling for the establishment of "an independent national state" in Palestine—rather than a secular democratic state *of* Palestine—and authorizing Palestinian attendance at an Arab-Israeli peace conference. Prime Minister Rabin of Israel responded "that the only place the Israelis could meet the Palestinian guerrillas was on the field of battle."[111]

The actual declaration was somewhat different: it confirmed the PLO's total rejection of UN Security Council Resolution 242, as well as "negotiations at the Arab and international levels based on this resolution"; its "determination to continue the armed struggle," i.e., terrorist atrocities against Israeli civilians; and its commitment to waging that struggle "*without any peace or recognition of Israel.*"[112] Only within these constraints was the PLO prepared to consider establishing an independent state or participating in an international conference. Even more revealing, however, is the second part of Chomsky's argument. If we turn to the source cited in his footnote, we discover that his summary of Rabin's response omits a rather crucial detail: "Prime Minister Yitzhak Rabin said the decisions adopted today by the Palestine National Council *showed that even when so-called moderates dominated it, the organization still called for the elimination of Israel.* He said that the only place the Israelis could meet the Palestinian guerrillas was on the field of battle."[113] Thus, far from spurning the PLO because of its commitment to the peace process, Rabin dismissed the declaration precisely because it rejected any possibility of peace with Israel. Would anyone understand this after reading Chomsky?

Other examples abound. Chomsky selectively quotes the Labor Party diplomat Abba Eban, who observed that as a result of Israel's reprisal policy, "there was a rational prospect, ultimately fulfilled, that affected populations would exert pressure for the cessation of hostilities." Chomsky reproduces the statement under the headline: "The Rational Basis For Attacking the Civilian Population."[114] Readers are informed that Eban "does not contest" the allegations he is discussing, namely the picture "of an Israel wantonly inflicting every possible measure of death and anguish on civilian populations," in a mood reminiscent of regimes he would not "dare to mention by name." Eban, of course, does contest these allegations, which he describes, in the very same article, as "a demonological version of Israel's history." Rejecting "the monster-image of Israel" concocted by Arab spokesmen, he adds with the utmost disdain: "I do not think it necessary to 'prove' that Israel's political and military leaders in our first decades were no senseless hooligans when they ordered artillery response to *terrorist concentrations* [emphasis added]," whereupon he launches into a detailed (and typically grandiloquent) discussion of the morality of warfare:

For as long as men and women have talked about war, they have talked about it in terms of right and wrong… the fact that even this tragic domain finds human beings engaged in such impulses as deliberation, choice, criticism and even remorse illustrates the paradox of war itself and points to its incompatibility with the human condition… Anyone who aspires to leadership must find a way of reconciling his political nature with his moral destiny.[115]

Are these the callous deliberations of a Zionist terrorist seeking to establish "The Rational Basis For Attacking the Civilian Population" in a mood reminiscent of Nazi Germany? Or has Chomsky supplied one more example of his compulsion to play fast and loose with facts and quotations?

In his obsessive need to prove that Israel is a demonic terror state, Chomsky is not content with mere distortion. Occasionally he resorts to outright invention:

The veteran paratroop commander Dubik Tamari, who gave the orders to level the Palestinian camp of Ain el-Hilweh by air and artillery bombardment "to save lives" of troops under his command (another exercise of the fabled "purity of arms"), justified the action with the comment that "the State of Israel has been killing civilians from 1947," "purposely killing civilians" as "one goal among others."[116]

As his source for these incredible statements, Chomsky cites an interview with Tamari in *Monitin*, a now-defunct Israeli tabloid magazine. The relevant issue of *Monitin* contains no such interview with Tamari; nor does it contain any article in which Tamari is quoted.[117] Has Chomsky manufactured the entire interview? Or has he merely concocted the source? Whatever the explanation, Chomsky knows that the vast majority of his readers will not take the time to verify alleged quotations from a little-known figure in a long-extinct Hebrew-language publication, which is now obtainable only in the largest libraries of a foreign country. What are we to make of the fact that such fabrications pass undetected?

Another Chomsky tactic involves reiterating statements that were reported in the media and then exposed as misquotations. Hence an example from the first Intifada:

Prime Minister Shamir warns that Palestinians who resist the occupation will be "crushed like grasshoppers," with their heads "smashed against the boulders and walls"; "We say to them from the heights of this mountain and from the perspective of thousands of years of history that they are like grasshoppers compared to us."[118]

Here Chomsky has recycled falsifications from a news story that had been discredited long before he wrote.[119] Contrast his version with Shamir's actual comments:

There are those who say… that the true owners of the land are the rioters, the murderers and the terrorists, who seek to destroy any remnant of the Jewish people in the land of Israel. We say to them—when we look from here on the thousands of years of our past and all that we have established in the present—that they are as grasshoppers in our sight.[120]

In other words, Shamir was pledging that Israeli Jews would not be defeated by "the rioters, the murderers, and the terrorists" who were fighting for their destruction, a point he illustrated with a well-known Biblical verse.[121] Nowhere did he describe "Palestinians who resist the occupation" as "grasshoppers"; nowhere did he say that they, or anyone else, would be "crushed like grasshoppers"; nowhere did he say that their heads would be "smashed against the boulders and walls"; and nowhere will readers who rely on Chomsky divine the true content of his remarks.

Comparable distortions appear in Chomsky's coverage of the peace process. To substantiate his argument that the Oslo Accords were a conspiracy to cement Israeli dominance in the West Bank and Gaza, he quotes two sources: Ariel Sharon, at that time a leading figure in the Likud opposition, and Yisrael Harel, a prominent Israeli settler.[122] Outlining the reception of the Oslo II agreement, Chomsky announces that "Sharon does not appear too dissatisfied with the outcome," quoting a news report which states the exact opposite: "Sharon's plan would differ from the current one in two key ways. No further land or authority would be handed over to the Palestinians and Israel would maintain the right of pre-emptive action and hot pursuit in Palestinian-controlled cities."[123] As for Harel, Chomsky alleges that he "agrees with Sharon and the governing Labor Party: 'If they keep to the current plan, I can live with it,' he says." But Harel's remarks, quoted at length, convey an altogether different message:

> "If they keep to the current plan, I can live with it," said Yisrael Harel, a founder of the Yesha Council and editor of a settler newspaper, *Nekudah*. But like many settlers, Mr Harel believed the Rabin Government was really moving toward *abandoning the settlements and the greater dream of the Land of Israel*... "I did not come to this country for this... to be under Arafat's sovereignty."

The headline of this newspaper report reads: "West Bank Settlers Talking of Betrayal: Religious or Not, West Bank Settlers Feel Betrayed by Israel."[124] Can there be any question at all whether Chomsky is intentionally deceiving his readers?

The same applies to another set of quotations that appears constantly in Chomsky's recent writings. This time the target is Shlomo Ben-Ami, key negotiator at the failed Camp David talks before the collapse of the Oslo Accords:

> Just before he joined the Barak government as Minister of Internal Security, historian Shlomo Ben-Ami observed in an academic study that "in practice, the Oslo agreements were founded on a neocolonialist basis, on a life of dependence of one on the other forever." With these goals, the Clinton-Rabin-Peres agreements were designed to impose on the Palestinians "almost total dependence on Israel," creating "an extended colonial situation," which is expected to be the "permanent basis" for a "situation of dependence." ... Step by step, the US and Israel have labored for 30 years to construct a system of permanent neocolonial dependency.[125]

Those inclined to accept Chomsky's portrayal of Ben-Ami as a remorseless advocate of colonial domination disguised as peace may be surprised to discover that Ben-Ami had firmly and explicitly attacked this very notion:

Another fallacy is the neo-colonialist approach that seeks salvation for the Palestinians only through economic development and foreign investments. Important as they are, these can never be a substitute for political rights and national dreams. It is now fair to say that economic co-operation with the Palestinians is accepted as the way to cement the peace process. Those among us who advocate a political separation between Israel and the Palestinians should support a policy of wise investments in the territories as the best way to free the Palestinians of their economic dependency on Israel, and to disentangle them from what is now a truly colonial situation: their absorption as unequal partners in the socio-economic tissue of Israeli life.[126]

Hence the true contents of the passage that Chomsky is so determined to mangle: "The economic protocol that was written immediately following Oslo is one of the expressions of this [error]. Instead of directing the focus of the Palestinian economy eastward, to Jordan and the Arab world, it fixed its sight on an almost total dependence on Israel." Ben Ami goes on to deplore the assumption that "even in a time of lasting peace between us and the Palestinians, there would be a situation of obvious inequality between the two entities."[127] To summarize, Ben-Ami's remarks explicitly affirmed that there could be no substitute for Palestinian self-determination; his goal was not to prolong the economic dependence of the Palestinian Authority, but to make it self-sufficient; and so he was not *advocating* a "permanent neocolonial dependency," but examining ways to *avert* such a solution—hardly the picture that Chomsky conveys to his unsuspecting audience.

Blatant misrepresentations also permeate Chomsky's polemics with his American Jewish critics. To the respected philosopher Michael Walzer he attributes the demand that "non-Jews must be expelled" from Israel. What is the basis for this scurrilous allegation?

The democratic socialist Michael Walzer observes with reference to Israel that "nation building in new states is sure to be rough on groups marginal to the nation," and sometimes "the roughness can only be smoothed… by helping people to leave who have to leave," even if these groups "marginal to the nation" have been deeply rooted in the country for hundreds of years, and constituted the overwhelming majority not many years ago.[128]

Chomsky gives no page reference in his footnote, and when we turn to Walzer's text, it is not hard to see why:

Having established boundaries, it remains to fight for *minority rights, equal protection, and all the liberal safeguards with them*… But whatever we do, nation building in new states is sure to be rough on groups marginal to the nation… For them, very often, the roughness can only be smoothed a little… by helping people to leave who have to leave, like the Indians of Kenya and Tanzania, the colons of North Africa, the Jews of the Arab world… *There must be a place to go; there must be havens for refugees.*[129]

Suppressing Walzer's insistence on minority rights and equal protection for all, Chomsky has perverted his observations on the need to help the *victims* of ethnic cleansing into an actual *demand* for ethnic cleansing! Indeed, far from maintaining that "non-Jews must be expelled" from Israel, Walzer was defending Israel's existence as a safe haven for *Jews expelled from the Arab world*. By quoting a few phrases out of context, Chomsky has simply reversed Walzer's meaning. How does he expect to get away with such crude defamations?

Sometimes Chomsky's misrepresentations of opponents border on the comical. There is, for example, his discussion of Zionist attitudes "familiar throughout the history of European colonialism," manifested by those who "fulminate over the Arab 'crazed in the distinctive ways of his culture' and committed to 'pointless' though 'momentarily gratifying' acts of 'bloodlust'" –statements which he attributes to Martin Peretz, editor of the *New Republic*.[130] The mind boggles: did the editor of America's most respected liberal magazine really denigrate Arabs in these terms? As his source on "Peretz's racist outpourings," Chomsky refers his readers to some comments by Christopher Hitchens in a seminar discussion recorded in the PLO's *Journal of Palestine Studies*. And here we discover that Peretz, far from engaging in "racist outpourings" against the Arab peoples, was offering a description of the portrayal of a fictional Arab character in a play performed at the American Repertory Theater![131] We may be forgiven for wondering whether Chomsky will shortly enlighten his disciples with his thoughts on the "sexist outpourings" of feminist drama critics who chronicle the murderous ways of Lady Macbeth.

In general, it is clear that the extensive apparatus of quotations and footnotes in Chomsky's polemical work is merely an elaborate hoax designed to mislead the unwary reader. Perhaps the most astonishing aspect of the whole charade is that Chomsky is almost never called to account for his deceptions.

The World's Leading Terrorist Commanders

> "The record of Israeli terrorism goes back to the origins of the state… The victims, by definition, are PLO 'partisans,' hence terrorists." — *Noam Chomsky*[132]

In recent years, Chomsky has surveyed the field of terrorism, where he discovers, yet again, that Israel is a paragon of evil. He makes his case by inflating or distorting each and every Israeli action involving civilian casualties. Thus, in his superficial review of the 1948 war, he tells us that Menachem Begin "took pride" in the infamous Irgun attack on Deir Yassin, "in which 250 defenseless people were slaughtered."[133] In fact, far from taking pride in slaughter, Begin had ordered his followers to give the villagers advance warning and "to keep casualties to a minimum." The Arab death toll was not 250 but 120, and the Jewish forces suffered forty casualties in the battle for this "defenseless" village.[134] But Chomsky is just getting started. He also refers to "the massacre of 250 civilians" at Lydda and Ramle, conclusively disproved by recent scholarship.[135] And he invokes "the massacre of hundreds of others at the undefended village of Doueimah [Dawayima]," citing a possible death toll of 1,000—a figure dismissed at the time by Arab officials, who reported twenty-seven killings, apparently carried out in revenge for atrocities against Jews.[136] Of course, while he casually inflates the rare Jewish excesses against Arabs, Chomsky has nothing to say about Arab terror which killed 2,000 Jewish civilians, let alone the fate of nearly 600 Jewish captives who were "slaughtered amid scenes of gang rape and sodomy... dismembered, decapitated, mutilated and then photographed."[137] These horrors are conveniently absent from his chronicles of Zionist barbarity.

Chomsky has other revelations in store, including a "recently-discovered Israeli intelligence report" which "concludes that of the 391,000 Arab refugees [in 1948]... at least 70 percent fled as a result of Jewish military operations..."[138] Turning to the scholarly literature, we learn that far from being an "intelligence report," this document was an unclassified "review" by anonymous authors found in the private papers of Aharon Cohen, who was "convicted of treason in 1960 for illegal contacts with Soviet agents"—surely "the last place to look for official IDF documents," as historian Shabtai Teveth observes.[139] No doubt the flight of Arab civilians during a war initiated by their own side with the intention of destroying the Jewish population was a major tragedy. Equally tragic was the Arab ethnic cleansing of 800,000 Middle Eastern Jews once the hostilities were over, a crime that elicits no great concern in Chomsky's writings.[140]

Very often, Chomsky's dishonesty is so extreme that the reader can only gasp in disbelief. Consider this example: "After the Six-Day War, Israel reportedly blocked a Red Cross rescue operation for five days, while thousands of Egyptian soldiers died in the Sinai desert."[141] Turning to his source, we find no trace of this atrocity. Instead we learn that Red Cross representatives in Tel Aviv were "investigating the possibility of using helicopters for dropping water and emergency rations to the stranded Egyptians," who were believed to number in the "hundreds rather than thousands." Meanwhile,

> Hundreds of Israeli lorries, in a vast rescue operation, were today collecting the remnants of the Egyptian Army in Sinai and carrying the rescued soldiers to the Suez Canal.... The Israel Air Force is to launch an operation tomorrow to recover soldiers still roaming about in the Sinai desert. Colonel Mosche Perlmann, the spokesman for General Dayan, the Defence Minister, said that Red Cross representatives would take part. Colonel Perlmann estimated that some 6,000 Egyptians had succeeded in reaching the canal across the desert during the past two days.[142]

Thus Chomsky's source contradicts him at every point. Far from blocking relief efforts while thousands of Egyptian soldiers died, Israel was using vast military resources to save them. This example alone is more than enough to justify Arthur Schlesinger's famous denunciation of Noam Chomsky—who had just admitted to faking "quotations" from President Truman—as an "intellectual crook."[143]

Chomsky's other examples of Israeli "terrorism" include "the expulsion by bombing" of "a million and a half civilians from the Suez Canal" during the War of Attrition in 1967-70.[144] In academic studies, however, we find that Egypt launched a massive artillery attack on Israeli forces, which "returned fire, targeting Egyptian artillery, the Suez refineries, and oil storage tanks," whereupon "Nasser continued to evacuate the canal cities," so that "by mid-September the town of Suez had only 60,000 of its original 260,000 citizens, and Ismailiya 5,000 of 173,000."[145] In other words, Israel was not perpetrating "the expulsion by bombing" of vast numbers of civilians but reacting to Egyptian attack, and it was not Israel but Egypt, which removed the population from the war zone. Again, Schlesinger's comment comes to mind.

Chomsky has further proof of Israel's depravity: the total number of victims of PLO atrocities in northern Israel "is approximately the same as the number killed when Israel shot down a civilian Libyan airplane over the occupied Sinai in February 1973; the plane had become lost in bad weather and was one minute flight time from the Suez Canal, towards which it was heading, when shot down by the Israeli air force."[146] This is a most barbaric crime in Chomsky's telling, although he does not explain how Israeli pilots were supposed to deduce that an innocent Libyan passenger plane had become lost in a war zone after receiving an erroneous weather forecast from its own meteorological service, incorrect information from an Egyptian control tower, and instructions from Egypt to land when it was already deep inside Israeli-controlled territory; or that an aircraft with no hostile intentions had managed to penetrate over 100 kilometers into an Israeli military no-fly area, approach an Israeli military base and then fly back towards Israeli positions along the Suez Canal, mistake Israeli fighters for Egyptian jets, and misinterpret repeated Israeli signals to land, followed by warning shots, as friendly gestures from an Egyptian air escort. Nor does Chomsky see fit to mention the testimony of Israel's chief of staff (had Israel known that it was a civilian airliner with passengers aboard that had lost its way, "there would have been no dilemma—we never would have used fire to force it down"), Israel's air force commander ("We tried desperately to force it down, not to shoot it down") and the Israeli fighter pilot ("I thought they would land easily"), confirmed by the international investigative committee (the Israelis were not trying to destroy the plane and kill the passengers but merely "to force the plane to land in the Sinai").[147] That Chomsky is prepared to equate this tragedy, in which there was no lethal intent, with deliberate PLO massacres in schools, synagogues, hotels, apartment buildings, airports and—of course—passenger aircraft, is a striking manifestation of his intellectual chicanery.

Of course, not all of Chomsky's propaganda claims are his own inventions. Sometimes they are other people's inventions. Witness his complaint that insufficient attention has been paid to "the 700 civilians reported killed in the Israeli bombing of Damascus" during the 1973 war.[148] His evidence consists of a single sentence in a newspaper column on post-war diplomacy by the notorious PLO apologist David Hirst, who supplies no citation or justification of any kind.[149] In contemporary reports, we learn that the major Israeli raid on Damascus was "an air attack against the Syrian general military headquarters and Syrian Air Force headquarters," with no suggestion of 700 dead civilians.[150] How seriously would we take an allegation of 700 civilian dead in a *Syrian* attack on an *Israeli* target, based on comparable evidence: a single sentence in a newspaper column on a different subject by a well-known supporter of far-right Jewish terrorists who offered no source or attribution, when other reports spoke of operations against military targets without even hinting at such a death toll? How seriously can we take anything Chomsky says?

Another Chomsky tactic involves alluding to selected PLO atrocities against Israeli civilians, which he sanitizes as far as possible, and then equating them with Israeli operations against terrorists, which he depicts as premeditated attacks on civilians. In May 1974, PLO terrorists attacked Ma'alot, murdering a father, a pregnant mother and their four-year-old child, and shooting their five-year-old daughter in the stomach. The terrorists then took over 100 schoolchildren hostage and threatened to slaughter them all unless their demands were met, ultimately murdering twenty-two teenagers before perishing in the Israeli rescue attempt.[151] Chomsky's version of the massacre is that "members of a paramilitary youth group were killed in an exchange of fire."[152] To this atrocity he counterposes the allegation that Israel was then engaged in "'napalm bombing of Palestinian refugee camps in southern Lebanon,' with over 200 killed." His source is Edward Said, a member of the PLO's ruling council. Not to be outdone, Chomsky reveals that Israel was involved in "large-scale scorched earth operations," with "probably thousands killed," although "no accurate figures are available," perhaps because his source for this claim is an article by a far-left journalist in a short-lived fringe publication which cites unverified estimates by anonymous "observers."[153] Then there is his claim that Israel bombed the Lebanese town of Nabatiya in 1975, "killing dozens of Lebanese and Palestinian civilians," citing a newspaper report that says nothing of the kind.[154] We might also mention his assertion that 2,000 people died when Lebanese cities, towns and villages were "mercilessly attacked" by Israel in 1978—a figure derived from a single uncorroborated guess in a magazine article, and contradicted by the Red Cross, which estimated 300 dead (terrorist and civilian); by other news reports, which gave death tolls in the low hundreds; and by PLO propagandists, who offered similar figures.[155] These examples are matched by his allegation that over 200 people were killed by Israeli bombing of Sabra and Shatila in June 1982, based on an "eyewitness account" by an anti-Zionist activist in the PLO's *Journal of Palestine Studies*.[156] The list is endless.

Many of Chomsky's judgments border on the surreal. In June 1976, PLO terrorists hijacked an Air France plane and diverted it to Idi Amin's Uganda, where the passengers were to be held hostage. A week later, Israeli commandos rescued the victims in the famous raid on Entebbe. Reacting to public admiration for this blow against international terrorism, Chomsky lamented "the outpouring of hatred and contempt for popular movements of the Third World." He felt that Israel's rescue mission should be compared with "other military exploits, no less dramatic, that did not arouse such awed admiration in the American press," notably the Japanese attack on Pearl Harbor. For Chomsky, the liberation of innocent hostages ranks with the fascist aggression that drew the United States into World War II.[157]

Extending his catalogue of Israeli "terrorism," Chomsky describes an Israeli bombing raid against Baalbek in Lebanon in January 1984, "killing about 100 people, mostly civilians, with 400 wounded, including 150 children in a bombed-out schoolhouse." He then ponders the likely reaction "if the PLO or Syria were to carry out a 'surgical strike' against 'terrorist installations' near Tel Aviv, killing 100 civilians and wounding 400 others, including 150 children in a bombed-out schoolhouse along with other civilian victims."[158] But his own sources report that the target area was "the headquarters of the militant Shi'ite Moslem group known as Islamic Amal. About 350 Iranian Revolutionary Guards have been operating there as well, reportedly helping to train Lebanese and foreign volunteers in terrorist tactics, especially the use of bombs." The Lebanese government (plainly a most impartial and reliable observer) claimed 100 dead in total (not 100 civilian dead, as Chomsky pretends) and 400 wounded, while a media correction the following day noted that "the figures were not independently confirmed" and that "the 'civilian' identification of the casualties was an assertion, not an agreed fact."[159] The Shi'ite militias had perpetrated suicide bombings that killed sixty-three people at the American embassy as well as 241 American peacekeepers and fifty-eight French soldiers, along with twenty-nine Israeli soldiers and thirty-two Arab prisoners, but these facts are of no interest to Chomsky, who is concerned solely with Israel's belated response.

Chomsky also describes an incident in which "Israel hijacked a ferryboat operating between Cyprus and Lebanon," but suppresses media reports that "the ferry was captured after intelligence information indicated several key Palestinian guerrillas were aboard" and that "there were indications the men were planning attacks on Israel."[160] These facts might be of interest to those who think that countries have the right to intercept vessels believed to be carrying terrorists preparing to slaughter innocent civilians in their territory. Having lambasted the Israeli interception of suspected terrorists who were promptly released unharmed when found to be innocent, Chomsky proceeds to compare the PLO massacre of schoolchildren at Ma'alot with Israeli bombardment of a Lebanese island near Tripoli, where casualties included "children at a Sunni boy scout camp" in his words.[161] The reader who attempts to verify this claim will find that the Israelis actually bombed an ammunition dump on the island, which was "known to be a training facility for the fundamentalist Sunni Moslem Tawheed faction," which "worked closely with pro-Arafat guerrillas." Sources in the terrorist faction "said that there had been 150 men on the island at the time and that twenty-five of the men were hit," with no hint of "children at a Sunni boy scout camp."[162]

Chomsky's coverage of other Israeli operations is equally inventive. He informs us that in Lebanon, Israel "carries out attacks with impunity and abandon," offering as evidence the fact that in July 1985, "Israeli warplanes bombed and strafed Palestinian camps near Tripoli, killing at least twenty people, most of them civilians..."[163] But the targets were not civilians: according to press reports, "Ahmed Jibril's Libyan-supported Popular Front for the Liberation of Palestine-General Command said seven of its guerrillas were killed and 20 others wounded," while the Syrian-backed Fatah rebel faction led by Abu Musa had its headquarters "demolished." The operation came after a series of Palestinian attacks on innocent Israelis, including "bombings of bus stops in two Tel Aviv suburbs, a bomb explosion on a Tel Aviv beach, two explosions in Jerusalem, the stabbing of a religious Jew in Jerusalem's Arab quarter and the killing of a couple in Bet Shemesh," all of which Chomsky ignores, as usual.[164]

Elsewhere in his catalogue of Israeli "hijacking," Chomsky draws attention to the fact that Syrians released during a prisoner exchange in June 1984 included Druze residents of the Golan Heights; a brief check reveals that he is referring to a dozen alleged terrorists who were released along with hundreds of Syrian POWs in return for a handful of Israelis.[165] He also relates that in April 1985, "several Palestinians were kidnapped from civilian boats operating between Lebanon and Cyprus and sent to secret destinations in Israel," a discovery which stems from his careful reading of *News From Within*, a Marxist-Leninist publication in Jerusalem.[166] And he laments that "Israel's hijacking of a Libyan civilian jet on February 4, 1986 was accepted with equanimity, criticized, if at all, as an error based on faulty intelligence"—not surprisingly, one might add, when we learn that the aircraft was an executive jet carrying official passengers after a major terrorist congress attended by PLO commanders such as George Habash, Ahmed Jibril, Nayef Hawatmeh and Abu Musa, and that the interception was based on intelligence information that the haul might include Abu Nidal.[167] As it happened, the wanted fugitives were not aboard, and Israel promptly released the travelers unharmed, permitting the Syrian Ba'ath Party officials to return to Damascus after their visit to a rogue dictatorship during a gathering of international terrorist leaders. Perhaps they were there to enjoy the scenery.

By falsifying facts and manipulating sources in his trademark fashion, Chomsky is able to generate his desired conclusion: that the American president and the Israeli prime minister—Ronald Reagan and Shimon Peres, respectively—are "two of the world's leading terrorist commanders."[168] The pretext for this claim is Israel's bombing of the PLO headquarters in Tunis. If Chomsky's verdict is accepted then this attack on a prime terrorist target—involving a few dozen casualties—is worse than the slaughter of 100,000 civilians during the years of PLO terror and destruction in Lebanon; worse than the massacre of up to 55,000 inhabitants of Hama by the neo-Nazi rulers of Syria; worse than the murder of 450,000 victims by the Ba'athist criminals in Iraq; worse than the execution of 30,000 opponents by the fundamentalist ayatollahs in Iran; worse than the genocide of 2 million people by theocratic fascists in Sudan.[169] These examples of Chomsky's mendacity can easily be multiplied.

The Treachery of the PLO

> "Before discussing prospects for peace in the Middle East, let me make a few preliminary comments…. If Hitler had conquered the world, there would be peace but not the kind we would like to see." — *Noam Chomsky*[170]

We turn, finally, to Chomsky's version of the Israeli-Palestinian peace process, whose successes were manifested in scenes of burning corpses and scattered body parts in Jerusalem and Tel Aviv. The origin of the so-called Oslo Accords lies in the events of 1988, when the PLO supposedly renounced terrorism and recognized Israel. In Chomsky's view, the PLO was "once again accepting Israel's existence in return for withdrawal from the occupied territories." Nevertheless, "the United States has imposed a satisfying form of humiliation on the victims of US-Israeli repression and rejectionism, righteously forcing them to concede that they, and they alone, have sinned," yet another symptom of the "imperial arrogance and racist contempt for those in our way."[171]

The PLO disagreed with Chomsky's verdict: "There was no PLO recognition of Israel," explained deputy leader Salah Khalaf (Abu Iyad), not long before Yasser Arafat issued a joint statement with Colonel Gaddafi announcing that "the so-called 'State of Israel' was one of the consequences of World War II and should disappear, like the Berlin Wall..."[172]

By 1993, a left-wing Israeli government had accepted the PLO's *bona fides* and agreed to permit the creation of a PLO dictatorship in the West Bank and Gaza.[173] Chomsky had a ready explanation for this *volte-face*. Having once lauded the PLO for its "heroism," he now made a shocking discovery: the PLO was crippled by "corruption, personal power plays, opportunism, and disregard for the interests and opinions of the people it claimed to represent... With its popular support in decline and its status deteriorating in the Arab world, the PLO became more tolerable to US-Israeli policymakers..."[174] In short, the PLO had sold out to the insidious forces of capitalism and Zionism. The Oslo Accords were "a complete capitulation to US-Israeli demands," while Arafat had become "a virtual Israeli agent," helping to re-enact "the traditional pattern of the European conquest of most of the world."[175] Worldwide support for the peace process merely indicated "the power of doctrinal management" and the fact that "the intellectual culture is obedient and unquestioning," as manifested by "the state of international opinion, now so submissive on this issue that commentators and analysts have literally forgotten the positions they and their governments advocated only a few years ago..."[176] Apparently the entire human race, apart from Chomsky and a few brave disciples, was now in the grip of Zionist propaganda.

In the midst of Chomsky's delirium, the Egyptian minister of war intimated that it was "important to use the phase of peace to prepare for emergencies," and a former chief of staff added: "The combined weaponry of the Arab states today exceeds that of Israel. If all these weapons were directed against Israel, the Arab states could defeat Israel."[177] The neo-Nazi regime in Syria anticipated the day when "the unjust, criminal Israeli terrorists breathe their last by Arab bullets or Arab knives."[178] And the PLO expressed similar thoughts. "We plan to eliminate the State of Israel," declared Arafat. "We will make life unbearable for Jews by psychological warfare and population explosion; Jews won't want to live among us Arabs."[179] Meanwhile terrorist atrocities escalated to unprecedented levels, and Israelis were subject to suicide massacres within their own borders for the first time in the history of their country.[180]

While damning the PLO for its "complete capitulation," Chomsky did not totally abandon his former heroes. "There has been *one* elected leader in the Middle East, *one*, who was elected in a reasonably fair, supervised election... namely Yasser Arafat," so he informed us. In Chomsky's parallel universe, the leaders of Israel and Turkey were mere usurpers, while the terrorist dictator who ran the Palestinian Authority—a man who rigged elections, silenced the media and crushed the opposition; a man whose own colleagues compared him to Idi Amin and Saddam Hussein—was the only true democrat in the Middle East![181]

As the Oslo Accords progressed toward their inevitable climax of bloodbath and slaughter, Chomsky ranted and raved about the "Labor/Likud program of establishing a Bantustan-style settlement" in the West Bank and Gaza. He placed great stress on the Israeli settlements, knowing full well that the vast majority of the settlers live next to the pre-1967 borders and pose no obstacle to a major withdrawal. And he portrayed Ehud Barak's two-state proposal as a "rejectionist" plan entailing "cantonization" of the disputed territories, with the Palestinian Authority now "playing the role traditionally assigned to indigenous collaborators under the several varieties of imperial rule."[182] But PLO strategist Faisal Husseini offered a rather different interpretation:

> Barak agreed to a withdrawal from 95% of the occupied Palestinian lands... no other party will be able to conduct a dialogue with us except from the point where Barak stopped, namely, from the right to 95% of the territory... our eyes will continue to aspire to the strategic goal, namely, to Palestine from the [Jordan] River to the [Mediterranean] Sea.[183]

Husseini was "a leading West Bank moderate" in Chomsky's eyes.[184] "We are ambushing the Israelis and cheating them," proclaimed this heroic figure: "our ultimate goal is the liberation of all historic Palestine from the river to the sea." As for the two-state solution, "we distinguish the strategic, long-term goals from the political phased goals, which we are compelled temporarily accept due to international pressure... Palestine in its entirety is an Arab land, the land of the Arab nation."[185] On similar lines, the chairman of the Palestinian Legislative Council, Ahmad Qurei (Abu Ala), boasted that "it was the first Intifada that brought about Oslo, and this is *an important and great achievement* because it did so *without us giving anything.*"[186] Evidently the leaders of the PLO have yet to be convinced by Chomsky's insights into their predicament.

The climax of the Oslo Accords was the second intifada, a savage campaign of massacres directed at innocent Israelis, including pregnant women and infants. This outcome would seem to belie Chomsky's thesis that the Palestinian Authority is "a virtual agency of the Israeli government."[187] As the burned and mutilated corpses of women and children lay scattered in Israel's buses and streets, its nightclubs and cafes, the Palestinian Authority demanded more of the same:

> All spears should be directed at the Jews, at the enemies of Allah, the nation that was cursed in Allah's book. Allah has described them as apes and pigs.... We blow them up in Hadera, we blow them up in Tel Aviv and in Netanya... until the Jew will hide behind a stone or a tree, and the stone or the tree will say: Oh Muslim, Oh servant of Allah, a Jew is hiding behind me, come kill him.[188]

Meanwhile Egypt offered "thanks to Hitler, of blessed memory" for his actions against "the most vile criminals on the face of the earth," while conceding that "we do have a complaint" against the Fuhrer, in that "his revenge on them was not enough." Lebanon's Hezbollah vowed "to finish off the entire cancerous Zionist project." Syria proclaimed that "the intifada is the countdown for the destruction of Israel." Saudi clerics affirmed the religious duty to "destroy the tyrant Jews" because "the Jews are the helpers of Satan."[189] But Chomsky's readers will search in vain for any acknowledgment of these facts in his writings on the Middle East.

Chomsky's fanatical hatred of Israel is such that even simple consistency is too much for him. At the height of the suicide bombings, he signed a petition demanding that American universities divest from Israel.[190] Critics pointed out that Chomsky had not proposed comparable measures against any of the racist and fascist dictatorships in the region: the terrorist Palestinian Authority, the apartheid regimes in Egypt or Saudi Arabia, the neo-Nazi rulers of Syria or the genocidal criminals in Sudan. Having initiated his campaign, Chomsky was then quick to renounce it: "I've probably been the leading opponent for years of the campaign for divestment from Israel," he averred, in a display of doublethink that would make Orwell cringe.[191]

Conclusion

> "The Hebrew press is much more open than the English language press, and there's a very obvious reason: Hebrew is a secret language, you only read it if you're inside the tribe. Like most cultures it's a tribal culture."
>
> — *Noam Chomsky*[192]

In light of this horrifying record of apologetics for Nazi-style fanaticism, we can only ask: What is Chomsky's motive for pretending that Arab regimes are falling over themselves to make peace, that the PLO is a bastion of moderation, that Israel is plotting the destruction of the whole world? Why does he demand that the Jewish state re-enact the "successful social revolution" which began with 70,000-100,000 murders in communist Yugoslavia? Why does he complain that Israel did not support the FLN terrorists who massacred 30,000-150,000 innocent people after Algerian independence?[193] Why does he spin his ridiculous tales of Zionist designs extending from the Nile to the Euphrates; his fables of Zionist conspiracies involving CIA money, the Italian Red Brigades, and the oil sheikhs of Saudi Arabia? Where is the method behind the madness?

A simple answer suggests itself. In his first writings on the subject, Chomsky warned that a key barrier to a "just peace" in the Middle East was "commitment to a Jewish state."[194] Shortly afterwards, he complained that his "peace" plan, entailing abolition of this Jewish state, had been thwarted by "the commitment of the Israeli government to Jewish dominance throughout the region."[195] He soon came to believe that the Jewish homeland was "a place where racialism, religious discrimination, militarism and injustice prevail," with non-Jews subject to persecution "all too reminiscent of the pogroms from which our forefathers fled."[196] As we have seen, he constantly equates Jews with Nazis, referring to "Israeli concentration camps" and the "genocidal texts of the Bible," and warning of a Zionist "final solution" that will annihilate the human race—an accusation without parallel even in the pages of *Mein Kampf.* At the same time, he believes that there are "no antisemitic implications in denial of the existence of gas chambers, or even denial of the holocaust," or in the claim "that the holocaust (whether one believes it took place or not) is being exploited, viciously so, by apologists for Israeli repression and violence."[197]

Nor can we forget the unadulterated bile that Chomsky has seen fit to pour upon his fellow Diaspora Jews. In a discussion of race and IQ, he wrote that it "might conceivably be the case" that "Jews have a genetically determined tendency toward usury and domination."[198] Subsequently he discovered that American Jews were "a substantial part of the dominant privileged elite groups in every part of the society... they're very influential, particularly in the ideological system, lots of writers, editors, etc. and that has an effect."[199] Asked why his books were ignored by the American Jewish press, he responded: "The Jewish community here is deeply totalitarian. They do not want democracy, they do not want freedom."[200] Elsewhere he invoked the status of New York, with its "huge Jewish population, Jewish-run media, a Jewish mayor, and domination of cultural and economic life."[201] And he offered a novel explanation for public concern about antisemitism: "By now Jews in the US are the most privileged and influential part of the population... privileged people want to make sure they have total control, not just 98% control."[202] Shocked by this injustice, the "dissident" from MIT will bravely struggle to protect the suffering masses from their privileged Jewish oppressors.

In sum, the entire corpus of Chomsky's writings on the Arab-Israeli conflict is simply a spectacular propaganda hoax, a mass of distortions, falsifications, and ludicrous fantasies, all of which serve to incriminate the victims and exonerate the aggressors in this ongoing tragedy. Every crime by Israel's foes is portrayed as a regrettable but understandable lapse, a mere detour from the course of moderation and compromise which they pursue with such extraordinary benevolence, notwithstanding the demonic depravity of the nation they are fighting to annihilate. It is hardly surprising that for the advocate of such a worldview, fellow Jews are hated enemies, and Holocaust deniers cherished allies.

Notes

1.   Interview, *Cambridge Chronicle*, April 9, 2003.
2.   For the different phases of this campaign, see Noam Chomsky, *Peace in the Middle East?* (London: Fontana, 1975); *Fateful Triangle: United States, Israel and the Palestinians* (1983; rev. ed. London: Pluto Press, 1999); *Pirates and Emperors, Old and New: International Terrorism in the Real World* (1986; rev. ed. London: Pluto Press, 2002); *Middle East Illusions* (Lanham, MD: Rowman & Littlefield, 2003). This is a mere sample.
3.   *Harvard Crimson*, November 30, 1972.
4.   *Fateful Triangle*, 21, 26, 29, 256-7n.
5.   *Middle East Illusions*, 179.
6.   *Fateful Triangle*, 217.
7.   Noam Chomsky and C.P. Otero, *Language and Politics* (Oakland, CA: AK Press, 2004), 670.
8.   Ibid., 676.
9.   Noam Chomsky, *Deterring Democracy* (London: Vintage, 1992), 438.
10.   *Fateful Triangle*, 208, 208n.
11.   Ibid., 271.
12.   *Pirates and Emperors*, 45.
13.   Interview, *Challenge*, No. 44, July-August 1997: http://www.chomsky.info/interviews/19970609.htm.
14.   *Language and Politics*, 499.
15.   Ibid., 568-9.
16.   *Pirates and Emperors*, 28-9. He adds that "Israeli intelligence apparently contributes to these efforts." *Fateful Triangle*, 11n.
17.   *Peace in the Middle East*, 119.
18.   Ibid., 17.
19.   See his remarks in *Dissent, Power and Confrontation*, ed. Alexander Klein (New York: McGraw-Hill, 1971), 118; Noam Chomsky and Edward Herman, *The Washington Connection and Third World Fascism* (Boston: South End Press, 1979), 20-1, 28; Chomsky and Herman, *After the Cataclysm* (Boston: South End Press, 1979), 140, 149, 205.
20.   Noam Chomsky, Bernard Avishai, "An Exchange on the Jewish State," *New York Review of Books*, July 17, 1975.
21.   See the constitutions of Armenia, arts. 11, 14; Lithuania, art. 32; Poland, art. 52; Ukraine, arts. 11, 12. Also relevant are the constitutions of Albania, art. 8; Bulgaria, art. 25; Hungary, art. 6; Macedonia, preamble, art. 49; Romania, art. 7. Online index: http://confinder.richmond.edu.

22. Chomsky and Avishai, "An Exchange on the Jewish State."

23. This factual blunder recurs in Chomsky's writings: "While it is commonly argued that Israel is Jewish only in the sense that England is English... that is a flat falsehood. A citizen of England is English..." *Fateful Triangle*, 157.

24. See, for example, Henry Kamm, *New York Times*, July 22, 1979 (ethnic cleansing in Vietnam); *San Diego Union*, July 20, 1986 (boat people deaths, citing UN figures); Ben Kiernan, *The Pol Pot Regime: Race, Power and Genocide in Cambodia under the Khmer Rouge, 1975-79* (New Haven, CT: Yale University Press, 1998).

25. *Fateful Triangle*, 160.

26. Ben-Gurion, "Lines of Action," Jewish Agency Executive, June 7, 1938, quoted in Efraim Karsh, *Fabricating Israeli History: The "New Historians"* (London: Frank Cass, 1997), 54-5.

27. Vladimir Jabotinsky, "The Social Question," *Hayarden*, October 21, 1938, quoted in *The Political and Social Philosophy of Ze'ev Jabotinsky*, ed. Mordechai Sarig (London: Vallentine Mitchell, 1999), 50.

28. *Peace in the Middle East?*, 43, 39, 114.

29. Ibid., 69 (successful social revolution); *New York Times*, July 9, 1990 (Yugoslav massacres).

30. *Peace in the Middle East?*, 69, 115.

31. Carl Gershman, "Matzpen and its Sponsors," *Commentary*, August 1970; Arie Bober, Noam Chomsky, Letters, *Commentary*, October 1970.

32. *Fateful Triangle*, 39-40.

33. Noam Chomsky, "Advocacy and Realism: A Reply to Noah Cohen," ZNet, August 26, 2004: http://www.zmag.org/content showarticle.cfm?SectionID=22&ItemID=6110.

34. *Peace in the Middle East*, 70.

35. Jamal Husseini, of the Arab Higher Committee of Palestine, informed the United Nations: "The representative of the Jewish Agency told us yesterday that they were not the attackers, that the Arabs had begun the fighting. We did not deny this. We told the whole world that we were going to fight." Security Council Official Records, April 16, 1948.

36. BBC News Broadcast, May 15, 1948. On the mendacity of far-left "revisionist historians" who deny the facts, see Karsh, *Fabricating Israeli History*; id., *Rethinking the Middle East* (London: Frank Cass, 2003), 107-203.

37. Yehoshafat Harkabi, *Arab Attitudes to Israel* (London: Valentine Mitchell, 1972), 38, 279 (Egypt, Jordan); Bernard Lewis, *Semites and Anti-Semites* (London: Weidenfeld and Nicolson, 1986), 162 (Saudi Arabia); Michael B. Oren, *Six Days of War: June 1967 and the Making of the Modern Middle East* (Oxford: Oxford University Press, 2002), 78 (Syria).

38. *Fateful Triangle*, 32.

39. Palestine National Charter, 1968, arts. 9, 19, 22; for text and commentary, see Yehoshafat Harkabi, *The Palestinian Covenant and its Meaning* (London: Vallentine Mitchell, 1979).

40. *Fateful Triangle*, 164; also *Language and Politics*, 407.

41. *Fateful Triangle*, 3.

42. Noam Chomsky, *Necessary Illusions: Thought Control in Democratic Societies* (Boston: South End Press, 1989), 289. Chomsky repeatedly cites the assessments of Israeli "doves" as evidence of Arab moderation, just as Nazi apologists might have illustrated the Führer's peaceful intentions by invoking the delusions of British appeasers in the 1930s.

43. *Fateful Triangle*, 64.

44.   *Radio Cairo*, March 17, 1968, quoted in Gil Carl AlRoy, "Do the Arabs Want Peace?" *Commentary*, February 1974.
45.   Oren, *Six Days of War*, 319, 326.
46.   *Fateful Triangle*, 64; see also *Language and Politics*, 411, 511, 703, 747; *Pirates and Emperors*, 25-6, 73, 116, 167-8; *Middle East Illusions*, 180-1.
47.   *Al-Ahram* (Egypt), February 25, 1971, quoted in Theodore Draper, "The Road to Geneva," *Commentary*, February 1974.
48.   *Fateful Triangle*, 99.
49.   *Radio Damascus*, October 15, 1973, reprinted in *The Israel-Arab Reader*, ed. Walter Laqueur (New York: Bantam Books, rev. ed., 1976), 459, emphasis added.
50.   *Al-Ahram* (Egypt), October 19, 1973, quoted in Draper, "Road to Geneva," and AlRoy, "Do the Arabs Want Peace?"
51.   *Wafa* (Beirut), June 9, 1974; *Journal of Palestine Studies*, Summer 1974, 224.
52.   *Fateful Triangle*, 67; see also *Language and Politics*, 746; *Pirates and Emperors*, 23; *Deterring Democracy*, 424; *Middle East Illusions*, 182.
53.   UN Security Council Draft Resolution, January 26, 1976; text in *Times* (London), January 28, 1976. Similar considerations apply to the 1982 Fez Plan (based on the 1981 Fahd Plan), which calls for "peaceful coexistence," according to Chomsky, *Fateful Triangle*, 344. This plan also included a thinly veiled endorsement of the "Right of Return."
54.   Kaddoumi, *Newsweek*, January 5, 1976; Khalaf, *New York Times*, February 17, 1976; Chomsky, *Fateful Triangle*, 68.
55.   Associated Press, March 12, 1979.
56.   *El Mundo*, Venezuela, February 11, 1980; cited in John Laffin, *The PLO Connections* (London: Corgi Books, 1982), 43-4.
57.   Associated Press, June 5, 1980.
58.   Ibrahim Souss, PLO representative in Paris, *Europe No. 1 Radio* (France), June 16, 1980; *Times* (London) August 5, 1980.
59.   *Fateful Triangle*, 41.
60.   Ibid., 161 ("constant themes"); *Pirates and Emperors,* 58 ("Nile to Iraq"); *Deterring Democracy*, 435 ("Nile to Euphrates"). Ben-Gurion's views were the exact opposite: "There is no reason for including the Sinai Peninsula, Lebanon, or regions of Syria and Saudi Arabia." Further, "The State of Israel is not identical with Eretz Israel [Hebrew: The Land of Israel]." Zaki Shalom, *David Ben-Gurion, the State of Israel and the Arab World, 1949-1956* (Brighton, UK: Sussex Academic Press, 2002), 150. See Daniel Pipes, "Imperial Israel: The Nile-to-Euphrates Calumny," *Middle East Quarterly*, March 1994.
61.   *Fateful Triangle*, 455, 467-9 ("The Road to Armageddon" is the chapter title); see also *Deterring Democracy*, 438.
62.   *Fateful Triangle*, 230.
63.   Ibid., 186-8, also citing two left-wing Israeli journalists who made the same points, again writing in the midst of the Israeli invasion, not during the peak years of PLO barbarism and massacre. Worse still, his footnote, 316n10, cites a report by David K. Shipler, *New York Times*, July 25, 1982, as if it supports his claims; in fact Shipler's article is devoted to accounts of PLO tyranny and oppression.
64.   Jillian Becker, *The PLO: The Rise and Fall of the Palestine Liberation Organization* (London: Weidenfeld & Nicholson, 1984), 123-6.
65.   *Washington Post*, July 17, 1976 (100 civilians); Becker, *PLO*, 264n9 (65 villagers).
66.   Becker, *PLO*, 154.
67.   Ibid., 143, 153, 159, 268n13; *PLO in Lebanon: Selected Documents*, ed. Raphael Israeli (London: Weidenfeld & Nicholson, 1983), 240, 244-6, 234-53 *passim*.

68. American Lebanese League, "The PLO Must Quit Lebanon!" *New York Times*, July 14, 1982, advertisement.
69. World Lebanese Organization et al., "Who is the Oppressor in the Middle East?" *Washington Times*, October 7, 1996, advertisement.
70. *Fateful Triangle*, 314.
71. Becker, *PLO*, 153.
72. Ze'ev Schiff and Ehud Ya'ari, *Israel's Lebanon War* (New York: Simon and Schuster, 1984), 147.
73. Becker, *PLO*, 280n10.
74. *New York Times*, July 25, 1982.
75. *Fateful Triangle*, 309.
76. Schiff and Ya'ari, *Israel's Lebanon War*, 220.
77. *Fateful Triangle*, 206.
78. Ibid., 217, referring to a hypothetical Syrian conquest of northern Israel. On the "destruction" caused by Israeli tactics, he cites a report by David Shipler, who in fact stresses that the PLO had caused the carnage by placing military targets beside churches, mosques, schools and other civilian locations; *New York Times*, July 3, 1982.
79. Ibid., 313n (points of similarity); 141, 217, 230, 233, 240, 307, 333, 335, 390, 398, 404, 417 (concentration camps); 444 (Bible).
80. Ibid., 229 (Israeli conduct); *After the Cataclysm*, 160 ("saved many lives").
81. Richard A. Gabriel, *Operation Peace for Galilee* (New York: Hill & Wang, 1984), 86-7.
82. Trevor N. Dupuy and Paul Martell, *Flawed Victory: The Arab-Israeli Conflict and the 1982 War in Lebanon* (Fairfax, VA: Hero Books, 1986), 173.
83. W. Hays Parks, "Air War and the Law of War," *Air Force Law Review*, Winter 1990, 165-6.
84. *Fateful Triangle*, 31.
85. Ibid., 229-30; *New York Times*, July 14, 1982 (Palestine Red Crescent Society); "Notebook," *New Republic*, March 5, 1984 (Arafat contacts).
86. *Fateful Triangle*, 229-30, 322n144; "Eyewitness: Israeli Captivity – A Report by Dr. Steinar Berge and Oyvind Moller From Norway," *Journal of Palestine Studies*, Summer/Autumn 1982, 85.
87. *New York Times*, July 14, 1982.
88. *New York Times*, July 26, 1982.
89. That is, 12,310 killed outside Beirut and 6,775 dead inside Beirut; Associated Press, December 1, 1982; *Christian Science Monitor*, December 21, 1982.
90. *Fateful Triangle*, 221.
91. *Necessary Illusions*, 170, emphasis added. See also Noam Chomsky, "Middle East Diplomacy: Continuities and Changes," *Z Magazine*, December 1991: "The 1982 invasion was far more devastating, with over 20,000 killed, mostly civilians."
92. *Washington Post*, *Times* (London), November 16, 1984. Presumably this number excludes the PLO terrorists and the Phalangist killings at Sabra and Shatila.
93. *Fateful Triangle*, xx, xxii n20, citing Aliza Marcus, *Boston Globe*, March 1, 1999, who writes: "More than 900 Israeli soldiers have died since 1982. As many as 25,000 Lebanese and Palestinians have been killed during the same period, according to Lebanese officials and international relief agencies."
94. Noam Chomsky, "The Current Crisis in the Middle East," Lecture, Massachusetts Institute of Technology, December 14, 2000: http://web.media.mit.edu/~nitin/mideast/chomsky_lecture.html. See also *Pirates and Emperors*, 8: "Some 20,000 were killed during the 1982 Israeli invasion… The Lebanese government reports 25,000 killed after the 1982 invasion."

95.   Noam Chomsky, *Hegemony or Survival: America's Quest for Global Dominance* (London: Penguin Books, 2004), 167.

96.   *Fateful Triangle*, 74.

97.   Walter Laqueur, "The Politics of Adolescence," *New Republic*, March 24, 1982. Laqueur goes on to describe the Chomsky volume he is reviewing as "a squalid tract… a clumsy piece of propaganda, such a ludicrous fabrication, intellectually worthless and morally grotesque, a parody of scholarship that reminds me of the worst excesses of Hitlerism and Stalinism…"

98.   *Fateful Triangle*, 405.

99.   "Report of the Commission of Inquiry into the Events at the Refugee Camps in Beirut (The Kahan Commission)," February 8, 1983; text in the *Jerusalem Post*, February 9, 1983.

100. *New York Times*, January 25, 1985.

101. See the report by the Jerusalem Center for Public Affairs, "Elie Hobeika's Assassination: Covering Up the Secrets of Sabra and Shatilla," *Jerusalem Issue Brief*, January 30, 2002. Hobeika was assassinated before testifying to Belgian investigators: he had "specifically stated that he did not plan to identify Sharon as being responsible for Sabra and Shatilla." Ibid.

102. *New York Times*, March 10, 1992, citing figures from the Lebanese police, who added that another 144,000 died in the civil war, 1975-90, with 13,968 abducted by Christian and Muslim militias, most presumed dead, and 857 killed in the 1982 Sabra and Shatila massacre.

103. *Fateful Triangle*, 409.

104. "The Responsibility of the Intellectuals," *New York Review of Books*, February 23, 1967.

105. *Fateful Triangle*, 161-2.

106. Jewish Agency Executive, June 7, 1938; reproduced in Karsh, *Fabricating Israeli History*, 44-5. Emphases added.

107. Shabtai Teveth, *Ben-Gurion and the Palestinian Arabs* (Oxford: Oxford University Press, 1985), 170. Emphasis added. There is, incidentally, an important error on page 189, where Ben-Gurion is quoted as saying: "We must expel the Arabs and take their places." The actual quote reads: "We do not wish and do not need to expel Arabs and take their place." Karsh, *Fabricating Israeli History*, 49.

108. *Fateful Triangle*, 182, 382; also *Pirates and Emperors,* 73.

109. Protocol of Meeting Concerning Arab Affairs, January 1-2, 1948, Kibbutz Meuhad Archive, Ramat Efal, Israel; quoted in Efraim Karsh, "Benny Morris and the Reign of Error," *Middle East Quarterly*, March 1999. Emphasis added.

110. Protocol of Mapai Central Committee Meeting, September 16, 1954, Ben-Gurion Archive, Sdeh Boker, Israel; quoted in David Tal, "Israel's Road to the 1956 War," *International Journal of Middle East Studies*, February 1996, 67. Emphasis added.

111. *Fateful Triangle*, 68.

112. Political Resolutions of the 13th Palestine National Council, arts. 1, 2, 9; reproduced (with commentary) in Harkabi, *The Palestinian Covenant and its Meaning*, 149-59. Emphasis added.

113. *New York Times*, March 21, 1977. Emphasis added.

114. *Fateful Triangle*, 182; also *Pirates and Emperors,* 73, 132; *Language and Politics*, 703; *Middle East Illusions*, 184, 237, where Eban's statement is further twisted into a reference to Israeli operations in Lebanon.

115. Abba Eban, "Morality and Warfare," *Jerusalem Post*, August 16, 1981. Eban's article was a reply to a self-serving column by Menachem Begin that sought to deflect criticism of Israeli air strikes in Lebanon by accusing Labor leaders of deliberately bombing civilians when in government.

116. *Pirates and Emperors*, 73-4, 197n95.

117. *Monitin*, October 1985.

118. *Fateful Triangle*, 482.

119. The misquotation originated in the *New York Times*, April 1, 1988, and was repeated many times over the next few days. It was exposed by Charles Krauthammer, *Washington Post*, April 15 and 21, 1988.

120. See Moshe Yegar, Israeli Consul-General, Letters, *New York Times*, April 20, 1988.

121. Numbers 13:33: "And there we saw giants... and we were in our own sight as grasshoppers, and so we were in their sight."

122. *Fateful Triangle*, 543, 566n15.

123. *Boston Globe*, November 17, 1995.

124. *New York Times*, November 17, 1995. Emphasis added.

125. *Pirates and Emperors*, 180. See also *Language and Politics*, 743; *Middle East Illusions*, 215, 227-8; *Hegemony or Survival*, 170; Interview, *Haaretz*, December 29, 2000; "Neocolonial Invitation to a Tribal War," *Los Angeles Times*, August 13, 2001; "Back in the USA," *Red Pepper* (UK), May 2002; "The Solution is the Problem," *Guardian* (UK), May 11, 2002; "Reshaping History," *Al-Ahram Weekly* (Egypt), November 18-24, 2004; etc.

126. Shlomo Ben-Ami, "From Oslo to a Lasting Peace," *Independent* (UK), December 7, 1994.

127. Shlomo Ben-Ami, *Makom Le-Khulam* [Hebrew] (Ha-Kibuts Ha-Me'uhad, 1998), 113.

128. Noam Chomsky, *Towards a New Cold War* (New York: Pantheon Books, 1982), 236; see also *Fateful Triangle*, 117; *Pirates and Emperors*, 186n8.

129. Michael Walzer, "Nationalism, Internationalism and the Jews: The Chimera of a Binational State," in Irving Howe and Carl Gershman, eds., *Israel, the Arabs and the Middle East* (New York: Bantam Books, 1972), 195. Emphases added.

130. *Fateful Triangle*, 482, 511n23.

131. *Journal of Palestine Studies*, Winter 1987, 97.

132. *Pirates and Emperors*, 78.

133. *Fateful Triangle*, 95-6.

134. Michael S. Arnold, *Jerusalem Post*, April 3, 1998 (advance warning, minimum casualties); Danny Rubinstein, *Ha'aretz,* January 28, 1998 (Arab death toll, citing historians at Bir Zeit University).

135. *Pirates and Emperors,* 78; the massacre allegation was demolished by Alon Kadish, Avraham Sela and Arnon Golan, *Kibush Lod, 1948* (Tel Aviv: Haganah Archive, 2000) [in Hebrew]. The figure of 250 dead was the number of Arab casualties reported by the local Israeli commander after the suppression of an armed rebellion. Arab propaganda initially claimed that 3,000 had been massacred. Israel's far-left "new historians" have produced some noteworthy atrocity fabrications; see Meyrav Wurmser, "Made-Up Massacre," *Weekly Standard*, September 10, 2001, discussing the Tantura hoax.

136. *Pirates and Emperors,* 30, 78; Noam Chomsky, *Turning the Tide* (Boston: South End Press, 1985), 76; Yoav Gelber, *Palestine 1948* (Brighton, UK: Sussex Academic Press, 2001), 209 (27 killings; 80 died in the conquest of the village); Associated Press, August 24, 1984 (revenge for anti-Jewish atrocities).

137. Netanel Lorch, *The Edge of the Sword: Israel's War of Independence, 1947-1949* (New York: G.P. Putnam's Sons, 1961), 450 (2,000 civilians); Sarah Honig, *Jerusalem Post*, March 1, 2001 (600 captives).

138. *Pirates and Emperors,* 198n105; also http://www.understandingpower.com/Chapter4.htm#f62.

139. Shabtai Teveth, "The Palestine Arab Refugee Problem and its Origins," *Middle East*

Studies, April 1990, 216-7.

140. Ya'acov Meron, "Why Jews Fled the Arab Countries," *Middle East Quarterly*, September 1995; Moshe Gat, *The Jewish Exodus from Iraq, 1948-1951* (London: Frank Cass, 1997); *The Forgotten Millions: The Modern Jewish Exodus from Arab Lands*, ed. Malka Hillel Shulewitz (New York: Continuum, 2001); Itamar Levin and Rachel Neiman, *Locked Doors: The Seizure of Jewish Property in Arab Countries* (Westport, CT: Praeger, 2001).

141. *Peace in the Middle East?*, 182n20. See also *Fateful Triangle*, 236.

142. *Times* (London), June 15, 1967.

143. Letters, *Commentary*, December 1969.

144. *Pirates and Emperors,* 73.

145. Jonathan Shimshoni, *Israel and Conventional Deterrence: Border Warfare From 1953 to 1970* (Ithaca, NY: Cornell University Press, 1988), 137-8.

146. *Fateful Triangle*, 74; also *Pirates and Emperors*, 77-8.

147. *New York Times*, February 23, 24, 25, June 7, 1973; *Washington Post*, February 23, 1973; *Hotam* (Israel), February 10, 1984.

148. *Peace in the Middle East?*, 182n20.

149. *Guardian* (London), January 26, 1974.

150. *Times* (London), October 10, 1973.

151. Becker, *PLO*, 186-7.

152. *Pirates and Emperors,* 65.

153. *Fateful Triangle*, 189; *Pirates and Emperors,* 65, 132; Chomsky's source for the claim of "thousands killed" appears to be the article by far-left writer Judith Coburn quoted in *Fateful Triangle*, 190-1.

154. *Pirates and Emperors*, 51, 191n41, citing James Markham, *New York Times*, December 4, 1975 (9 dead according to the local hospital, 17 according to the PLO press service, with no breakdown between combatants and civilians).

155. *Towards a New Cold War*, 296, 452n115 (citing *Time*, April 3, 1978, which gives no source); *Fateful Triangle*, 99, 192 (citing *TNCW*); *Washington Post*, March 19, 1978 (Red Cross, 300 dead); *US News & World Report*, March 27, 1978 (400 dead, no source); Paul Findley, "Arab Victims of Recent Israeli Raids," *Journal of Palestine Studies*, Spring 1980, 202 (list of 344 dead in total, 1977-80).

156. *Fateful Triangle*, 197, 318n42.

157. *Seven Days*, July 1976; reprinted in *Journal of Palestine Studies*, Autumn 1976.

158. *Pirates and Emperors,* 76; also *Language and Politics*, 417, 474, where the figures escalate to "about 500 casualties, including approximately 200 children who were killed or wounded in an attack which destroyed a schoolhouse."

159. *New York Times*, January 5 and 6, 1984; also *Boston Globe*, January 5, 1984: "Most of the targets were strongholds of the Islamic Amal Movement and the Hezbollah, or Party of God—Lebanese extremist groups whose members are Shi'ite Moslems. They are supported by Iranian Revolutionary Guards who preach Ayatollah Ruhollah Khomeini's brand of revolution."

160. *Pirates and Emperors,* 64 (hijack); *Boston Globe*, July 3, 1984 (guerrillas).

161. *Pirates and Emperors,* 64-5.

162. *Washington Post*, June 28, 1984. Chomsky cites the *New York Times*, June 30, 1984, which naively reports the Lebanese police claim that the casualties were "boy scouts belonging to a militant Moslem fundamentalist faction, Al Tawhid." In Chomsky's dictionary of distortion, this becomes "children at a Sunni boy scout camp."

163. *Pirates and Emperors,* 75.

164. Associated Press, July 11, 1985.

165. *Pirates and Emperors,* 64-5; *New York Times*, June 28, 1984.

166. *Pirates and Emperors,* 64, 194n71.
167. Ibid., 64 (hijacking); *New York Times, Los Angeles Times,* February 5, 1986 (terror-
     ist congress).
168. *Pirates and Emperors,* 38.
169. On Syria, see *The Massacres of Hama: Law Enforcement Requires Accountability,*
     Syrian Human Rights Committee, London, 2002, reporting 30,000-40,000 massa-
     cred and 10,000-15,000 disappeared; on Iraq, Gerard Alexander, "A Lifesaving
     War," *Weekly Standard,* March 29, 2004; on Iran, Christina Lamb, "Khomeini
     Fatwa 'Led to Killing of 30,000 in Iran,'" *Sunday Telegraph* (UK), February 4,
     2001; on Sudan, *Quantifying Genocide in Southern Sudan and the Nuba Moun-
     tains, 1983-1998,* US Committee for Refugees, 1998.
170. *Middle East Illusions,* 199.
171. *Necessary Illusions,* 296, 311.
172. Khalaf, *Al-Watan* (Kuwait), February 11, 1989; Arafat, BBC *Summary of World
     Broadcasts,* January 8, 1990. See Jeane Kirkpatrick, "How the PLO Was Legiti-
     mized," *Commentary,* July 1989.
173. For an account of Israel's surrender in the negotiations, see Yigal Carmon, "The
     Story Behind the Handshake," *Commentary,* March 1994.
174. *Fateful Triangle,* 536.
175. Noam Chomsky, *Powers and Prospects* (Boston: South End Press, 1996), 148,
     150. These absurdities were compounded by blatantly erroneous predictions, e.g.:
     "It is also hardly to be expected that Israel will end its illegal occupation of southern
     Lebanon," 231. Israel withdrew to the international border soon afterwards.
176. *Fateful Triangle,* 558.
177. *Ruz-el-Yusuf* (Egypt), January 23, 1995; see David Bar-Illan, "Egypt Against Is-
     rael," *Commentary,* September 1995.
178. BBC *Summary of World Broadcasts,* March 25, 1995.
179. *Jerusalem Post,* February 23, 1996. See Yedidya Atlas, "Arafat's Secret Agenda Is
     to Wear Israelis Out," *Insight on the News,* April 1, 1996, citing multiple Israeli and
     Scandinavian reports. Ehud Ya'ari, "Bend or Break!" *Jerusalem Report,* April 4,
     1996, confirmed the authenticity of the speech. See also Efraim Karsh, *Arafat's
     War: The Man and His Struggle for Israeli Conquest* (New York: Grove Press,
     2003).
180. For documentation of the Palestinian Authority's alliance with Hamas, see Morton
     A. Klein, "Focus on Hamas: The PLO's Friend or Foe?" *Middle East Quarterly,*
     June 1996. In the words of Farouk Kaddoumi, head of the PLO's political depart-
     ment, "We were never different from Hamas. Hamas is a national movement. Stra-
     tegically, there is no difference between us." *Kul Al-Arab* (Israel), January 3, 2003;
     Jerusalem Post, January 4, 2003.
181. Chomsky interview, February 17, 2004, http://www.usamnesia.com/interviews/nc/
     chomsky.htm, http://www.chomsky.info/interviews/20040217.htm (one elected
     leader); Daniel Polisar, "Yasser Arafat and the Myth of Legitimacy," *Azure,* Sum-
     mer 2002 (rigged elections); *US News and World Report,* December 27, 1993 (Idi
     Amin/Saddam Hussein analogy from senior PLO official Yasser Abd Rabbo).
182. *Fateful Triangle,* 563 (Bantustans); *Middle East Illusions,* 217 (Barak offer). Israel
     could abandon 89 percent of the West Bank while annexing over 70 percent of the
     settlers, according to the former director of the Jaffee Center for Strategic Studies at
     Tel Aviv University: *Jerusalem Post,* July 27, 1998. Settlements take up only 1.36
     percent of the West Bank, according to Peace Now: David Makovsky, "Middle East
     Peace Through Partition," *Foreign Affairs,* March/April 2001.
183. *Al-Safir* (Lebanon), March 21, 2001. For analysis of the negotiations, see Saul

Singer, "Camp David, Real and Invented," *Middle East Quarterly*, Spring 2002, debunking the claims of Arafat apologists Robert Malley and Hussein Agha.

184.   *Necessary Illusions*, 298.
185.   *Al-Arabi* (Egypt), June 24, 2001.
186.   *Al-Nahar* (Lebanon), June 12, 2003, emphasis added.
187.   *Powers and Prospects*, 162.
188.   Palestinian Authority Television, August 3, 2001.
189.   *Al-Akhbar* (Egypt), April 18 and 25, 2001 ("most vile criminals"); *Financial Times*, Europe Edition, April 25, 2001 (Hezbollah); *Agence France Presse*, July 25, 2001 (Syria); Kenneth R. Timmerman, *Preachers of Hate: Islam and the War on America* (New York: Crown Forum, 2003), 147 ("tyrant Jews"); "Friday Sermons in Saudi Mosques: Review and Analysis," Middle East Media Research Institute, September 26, 2002 ("helpers of Satan").
190.   Vicky Hsu, "MIT, Harvard Faculty Petition Universities' Israel Investments," *Tech* (MIT), May 1, 2002; George Bradt, "Hundreds Support Call For Divestment," *Harvard Crimson*, May 8, 2002; Alan Dershowitz, "Noam Chomsky's Immoral Petition," *Jerusalem Post*, May 15, 2002.
191.   David Weinfeld, "Chomsky's Gift," *Harvard Crimson*, December 12, 2002.
192.   Noam Chomsky, Speech to the Scottish Palestine Solidarity Campaign (delivered by live video from MIT), October 11, 2002; published as "Anti-Semitism, Zionism and the Palestinians," *Variant* (a Scottish arts magazine), Winter 2002.
193.   *Peace in the Middle East?*, 73; on the FLN massacres, see Alistair Horne, *A Savage War of Peace: Algeria 1954-1962* (New York: Viking Press, 1977), 538.
194.   *Peace in the Middle East?*, 33.
195.   "An Exchange on the Jewish State," *New York Review of Books*, July 17, 1975.
196.   "Time to Dissociate From Israel," *Christian Science Monitor*, March 4, 1988, advertisement signed by Noam Chomsky et al.
197.   See W.D. Rubinstein, "Chomsky and the Neo-Nazis," *Quadrant*, October 1981. This comment alone belies the subsequent pretense that his writings on Holocaust deniers were limited to the issue of "free speech."
198.   Noam Chomsky, "The Fallacy of Richard Herrnstein's IQ," *Social Policy*, May/ June 1972.
199.   *Language and Politics*, 570.
200.   Ibid., 685.
201.   Noam Chomsky, "The Middle East Lie," *Lies of Our Times*, January 1990.
202.   "Anti-Semitism, Zionism and the Palestinians," *Variant*, Winter 2002.

7

Chomsky's Ayatollahs

Paul Bogdanor

"Jews Worship Satan": The Blood Libels of Israel Shahak

"I am indebted to several Israeli friends, primary among them Israel Shahak, for having provided me with a great deal of material… as well as much insightful comment." —*Noam Chomsky*[1]

"If we believe the rabbis, they will restore the old Jewish barbarism."
—*Israel Shahak*[2]

In his many chronicles of the various plots and conspiracies by which the Jewish state seeks to bring about a global "final solution" for the human race, Noam Chomsky projects an aura of scholarly integrity by quoting massively from sources identified as "Israeli doves." These individuals are, almost without exception, notorious cranks from Israel's radical fringe left. Many are the "thoughtful and courageous" Israelis who have helped to expose the malevolence and depravity of their countrymen. There is Uri Avnery, long-time publisher of a semi-pornographic tabloid, who ruminates on Israel's contribution to "Semitic suicide." There is Dov Yirmiah, Marxist activist, who judges, after careful consideration, that his homeland is "a nation of vicious thugs, whose second nature is fire, destruction, death and ruin." There is Meir Pail, leader of the communist Moked faction, who concludes that Israelis are "spiritual slaves to the culture of physical force." There is Boaz Evron, left-wing scribbler, for whom "the true symbol of the state is no longer the Menorah with seven candlesticks; the true symbol is the fist." There is Mattityahu Peled, anti-Zionist politician and former general, who reveals that "the Israelis have become the Mongols of the Middle East," even as he excuses the PLO for refusing to alter its genocidal covenant. There is Yeshayahu Leibowitz, theology professor, who coined the term "Judeo-Nazi" as the only adequate means to express the unholy wickedness of the state founded by the victims of the Holocaust. And there are "serious commentators" such as the sociologist Baruch Kimmerling, who describes his homeland as a "*Herrenvolk* Republic" with a "Thatcherist and semi-fascist regime," and who also happens to be active in Hadash, Israel's Communist Party.[3] No doubt important and reliable conclusions are to be drawn from the subtle meditations of these Olympian moral giants, whose failings would hardly escape notice if they were not telling Chomsky what he wanted to hear.

Pride of place in Chomsky's list of Israeli truth-tellers who dare to expose the evils of Zionism goes to the late Israel Shahak, applauded for "commitment to human rights that few people anywhere can equal."[4] The indefatigable Shahak was famous for devoting several decades of his life to sifting, cataloguing, and translating sensationalist tidbits from the less respectable sectors of the Israeli press, which he duly mailed to legions of anti-Israel obsessives on the far corners of the earth. Appended to each mailing would be a lengthy commentary explaining how the enclosed items afforded yet more proof of the iniquity of the Elders of Zion. If his supporters regarded this preoccupation (so typical of conspiracy-minded cranks throughout the world) as the diligent labors of a brave humanitarian, serious observers noted that Shahak was a caricature and a cartoon figure to the countrymen whose wickedness he sought to expose. In real life, Shahak may have endured a humdrum existence as a professor of organic chemistry; but it was in his political writings that his most intriguing concoctions were to be found.

What was the reason for this extraordinary, lifelong campaign? Shahak believed that "a majority of my people has left God, and has substituted an idol in its place, exactly as happened when they were so devoted to the Golden Calf in the desert that they gave away their gold to make it. The name of this modern idol is the State of Israel." A sign of this idolatry was "the excessive—indeed almost the exclusive—concern with money and the flattery of the rich.... The force of Jewish devotion in assembling money is thought to be infinite" - so much so that the Zionists had even established "a special school for people who will gather money from rich Jews."[5] But if much of the time Israel displayed the idolatrous visage of a capitalist Golden Calf, its socialist attributes were no less despicable; a crucial component in the machinery of Zionist repression was the kibbutz, which functioned as a training ground for "the population of an Orwellian state... the Israeli analogue to the class of armed nobility during the heyday of feudalism." All kibbutz members were subjected to a rigorous program of brainwashing, whereupon they were put to work on tasks requiring "inhuman behavior," in accordance with "the totalitarian and militaristic character of kibbutz education."[6] In Shahak's hall of ideological mirrors, Israel was simultaneously a capitalist Golden Calf and a socialist Gulag—and in both cases, demonic.

Yet for Shahak, the true source of Zionist depravity was more profound: "The majority of the Jewish public in Israel (and also out of it) believes that only Jews are human beings, and therefore deserve to be trusted, while the

Gentiles usually lie, as stated in most cases throughout Talmudic Law." Furthermore,

> I am not afraid to say publicly that Israeli Jews, and with them most Jews throughout the world, are undergoing a process of Nazification… according to Jewish Talmudic law, legally valid in Israel today, any Gentile woman is considered as impure, a slave, a Gentile and a whore…. The argumentation provided by Talmudic law to back that judgement… can only be compared to Julius Streicher…

Indeed, according to Shahak, the hate-mongers of *Der Stürmer* were rather soft in comparison with their Jewish counterparts: "jurists in Nazi Germany accepted the Nuremberg Laws," but these were "infinitely more moderate than the 'Gentile' regulations in Talmudic Law," so he assured his readers. Enacting the requirements of their faith, which surpassed the bigotry of Nazism, the Jews had constructed the most hideous society that the human mind could possibly imagine: "Everything is divided into 'Jewish' and 'non-Jewish.' In Israel there are (officially) no Israeli babies. There are equally no Israeli tomatoes (or potatoes, or corn or any other produce)—there are only tomatoes from Jewish farms, and tomatoes from non-Jewish farms." If only the consumers of Jaffa Oranges had been alerted to these facts! But here, too, Shahak was ready with an explanation, namely "the Jewish establishment in the USA and its intellectual slaves…. The totalitarian pressure of the USA Jewish establishment, together with its slaves and flatterers, pushes Israel towards extreme courses…" After all, "Jewish terror is very kosher in the USA!"[7] Would any fascist disagree?

Shahak—whose supporters never failed to advertise his wartime experiences in a concentration camp[8]—strenuously denied that his views on the kosher terror qualified him as a Nazi. That is hardly surprising, since he was one of the most splenetic proponents of the anti-Zionist cliché that the Jewish state is the true successor of the Third Reich. The principle was established at the outset of his political campaigns, when he predicted that if Israel failed to lose the next war, "we will become Nazified. We will become to Arabs like Nazi Germany was to the Slavic people… I think the comparison with Germany is a very apt historical one… I use the word Nazi very frequently about Israeli policies."[9] This last observation was correct. Sometimes it seemed as if Shahak could hardly write a sentence, let alone a page, without denouncing the Jewish state as racist and Nazi. On occasion, however, he managed to conjure up a novel comparison:

> The immediate analogy which a lot of people are making in Israel is Germany. Not only the Germany of Hitler and the Nazis but even the former German Empire wanted to dominate Europe. What happened in Japan after the attack on China is that they wanted to dominate a huge area of Asia.[10]

Thus Shahak, if only for an instant, was able to grant the possibility that the appropriate analogue for the Jewish state was Imperial Germany or Fascist Japan. But such concessions were short-lived. Indeed, Shahak's compulsion to equate Jews with Nazis could be re-ignited by the strangest provocations. The

deportation of bearded Hamas terrorists sent the professor into further parox-
ysms of demented fury: "at an early stage of the Nazi occupation of Poland, in
1939, well before the Jews were rounded up into the ghettoes, Nazi soldiers
often beat up or harassed particularly those Jews (and occasionally Poles) who
wore beards..." Railing against this latest crime by the "Judeo-Nazis" of the
Jewish state, he concluded: "As long as the United States continues to support
Israel, it can only be surmised that this tendency will culminate either in a
transfer or in another Holocaust..."[11]

Not content with execrating the Jewish state as the reincarnation of Nazi
Germany and the likely perpetrator of a new Holocaust, Shahak proceeded to
vilify each and every Jewish writer, thinker, leader or rabbi whose opinions
incurred his displeasure. Moses Hess, one of the first socialist thinkers in Germany, was "an extreme Jewish racist," whose views "were not unlike comparable bilge about the 'pure Aryan race.'"[12] Chaim Weizmann's "anti-Arab racism... can only be compared to Nazi anti-Semitic outbursts."[13] Martin Buber
"glorified a movement holding and actually teaching doctrines about non-
Jews not unlike the Nazi doctrines about Jews." Bible scholar Yehezkel Kaufmann
was "an advocate of genocide on the model of the Book of Joshua." The
Lubavitcher Rebbe was the "hereditary Fuehrer of Habbad," guilty of publishing "the most rabid bloodthirsty statements and exhortations against all Arabs."[14] Ignoring the standard pretense that anti-Zionism is distinct from
antisemitism, Shahak hastened to declare that "there are Nazi-like tendencies
in Judaism..."[15] Finally, when his readers must have been wondering whether
there was a single Jewish person on the face of the earth he did *not* regard as a
Nazi, Shahak provided some relief: echoing Chomsky, he explained that American Jews "have been compared by the Hebrew press to communists under the
Comintern, with their loyalty to Stalin."[16]

Shahak had many other insights into the malevolent practices of the Judeo-
Nazis. Writing in the PLO's *Journal of Palestine Studies*, he explained that "all
Zionists—the so-called leftist Zionists as much as any others—claim for the
Jews by 'historical right' both Palestine and Jordan..." Ben-Gurion, "who was in
the Zionist sense a real moderate," added parts of Syria, Lebanon, and Egypt,
but the claws of Zionism extended much further than "from the Nile to the
Euphrates"; there was the danger that "even Cyprus is to be included" in the
quest for Jewish *Lebensraum*. Pursuing their dreams of empire, the Zionist Jews
were given to invoking the principles of the Bible, according to which "all
inhabitants have to be exterminated, including babies..." The "other Holocaust"
recounted in the Torah—i.e., the destruction of the Canaanites—was being
"used in order to accustom Israeli Jewish opinion to possible acts of terror..."
Even more worrying was "the use of biblical examples of mass extermination"
to justify the murder of millions of Arabs: "It is this insistence on the biblical
historical right and on the rightness of biblically-justified genocide which
makes such a proposal in Israel a serious danger, the source of whose social

respectability demands to be known in detail."[17] How fortunate that Israel Shahak was available to explain to would-be PLO terrorists that their future victims were not the children of Holocaust survivors from Europe or dispossessed refugees from Arab countries, but participants in a biblical conspiracy extending from Cyprus to Iraq and entailing the murder of millions of people in a repetition of the ancient massacres of the Canaanites!

Although his substantive views were clearly the product of a disturbed mind, Shahak's propaganda technique would have been familiar to students of radical left-wing "activism" everywhere. Assuming the mantle of the persecuted dissident, the brave non-conformist ostracized by an oppressive society for daring to reveal its ugly crimes and hypocrisies, Shahak regaled his audience with a stream of outrageous libels, ludicrous fabrications and transparent hoaxes. As each successive allegation was exposed and discredited, he would simply proceed to a new invention.

The effects of his fantasies were not slight. When Senator Fulbright saw fit to conduct Congressional hearings on dangers to the world's oil supplies, he was able to cite Israel Shahak in support of the claim that the Jewish state was poised to resolve the energy crisis "by taking over Kuwait, there being no force in the desert between Israel and the Persian Gulf capable of resisting the Israeli Army."[18] Similarly, when Middle East correspondent John K. Cooley sought to enlighten his readers on the prospects for peace in the region, he was able to quote an unimpeachable source:

> Dr. Shahak says he suspects that Israel's economic and social difficulties… may be setting the scene for a new Israeli-launched war against the Arab countries, this time Syria and Jordan. The war would be started by Israeli military men on the ground that this might be the only way to renew the flow of support by US and world Jewry for the state of Israel, he says.[19]

Needless to say, when PLO publications wanted further proof of Zionist malevolence, they could rely on the good chemistry professor to warn that Israeli strategists were focused on "dismembering Syria… they hope that they will find Arabs who will play the role of Indian maharajahs." Furthermore, "by the conquest of Jordan, Israel could really cut the Arab world in two… Jordan has borders with Kuwait and the UAE," and so "Israel could levy blackmail on Arab oil countries one way or another."[20] Obsessed with exposing Zionist plans to control the Middle East, Shahak evidently had no time to acquire a basic knowledge of geography.

That Israel never even came close to a combined invasion of Syria and Jordan—let alone a military occupation of Kuwait—did not diminish Shahak's confidence (or his audience) in the slightest. Instead he continued to warn that "the domination of the whole Middle East by Israel is the constant aim of Israeli (and before this of Zionist) policies.… This can best be shown… in the cases of Egypt, Syria and even Iraq…"[21] More than a decade after his original prediction, he was still asserting that "the current government of Israel, through its loyal

American Jewish servants, intends to conquer Jordan...”[22] For good measure, he referred to “Israeli genocidal meddling in Central America or in countries like Zaire.”[23] Was it for these pearls of wisdom that Shahak was cited in Senate hearings on the oil crisis or invited to testify before a Congressional subcommittee on foreign affairs?[24]

Shahak’s admirers were even more impressed by his (frequently hilarious) fictions concerning Israel’s human rights record. How many dime-store novelists could rival the sheer audacity of his tales of Zionist oppression? In the 1970s, Shahak was anxious to chronicle the laws of the conqueror for his credulous disciples:

> Does one want to punish the area of Hebron? Grapes are not allowed to be transported on the roads during harvest time.... Does one want to punish the city of Ramallah? The sale of mutton is forbidden in that town for two months.... Does one want to punish the town of al-Bira? An order is issued to take pictures of Palestinian folklore off the walls of the city hall, and to hide them in a cellar!

He also reported that “the Gaza Strip constitutes a concentration camp (and just like a concentration camp it is surrounded by barbed wire)...”[25] And more was to follow. By the early 1980s, Shahak was prepared to announce some astonishing discoveries about “the real conditions of life” in the West Bank and Gaza:

> The four colors of which the Palestinian flag is composed—white, black, green and red—are prohibited to be used too closely in any painting publicly displayed. It is forbidden to the Palestinian painters of the occupied territories to paint a surrealist flower in which one petal will be white, the other black, the third green and the fourth red; or alternatively pictures of wildlife with white, black, green and red flowers too close one to the other.

He further alleged that Israeli censors confiscated a picture of a horse because it constituted a “nationalistic incitement”; that they banned a painting of a dove because it was depicted in the wrong colors; that Israel’s security concerns were a mask for repressive control over “the patterns of postage stamps” as well as “controls of art forms and songs to be sung on the radio”; that “a system resembling slavery exists”; and so on.[26]

When Israel went to war against PLO forces on its northern border, Shahak was able to impart a new revelation: “A killing of the Palestinians in Lebanon, specially of males, has begun and is being carried on. There is very little doubt that many of the Palestinians who were ‘arrested’ or who ‘disappeared’ will not be seen again, and their very existence will be denied.” (Chomsky observed that “Shahak’s speculation does not appear to be too far-fetched...”)[27] Similarly, when Israel retaliated against Hezbollah shelling of its towns and villages, Shahak was ready with further insights. “The main Israeli aim in Lebanon is the economic exploitation of this country and other Middle Eastern states,” he explained to his American readers, before turning to a learned disquisition on the Zionist rationale for drug-dealing:

the Israeli involvement in the drug trade warrants some conclusions in regard to the nature of political realities in the Middle East.... Part of the motivation must be to weaken the disaffection of Middle Eastern masses by encouraging drug addiction and thus promoting political apathy... The Israeli wars in Lebanon should be compared to the Opium Wars of the 19th century.[28]

Thus Shahak maintained that Israel was engaged in a secret genocide of Palestinian refugees, and that Israel's operations against Shi'ite terrorists were simply a cover for the economic enslavement of the Middle East and the corruption of the Arab masses through drug addiction. What could be more obvious? And yet these ludicrous fictions—which would be an embarrassment to Radio Damascus—were greeted with awe and enthusiasm by his foreign devotees.

Shahak always seemed to have a limitless supply of his esoteric "facts." "I could go on indefinitely, and give innumerable examples," he vouchsafed to his readers.[29] "Without too much difficulty," his critics might have replied, "if you simply make it up as you go along."

The predictable nadir of Shahak's political activities was the publication of his book *Jewish History, Jewish Religion: The Weight of Three Thousand Years*. In this work—issued, as we shall see, to a chorus of acclaim from radical left-wing haters of Israel—Shahak dispensed, once and for all, with the pretense that Israelis or Zionists, rather than Jews as such, are the true source of the evils that beset the human race. He began as he meant to continue—with an antisemitic fabrication. In the 1960s, he related, he had "personally witnessed" an Orthodox Jew's refusal to allow the use of his telephone on the Sabbath to call an ambulance for a non-Jew who had collapsed nearby. On seeking a ruling from the religious authorities, the outraged witness was instructed that according to rabbinical law, "a Jew should not violate the Sabbath in order to save the life of a Gentile." Shahak professed that he had "reported the incident to the main Hebrew daily, *Haaretz*, whose publication of the story caused a media scandal."[30] What he did not tell his readers is that, challenged to substantiate his "eye-witness account," he had been forced to admit that it was a straightforward hoax and that the Orthodox Jew in question did not exist. He also neglected to disclose that the rabbinate, far from confirming his interpretation of Jewish law, had in fact ruled that it was mandatory for a Jew to violate the Sabbath in order to save a human life, whether Jewish or Gentile. In the words of one commentator, "The whole incident had been fabricated in true *Protocols* style."[31]

The analogy was appropriate. For according to Shahak, Israel's Jewish character constitutes a danger not only to its own population, "but to all Jews and to *all other peoples and states in the Middle East and beyond*."[32] In his view, the essence of the "Jewish ideology" is expansion of Israel's borders throughout the region, coupled with the enslavement (under apartheid conditions) of non-Jewish populations. This belief, he maintained, is so deeply entrenched that not only Israelis but even Diaspora Jews display "a strong streak of totalitarianism in their character."[33] (In fairness, it must be noted that Shahak subsequently had second thoughts about the Israeli half of the equation. "In the old days of Zionist purity," he explained, apartheid was observed to the letter, but this did not last, for "it was then found that apartheid, especially if strictly enforced, interferes with money-making." Thus "Jewish apartheid" had now given way to Jewish greed.)[34]

Given his premise, it is not surprising that Shahak's argument quickly degenerated into stereotypical antisemitic smears. He proclaimed that "Jewish children are actually taught" to utter a blessing near a Jewish cemetery, but "to curse the mothers of the dead if it is non-Jewish.... A pious Jew arriving for the first time in Australia, say, and chancing to pass near an Aboriginal graveyard, must—as an act of worship of 'God'—curse the mothers of the dead buried there."[35] He asserted that Judaism was riddled with sexual obscenity: "The duty of pious Jews is to restore through their prayers and religious acts the perfect divine unity, in the form of sexual union, between the male and female deities... at one point the goddess approaches with her handmaidens, at another the god puts his arm around her neck and fondles her breast, and finally the sexual act is supposed to take place."[36] And he warned that Jews worship the Devil: "both before and after a meal, a pious Jew ritually washes his hands, uttering a special blessing. On one of these two occasions he is worshipping God... but on the other he is worshipping Satan... some of the sacrifices burnt in the Temple were intended for Satan."[37] He added that "kidnapping of Gentiles by Jews is allowed by talmudic law," that "a Jew is in general forbidden to save the life of a Gentile" and that Jews have "no respect towards non-Jewish corpses and cemeteries."[38] He further disclosed that Judaism is based on "deception of God" as well as "deception of other Jews, mainly in the interest of the Jewish ruling class," and that Judaism is "obviously motivated by the spirit of profit"; indeed, "Marx was quite right" when he portrayed Judaism as "dominated by profit-seeking."[39] Not since the genocidal ravings of Goebbels and Streicher had a Western author drawn such a horrible portrait of grave-cursing, lust-wallowing, Devil-worshipping, man-stealing, corpse-defiling, money-grubbing Jewish monsters.

From justifying antisemitic ideology, it was only a short step to justifying antisemitic mass murder. Shahak finally took that step. In *Jewish History, Jewish Religion*, he hastened to rationalize the pogroms, which he characterized as "popular anti-Jewish manifestations of the past." Since the Jews of Eastern Europe were mercilessly exploiting the peasants, according to Shahak, it was only natural that they became the targets of popular fury. Referring to the Chmielnicki uprising in which tens of thousands of Jews were slaughtered with incredible brutality, Shahak invoked popular rebellions against English colonizers and French slave-owners, lamenting that in the historiography of the pogroms, "an enslaved peasant is transformed into a racist monster, if Jews profited from his state of slavery and exploitation."[40] By now he was simply recycling Soviet antisemitic propaganda. (In the words of one such propagandist, "Polish, Ukrainian and Byelorussian peasants, reduced to despair by merciless exploitation, sometimes rebelled and avenged themselves on their oppressors... the personification of which were the rapacious Jewish lease-holders, tax-farmers, money-lenders and inn-keepers.")[41] And this was plagiarism with a definite purpose. In a striking innovation, Shahak extended his analogy to the present:

> The State of Israel now fulfils towards the oppressed peasants of many countries—not only in the Middle East but also far beyond it—a role not unlike that of the Jews in pre-1795 Poland: that of a bailiff to the imperial oppressor... It seems that Israel and Zionism are a throwback to the role of classical Judaism—writ large, on a global scale, and under more dangerous circumstances.[42]

The implications were clear: if East Europeans were justified in annihilating the Jewish communities in their midst, the peoples of the world are now entitled to inflict the same fate on the population of Israel. So it is that Israel Shahak, an obscure chemistry professor in Jerusalem, laid before an international audience the case for a second Holocaust.

Reactions to Shahak's antisemitic diatribes were almost as shameful as their contents. Far from being dismissed as the ravings of a Jew-baiting crank, *Jewish History, Jewish Religion* was festooned with plaudits from the argute aficionados of anti-Zionism. Gore Vidal, that exemplar of redneck bigotry raised to the level of literacy, ruminated on "the great Gentile-hating Dr. Maimonides" and found space to explain that President Truman had recognized Israel solely because "an American Zionist brought him two million dollars in cash," before hailing Shahak as "a humanist who detests imperialism [conducted] in the name of the God of Abraham... a highly learned Thomas Paine.... He is the latest, if not the last, of the great prophets."[43] Edward Said, formerly of the PLO's ruling council, acclaimed "one of the most remarkable individuals in the contemporary Middle East... he alone stated the unadorned truth, without consideration for whether that truth, if stated plainly, might not be 'good' for Israeli [sic] or the Jews."[44] Not to be surpassed, Noam Chomsky opined that "Shahak is an outstanding scholar, with remarkable insight and depth of knowledge. His work is informed and penetrating, a contribution of great value."[45]

If Shahak's life occasioned these extravaganzas of unctuous flattery, his death evoked scarcely believable raptures from the faithful. In his soon-to-be-defunct column in *The Nation*, Christopher Hitchens remembered his "dear friend and comrade Dr. Israel Shahak," whose home was "a library of information about the human rights of the oppressed.... If he [had] admitted to any intellectual model, it would have been Spinoza... [He was] a great and serious man."[46] In Britain, respectful obituaries appeared in the *Guardian* and the *Independent*, where veteran anti-Israel propagandist Michael Adams canonized this "lifelong campaigner in the cause of human rights," who "had something of the character of an Old Testament prophet."[47] Writing in the *New Statesman*, John Pilger extolled "the indomitable peace campaigner Israel Shahak," before castigating Westerners for "allowing the lessons of the Holocaust to serve only the oppressor," meaning the Jews.[48] The Arabist *Washington Report on Middle East Affairs* paid tribute to this "genuinely prophetic Jewish voice," adding that future generations would remember him alongside the Germans who tried to assassinate Hitler.[49] But while some compared Shahak to the victims of Hitler, the present-day disciples of Hitler were equally enthusiastic: "Dr. Israel Shahak risked all to bring what he calls 'decent humanity' to Judaism and the Zionist State," mourned the American Nazi leader David Duke, noting that Shahak had exposed "numerous examples of hateful Judaic laws... that permit Jews to cheat, to steal, to rob, to kill, to rape, to lie, even to enslave Christians."[50]

Thus Shahak, having devoted his life to exposing the kosher terror and the Devil-worshipping Jews, found himself mourned in death by the far-left supporters of the PLO and the far-right admirers of Nazi Germany. *Les extremes se touchent.* What further proof do we need that it is not "the Jewish religion" but the writings of Dr. Israel Shahak that have been "poisoning minds and hearts" throughout the world?[51]

"A Slow, Steady Genocide": Tanya Reinhart Unveils the Zionist Conspiracy

"Deeply informed and carefully argued, Tanya Reinhart's expert and chilling analysis could hardly be more timely." —*Noam Chomsky*[52]

"What is happening in the Territories is a process of slow and steady genocide." —*Tanya Reinhart*[53]

In November 2004, shortly after playing host to a conference by the openly pro-terrorist Palestine Solidarity Movement, Duke University was thoughtful enough to subject its students to another barrage of propaganda. Guest of honor at the university's latest colloquy on the Middle East was one Tanya Reinhart, identified as "a professor emeritus at Tel Aviv University" who "received her Ph.D. in linguistics from the Massachusetts Institute of Technology, where Professor Noam Chomsky served as her thesis advisor." Shortly before her visit, Reinhart had announced that Israel's policies were "incomparably worse" than the crimes of the Milosevic regime in Yugoslavia.[54] In her Duke lecture—sponsored, *inter alia*, by the Departments of Cultural Anthropology, Literature and Women's Studies—she "called for a general boycott of Israel, including its military, businesses and universities." But she also found it convenient to make a little exception to her demand: "In response to a question, Reinhart clarified that the boycott she advocates applies to academic conferences put on by Israeli universities, but not individual Israeli faculty members. Thus, she explained, she was not breaking her own boycott by accepting the invitation to speak at Duke."[55] In short, Israel would be isolated, its defenders disarmed, its economy starved and its institutions humiliated, but Reinhart would remain free to travel the world in order to expose the demonic evils of the country whose citizens were, at that very moment, being bombed, shot, knifed, incinerated and massacred.

If her practical proposals display no shortage of hypocrisy, Reinhart's avowed beliefs bear the mark of sheer fanaticism. For Reinhart, there are "two poles" in Israeli politics: "preservation of the present apartheid situation under the cover of negotiations, or ethnic cleansing and mass evacuation" (that is, evacuation of Palestinians; Reinhart has no qualms about the expulsion of Israelis from their homes in the West Bank and Gaza). Apartheid, according to Reinhart, is the policy of Shimon Peres and Yossi Beilin; ethnic cleansing is the goal of Ariel Sharon and the IDF. This view of the world has placed her in a difficult dilemma: "I confess that often in the dark months of Israel's brutality, when the ethnic cleansing pole seemed to be winning, I prayed that Beilin would manage to take us back to the road of apartheid." She finds no solace in the existence of organizations such as Peace Now, which merely provide a convenient façade for Israel's malevolent crimes: "The political leadership of Israel's peace camp has years of experience diverting the majority of the occupation's opponents toward the route of preserving the status quo." But whereas Israeli society oscillates between apartheid and ethnic cleansing, with Peace Now campaigning to preserve the "occupation," Palestinian nationalism is the epitome of moderation; were Israel to withdraw, the resulting PLO-controlled state would hasten to "construct democratic institutions" and to "conduct negotiations with mutual respect."[56] Recall that the Palestinian Authority openly proclaims that "the Resurrection will not take place until the Muslims fight the Jews and the Muslims kill them."[57]

It is obvious that Reinhart's message is aimed at a relatively narrow audience. If there is anyone who still believes that that the PLO "had developed in the Palestinian refugee camps in Lebanon"; or that Israel demolished the PLO Research Center in Beirut for the purpose of "effacing virtually the entire record of collective Palestinian life" (quoting Edward Said); or that the Oslo War was "triggered" by Ariel Sharon's "provocative" visit to the Temple Mount in Jerusalem; or that twelve-year-old Muhammad al-Durra was killed by Israeli bullets; or that "no Palestinian terror attacks on Israeli civilians had yet taken place" before the breakdown of the peace process; or that Fatah commander Thabet Thabet was killed by Israel because he was a "renowned moderate leader"; or that "the US forced starvation on millions of people" in Afghanistan—then for such a person, Reinhart will be a valued resource.[58] Others will be less favorably disposed. Clearly not much is to be expected from a writer who cannot even spell the names of a well-known Israeli intellectual (Yeshayahu Leibowitz) or a longstanding Knesset member (Zerach Warhaftig), and who provides different spellings (both erroneous) for the last names of two related Palestinian leaders (Marwan and Mustafa Barghouti).[59] Nor can we place much faith in a commentator who derives her information from the likes of Edward Said (of the Palestine National Council), Hanan Ashrawi (through her propaganda outlet MIFTAH), Ran Hacohen (of Tel Aviv University's Department of Comparative Literature) or Ronnie Kasrils (of the South African Communist Party), let alone one who regards Noam Chomsky and Arundhati Roy as serious observers of world affairs.[60]

That Reinhart herself need not be taken very seriously is confirmed by the farrago of fiction that constitutes her analysis of recent history. Consider her treatment of the breakdown of the Oslo peace process at the Camp David and Taba summits in 2000. In the standard version of events, after eight years of unilateral Israeli withdrawals accompanied by Palestinian massacres of Israeli women and children, Ehud Barak agreed to surrender all but a microscopic fraction of the West Bank and Gaza, to connect the two territories with a secure route bisecting Israel, to recognize an independent Palestinian state, to establish a Palestinian army, to re-divide Jerusalem and to absorb tens of thousands of Palestinian exiles within Israel's pre-1967 borders; Arafat flatly rejected the offer, presented no counterproposal, and began preparing for war.[61] But Reinhart, who regards Israel's criminality as an *à priori* truth, will have none of it. According to her, Barak wanted to restrict the Palestinian state to "five isolated cantons (including Gaza) inside Israel," and to guarantee that within the state's territory, "the settlements will be expanded… the Israeli army will stay to protect them, and thus the situation will remain as it is now…" This was the "biggest fraud of Barak's plan." Another fraud was Israel's "verbal trick" over partition of its capital city: "It is hard to understand how so many have swallowed the story about Barak's willingness to divide Jerusalem." As for domestic protests against his concessions, here was yet another sign of Barak's cunning: "The crisis with Israel's right wing on the eve of the Camp David summit contributed further to the false impression that Barak made an unprecedented offer." When Barak failed to secure the Palestinian Authority's surrender, he provoked the second intifada so that he could launch a campaign of state terror. After all, Reinhart observes, "the easy way to exterminate a weak nation has always been to drag it into a hopeless war."[62]

Unfortunately for her argument, Reinhart neglected to inform the PLO leadership of these discoveries. The latter were under the impression that they had fooled the Israelis into making unprecedented concessions without offering anything in return. Thus Fatah Central Committee member Sakher Habash declared that a Palestinian state on the pre-1967 borders was merely a "temporary political goal… The Palestinian state, whatever it will be, will constitute the beginning of the dismantling of the Zionist enterprise." Palestinian strategist Faisal Husseini announced that "Barak agreed to a withdrawal from 95% of the occupied Palestinian lands" and boasted that "no other party will be able to conduct a dialogue with us except from the point where Barak stopped, namely, from the right to 95% of the territory." Palestinian commentator Abdel Bari

Atwan reported that Arafat rejected the Camp David proposals "because he wasn't prepared to sign a final agreement with the Jewish state." But for Reinhart, obsessed with Zionist conspiracies, the only relevant issue is "Barak's mastery of schemes of deception."[63]

Even the Temple Mount is merely another cog in the sinister Barak's machinations. Since 1967, according to Reinhart, Israel has deliberately manufactured a religious mystique about the Western Wall with the aim of forestalling demands to demolish the Al-Aqsa Mosque and rebuild the Temple. But at Camp David Barak insisted on raising a claim to the Temple Mount itself to sabotage negotiations and provoke a new conflict.[64] So extreme is Reinhart's paranoia that even the holiest site in Judaism is a figment of the Zionist conspiracy. Needless to say, she firmly endorses the PLO propaganda line that it was Sharon's visit to the Temple Mount—or rather (as she neurotically reminds us) Barak's approval of Sharon's visit—that triggered the second intifada.[65] And in this instance, she surpasses the PLO itself in her talents for dissimulation. More than two weeks before the Sharon visit, the Palestinian Authority officially declared that "the time for the intifada has arrived, the time for jihad has arrived." Yasser Arafat's adviser told the French media that "a few days before the Sharon visit to the Mosque," Arafat had "requested that we be ready to initiate a clash…" Palestinian Authority cabinet minister Imad Faluji announced that the violence "had been planned since Chairman Arafat's return from Camp David…" Fatah commander Marwan Barghouti asserted that "the intifada did not start because of Sharon's visit," but because its instigators "did not approve of the peace process in its previous form."[66] But why should Reinhart be bothered by such trivial matters as facts?

Reinhart is aware that her claims tend to arouse skepticism: "It is still difficult for many to believe that a deception of such magnitude is possible… it looks like it would take a sick mind to intentionally conceive and execute such a plot, the type found only in absurd conspiracy theories." But she apparently believes that her conspiracy theory—in which Barak single-handedly beguiles both the PLO and the Israeli public, not to mention the State Department, the international community and virtually every other living soul on the planet, apart from Tanya Reinhart—is not nearly absurd enough. For the truth of the matter—revealed to us exclusively by the linguistics professor from Tel Aviv—is that Barak and Sharon are running the conspiracy together! Although they "have always been perceived as political rivals," she informs us, the nefarious duo share "a long history of cooperation and a common worldview."[67] So extensive is this collaboration that Reinhart finds it necessary to supply an entire chapter on the subject of "Barak's Version of Sharon." Here we learn that Barak's precipitous retreat from southern Lebanon was just another artfully induced misperception. Indeed, now "even the slightest incident will be viewed as a legitimate reason for Israel to launch a devastating attack against both Lebanon and Syria." In lieu of evidence, she poses a question: "why wasn't the border fortified? There are two options: either there has been a very big goof-up, or Barak is executing, in practice, Sharon's plan."[68] What more proof do we need that Barak and Sharon are collaborators, or that the withdrawal from Lebanon is actually part of a dastardly scheme to invade Lebanon, with Syria falling victim along the way? Are there no limits to fantasy?

But Reinhart's thesis that Barak was in league with Sharon is merely the entrée to a much more elaborate conspiracy theory. In her view, Israel is really a secret military dictatorship. "It is often apparent that the real decisions are made by the military rather than the political echelon," she explains. Her proof? "In all televised coverage of meetings of the Israeli government or cabinet, one sees at least an equal number of uniformed representatives of the various branches of the military and the security forces."[69] In other words, count the uniforms! As for the objectives of this carefully disguised military junta, Reinhart is in no doubt: "the political generals… may believe that under the appropriate conditions of regional escalation, it would be possible to execute the transfer option—the mass evacuation of the Palestinian residents, as happened in 1948…" This would require "the umbrella of an extensive regional war," but of course, "Israel has been preparing for such a war, and is awaiting US approval." Duplicating Israel Shahak's lifelong delusion, she initially predicted that the target would be Syria.[70] But the buildup to war in Iraq caused her to reorient her laser-like perceptions. In late 2002, Reinhart was among scores of Israeli academic leftists who issued an "Urgent Warning" that an American invasion of Iraq would be "exploited by the Israeli government" to commit "full-fledged ethnic cleansing."[71] On this occasion—as on so many others—the predictions of the professional haters of Israel proved to be worthless, but Reinhart has yet to be deterred. After all, she is privy to the most closely guarded information: "Israel's course," she reveals, "is currently directed by an all-powerful group of fanatical generals who keep their plans secret from even the full forum of the Israeli government. These are the generals who are authorized to unleash Israel's nuclear arsenal."[72] How many Middle East spies could hope to achieve the penetrating insights of the linguistics professor from Tel Aviv University?

It is when she turns to Israel's reaction to PLO-instigated violence that Reinhart really comes into her element. In her view, there is virtually no limit to the atrocities of the Israeli junta. "More than seven thousand Palestinians were reported injured… many in the head, legs or knees by carefully aimed shots," she avers. But this is hardly the climax of Israeli sadism: "A common Israeli practice," she explains, "is to shoot a rubber-coated metal bullet straight into a Palestinian's eye—a little game played by well-trained soldiers that requires maximum precision." Her source for these tales is the Palestinian "human rights" group LAW, infamous for engaging in "anti-Zionist and anti-Semitic" incitement and for misappropriating millions of dollars in charitable donations.[73] Having reproduced these concoctions from a discredited hate group, Reinhart turns to the testimony of an IDF officer who announces: "We are very much trying not to kill them." From this she deduces that Israel has a deliberate policy of maiming: "Specially trained units... shoot in a calculated manner in order to cripple, while keeping the statistics of Palestinians killed low...Their fate is to die slowly, away from the cameras... an act of ethnic cleansing... by which people are slowly forced to perish or flee." Feigning outrage at this horrible crime, Reinhart conveniently omits the officer's statement that his soldiers "only shoot to wound Palestinians who are firing at them or throwing firebombs."[74]

Not content with these defamations, eminently worthy of *Der Stürmer*, Reinhart proceeds to unveil her newest discovery: the "untold crime" of Jenin. "Ordinary language allows the use of the word 'massacre' for such cases of indiscriminate killing of civilians," she writes of the battle that claimed fifty-two enemy dead, according to United Nations figures, including thirty-eight armed terrorists.[75] That Reinhart is prepared to resurrect such long-refuted fictions is a testament to her belief that she can get away with anything. Her evidence for the "massacre" allegation consists of an Internet posting by an "activist" based in Germany and an interview with a disgruntled army driver and self-described madman who calls himself "Kurdi Bear."[76] And this weighty documentation is counterposed to the unanimous findings of every single independent investigation, including the prosecutorial inquisitions of such venomously anti-Israel NGOs as Human Rights Watch! It is tempting to argue that no propagandist ever went lower for a proof, but how then do we characterize Reinhart's tales of the "little game" of shooting special bullets into people's eyes, based on stories from an antisemitic hate group? Or her conclusion that "specially trained units" shoot to cripple, based on an officer's statement that they were trying their best not to kill?

Where Reinhart's allegations are not simply too absurd to discuss, they can be exposed as false with but a moment's investigation. Consider her charge that Israel is implementing a deliberate policy of mass starvation:

> What we are witnessing in the occupied territories—Israel's penal colonies—is the invisible and daily killing of the sick and wounded who are deprived of medical care, of the weak who cannot survive in the new poverty conditions, and of those who are approaching starvation... Pushing the Palestinians to starvation is not just a tragic outcome of Israel's "war against terror." It is a systematic policy... It is a well-calculated strategy of ethnic cleansing.[77]

Reinhart's evidence that Israel is deliberately starving millions of people to death consists of statistics on child malnutrition. Yet World Bank figures show that child malnutrition rates in the West Bank and Gaza are surpassed in Argentina, Bolivia, Brazil, China, Colombia, Egypt, Indonesia, Iran, Iraq, Jordan, Libya, Malaysia, Mexico, Morocco, Nicaragua, Oman, Panama, Peru, Russia, South Africa, Syria, Turkey, Venezuela, Yemen, and most of Africa and Asia.[78] By Reinhart's standards, it follows that most of the world's governments—and virtually all Arab states—are pursuing "a well-calculated strategy of ethnic cleansing" against their populations. But what else can we expect from an author who is still peddling Noam Chomsky's claim that the Bush Administration "forced starvation upon millions of people" in Afghanistan, where UNICEF estimates that the deaths of 112,000 children and 7,500 pregnant women will be prevented every year as a result of the American occupation?[79]

That Reinhart's tales of Israeli cruelty and sadism are completely without foundation should be obvious to any sane person. According to Ze'ev Schiff, Israel's most respected military commentator, Ariel Sharon's government gave the IDF strict instructions to the effect that "one of the criteria for judging the success of your operation in the refugee camps will be the lowest possible number of civilian casualties."[80] Reinhart, so assiduous in collecting newspaper clippings from *Ha'aretz*, apparently missed this particular item. Or did she?

It should be stressed that Reinhart does not restrict her focus to the Palestinian victims of Israeli terror. She also mentions the Israeli victims—of Israeli terror. Recording the opening battles of the Oslo War, she notes that the "pretext for Israeli military action was a Palestinian shooting from Beit Jala into Gilo." She dismisses this as "an Israeli provocation," citing the assurances of the local PLO commander. She observes that "it remains a mystery how the sophisticated and well-equipped Israeli army was not able to directly hit the Palestinian snipers."[81] The logic is inescapable: the Palestinian snipers must have been working for the Israelis! But this only scratches the surface of the IDF's devilish designs. Even more sinister is the tactic of targeted killings, employed—according to Reinhart—for the purpose of *increasing* terrorism against Israeli civilians. On the one hand, "the assassination of a moderate leader is a signal… that the days of 'peace games' are over." On the other hand, targeted killings of terrorists are intended to provoke "a bloodbath of terrorist retaliation… It is not just Palestinian life that does not count in Israel; those in the military sect have no reservations about sacrificing their own people."[82] Thus the IDF uses Palestinian snipers to fire into Israeli neighborhoods; it assassinates Palestinian moderates in order to prevent peace negotiations with Israeli politicians; it kills Palestinian terrorists in order to provoke massacres of Israeli women and children. Reading these conspiratorial lunacies, one is almost grateful for the conventional insanity of an ex-Congressman like Paul Findley, who expatiates on the question of Mossad responsibility for the Kennedy assassination, or of Reinhart's mentor Noam Chomsky, who explains that Israel sponsored the Red Brigades in a plot to destabilize Italy.[83]

In reviewing this cornucopia of ideological inventions, obscene libels and embarrassing factual blunders, it is tempting to ask how it is possible that such allegations can be made—perhaps even believed—by an academic teaching at a respectable university. But to pose such questions is to miss the essence of the Chomskyan enterprise. For Chomsky, Reinhart and their many sycophants, disciples and imitators, there is no need to *prove* that the peace process is a Zionist deception of the PLO, that Barak is in league with his fellow-conspirator Sharon, that Israel is ruled by a military sect, that Peace Now is an instrument of Israeli expansionism, that the Jewish state has a policy of "slow, steady genocide," that the IDF has a "little game" of shooting people in the eyes, that there was a massacre in Jenin, or that Israeli soldiers employ Palestinian snipers to fire into Israeli neighborhoods. All that is required is an audience of sufficient credulity and the most hysterical anti-Israel charges will enter the realm of respectable discourse. Then we will encounter the predictable plaudits: "Reinhart accomplishes the formidable task of adding insight to a subject that is written about endlessly" (the *Nation*); "Reinhart's conclusions become inescapable... Intensely researched and energetically argued..." (*Tikkun*); "She talks about facts... in a manner similar to examining a scientific theorem, through the refinement of awareness..." (*Ha'aretz*).[84] And we will be left with a melancholy conclusion: the only thing needed for evil to triumph is for fools to sing its praises.

Notes

1.   Noam Chomsky, *Fateful Triangle* (rev. ed., London: Pluto Press, 1999), 3n.
2.   Letters, *Jerusalem Post*, February 16, 1989.
3.   Chomsky, *Fateful Triangle*, 3n, 69, 147, 240-1, 258, 396, 447; id., *Middle East Illusions* (Lanham, Maryland: Rowman & Littlefield, 2003), 227-8; Baruch Kimmerling, *Politicide: Ariel Sharon's War Against the Palestinians* (London and New York: Verso, 2003), 5, 35.
4.   *Fateful Triangle*, 142.
5.   Shahak, "A Jewish Duty or Jewish Apostasy?" *Times* (London), January 27, 1973.
6.   Shahak, "Palestine-Israel in Oslo," *Journal of Palestine Studies*, Summer 1984, 177-83.
7.   Shahak, "Human Rights in Israel," *Journal of Palestine Studies*, Spring 1975, 161-71.
8.   In this respect, he was hardly unique. One of the first exponents of Holocaust denial, the French socialist Paul Rassinier, was a former concentration camp inmate. See Michael Shermer and Alex Grobman, *Denying History: Who Says the Holocaust Never Happened and Why Do They Say It?* (Berkeley: University of California Press, 2000), 41.
9.   Interview, *Journal of Palestine Studies*, Spring 1975, 6, 9.
10.   Interview, *Middle East Policy*, Summer 1989.
11.   Shahak, "The Deeper Significance of the Mass Expulsions," *Middle East Policy*, June 1993.
12.   Shahak, *Jewish History, Jewish Religion: The Weight of Three Thousand Years* (1994; rev. ed., London: Pluto Press, 1997), 30.
13.   Shahak, "The Continuing Aims of Zionist Policies in the Middle East," *Middle East Policy*, Spring 1986.
14.   *Jewish History*, 27-8.
15.   Interview, "A Survivor For Whom Never Again *Means* Never Again," *Link*, May/June 1995.
16.   Interview, *Middle East Policy*, Summer 1989; see also *Jewish History*, 101, 103.
17.   Shahak, "The 'Historical Right' and the Other Holocaust," *Journal of Palestine Studies*, Spring 1981, 27-34.

18.   Dana Adams Schmidt, "Fulbright Sees Risk of Blow to Seize Oil," *Christian Science Monitor*, May 31, 1973.
19.   John K. Cooley, "Political Dissenter in Israel Fearful of Another War," *Christian Science Monitor*, July 14, 1976. That Cooley takes such fabrications seriously is an apt comment on the quality of the reporting provided by this veteran PLO apologist.
20.   Interview, *Journal of Palestine Studies*, Spring 1978, 6, 8.
21.   "The Continuing Aims of Zionist Policies in the Middle East."
22.   Interview, *Middle East Policy*, Summer 1989.
23.   "The Deeper Significance of the Mass Expulsions."
24.   For the latter, see *New York Times*, April 5, 1974.
25.   "Human Rights in Israel," 164.
26.   Shahak, "Banning the 'Terrible' White, Black, Green and Red," *Christian Science Monitor*, March 3, 1981.
27.   Shahak, Letters, *Economist*, July 10, 1982; cited in Chomsky, *Fateful Triangle*, 410, 411.
28.   Shahak, "The Real Israeli Interest in Lebanon," *Washington Report on Middle East Affairs*, July 1996.
29.   "Human Rights in Israel," 163.
30.   *Jewish History,* 1.
31.   Immanuel Jakobovits, "A Modern Blood Libel – *L'Affaire* Shahak," *Tradition*, Summer 1966.
32.   *Jewish History,* 2. Emphasis added.
33.   Ibid., p10.
34.   Shahak, "Israeli Discrimination Against Non-Jews is Carefully Codified in State of Israel's Laws," *Washington Report on Middle Eastern Affairs*, January/February 1998.
35.   *Jewish History*, 23-4.
36.   Ibid., 33-4.
37.   Ibid., 34.
38.   Ibid., 36-7.
39.   Ibid., 48-9.
40.   Ibid., 73.
41.   *Soviet Antisemitic Propaganda: Evidence From Books, Press and Radio* (London: Institute of Jewish Affairs, 1978), 95.
42.   *Jewish History*, 73-4.
43.   Ibid., Foreword to the First Printing.
44.   Ibid., Foreword to the Second Printing.
45.   Ibid., cover endorsement.
46.   Christopher Hitchens, "Israel Shahak, 1933-2001," *The Nation*, July 23/30, 2001. See also Alexander Cockburn, "Remembering Israel Shahak," *Antiwar.com*, July 13, 2001: http://www.antiwar.com/cockburn/c071301.html.
47.   Elfi Pallis, *Guardian* (London), July 6, 2001; Michael Adams, *Independent* (London), July 26, 2001.
48.   John Pilger, "Far From Being the Terrorists of the World, the Islamic Peoples Have Been Its Victims," *New Statesman*, September 17, 2001. This article is also noteworthy for its trademark Pilger fabrications:

At least a million civilians, half of them children, have died in Iraq as a result of a medieval embargo imposed by the United States in Britain... the terrorist training camps where Osama Bin Laden, "America's most wanted man," *allegedly* [emphasis added] planned his attacks, were built with American money and backing... Hamas... did not exist until Israel's outright rejection of a Palestinian state.

And so on. As the Sovietologist Leopold Labedz observed (*Encounter*, February 1980), "'Progressive' rationalizations give one the best idea of infinity. The making of ideological myths is, alas, endless."

49.   Allan C. Brownfeld, "With Israel Shahak's Death, A Prophetic Voice is Stilled," *Washington Report on Middle East Affairs*, October 2001. A notice by Norton Mezvinsky had already appeared in the August/September 2001 issue; Mezvinsky was co-author of Shahak's final work, *Jewish Fundamentalism in Israel* (London: Pluto Press, 1999).

50.   http://www.davidduke.com/index.php?p=148.

51.   *Jewish History*, 74.

52.   Cover endorsement, Tanya Reinhart, *Israel/Palestine: How to End the War of 1948* (New York: Seven Stories Press, 2002).

53.   Interview, "A Slow, Steady Genocide," *FromOccupiedPalestine.org*, September 10, 2003.

54.   *Yediot Aharanot*, November 6, 2000: http://www.tau.ac.il/~reinhart/political/DontSayYouDidntKnow.html.

55.   James Todd, "Speaker Urges Boycott of Israel," *Duke News & Communications*, November 23, 2004: http://www.dukenews.duke.edu/mmedia/features/mideast/reinhart_1104.html.

56.   *Israel/Palestine*, 222, 232, 228.

57.   Palestinian Authority TV, September 10, 2004.

58.   *Israel/Palestine*, 9, 130, 88, 108, 95, 124-5, 179.

59.   Ibid., 8, 89-90, 125-8.

60.   Ibid., 15, 130, 118-9, 141, 175, 179-80.

61.   See e.g.., *New Republic*, August 7, 2000.

62.   *Israel/Palestine*, 42-6, 38-41, 51, 96.

63.   Habash, *Al-Hayat Al-Jadida* (Palestinian Authority), November 17, 2000; Husseini, *Al-Safir* (Lebanon), March 21, 2001; Atwan, *Jerusalem Post*, November 20, 2004; Reinhart, *Israel/Palestine*, 61.

64.   *Israel/Palestine*, 89, 92.

65.   Ibid., 93-4.

66.   *Al-Sabah* (Palestinian Authority), September 11, 2000; Mamduh Nufal, *Nouvel Observateur* (France), March 1, 2001; Imad Faluji, *Jerusalem Post*, March 3, 2001; Marwan Barghouti, *Jerusalem Times*, June 8, 2001.

67.   *Israel/Palestine*, 78.

68.   Ibid., 83, 85.

69.   Ibid., 199-200.

70.   Ibid., 203-4.

71.   For the full text, see http://www.columbiadivest.org/pdfs/israeliacademicstatement.pdf.

72.   *Israel/Palestine*, 206.

73.   Ibid., 113-4, 251; see also 93-6. On LAW, see Edwin Black's award-winning series "Funding Hate" (Parts 1 and 4), *New York Sun*, October 17 and 22, 2003.

74.   *Israel/Palestine*, 114-6; for the officer's interview, see *Jerusalem Post*, October 27, 2000.

75.   Ibid., 155. The most detailed examination of the Jenin operation is Yagil Henkin, "Urban Warfare and the Lessons of Jenin," *Azure*, Summer 2003, 33-69, from which these figures are taken.

76.   *Israel/Palestine*, 152-3 (Indymedia posting by Irit Katriel), 161-5 (interview with "Kurdi Bear," who describes himself as "driven by madness, by desperation... For almost half a year I am suspended from work...").

77.   Ibid., 175-7.

78.   World Bank, *World Development Indicators 2005*, Table 2.17: Nutrition, available at http://www.worldbank.org/data/wdi2005/wditext/Table2_17.htm. The child malnutrition figures employ data for the most recent year, up to 2003.

79.   *Israel/Palestine*, 179-80; Nicholas D. Kristof, "A Merciful War," *New York Times*, February 1, 2002.

80.   *Haaretz*, March 3, 2002; cited in Henkin, "Urban Warfare," 54.

81.   *Israel/Palestine*, 101-2.

82.   Ibid., 126, 140-1.

83.   See Paul Findley, "In Kennedy Assassination, Anyone But Mossad is Fair Game For US Media," *Washington Report on Middle East Affairs*, March 1992; Noam Chomsky, *Fateful Triangle*, 256-7n.

84.   Robert Jensen, "Occupation Blues," *Nation*, January 6, 2003; Joel Schalit, "Three Women Writers, One War," *Tikkun*, May/June 2004; Yitzhak Laor, "In Praise of the Facts," *Haaretz*, February 25, 2005.

8

Norman G. Finkelstein: Chomsky for Nazis

Paul Bogdanor

"I can't imagine why Israel's apologists would be offended by a comparison with
the Gestapo. I would think that, for them, it is like Lee Iacocca being told that
Chrysler is using Toyota tactics." —*Norman G. Finkelstein*[1]

That Norman G. Finkelstein considers friends of Israel the moral equivalent
of Gestapo torturers and mass murderers might be an occasion for surprise among
normal people. Scarcely less amazing, then, is a parallel observation that appears in his subsequent writings on the Jewish state. Reflecting on the excuses
offered by a leading Nazi tried at Nuremberg, Finkelstein declares: "the Germans could point in extenuation to the severity of penalties for speaking out
against the crimes of state. What excuse do *we* have?"[2] The burden of his
insinuation is that Jewish supporters of Israel are morally *worse* than the Nazi
perpetrators of the Final Solution. And this is merely a sampling of the intellectual rationalizations which have led him from the proposition that Israel is a
Nazi state to the claim that pro-Israeli Jews are worse than Nazis to the discovery that the field of Holocaust studies is merely a Zionist "propaganda enterprise,"[3] and thence to the suggestive remark, "Hitler's war against the Jews,
even if irrational (*and that itself is a complex issue*)."[4]

Finkelstein's tract *Image and Reality of the Israel-Palestine Conflict*—greeted
with extravagant praise by William Quandt, Noam Chomsky, and other veter-
ans of the anti-Israel lecture circuit—is distinguished by the author's exploitation of every conceivable opportunity to compare Jews with Nazis. To take one
of many examples, he proposes to discredit the Israeli doctrine of "purity of
arms" (i.e., protection of innocent human life) with the asseveration that its
"closest analogue was, ironically, Nazism." Similarly, Jewish claims of a historical right to the land of Israel were deployed "with a vengeance, by the Nazis
themselves, to justify the conquest of the East." As for the argument that Jews
were defending themselves against Arab aggression, "the Nazis justified the
genocide against the Jews as an act of self-defense... Even the murder of Jewish

135

children was rationalized by Himmler... on defensive grounds." Meanwhile, the absence of anti-Arab racism among Israeli soldiers merely parallels the discovery that "contrary to widespread belief, abusive force was not truly integral to the Final Solution."[5] What more do we need to establish the fundamental parity between purity of arms and mass extermination; Zionism and *Lebensraum*; Moshe Dayan and Heinrich Himmler?

Finkelstein denies that he is a Jewish antisemite. And with good reason. For this self-proclaimed expert on the Jews and their enemies, it is not proof of antisemitism that German Jews were charged with the ritual murder of children, just so long as no criminal convictions resulted; it is not proof of antisemitism that there were campaigns against Jewish emancipation, just so long as these were "orchestrated" by "anti-Jewish agitators"; it is not proof of antisemitism that German writers advocated the physical extermination of Jews, just so long as the majority contented themselves with lesser forms of hatred; it is not proof of antisemitism that German Jews were subjected to "episodic spasms of anti-Jewish violence," just so long as there was no repeat of the Dreyfus case or the Russian pogroms; nor is it proof of antisemitism that the centers of power were "packed with insane Jew-haters," because if this was the case, "Jewish blood should have been flowing in German streets."[6] Nor, finally, is there any hint of prejudice when an aspiring university teacher sneers at "arriviste and shtetl-chauvinist Jews of Eastern European descent," or when he complains that "the hoped-for revival of Jewish life is thus coming to pass as Eastern European Jews parlay their newly discovered roots into a cut of the Holocaust booty"—especially when that teacher is Finkelstein himself.[7]

Quite understandably, Finkelstein's opinions on Jewish subjects have not made him popular in respectable academic circles. According to Chomsky, his mentor, the student Finkelstein's professors "stopped talking to him: they wouldn't make appointments with him, they wouldn't read his papers." Such was his reputation for learning that "when he got to the point of writing his thesis he literally could not get the faculty to read it... Finally, out of embarrassment, they granted him a PhD..." Subsequently, the aspiring Erasmus found himself "working part-time with disturbed teenaged kids for a couple [of] thousand dollars a year."[8] Finkelstein is equally candid about his resumé: "I'm in exile in Chicago because I was thrown out of every school in New York," he laments. He is "not happy" there and longs for a teaching position in his home city. "I'm still praying for a miracle," he adds.[9] Tragically, the gatekeepers of scholarly standards have not seen fit to admit this intellectual colossus into their ranks. After all, as one witness testified, "Finkelstein appears to suffer from an almost total lack of self-control. His readers might find him harder to take seriously if they had watched him screaming questions as a heckler at the back of the audience."[10] That certain readers are inclined to take him seriously even *without* witnessing his malevolent outbursts against the Jews might be thought sufficient cause for dismay.

Finkelstein's Image and Israel's Reality

"I don't really know much about Israel."
—*Norman G. Finkelstein*[11]

Finkelstein's candid confession has not prevented him from publishing multiple books and essays concerning the object of his ignorance. And in these works, his nescience is on full display. His *magnum opus* on the Jewish state, *Image and Reality of the Israel-Palestine Conflict*, displays little or no familiarity with any of the established authorities in the field: Shlomo Avineri, Arthur Hertzberg, Walter Laqueur or David Vital on Zionism; J.C. Hurewitz or Christopher Sykes on the British Mandate; Rony Gabbay or Nadav Safran on the early Arab-Israeli wars; Yehoshafat Harkabi, Bernard Lewis, Daniel Pipes, Barry Rubin, and all too many others on the dynamics of the conflict. Finkelstein is not a professional historian, has conducted no archival research, and makes no reference to primary or secondary sources in Hebrew or Arabic, with the exception of the occasional newspaper article translated by a far-left comrade in Israel. Not surprisingly, academic journals have kept their distance from this P.T. Barnum of Middle East historiography.

Where Finkelstein does attempt to draw on mainstream scholarship, the result is unalloyed embarrassment. His first chapter purports to be a study of Zionist thought, based on the work of Israeli scholar Yosef Gorny. In this discussion we find scarcely any mention, let alone analysis, of the ideas of Pinsker, Herzl, Nordau, Katznelson, Gordon and other Zionist luminaries. Instead we learn that Zionism originated in the "reaction to Enlightenment rationalism and liberalism… [its] point of departure was the presumed bankruptcy of the democratic idea."[12] As every student of the subject knows, Zionism originated precisely in the Enlightenment rationalist ethos of the Russian-Jewish *maskilim*, and its point of departure was the need to complete the process of Jewish emancipation which democratic ideas had made possible.[13] Indeed, in a striking display of doublethink, Finkelstein recites the very evidence that destroys his thesis. As Gorny documents at length, Zionist leaders, far from abjuring the "democratic idea," defended it even in the most difficult circumstances. Weizmann favored "Jewish-Arab cooperation in running the country on the basis of political equality." Ben-Gurion "promised the Arab inhabitants of the state total civil and national equality, and autonomy in education, culture and religion." And Jabotinsky envisioned that in a Jewish state, "there would be no reason to deny the Arab inhabitants full and equal rights as a national entity."[14]

But Finkelstein is unmoved. In his eyes, Jews are not a people, they have no common identity, no historical homeland, and no national claims; they have to right to band together for self-defense, and they have no right to return to their country of origin. The demand for Jewish statehood merely "duplicated the reasoning" of antisemites, who "invoked the same argument to justify Jew-hatred."[15] With his insistence that Jews, alone among the world's persecuted groups, must remain always and everywhere a powerless minority—and this in the aftermath of the Holocaust—it is Finkelstein who "duplicates the reasoning" of the antisemites he affects to criticize. And this reasoning leaves little to the imagination:

> Israel has not resolved the Jewish Question; if anything, the enthrallment of the self-described "Jewish state" to Western imperialism and its local satraps has exacerbated it... Israel has not remade the Jewish people into a "working nation"; if anything, it is transforming Israeli Jews into a parasitic class...[16]

In his contention that Israeli Jews are simultaneously the running dogs of imperialism and the germ cells of a parasitic class, Finkelstein has produced a novel synthesis of communist and Nazi propaganda.

Proceeding from this unique starting point, Finkelstein dismisses the Jewish claim to the land of Israel, which, as noted, he equates with the Nazi quest for *Lebensraum*. "Zionism's 'historical right' to Palestine was neither historical nor a right," so he informs us.[17] It was not historical because it "voided" two millennia of non-Jewish rule in Palestine; it was not a right because it rested on a "Romantic mysticism" of "blood and soil." These "arguments" raise some intriguing dilemmas. If Jews no longer have any right to their homeland because it was appropriated by others, then the same reasoning must apply to the peoples of Portugal, Spain, Sardinia, Sicily, Crete, and the southern areas of France and Italy, which also fell victim to Arab-Islamic conquest. Indeed, the Ottoman Empire expanded its territory as far as Hungary and southern Poland, as well as the whole of central Europe, including parts of Greece, the former Yugoslavia, Romania and Bulgaria. By Finkelstein's logic, it would seem that Europeans have no historical claim to any of these countries, which should be returned to their former Muslim owners at once. Such are the absurdities that arise when dreams of Israel's destruction are justified in the language of anti-imperialism.

Aggression and Self-Defense

If, as he insists, Israeli Jews are a "parasitic class" surviving through the victories of a "conquest regime," then Finkelstein is in fundamental agreement with Nasser's famous pronouncement that "Israel's existence is in itself an aggression." Therefore nothing the Jewish state does, no matter what the provocation, can ever be interpreted as an act of self-defense. And this is precisely Finkelstein's position. To illustrate, I will consider in detail his treatment of the 1967 Six Day War.[18] Here we see the essence of the Finkelstein syndrome: mutilation of the historical background; fabrication of facts and quotations; and suppression of crucial information.

Clashes with Syria

The trigger for the 1967 crisis was a series of border clashes between Syria and Israel. To Finkelstein, it is obvious that Syrian shelling of Israeli civilians was a manifestation of Israeli belligerence. The explanation could not possibly lie in the Syrian announcement, in January 1967, that "Syria has changed its strategy, moving from defense to attack.... We will carry on operations until Israel has been eliminated." Or in the April addendum: "Our known objective is the freeing of Palestine and the liquidation of Zionist existence there."[19] For Finkelstein, the only "evidence" worthy of consideration is the Israeli response to these Hitlerian outbursts—and his evidence, under scrutiny, is less than compelling. Thus he quotes Israeli chief of staff Yitzhak Rabin, who was "alleged to have announced on Israeli radio that 'the moment is coming when we will march on Damascus to overthrow the Syrian government.'" Hidden in his footnote is the qualification that there is "some dispute as to whether Rabin actually issued the quoted threat," although "the point would seem to be academic."[20] The Rabin threat is, of course, a fabrication: no published text exists for the statement, which has been attributed to a misquotation from a wire service report of an IDF press briefing.[21] In fact, as serious historians repeatedly emphasize, there was "no Israeli threat to overthrow the Damascus government," and the warnings actually issued were feeble in comparison with Syria's constant exhortations to invasion and genocide.[22] Yet Finkelstein, so diligent in recording non-existent Israeli threats, is happy to conceal Arab demands for "the liquidation of Zionist existence."

Indeed, no invention is so absurd, no falsehood so discredited, that Finkelstein will not try his very best to revive it. Consider the Soviet "warning" in May that Israel was poised to invade Syria—perhaps the most notorious diplomatic hoax of the twentieth century. In Finkelstein's account, "although apparently erring in details, the Soviet intelligence report was not wide of the mark in its general thrust... the Israeli threats against the Damascus regime impelled Nasser to act."[23] Always the scrupulous scholar, he even suggests a source for the Soviet report:

> In early May 1967, Israel's cabinet reportedly decided to attack Syria... The Soviets apparently got wind of the Israeli cabinet decision [through KGB spies? through telepathy?] and conveyed a warning—albeit overblown—to Nasser...[24]

Finkelstein is surely the last person on earth who affects to believe this tale. The Egyptians themselves gave it no credence. Inspecting the border between Israel and Syria, the Egyptian chief of staff found no hint of Israeli preparations and reported that the Syrian army was not even in a state of alert; identical conclusions were reached by Egyptian military intelligence.[25] Such is the basis for Finkelstein's claim that "the Israeli threats against the Damascus regime impelled Nasser to act."

UNEF and the Straits of Tiran

Fueled by his fantasy version of history, Finkelstein reports that "Nasser reacted in mid-May to the new Israeli threats by moving Egyptian troops into the Sinai and ordering the removal of [the UN peacekeeping force] UNEF from Sinai, Gaza and Sharm al-Shaykh overlooking the Straits of Tiran."[26] This was in breach of an international agreement that UN forces would guarantee demilitarization of Sharm al-Shaykh to prevent an Egyptian blockade of southern Israel.[27] Egypt's military liaison told the UNEF commander: "We have arrived at this decision after much deliberation and are prepared for anything. If there is war, we shall next meet in Tel Aviv."[28] Finkelstein, however, feigns innocence of the true import of the Egyptian move, citing the UN secretary-general's pusillanimous proposal to relocate UNEF in Israel: "It is hard to understand," he writes, "why stationing UNEF on the Egyptian side of the border preserved peace while stationing it on the Israeli side would not have or, put otherwise, why UNEF would deter Egyptian aggression on the Egyptian but not the Israeli side."[29] What is even harder to understand is how Finkelstein expects his readers to believe that UN forces stationed in Israel could have kept Egyptian troops out of strategic positions in Egyptian territory, or that non-existent Israeli troop concentrations were a threat to Syria while genuine Egyptian troop concentrations were not a threat to Israel.

Having dismissed the UN peacekeeping forces, remilitarized the Sinai Peninsula and reoccupied Sharm al-Shaykh, Nasser promptly barred Israeli shipping from the Straits of Tiran, effectively blockading southern Israel. "We knew that by closing the Gulf of Aqaba it might mean war with Israel," he announced, adding that if war came, "it will be total and the objective will be to destroy Israel."[30] This declaration is entirely suppressed by Finkelstein, who proceeds to offer one bogus defense after another for the Egyptian position. He mentions the UN secretary-general's proposal for "a two-week moratorium in the Straits of Tiran" (a concept which equated Egypt's aggression with Israel's right of free passage) while concealing the Soviet rejection of the plan and falsely reporting that Egypt accepted it.[31] He adds that Nasser "was open to World Court arbitration of the dispute," when his sources merely report that Egypt raised "no objection" and "did not rule out completely" such a hearing (and made no commitment to abide by the result).[32] He treats the legality of the blockade as a controversial issue, although, as one legal specialist observes, in 1950 Egypt had "explicitly and formally recognized the right of innocent passage through the Straits of Tiran," stating that this was "in conformity with international practice and with recognized principles of international law."[33] He ignores the most detailed legal study of the subject, which concludes that there was "no reason to doubt Israel's right to this part of its territory" and that Israel was "entitled to the use of its waters as well as ingress and egress through the Strait of Tiran."[34] And he denies that Israel was "mortally dependent on trade through Eilat," expressly contradicting Egypt's view of the matter, as announced by Radio Cairo:

> With the closing of the straits, Israel faces two possibilities, both of which are blood-soaked: either it will die by strangulation in the wake of the Arab military and economic blockade, or it will die by shooting from the Arab forces surrounding it in the south, north and east.[35]

With scholars like Finkelstein, who needs propagandists?

Arab Intentions and Capabilities

But the biggest insult is yet to come. Finkelstein announces, with great firmness: "there was no evidence at the time that Nasser intended to attack" and "even if he did, it was taken for granted that Israel would easily thrash him."[36] These assertions are a mark of his contempt for his readers. As every informed student of the period knows, the Arab dictators were virtually screaming their intention to wipe Israel off the face of the earth. Nasser proclaimed his goal openly: "We want to fight to liberate and regain Palestine."[37] Throughout the crisis, his regime boasted of its plans for bloody slaughter. Thus at one point:

> The Zionist barrack in Palestine is about to collapse and be destroyed... Every one of the hundred million Arabs has been living for the past nineteen years on one hope—to live to see the day Israel is liquidated... There is no life, no peace nor hope for the gangs of Zionism to remain in the occupied land.

And a day later: "It is our chance, Arabs, to direct a blow of death and annihilation to Israel and all its presence in our Holy Land. It is a war for which we are waiting and in which we shall triumph."[38] Other Arab rulers were thinking along the same lines. Syrian Defense Minister Hafez al-Assad pledged to "take the initiative in destroying the Zionist presence in the Arab homeland." King Hussein of Jordan boasted that all of the Arab armies now surrounded Israel. PLO founder Ahmed Shuqayri wanted to "destroy Israel and its inhabitants." Algerian Prime Minister Boumedienne demanded "the destruction of the Zionist entity." President 'Aref of Iraq declared: "Our goal is clear—to wipe Israel off the face of the map."[39] Truly, it requires the talents of Goebbels to pretend that there was "no evidence" of Arab plans to attack.

According to Finkelstein, Israel was certain of "a quick and easy victory regardless of which side initiated hostilities." Once again, he is highly selective in his mining of the documentary record. He cites Labor Minister Yigal Allon's faith in the IDF, but not Defense Minister Moshe Dayan's fear that if the Egyptians attacked first, Israel would be wiped out. He quotes the dismissal of Arab military forces by General Uzi Narkiss, but not the contrary assessments by Generals Avraham Yoffe and Rehavam Ze'evi. He mentions General Ariel Sharon's belief that the IDF could stop an Egyptian attack, but not his warning that surrender in the Straits of Tiran would open the door to Israel's destruction. He recalls Mossad chief Meir Amit's assurance to the United States that any war would be finished in two days, but not the prediction by military intelligence commander Aharon Yariv that the Arab states were about to threaten Israel's existence. He offers subsequent public claims by Generals Mattityahu Peled and Ezer Weizman that Israel's survival had not been at stake as correctives to their private views at the time, which were precisely the opposite.[40] Such are the methods employed (in the words of Lucy Dawidowicz) by the "predators of history, who plunder the historical storehouse for just those 'facts' which fit their political needs."[41]

Finkelstein contends that the "mortal threat that Nasser allegedly posed to Israel in 1967 is as chimerical as his intention to attack it."[42] The aggressors believed otherwise. The Egyptian Chief of Staff was ready "to destroy Israel's air force and occupy its territory." Nasser told the UN Secretary-General: "We will have all the advantages of attacking first. We are sure of victory." A high government official and Nasser associate commented on "the concept that had seized the leadership, namely that the destruction of Israel was a child's game." The American Ambassador to Egypt testified to the Arab belief that "victory is no tentative possibility, but a reality." Immediately before the outbreak of hostilities, Egypt's Field Marshal Amer expected to "destroy the Israeli army" and anticipated that "soon we'll be able to take the initiative and rid ourselves of Israel once and for all." The Syrian army predicted that "the UAR and Syria can destroy Israel in four days at most."[43] Moscow was even more confident. The Soviet defense minister proclaimed: "The fiftieth year of the Great October Socialist Revolution will be the last year of the existence of the State of Israel." The Soviet ambassador told the leader of Israel's Communist Party: "The war will last 24 hours only and no trace of the State of Israel will be left."[44] In short, a far cry from Finkelstein's image of a Zionist colossus poised to conquer the Middle East.

Imaginary War Crimes

Of course, no example of Marxist agitprop would be complete without faked allegations of war crimes, and Finkelstein is happy to oblige. Turning to "the Israeli combined air and naval assault on the USS *Liberty*," an American spy ship, he dismisses as "vulgar propaganda" the indisputable fact that the tragedy was a friendly-fire incident, as accepted by the American naval attaché in Tel Aviv at the time, his deputy, and the CIA station chief, and documented in multiple investigations by the American Navy, the CIA, the National Security Agency and both houses of Congress, among others, and in a definitive book-length study based on 500 interviews and 3,000 documents by a former member of the Navy's Judge Advocate General Corps. But mere facts are of no importance for Finkelstein, who announces that "just about every official and intelligence agency on the American side eventually concluded that the attack was intentional," gambling on his readers' ignorance. Unlike previous conspiracy theorists, he does not even pretend to offer an Israeli motive for deliberately attacking a friendly superpower—no doubt wisely, since every suggestion so far has been immediately discredited. The friendly-fire explanation was confirmed by the Israeli flight recordings and has now been vindicated beyond any possibility of debate by transcripts from the National Security Agency, which prove that the Israelis misidentified their target as an Egyptian supply ship.[45]

Not content with these long-refuted myths, Finkelstein invokes "unimpeachable eye-witness testimonies of Israeli soldiers, as well as the testimony of an

Israeli military historian, that the IDF executed scores of Egyptian POWs during the June War."[46] No further evidence is given, but his footnote cites press reports on the testimony of "eye-witness" Gabi Bron and "military historian" Aryeh Yitzhaki. Both sources had explicitly disavowed the statements attributed to them as media inventions. Egyptian POWs "were not shot, and there were no mass murders," asserted Bron. "In fact, we helped prisoners, gave them water, and in most cases just sent them in the direction of the [Suez] Canal." Yitzhaki, who was not a military historian but a clerk in a military archive, was even more emphatic: "In no case did Israel initiate massacres," he wrote. "On the contrary, it did everything it could to prevent them." The specific examples mentioned in Finkelstein's reports proved to be legitimate acts of war; thus an alleged mass killing of hundreds of POWs at El-Arish in the Sinai turned out to be a battle with enemy forces who attacked an Israeli convoy.[47] And all of this was known years before Finkelstein chose to repeat the allegations. The conclusions would seem to be obvious.

The Aftermath

Even if all of Finkelstein's falsifications were to pass scrutiny, rather than collapsing on inspection, none of this would avail him unless he could demonstrate that Israel's conquests served an expansionist purpose befitting the natural bloodlust of a "parasitic class." It would be most embarrassing if it could be shown that immediately after victory, the Zionist devil offered to abandon nearly all of its territorial gains for a genuine peace. Clearly the ideological exits must be sealed.

Thus, according to Finkelstein, "Israel's first policy decision regarding the conquered territories" was taken within days, when the cabinet voted to offer "a settlement on the pre-June 1967 borders with Syria and Egypt (Israel keeping Gaza), but made no mention of the West Bank." Meanwhile Moshe Dayan "declared in his 'private capacity' that Gaza would not be returned to Egypt or the West Bank to Jordan."[48] The implication is that Israel was planning to retain permanent control over the West Bank and Gaza; and the facts are exactly the reverse. By early July 1967, it was clear that the Israeli leaders wanted to implement the very two-state solution that the Arab world had contemptuously rejected two decades earlier:

> The majority [of the cabinet] favors creating a Palestinian state, in which the Gaza area would be included... It would have close economic ties with Israel, with joint development plans that would include resettlement of the 400,000-600,000 refugees in the area... The proposition for an independent Palestinian state seems to have the best chance [of approval]... It opens up the possibility of resettling the refugees now in camps into Palestinian towns and farms. Israeli specialists are working on such a plan, to be ready in a few weeks.

Here, then, was the position of the majority of Israeli decisionmakers: negotiations for peace and mutual recognition; complete withdrawal from the Sinai

Peninsula and the Golan Heights; abandonment of any claim to the West Bank and Gaza; agreement to an independent Palestinian state; immediate resettlement of Palestinian refugees.[49] Indeed, two days after this report, Prime Minister Levi Eshkol publicly confirmed his readiness to establish a Palestinian state extending to the Jordan River and containing every major West Bank population center, including Jenin, Jericho, Nablus, Qalqilya and Tulkarm, with an additional passage through Israeli territory to the Mediterranean Sea. Similar ideas were voiced by Yigal Allon, Yitzhak Rabin and Moshe Dayan.[50]

But none of Israel's proposals, either public or private, occasioned any interest from any Arab interlocutor, although Finkelstein would have us believe that Arab regimes were falling over themselves to make peace. On the eve of the Khartoum conference in late 1967, he writes, "Nasser called for an early peace settlement with Israel and threatened to 'go it alone' if rebuffed at the summit."[51] What Nasser actually told the summit was that in the wake of defeat, "his nation was virtually without money and the military potential to make war, but that, if the other Arab states pooled their resources with him, *he would be prepared to fight*." Failing this, "the primary goal of President Nasser and King Hussein would be to get Israel to withdraw from the Arab territories," albeit "*without recognizing or negotiating directly* with Israel."[52] Attention thus focused on Marshall Tito's efforts to obtain withdrawal without peace; and whereas Finkelstein predictably hails the Yugoslav "peace plan," contemporary observers noted that Tito had "failed to come up with any substantial Arab approval for ending the state of belligerency against Israel."[53] The principles governing Arab policy were enunciated with unanimous agreement at the close of the Khartoum summit: "No peace with Israel, no negotiation with Israel, no recognition of Israel"[54]—a declamation which even Finkelstein finds difficult to excuse. Although he does try.

In short, Finkelstein's image of Arab and Israeli positions after 1967 "exactly reverses the reality," to use his own formulation. And since the relevant background is easily discoverable, he can hardly be unaware of that fact. But what else can we expect from an author who defines Israeli Jews as a "parasitic class" and Arab dictatorships as the helpless victims of Zionist imperialism?

Freedom Through Slaughter

The outbreak of the first Intifada provided another outlet for Finkelstein's anti-Zionist fervor. Undertaking a prolonged sojourn in the West Bank, he related that "mothers joined their children at makeshift barricades singing patriotic songs and stoning soldiers" in a "struggle for what John Stuart Mill called the most basic of democratic freedoms."[55] Meanwhile Israeli civilians were attacked with rocks, knives, axes, and Molotov cocktails. In one case, "an Israeli mother and her three children burned to death" when "youths hurled five gasoline bombs at a passenger bus near the West Bank town of Jericho and flames engulfed the vehicle."[56] On another occasion, fourteen died after a bus was driven into a ravine: "Several of the victims were burned to death, while others were crushed," reported journalists on the scene, as a rescuer found "something black that just a few minutes ago was a human being."[57] Later still, Intifada thugs waited for an Israeli peace activist, "bashed her head in with axes, cut her throat with knives, pulled out her hair and smeared her blood on the dashboard," while in yet another attack, "one victim was beheaded, the other quartered and the third disemboweled."[58] Over 160 Israelis died in this manner, with 4,000 wounded in the first three years. But Finkelstein's support for the violence was undiminished.[59]

Then there were the Palestinian casualties: "the tortured, burnt, hanged, quartered and garroted victims of the Intifada," in the words of one commentary. These included "a man tied to a post and stabbed to death, an old man axed, a boy of five bloodied... At least 100 of the victims had been beaten to death. Others had been tortured with burning cigarettes, knives and boiling tar, and their limbs and genitals amputated." Other typical practices were "the beheading of prostitutes in the Nablus casbah, the evisceration of pregnant women, the 'honor' killings of straying teenage girls, and the torture-murder of children." The motivations were often obscure; in general, it was "difficult to tell whether the child victims are beaten, maimed and killed for their own crimes or those of their parents."[60] The respected journalist Steven Emerson reported that the population lived "in daily terror" because "hardly a day goes by without a brutal execution of a Palestinian by roving death squads," representing Fatah, Hamas and other fascist movements:

> Some common murder techniques are beheading, mutilation, gouging out eyes, cutting off ears or limbs, and pouring molten plastic or acid on a victim's face. Although the squads refer to their victims as "collaborators" (meaning with Israel), most of them are executed because of political, religious, and personal rivalries or because of suspected drug dealing or prostitution.[61]

Emerson related that over 800 people had died in these atrocities, but later estimates were much higher: a team of Palestinian and Israeli researchers identified 750 death-squad murders in Gaza and concluded that another 1,000 had been slaughtered in the West Bank.[62] Curiously, Finkelstein seems to have noticed none of these horrors during his pilgrimage of solidarity with the killers.

As the Intifada disintegrated into a carnival of internecine torture and massacre, Finkelstein exhorted his heroes to ever-greater atrocities against the Zionist foe. "The 'politically correct' response is that the Israeli citizens should not be held accountable for the crimes of the Israeli state. It is also, in my view, a politically invalid response," he declared, invoking the destruction of Japanese cities during the Second World War as an example of the "accountability" he had in mind for the men, women and children of Israel. He quickly found a suitable agent of retribution: Saddam Hussein, who "in attacking the Israeli heartland and openly defying the US," had "restored to Arabs their human dignity." Indeed, "as he stood poised to launch the Scud missiles at Tel Aviv, Saddam Hussein's list of grievances against Israel was a lengthy one." Israel's crimes were its backing for Kurdish freedom fighters and support for the liberation of Kuwait. Admittedly, Israelis may have had some complaints against Iraq; for example, past sponsorship of terrorist massacres in planes, airports and synagogues. Nevertheless, "The balance of legitimate grievances would seem to be clearly on the Iraqi side," and "Israel's pose of wounded innocence as the Iraqi missiles landed on Tel Aviv was pure hypocrisy," so the victims deserved whatever the Butcher of Baghdad had in store for them.[63]

But the Scud missiles failed to wreak on Israel's cities the kind of "accountability" imposed on Tokyo and Hiroshima, and Finkelstein was obliged to search for a sharper instrument of destruction. Nearly a decade after his meditations on Iraq, the wandering Jew-hater pitched his tent in Lebanon. There he paid tribute to the local gangsters: "I truly honor [Hezbollah] for having inflicted an exceptional and deserving defeat on their foreign occupiers," he declaimed. "It's another wonderful chapter in the long and painful struggle for human emancipation and even liberty and certainly one that every human being can take inspiration from." Perhaps fearing that the terrorists' bloodlust might be sated after the mass killings of American marines, the bombing of American and Israeli embassies, and the continuous shelling of Israeli towns and villages, Finkelstein eagerly imparted further revelations of Zionist depravity. "It's a Nazi-like prison," he said of the Israeli facility at Khiam in south Lebanon; "It's a concentration camp," he added, "and there are even some novelties to the Nazi experiments."[64] Challenged to repudiate his message, Finkelstein was quick to reaffirm it:

> I did make a point of publicly honoring the heroic resistance of Hezbollah to foreign occupation.... To my thinking the honorable thing now is to show solidarity with Hezbollah as the US and Israel target it for liquidation. Indeed, looking back my chief regret is that I wasn't *even more* forceful in publicly defending Hezbollah against terrorist intimidation and attack.[65]

So much for the population of northern Israel. As for the hundreds of thousands of Israeli civilians living across the pre-1967 borders, "I consider them legitimate targets of armed resistance (apart, of course, from the children)."[66] Pregnant women, the elderly, and the disabled—not to mention newlywed couples and mothers and fathers in the prime of life—are, in his view, legitimate targets for massacre.

Of course, we must not be unfair to Finkelstein, for the ambit of his terrorist ideology is not limited to Israelis. He also believes that "it's payback time for the Americans... we deserve the problem on our hands because some things Bin Laden says are true."[67] Seen in this light, his support for war crimes has a certain consistency: he defends Hezbollah against Israel, and al-Qaeda against America.

The Neo-Nazis' Favorite Jew

"Were it not for the fact that my late parents passed through the Nazi holocaust, I myself would probably be a skeptic by now." —*Norman G. Finkelstein*[68]

After decades of unbroken toil in the fetid swamps of left-wing extremism, Finkelstein suddenly emerged as the most popular Jew in the history of antisemitism. Celebrated by neo-Nazis all over the world, and a best-selling author in Germany, Finkelstein publicly announced an epoch-making discovery: "'The Holocaust' is in effect the Zionist account of the Nazi holocaust."[69] With this revelation, he prepared the world for *The Holocaust Industry*, his crowning achievement in the field of anti-Jewish incitement. In Britain, every major newspaper devoted at least a full page to the book, which was serialized in the *Guardian*. In France, it received two full pages plus an editorial in *Le Monde*. In Germany, the reaction was explosive: some 200 journalists attended the book's press launch, while over 130,000 copies were sold in the first few weeks, and three volumes of commentary were issued within months.[70] On publication of the paperback edition, the book was scheduled for translation into sixteen languages, including Danish, Swedish, Dutch, Portuguese, Polish, Romanian, Turkish, Japanese, and—of course—Arabic.[71]

Finkelstein quickly found other admirers. Jew-baiter Ernst Zundel exulted that "Finkelstein continues his one-man intifada against the Holocaust establishment and vigorously attacks the Holocaust profiteers [in his] ever-so-feisty volume."[72] Hitler-worshipper David Irving was equally impressed: "We have corresponded in past years… I am sure that many Americans will want to see and hear this brave man."[73] The neo-Nazi *Journal for Historical Review* was ecstatic: "the kinds of things that revisionists have been saying for years… one can find much of both Novick and Finkelstein prefigured in the early writings of Butz and Faurisson," the founding fathers of the Holocaust-denial cult.[74] Visitors to neo-Nazi websites can read the full text of *The Holocaust Industry*, alongside such classics as *The Hoax of the Twentieth Century* by Arthur Butz and *The International Jew* by Henry Ford.[75] The admiration is reciprocal: Finkelstein not only enjoys cordial relations with Hitler apologists such as Irving, but readily grants interviews to the kind of bigot who identifies his work as "a comprehensive picture of the great plot of international Jewery [sic]… [a] blessing for all Holocaust deniers… The book really provides all a professional negationist requires: Jewish plot, Israeli zionism, greed."[76]

How did Finkelstein win such allies? What is the source of their morbid fascination?

Finkelstein sees the Holocaust as an "ideological representation" whose "central dogmas serve significant political and class interests."[77] He argues that American Jews are the class enemy, ruthless collaborators with capitalism and imperialism, who use the memory of the gas chambers to oppress their victims.[78] The result is a gruesome parody of ethnic self-hatred: "Lording it over those least able to defend themselves: that is the real content of organized American Jewry's reclaimed courage."[79] Moreover: "By conferring total blamelessness on the Jews, the Holocaust dogma immunizes Israel and American Jewry from legitimate censure." The Holocaust "dogma" must be overcome, so that the Jews can once again be "censured" with impunity. If Arab fanatics wish to annihilate the Israelis, then the Israelis must have provoked them. If black racists blame the Jews for their problems, then the Jews must be at fault. "Ever chastised, ever innocent," he sneers, "this is the burden of being a Jew."[80]

Like many examples of the genre, Finkelstein's book is replete with falsehoods. Consider his thesis that in post-war America there was "public silence on the Nazi extermination" as a result of "the conformist policies of the American Jewish leadership," which turned the Holocaust into "a taboo topic."[81] To accept this claim, we would have to believe that the Nuremberg tribunal and the Eichmann trial went unreported. We would have to ignore the classic studies by Max Weinreich (*Hitler's Professors*), Eugen Kogon (*The Theory and Practice of Hell*), Gerald Reitlinger (*The Final Solution*), Leon Poliakov (*Harvest of Hate*), Raul Hilberg (*The Destruction of the European Jews*) and Hannah Arendt (*Eichmann in Jerusalem*). And we would have to dismiss the testimonies of Anne Frank (*Diary*), Emmanuel Ringelblum (*Notes From the Warsaw Ghetto*), Viktor Frankl (*From Death-Camp to Existentialism*), Primo Levi (*If This is a Man*), Bruno Bettelheim (*The Informed Heart*) and Elie Wiesel (*Night*). All were published in America between 1945 and 1967. Plainly the Jews were not very successful in the task of enforcing "public silence" on the "taboo topic" of their own suffering.

Finkelstein's tract is also riddled with self-contradictions. He maintains that American Jews discovered the Holocaust only after the Six Day War, but he adds that in previous years they embraced "the universalist message" of concentration camp survivor Bruno Bettelheim.[82] He announces that the "historical evidence for a murderous Gentile impulse [towards Jews] is nil," but then he excoriates the United States Holocaust Museum because it "mutes the Christian background to European anti-Semitism."[83] He is enraged by the fake memoirs of Jerzy Kosinski and Binjamin Wilkomirski, but he endorses the fake history of Arno Mayer.[84] What are we to think of a book which explains that "much of the literature on Hitler's Final Solution is worthless as scholarship," only to announce that "[n]ot all" the arguments of Holocaust deniers are devoid of value? And how should we react to an author who can dismiss the work of Deborah Lipstadt, only to endorse the view that David Irving plays "an indispensable part" in the "historical enterprise"?[85]

The book systematically falsifies quotations and references. We are told that in a 1961 *Commentary* symposium on Jewish identity, only two contributors stressed the Holocaust; in fact, at least six did and this in a highly unrepresentative sample of Jewish intellectuals.[86] Daniel Goldhagen supposedly thinks that Serbian crimes in Kosovo "are, in their essence, different from those of Nazi Germany only in scale." In fact he is referring to Bosnia as well as Kosovo, both of which he explicitly distinguishes from the Holocaust.[87] Guenter Lewy is cited as authority for the claim that the Nazis "murdered as many as a half-million Gypsies," a figure which Lewy rejects as baseless.[88] Yehuda Bauer supposedly maintains that the Gypsies "did not fall victim to the same genocidal onslaught as the Jews." His actual position is that the Gypsies *were* victims of *genocide*, or partial destruction, while Jews were singled out for *Holocaust*, or total annihilation.[89] Elie Wiesel is mocked because he claims to have read the works of Kant in Yiddish, when they were never published in that language. In fact parts of Kant's *Critique of Practical Reason* were translated into Yiddish, as Finkelstein was later forced to admit.[90] The list goes on.

Finkelstein is indignant at the suggestion that he is aiding Holocaust deniers. Yet he enjoys cordial relations with neo-Nazis, grants them interviews, allows his books and articles to be posted on their websites, dismisses the findings of legitimate Holocaust historians while heaping praise on the deniers, and repeatedly insists that the deniers' positions are entirely reasonable, in light of the "profiteering" and "hucksterism" of the privileged Jewish elite. "Given the nonsense churned out daily by the Holocaust industry, the wonder is that there are so *few* skeptics," he remarks.[91] He is even prepared to ridicule the "Holocaust industry luminaries" who signed a public statement condemning "Syria's Denial of the Holocaust." The statement read in part:

> [Syria] declared that Israel invented "the myth of the Holocaust" and "invents stories about the Holocaust and exaggerates it to astronomical levels" in order "to receive more money from Germany and other Western establishments" and to silence "anyone opposed to Zionism and its expansionist policies."[92]

"Regrettably," concludes Finkelstein, "the Syrian charge is true."[93]

The "Double Shakedown"

Finkelstein's central allegation is that the pursuit of Holocaust reparations is a "double shakedown of European countries as well as legitimate Jewish claimants."[94] Determined to play on the fears of elderly survivors, he fails to notice the obvious contradiction: if Jewish claimants have a right to the money, then it has not been stolen from European countries; but if European countries have a right to the money, then it cannot be stolen from Jewish claimants. Since Finkelstein's "double shakedown" is a logical impossibility, one wonders how anyone can take it seriously. But such is the malevolent power of the Jewish "Holocaust industry" that it could never be restrained by the laws of logic, let alone the sovereignty of states:

> The shakedown of Switzerland and Germany has been only the prelude to the grand finale: the shakedown of Eastern Europe... the Holocaust industry has sought to extort billions of dollars from these already impoverished countries... it can easily break the feeble resistance of prostrate nations.[95]

Not since the *Protocols of the Elders of Zion* have the Jews been credited with the power to crush continents.

The Ordeal of the Swiss Banks

To sample Finkelstein's methods, consider his treatment of restitution from the Swiss banks. The search for Jewish assets deposited in Swiss accounts before and during the Holocaust is presented as yet another proof of Jewish power and malevolence. "Switzerland was easy prey," writes Finkelstein: "Few would sympathize with rich Swiss bankers as against 'needy Holocaust survivors.'"[96] With this observation, Finkelstein becomes the first Marxist in history to defend the interests of corrupt financiers against the rights of their defrauded customers.

The Swiss banks initially claimed that they could identify only 775 unclaimed dormant accounts, with a combined value of $32 million.[97] This pretense was quickly abandoned in the face of universal ridicule. Faced with U.S. Senate hearings, the banks hurriedly agreed to establish an investigative body (the Volcker Committee) and implement its recommendations. These findings (the Volcker Report) are the centerpiece of Finkelstein's case for the spotless innocence of Swiss bankers and the criminal guilt of American Jews.[98] That is curious, for the Report concluded that the number of properly documented accounts with a "probable or possible relationship to victims of Nazi persecution" was not 775, as the banks had claimed, but 53,886.[99] Furthermore, the current value of these accounts was not $32 million, as the banks had claimed, but up to $1.2 billion.[100]

But that is not all. Absent from Finkelstein's book is the rather significant finding that the records for no less than 2.8 million accounts opened in the Nazi era—two-fifths of the total—had completely vanished.[101] Under Swiss law, the banks were obliged to maintain their records for only ten years;[102] but since the banks knew full well that most of their Jewish depositors had been murdered by the Nazis, it was highly convenient that the heirs of these unfortunate customers would be unable to trace the funds. Without the records, the banks automatically kept the victims' money, because Switzerland has no escheat law, whereby unclaimed assets would revert to the state.[103] As the Report noted, there is an "unfillable gap" of millions of accounts "that can now never be known or analyzed for their relationship to Holocaust victims."[104] Not one of these facts is disclosed by Finkelstein.

Finkelstein purports to be greatly impressed by the fact that the Volcker Report exonerated its financial sponsors from the charge of deliberate plunder, a wholly predictable outcome.[105] He is somewhat less enthusiastic about its other findings, as shown by his decision to suppress them in their entirety. For the Report also documented a mass of "questionable and deceitful actions" on the part of the banks, including:

withholding of information from Holocaust victims or their heirs about their accounts, inappropriate closing of accounts, failure to keep adequate records, many cases of insensitivity to the efforts of victims or heirs of victims to claim dormant or closed accounts, and a general lack or diligence—even active resistance—in response to earlier private and official inquiries about dormant accounts.[106]

The Report also found that most of the "deceitful actions" occurred not in small financial boutiques, but in the large commercial banks.[107] Recall that these are not the accusations of the "Holocaust industry," but the verdict of an investigation financed to the tune of hundreds of millions of dollars by the Swiss banks themselves. Could Finkelstein's readers possibly guess the true contents of the Volcker Report from his book? Would they realize that the Swiss banks themselves had therein admitted to deceitful behavior with respect to many hundreds of millions of dollars belonging to Holocaust victims?

The "Devilish Reality" of Compensation.

The second half of the "double shakedown" is the alleged robbery of Holocaust survivors. Here Finkelstein addresses the so-called Gribetz Plan for the distribution of the $1.25 billion compensation agreed by the Swiss banks.[108] He admits that the scheme "seemed to belie pervasive fears that the monies would be appropriated by Jewish organizations." But then he announces a shocking discovery: hidden in the details of the Gribetz Plan is "the devilish reality" that "probably but a small fraction of the Swiss monies" will be paid directly to victims of Nazism.[109] The reader is primed to expect massive documentation of this "devilish reality." So where is it? Finkelstein accepts that from the $1.25 billion fund, $800 million will cover dormant bank accounts, with another $400 million for looted assets, slave labor and refugees. This might be thought to present a certain difficulty for his position. It is instructive to see how he resolves it.

On the $800 million, Finkelstein admits that money will be paid directly to owners of dormant bank accounts. But he says that this will amount to only a minuscule fraction of the total; the remainder will go to Jewish groups, not only because "the Holocaust industry will have the final say," but also because the funds "won't be distributed until many years from now, when few actual Holocaust survivors will be alive."[110] Not a shred of evidence is provided for these stunning assertions. Instead Finkelstein simply speculates—without any justification at all—that most of the funds will be misappropriated thanks to the wickedness of the "Holocaust industry."

On the $400 million, Finkelstein is enraged that the money will be held in abeyance until the legal appeals are over. Does he seriously expect that money will be irrevocably surrendered while it is still the subject of litigation? Or does he think that the funds should be distributed to elderly Holocaust survivors and then retrieved if the courts rule otherwise? He predicts that the survivors will be so determined to appeal that few will be alive to benefit even if they win;

meanwhile the "Holocaust industry," already the "main beneficiary" of the Gribetz Plan, can only gain from the delay.[111] His guess becomes plausible only if we assume what he has to prove, that Jewish groups are run by heartless profiteers whose only concern is to swindle Holocaust victims, doubtless including their own relatives. The fact is that he has produced no evidence whatsoever.

Building on these absurdities, Finkelstein creates an imposing edifice of disinformation. Of the $400 million just mentioned, $100 million will go to the looted assets class. According to Finkelstein,

> In the 'looted assets' class, $90 million is earmarked not for direct payments to Holocaust survivors but for Jewish organizations servicing Holocaust communities 'broadly defined.' The largest allocation will go to the Claims Conference...[112]

This is the exact opposite of the truth. What the Gribetz Plan actually says is that $90 million will be spent on "food packages, medical care, winter relief and other *direct assistance* to impoverished and ill elderly Nazi victims in the former Soviet Union" (75 percent) and on "*direct emergency relief* to needy Holocaust survivors in other parts of the world" (25 percent).[113] Furthermore, the distribution will be managed not only by the Claims Conference, but also by the Joint Distribution Committee, with the input of Holocaust survivors and under court supervision; and the reason for this arrangement is precisely that it will avoid the unnecessary expense of establishing an additional bureaucracy, thus guaranteeing that the assistance will reach the people who need it.[114]

By playing on his suspicions and innuendoes—liberally augmented with falsehoods—Finkelstein is able to conclude[115] that upon "close analysis" the Gribetz Plan "confirms" his argument, i.e., "the devilish reality" that "probably but a small fraction of the Swiss monies" will be paid directly to the victims. But the only "devilish reality" involved is Finkelstein's readiness to exploit the fears of elderly Holocaust survivors to advance his own political agenda.

The Number of Survivors

A final theme in Finkelstein's crusade on behalf of Swiss bankers and German industrialists persecuted by the international Zionist conspiracy is the alleged inflation of the number of Holocaust survivors by Jewish organizations. Finkelstein promotes this allegation by means of a series of ingenious distortions and outrageous conclusions.

Thus, he tells us that Stuart Eizenstat, chief American envoy at the German slave-labor negotiations, "put the total number of slave laborers, Jewish and non-Jewish, still alive at 'perhaps 70-90,000.'... This would put the total number of still living Jewish slave laborers at 14,000-18,000 (20 percent of 70-90,000)." Finkelstein then ridicules the fact that "as it entered into negotiations with Germany, the Holocaust industry demanded compensation for 135,000 still living former Jewish slave laborers... the number of former Jewish slave laborers still alive increased nearly tenfold..."[115] So Finkelstein is claiming that 14,000-18,000 surviving Jewish slave laborers magically increased to 135,000 within months, thanks to the mendacity of the "Holocaust industry."

But the only deception here is being practiced by Finkelstein. Eizenstat actually said: "For those who are so-called *slave laborers... generally—although not exclusively—Jewish concentration or ghetto survivors*, my understanding is that there are somewhere under 100,000; perhaps 70,000 to 90,000." For non-Jewish *forced* laborers (people who had not been sent to camps or ghettos) Eizenstat mentioned an estimate of 500,000 Poles alone, many of whom were agricultural workers.[117] Contrary to Finkelstein, Eizenstat clearly stated that most of the 70,000-90,000 surviving slave laborers were Jews. Contrary to Finkelstein, no one alleged a tenfold increase in their numbers within the space of months. Moreover, the larger "Holocaust industry" figure of 135,000 surviving Jewish slave laborers appears to have been an underestimate, since the existing German Holocaust compensation program was already paying monthly pensions to 170,000 survivors, "many of whom may be presumed to have performed slave labor."[118]

Having perpetrated this distortion, Finkelstein then asserts, without explanation, that "if 135,000 former Jewish slave laborers are still alive today, some 600,000 must have survived the war..." After conjuring the 600,000 figure out of thin air, he adds: "[if] 600,000 Jewish *inmates* survived the war, then fully 3 million *inmates* in total must have survived. By the Holocaust industry's reckoning, *concentration camp* conditions couldn't have been harsh at all..."[119] By conflating *slave laborers* (many of whom worked in ghettos, factories, or comparable places of confinement, not in the camps)[120] and *forced laborers* (non-Jews who had never been sent to the camps) with *concentration camp inmates*, Finkelstein is able to attribute wholly imaginary claims to the "Holocaust industry." In this farrago of deceit, the only issue that merits discussion is his own ability to manipulate definitions and statistics.

Other examples abound. Finkelstein laments that "the Gribetz Plan now deems every Russian Jew who survived World War II to be a Holocaust survivor," citing a statistical table which deems nothing of the kind.[121] As a consequence of this decision, "Russian Jews who fled in advance of the Nazis or served in the Red Army now qualify as Holocaust survivors because they faced torture or death if captured"—how ridiculous. Apparently, Finkelstein thinks that no wrong has been committed against people described in the Gribetz Plan as "destitute, elderly victims of Nazi persecution still living in the former Soviet Union" who "lost virtually all their material possessions to the Third Reich's plunder."[122]

Fortified by this disgraceful assumption, Finkelstein rails against the Gribetz Plan's figures of 832,000-960,000 "Jewish Nazi victims living in the world today."[123] He also accuses Burt Neuborne ("lead counsel for the Holocaust industry") of pretending that the Gribetz figures refer mainly to non-Jews, and calls for his disbarment.[124] But the diligent reader who investigates this supposed misrepresentation will find that Neuborne was not citing the Gribetz figures at all; he was quoting a German foundation's estimate of surviving *victims of slave labor and forced labor*, most of whom are indeed non-Jews, as we have already seen.[125] Is there is any limit to Finkelstein's capacity for fakery?

The Verdict of the Historians

To any serious reader, it is clear that *The Holocaust Industry* is not a courageous exposé by a marginalized dissident but a toxic stream of defamations, falsifications, and fabrications aimed at his fellow Jews. That is also the verdict of historians.[126] According to Ronnie Landau, it is "an ideological rant, masquerading as scholarship… a dance on the graves of the Jewish dead." According to David Cesarani, its "flimsy" argument "rests on the misinterpretation of history and questionable use of sources" and is "distorted by a venomous dislike of the 'American Jewish elites.'" According to Omer Bartov, it is "an ideological fanatic's view of other people's opportunism" by a writer who is "reckless and ruthless in his attacks." According to Israel Gutman, it is "a lampoon, which takes a serious subject and distorts it for improper purposes. I don't even think it should be reviewed or critiqued as a legitimate book." According to Hans Mommsen, it is "a most trivial book, which appeals to easily aroused antisemitic prejudices." According to Ronald W. Zweig, "Finkelstein's falsifications" are in danger of becoming "the twenty-first century version of the *Protocols of the Elders of Zion*."[127]

Such a bill of indictment would give pause to an honest author. But what is the combined weight of the historical profession when set against the anti-Jewish conspiracy theories of Norman G. Finkelstein?

Conclusion

Throughout his long and inglorious career, Finkelstein has been sustained by a simple thesis. "In the Holocaust framework," he laments, antisemitism is "always irrational," but such propositions "do not withstand even superficial scrutiny." Rather, hatred of Jews "develops in a specific historical context with its attendant interplay of interests."[128] Finkelstein does not explain how Jews threatened the "interests" of the Third Reich. But why should he? This is surely self-evident to the neo-Nazis who sing his praises, to the Holocaust deniers who republish his books on their websites, to the legions of enthusiasts eager to hear that the wicked Zionists are the source of all the evils that beset the human race. In Finkelstein's mental universe, Israeli Jews are a "parasitic class," but Hezbollah terrorists are the paragons of liberation. In his scholarly judgment, "abusive force was not truly integral to the Final Solution," but Israeli prisons are the scene of "novelties to the Nazi experiments." In his moral calculus, Tel Aviv deserves the fate of Hiroshima and pregnant women are "legitimate targets" for mass murder. In his version of reality, supporters of the Jewish home-land are worse than the Gestapo, and the governments of Europe are helpless in the face of a Jewish conspiracy so powerful that "it can easily break the feeble resistance of prostrate nations." What are we to make of the fact that such a man is a best-selling author in sixteen languages?

Recently, Finkelstein has identified yet another Jewish assault on the "inter-ests" of the world. "There are now more Holocaust museums in the United States than there are Burger Kings," he warns. "And it is only a matter of time that there are more Holocaust museums than there are McDonalds."[129] As long as humanity is threatened by the memory of the Holocaust, Norman G. Finkelstein will be at hand to remind us of the "rationality" of anti-Jewish fanaticism.

Notes

1. John Dirlik, "Canadian Jewish Organizations Charged With Stifling Campus De-bate," *Washington Report on Middle East Affairs*, May/June, 1992.
2. Norman G. Finkelstein, *Image and Reality of the Israel-Palestine Conflict* (London and New York: Verso, 1995), 4. Emphasis added. Finkelstein later contradicts himself by pointing out that Germans were not punished for refusing to participate in atrocities against Jews, 209n72.
3. Norman G. Finkelstein, "Daniel Jonah Goldhagen's 'Crazy' Thesis," *New Left Review*, July/August, 1997, 83.
4. Norman G. Finkelstein, *The Holocaust Industry: Reflections on the Exploitation of Jewish Suffering* (London and New York: Verso, 2001), 52n29.
5. *Image and Reality*, 88, 100-1, 107, 116; cf. 116-20 *passim*. On "abusive force," cf. Primo Levi's famous essay on "useless violence" in the Nazi death camps, where the goal was to inflict "the greatest physical and moral suffering. The 'enemy' must not only die, he must die in torment." *The Drowned and the Saved* (New York: Vintage, 1989), 120.
6. "Daniel Jonah Goldhagen's 'Crazy' Thesis," 48-52.
7. *Holocaust Industry*, 35-6n56, 135.
8. Noam Chomsky, *Understanding Power: The Indispensable Chomsky* (New York: The New Press, 2002), 244-8.
9. Interview, *Irish Times*, July 1, 2003.
10. John Authers, *Financial Times*, August 23, 2003.
11. Interview, *Jerusalem Report*, August 28, 2000.
12. *Image and Reality*, 7-8.
13. On this point, see Shlomo Avineri, *The Making of Modern Zionism: Intellectual Origins of the Jewish State* (New York: Basic Books, 1981). Finkelstein acknowl-edges the existence of Avineri's book in two footnotes, the first of which (predict-ably) compares him to Hitler: 175n14, 178n28.
14. Yosef Gorny, *Zionism and the Arabs, 1882-1948: A Study of Ideology* (Oxford: Oxford University Press, 1987), 206, 234, 307; *Image and Reality*, 10-11.
15. *Image and Reality*, 8.
16. Ibid., 20.
17. Ibid., 101.
18. I pass over two of Finkelstein's chapters: "A Land Without a People," ibid., 21-51 (an assault on the journalist Joan Peters), and "Born of War, Not by Design," 51-88 (a commentary on the historian Benny Morris), because his arguments have been refuted elsewhere. On his woefully incompetent attack on Peters, see Erich and Rael

Jean Isaac, "Whose Palestine?" *Commentary*, July 1986; Letters, *Commentary*, October 1986. On Morris' record of scholarly falsification, see e.g., Efraim Karsh, "'Falsifying the Record': Benny Morris, David Ben-Gurion, and the 'Transfer' Idea," *Israel Affairs,* Winter 1997, and Karsh's essay in this book.

19.   Michael B. Oren, *Six Days of War: June 1967 and the Making of the Modern Middle East* (Oxford: Oxford University Press, 2002), 42, 45.

20.   *Image and Reality*, 125, 213n6.

21.   Richard B. Parker, *The Politics of Miscalculation in the Middle East* (Bloomington and Indianapolis: Indiana University Press, 1993), 15; Isabella Ginor, "The Cold War's Longest Cover-Up: How and Why the USSR Instigated the 1967 War," *Middle East Review of International Affairs*, September 2003, 38.

22.   Walter Laqueur, *The Road to War: The Origins and Aftermath of the Arab-Israeli Conflict 1967-8* (London: Pelican Books, 1969), 89.

23.   *Image and Reality*, 126-7.

24.   Norman G. Finkelstein, "Abba Eban With Footnotes," *Journal of Palestine Studies*, Spring 2003, 78.

25.   Oren, *Six Days of War*, 64; see also Laqueur, *The Road to War*, 98; Parker, *The Politics of Miscalculation in the Middle East*, 95.

26.   "Abba Eban With Footnotes," 78.

27.   Laqueur, *The Road to War*, 104.

28.   Oren, *Six Days of War*, 69.

29.   "Abba Eban With Footnotes," 78-9; also *Image and Reality*, 128.

30.   *Washington Post*, May 27, 1967.

31.   *Image and Reality*, 129 (moratorium); Oren, *Six Days of War*, 126 (Soviet and Egyptian rejection).

32.   *Image and Reality*, 129, 215n17; Parker, *The Politics of Miscalculation in the Middle East*, 234, 236.

33.   *Image and Reality*, 138-9; Leo Gross, "The Geneva Conference on the Law of the Sea and the Right of Innocent Passage Through the Gulf of Aqaba," *American Journal of International Law*, July 1959, 565 (Egyptian admission).

34.   Leo Gross, "Passage Through the Strait of Tiran and in the Gulf of Aqaba," *Law and Contemporary Problems*, Winter 1968, 133.

35.   *Image and Reality*, 139 ("mortally dependent"); *Radio Cairo*, May 27, 1967, quoted in Moshe Shemesh, "Did Shuqayri Call For 'Throwing the Jews into the Sea?" *Israel Studies*, Summer 2003, 79 ("two possibilities").

36.   *Image and Reality*, 134.

37.   Oren, *Six Days of War*, 56.

38.   Laqueur, *The Road to War*, 105.

39.   Oren, *Six Days of War*, 78, 132, 136-37, 163-64.

40.   "Abba Eban With Footnotes," 82; Oren, *Six Days of War*, 87, 133-34, 156.

41.   Letters, *Commentary*, September 1983.

42.   *Image and Reality*, 135.

43.   Oren, *Six Days of War*, 57, 86, 92, 95, 160, 163.

44.   Ginor, "The Cold War's Longest Cover-Up," 50.

45.   "Abba Eban With Footnotes," 85, 89n37. See Hirsh Goodman and Ze'ev Schiff, "The Attack on the *Liberty*," *The Atlantic Monthly*, September 1984; Michael B. Oren, "The *USS Liberty*: Case Closed," *Azure*, Spring 2000; id., "Unfriendly Fire: Why Did Israeli Troops Attack the USS *Liberty*?" *New Republic*, July 23, 2001; id., Letters, *New Republic*, September 17, 2001; A. Jay Cristol, *The Liberty Incident* (Dulles, VA: Brasseys, 2002); *Jerusalem Post*, June 3, 2004 (flight recordings); *Ha'aretz*, July 9, 2003, *Jerusalem Post*, July 10, 2003 (NSA transcripts); Richard B. Parker, Communications, *Middle East Journal*, Autumn 2003.

46. "Abba Eban With Footnotes," 86, 89n38.
47. Alon Pinkas, *Jerusalem Post*, August 17, 1995; Michael B. Oren, *New Republic*, July 23, 2001.
48. *Image and Reality*, 151.
49. *Washington Post*, July 6, 1967.
50. Reuven Pedatzur, "Coming Back Full Circle: The Palestinian Option in 1967," *Middle East Journal*, Spring 1995, 273-76, 278.
51. *Image and Reality*, 154.
52. *New York Times*, August 31, 1967, emphasis added. This report carries the Orwellian headline, "Nasser and Hussein Urge Compromise With Israel at Arabs' Summit Parley."
53. *Washington Post*, September 1, 1967. In the end, the Arab states "rejected for the present a mild proposal in Marshal Tito's plan for a new Arab declaration of allegiance to the United Nations Charter – a move tantamount to recognizing Israel's right to exist," Editorial, *New York Times*, September 2, 1967. Yet again, Arab regimes conceded that they were the aggressors in the conflict.
54. *New York Times*, September 2, 1967.
55. Norman Finkelstein, "Bayt Sahur in Year II of the Intifada: A Personal Account," *Journal of Palestine Studies*, Winter 1990, 64, 74.
56. *Los Angeles Times*, October 31, 1988.
57. *Washington Post*, July 7, 1989.
58. *Jerusalem Post*, April 9, 1993.
59. *Time*, June 5, 1995 (160 killed); *Jerusalem Post*, December 4, 1990 (4,000 injured).
60. *Jerusalem Post*, May 21, 1991.
61. Steven Emerson, "Meltdown: The End of the Intifada," *New Republic*, November 23, 1992.
62. Yosif Mahmoud Haj-Yahia, Edy Kaufman and Sufian Abu Nijaila, *Alleged Palestinian Collaborators With Israel and Their Families*, Peace Papers, No. 12, Truman Institute, Hebrew University of Jerusalem, Summer 1999, 18-9.
63. Norman G. Finkelstein, "Reflections on Palestinian Attitudes During the Gulf War," *Journal of Palestine Studies*, Spring 1992, 55, 64-5, 67.
64. Associated Press, December 10, 2001.
65. Norman G. Finkelstein, "A Reply to Michael Young," http://www.normanfinkelstein.com, emphasis added.
66. Norman G. Finkelstein, "Postscript to German Edition of *The Rise and Fall of Palestine*," http://www.normanfinkelstein.com.
67. "How to Lose Friends and Alienate People: A Conversation With Professor Norman Finkelstein," *CounterPunch*, December 13, 2001: http://www.counterpunch.org/finkelstein1.html.
68. Online interview with Giovanni De Martis, http://www.olokaustos.org/saggi/interviste/finkel-en4.htm.
69. "Daniel Jonah Goldhagen's 'Crazy' Thesis," 84.
70. *Gibt es wirklich eine Holocaust-Industrie?* ed. Ernst Piper (Zurich: Pendo, 2001); *Die Finkelstein-Debatte*, ed. Petra Steinberger (Munich: Piper, 2001); *Das Finkelstein-Alibi*, ed. Rolf Surmann (Cologne: Papyrossa, 2001).
71. Joseph Croitoru, "Holocaust Memories," *Frankfurter Allgemeine Zeitung*, May 14, 2001; Finkelstein, "Foreword to the Paperback Edition," *Holocaust Industry*, vii.
72. Ernst Zundel, "ZGram," October 15, 2000: http://www.zundelsite.org/english/zgrams/zg2000/zg0010/001015.html.
73. David Irving's Action Report Online, August 10, 2002: http://www.fpp.co.uk/docs/Irving/RadDi/2002/110802.html.

74.   Samuel Crowell (pseud.), "Making Room for the Revisionists," *Journal for Historical Review*, January/February 2001: http://www.ihr.org/jhr/v20/ v20n1p41_Finkelstein.html.
75.   "Holocaust Revisionism in English," http://www.vho.org/aaargh/engl/engl.html.
76.   Giovanni De Martis, "From the Book to the Interview," http://www.olokaustos.org/ saggi/interviste/finkel-en2.htm.
77.   *Holocaust Industry*, 3.
78.   For example: "Moving aggressively to defend their corporate and class interests, Jewish elites branded all opposition to their new conservative policies anti-Semitic.... In this ideological offensive, The Holocaust came to play a critical role... Thus American Jewish elites could strike heroic poses as they indulged in cowardly bullying." Ibid., 37.
79.   Ibid., 38.
80.   Ibid., 52-3.
81.   Ibid., 13-4.
82.   *Holocaust Industry*, 16, 54.
83.   Ibid., 49, 73.
84.   Ibid., 55-62, 71. For analysis of Arno Mayer's ideologically motivated falsifications, see Daniel Jonah Goldhagen, "False Witness," *New Republic*, April 17, 1989; Christopher Browning, "The Holocaust Distorted," *Dissent*, Summer 1989; and Lucy Dawidowicz, "Perversions of the Holocaust," *Commentary*, October 1989. Mayer asserts that more Jews died from "natural" causes (e.g., disease) than "unnatural" causes (gassing, shooting, etc.). As Browning observes: "This extraordinary allegation... finds no support whatsoever in any documents or historical studies that I have seen, and Mayer's book – without footnotes – provides no evidence for it."
85.   Ibid., 55, 68-72.
86.   Ibid., 13. See Lawrence Baron, "The Holocaust in American Public Memory, 1945-1960," in *Holocaust and Genocide Studies*, Spring 2003 for a thorough demolition of the thesis of Jewish indifference to the topic before 1967.
87.   *Holocaust Industry*, 70; Daniel J. Goldhagen, "A New Serbia," *New Republic*, May 17, 1999.
88.   *Holocaust Industry*, 76; Guenter Lewy, *The Nazi Persecution of the Gypsies* (Oxford: Oxford University Press, 2001), 221-22.
89.   *Holocaust Industry*, 76; Yehuda Bauer, *Rethinking the Holocaust* (New Haven, CT: Yale University Press, 2002), 66. Bauer notes that after a discussion with Hitler in 1942, Himmler wrote in his diary: "*Keine Vernichtung der Zigeuner*" (No extermination of the Gypsies).
90.   *Holocaust Industry*, 82; Viktor Frike, "Shoah Business," *Salon.com*, August 30, 2000. Finkelstein also compares Elie Wiesel, the Auschwitz survivor, to Rudolf Hoess, the Auschwitz commandant: see *Image and Reality*, 208n71.
91.   *Holocaust Industry*, 68.
92.   "We Condemn Syria's Denial of the Holocaust," *New York Times*, February 9, 2000, advertisement.
93.   *Holocaust Industry*, 129.
94.   Ibid., 89.
95.   Ibid., 130-31.
96.   Ibid., 90.
97.   *New York Times*, February 9, 1996.
98.   Independent Committee of Eminent Persons, *Report on Dormant Accounts of Victims of Nazi Persecution in Swiss Banks*, December 6, 1999 ("Volcker Report").

99. Ibid., para. 30; Table C. The figure is highly conservative, not least because accounts opened using a Swiss address and small savings accounts were disregarded, Annex 4, para. 8. This excluded 1.9 million of the 4.1 million accounts for which records remain, despite the likelihood that some were opened by Jewish depositors using false Swiss addresses or the addresses of Swiss intermediaries for purposes of concealment.
100. Ibid., Annex 4, para. 42n23; I converted the Report's figure of SFr 1.9 billion (calculated using the mean value of known account values) to US$ with the December 6, 1999 exchange rate. *Washington Post*, December 7, 1999, gives a figure of $1.3 billion.
101. Ibid., para. 20; Table A. Finkelstein makes much of the finding that there was "no evidence of systematic destruction of account records *for the purpose of concealing past behavior*," para. 22, emphasis added, but he suppresses evidence that in some instances, "document destruction was conducted regularly and systematically," Annex 7, para. 11. As Judge Korman observed, "The destruction was part of the banks' ordinary course of business, and it was massive… for 40% of bank accounts open or opened in Switzerland between 1933 and 1945, there is no record at all, and for the rest, there is often no more than a customer registry card." See Judge Edward R. Korman, "Memorandum & Order," *In re Holocaust Victim Assets Litigation* (Eastern District of New York, February 19, 2004), 20, 23: http://www.swissbankclaims.com.
102. Volcker Report, para. 23.
103. Ibid., para. 45. Incredibly, the Report treats the banks' ability to retain unclaimed assets as a *mitigating* factor in their conduct.
104. Ibid., para. 38.
105. *Holocaust Industry*, 111-14. Compare Paul Volcker's own verdict: "They were lackadaisical, to say the least. The banks had no incentive to find out the truth about the assets because they felt they should protect the honor of Switzerland. They could have solved this problem a long time ago if they really wanted to." *Washington Post*, December 7, 1999.
106. Volcker Report, para. 41.
107. Ibid., para. 44.
108. "Postscript to the Paperback Edition," *Holocaust Industry*, 154-67. Judah Gribetz, *Special Master's Proposed Plan of Allocation and Distribution of Settlement Proceeds*, September 11, 2000 ("Gribetz Plan"): http://www.swissbankclaims.com.
109. *Holocaust Industry*, 154-55.
110. Ibid., 163-64.
111. Ibid., 165.
112. Ibid., 165-66. The remaining $10 million goes to Gypsies, Jehovah's Witnesses, and homosexuals.
113. Gribetz Plan, 26. Emphases added.
114. Ibid., 120-2: "virtually all of the recommended programs for the needy are already functioning, and will incur no start-up costs and relatively low administrative expenses, a crucial concern in light of the Special Master's duty to minimize such deductions from the Settlement Fund."
115. *Holocaust Industry*, 167.
116. Ibid., 126.
117. Stuart E. Eizenstat, State Department Briefing, May 12, 1999: http://www.state.gov/www/policy_remarks/1999/990512eizenstat_slavelabor.html. Emphases added.
118. Gribetz Plan, 145. Finkelstein is now aware of the facts: see *Holocaust Industry*, 162, 166.
119. *Holocaust Industry*, 127. Emphases added.

120. Gribetz Plan, 144-5. Gribetz points out that some sources distinguish slave labor from forced labor, whereas others do not: see 142n387. This naturally causes confusion.

121. *Holocaust Industry*, 160; Gribetz Plan, Annex C, C-7, Table 3. This table presents estimates of Jewish population losses in the Holocaust. There is no category for "Russian Jews," but there is an entry recording that a pre-war Soviet Jewish population of 3.02 million fell by 1-1.1 million. Nowhere does the table state or imply that "every Russian Jew" surviving the war qualifies as a Holocaust survivor.

122. Gribetz Plan, 122-3.

123. Ibid., Annex C, C-8.

124. *Holocaust Industry*, 168-69.

125. Neuborne, Letters, *The Nation*, December 25, 2000. See also Neuborne, Letters, *Nation,* February 18, 2002.

126. *The Holocaust Industry* secured one serious scholarly endorsement, from political scientist Raul Hilberg, a writer whose expertise on the Nazi bureaucracy notoriously outweighs his knowledge of Jewish history.

127. Ronnie Landau, "A Grubby Story?" *Spectator* (London), July 22, 2000; David Cesarani, "Finkelstein's Final Solution," *Times Higher Education Supplement* (London), August 4, 2000; Omer Bartov, "A Tale of Two Holocausts," *New York Times*, August 6, 2000; Yair Sheleg, "The Finkelstein Polemic," *Ha'aretz Magazine*, March 30, 2001 (Gutman, Mommsen); Ronald W. Zweig, Review, *The Journal of Israeli History*, Summer-Autumn 2001, 210.

128. *Holocaust Industry*, 51-2.

129. Interview, CBC News, January 23, 2005.

9

Peter Novick: Blaming Israel for "Too Much" Holocaust Awareness

David G. Roskies

I

Must every major city in the United States boast its own museum of the Holocaust? Must every high school offer a mandatory curriculum on the destruction of European Jewry, every college campus have an endowed chair of Holocaust studies? Should a so-called Week of Remembrance in mid-April be observed, as Martin Luther King Day is now observed in mid-January? How many movies and books are enough?

To Peter Novick, the point of saturation has already been reached. A professor of history at the University of Chicago, Novick has set out to write the story of Holocaust consciousness in America, beginning in the war years and ending with a glimpse at the future. In his book *The Holocaust in American Life*,[1] the first thing he reminds us is that the Holocaust did not always occupy such a prominent place in our urban landscape, on college campuses, in our civil religion, in cinemas and bookstores, or on the op-ed page of the *New York Times*. Even to think about World War II in terms of the fate of the Jews, as we tend to do now, is, he admonishes, to impose present preoccupations onto a very different past.

Defending certain elements of that past, and decrying the Holocaust-obsessed present, is the burden of this book. In his opening chapters, Novick returns us to an era when a public emphasis on ethnicity was viewed, not least by American Jews themselves, as politically counterproductive and perhaps intrinsically suspect. And with reason: although, nowadays, it is commonplace to hear that American Jews did not do nearly enough to help their co-religionists during the war, Novick argues otherwise. Basing himself on the minutes and internal memoranda of the American Jewish Committee, the American Jewish Congress, the Jewish Labor Committee, and the National Community Relations Advisory Council, he concludes that organized Jewry acted vigorously and responsibly in light of the actual political landscape at home and, especially, the intractable conditions abroad.[2]

Similarly in the immediate postwar period, when the Jewish community rallied behind Washington to confront the new threat of Soviet totalitarianism. Under the impact of the cold war, Novick writes, American Jewish discourse about the Holocaust was necessarily "either muted or turned to anti-Soviet purposes."[3] As for Holocaust survivors who had made their way here, to the extent they were talked about at all they were upheld not as figures of martyrdom but as model citizens who were taking full advantage of the American dream.

It was during the 1960's and 70's, the period Novick calls "The Years of Transition," that things changed. The catalysts were two events that occurred halfway around the globe, in the state of Israel. The first was the trial of Adolf Eichmann, which etched the details of the German killing machine into the collective Jewish psyche. The second was the Six-Day war of 1967, when American Jews relived the trauma of mass annihilation in the belief (false, according to Novick) that the Israeli army was in imminent danger of defeat.[4]

What resulted from these two events was an American Jewish fixation with the horrors of the Holocaust that would mark—or, in Novick's view, disfigure— the decades to come, legitimating a whole new orientation to communal affairs. At the extreme, he writes, fears based on the Holocaust impelled Jewish organizations more or less to invent a surge in domestic antisemitism, with the Anti-Defamation League of B'nai B'rith being "especially assiduous in giving wide circulation to anti-Semitic remarks by obscure black hustlers and demagogues."[5] Similarly inflated notions of Jewish insecurity lay behind the hysterical campaigns to rally support for Israel and Soviet Jewry ("Never Again!"), and to warn against the dangers of assimilation.

And this, says Novick, is where we still are today. American Jews who themselves have abandoned any but the most rudimentary religious practices, and are as fuzzy in their grasp of history as their fellow non-Jewish Americans, have created an entire surrogate religion around the Holocaust, complete with saints (survivors), scripture (*Schindler's List*), and shrines (those ubiquitous museums). A community more secure, and more affluent, than Jews have ever been in all of history has given itself over to an utterly irrational scenario of destruction and victimization, in disregard of political reality and to the detriment of its own best interests and values.

II

As this brief summary suggests, Israel and Zionism are the combined *bête noire* of Novick's account of the career of the Holocaust in American consciousness. The sea change that occurred between the 1940s, when the murder of European Jewry still lacked a name, and the 1970s, when the whole world began to suffer from Holocaust-envy, was, in his view, the work of the Zionist lobby. Even the word "Holocaust," he contends, did not gain currency in America until it was imported from Israel during the Eichmann trial.[6]

Likewise, the campaign to vilify Hannah Arendt for her 1963 book, *Eichmann in Jerusalem*[7]—a work whose thesis "that the typical Holocaust perpetrator was terrifyingly normal and by no means a driven anti-Semite" is, Novick airily asserts, now accepted by "almost all scholars"[8]—was launched by the Zionist lobby, in conjunction with Israel. As he tells it, the Anti-Defamation League launched the first prong of the attack, with Nahum Goldmann, head of the World Zionist Organization, responsible for the second.[9] And only a few pages later, he quotes "a long-time official of the Anti-Defamation League" who wrote in a letter to a friend "that by the 1970s organized American Jewry had become 'an agency of the Israeli government . . . follow[ing] its directions from day to day.'"[10] What more proof could the discerning reader possibly demand?

After the Six-Day War, he adds, American Jewish organizations routinely took their marching orders from Israel, sometimes literally so: the annual March of the Living, a worldwide effort to rescue Jewish teenagers from assimilation by leading them on a pilgrimage to the Nazi death camps and then to Israel, is a transparent Zionist product.[11] Novick also cites corroborating evidence from "changes" in "popular Jewish attitudes": the "mandatory" presence of Israeli artifacts in every American Jewish living room; the blind and totally uninformed American Jewish "commitment to Israel," and so forth. He even blames the Zionists for doing away with the last vestiges of authentic Jewish American speech patterns, replacing the beloved *yarmulke* with *kippa* and the homey *shabbes* with the harsh-sounding *shabbat*.[12]

All the main villains in Novick's story are either "Zionists" or "neo-conservatives," or both. The late Lucy S. Dawidowicz, for example, the formidable historian of the Holocaust, appears here only as a neoconservative "expert on Communism."[13] Novick has mined archival sources for every letter-to-the-editor Dawidowicz ever wrote, every internal memorandum she ever prepared for a Jewish organization; yet nowhere does he so much as mention her classic 1975 book, *The War Against the Jews, 1933-1945*, a work whose sobriety, rigor, and uncompromising argumentation set a gold standard for the then-infant field of Holocaust studies.[14]

In short, the real subject of Novick's book is not the Holocaust at all but rather the politics of memory. This, however, is an area in which his own credentials rather severely qualify his competence to pass judgment. As a resolutely secular Jew, with, apparently, little if any command of traditional sources, Novick demonstrates no feel whatsoever for the processes of covenantal memory whereby Jews have always apprehended historical events under such constituent rubrics as exile, martyrdom, redemption. If, for example, during the Yom Kippur war of 1973, Jews the world over instinctively "remembered" the Holocaust, Novick assumes that Zionist propaganda was somehow to blame.[15] That the Egyptians themselves chose the holiest day in the Jewish calendar to launch their near-fatal attack on the Jewish state does not even enter into his historical equation. They remembered, but he does not.

As a stranger to the inner life of the Jews, Novick also demonstrates no feel for their habitual patterns of collective behavior. Discussing the postwar displaced-persons (DP) camps, for example, he documents the efforts of Zionist chaplains and emissaries from the Jewish Agency to influence refugees to emigrate to Palestine, castigating these officials for manipulating the naive sensibilities of the traumatized and helpless refugees. What he does not know or does not acknowledge is that the majority of Jews who survived the war had in fact been members of one or another highly politicized prewar youth movement, and that the second thing they organized in the DP camps, after a quorum to recite *kaddish*, was political parties. If some proportion ended up going to Palestine, it was not out of naivete but out of informed conviction.

But this particular set of convictions is not much to Novick's liking. Nor does he like it any better in its present-day manifestation, when it takes the form of a Holocaust-inspired preoccupation with Jewish self-interest. American Jews, Novick argues throughout his book, have become increasingly insular, using the "lessons" of the Holocaust and the defense of Israel as reasons to abdicate their proper, liberal agenda. As a Left-liberal, he complains that this overmindfulness of their own sorrows commits Jews to nothing positive as Americans.

Worse, by "raising the threshold of outrage," the emphasis on remembering the Holocaust has desensitized Jews to their moral obligation toward those less fortunate than themselves. In an outburst of passion, he asks why the American Jewish community does not labor to rescue the millions upon millions of innocent children who are dying of starvation today. Indeed, why does the annual loss of over ten million children to hunger and preventable disease make no moral claim on the wider American conscience? Because, he suggests, they are too "unholocaustal."[16] The Jews, in other words, are guilty not only of having betrayed themselves but of having unwittingly contributed to the self-betrayal of all socially conscious Americans. This, of course, is the purest cant—and, as a glance at the agenda of any major Jewish organization would confirm, a wild distortion of the truth to boot.

III

Perhaps the best illustration of Novick's warped conception of American Jewish life is the striking contrast in his respective verdicts on Hannah Arendt and Lucy Dawidowicz. Only a few references to Dawidowicz lie scattered throughout the book (many of them are in the footnotes). Dawidowicz comes across as - at best - a political pundit. This, in a book about the Holocaust in American life that devotes nine pages to Arendt's *Eichmann in Jerusalem*. Since Novick labors so valiantly to defend Arendt's reputation but clearly fails to learn anything from Dawidowicz's example, a brief comparison may be in order.

Hannah Arendt remained wedded to a narrow conception of European Jewish life, which she enunciated in her essay, "The Jew as Pariah."[17] From its purview, she issued a sweeping indictment of the entire European Jewish leadership in wartime. As for Adolf Eichmann, he must have cut a banal figure indeed next to the demonically seductive Martin Heidegger, the philosopher and Nazi sympathizer who was Arendt's teacher and former lover. But none of this matters for Novick: to him Arendt represents the historian as gadfly, and in defending her he is defending his own left flank.

Lucy Dawidowicz, by contrast, spent half a lifetime researching and writing *The War Against the Jews, 1933-1945*, which—to repeat—Novick fails to mention. On the strength of this great book, she fully achieved the authority to speak to Americans, and to American Jews, about the Holocaust; in her, it is not too much to say, the scholar became the moral counterpart to the eyewitness. In the course of writing that book, moreover, Dawidowicz become a religiously observant Jew and a passionate defender of Israel. Perhaps that is why Novick declines to honor her, for to do so would cede something of the moral high ground that he is so determined to occupy with so much bluster.

IV

Despite the multiple deformations under which Novick labors, has he nevertheless stumbled onto an important point? Is there not something deeply troubling about an American Jewish community that has been spending exponentially more money erecting monuments to the dead than to educating its young, or about the proliferation of Holocaust courses that teach about the Jews only as a community marked for destruction, and then often in the context of a competition for victim status in today's multicultural America? There is, indeed. Nor has Novick been the only one to be troubled by this state of affairs.

But in this respect *The Holocaust in American Life* may in fact be a symptom of a subtle, and still largely unarticulated, shift in mood. What, after all, explains the huge success of the Oscar-winning escapist fantasy, *Life Is Beautiful*? Although the Italian comic Roberto Benigni may seem to make a strange bedfellow with the dour professor Peter Novick, each in his own way is urging us to bring closure, as it were, to the Holocaust, the one by means of zany antics and the mindless message that love and laughter will save a child from the hangman, the other by demystifying Jewish memory itself as nothing but a tool of Zionist politics.

Novick is also not wholly wrong in focusing on the pivotal role played by Zionism in the resurgence of Jewish collective memory in our day, though he is blind to the reciprocal nature of the dynamic. Jewish political sovereignty itself would never have been achieved in the land of Israel had it not been for Zionism's ability to appeal to such ancient and ineradicable Jewish archetypes as the ingathering of the exiles, Ezekiel's vision of the dry bones, and the tradition of *kiddush haShem*, the sanctification of God's Name through martyrdom. Nor would the campaign to free Soviet Jewry have succeeded in mobilizing the energies of hundreds of thousands of American Jewish youngsters without the powerful reverberations of the biblical injunction, "Let My People Go!," a more compelling slogan by far, incidentally, than "Never Again!" The airlift of Ethiopian Jews to Israel is similarly unimaginable in the absence of the sanction implied by the very name of "Operation Exodus."

It stands perfectly to reason, in other words, that American Jewish organizations should have drawn upon Israel and Zionism in their own efforts to forge a sense of a shared Jewish past, present, and future. The use—and abuse—of Holocaust memory forms part of a much larger mobilization of group memory for the sake of group survival. But what this means is that, as the power of the Zionist appeal wanes—and it is demonstrably waning—so, too, will the power of the Holocaust.

And then where will American Jews be? If they follow the instruction of Peter Novick, they will be good Americans—of his stripe—and they will be even more bereft of their own history and memory than they already are.

Notes

1.   Peter Novick, *The Holocaust in American Life* (Boston: Houghton Mifflin, 1999); also published as *The Holocaust and Collective Memory* (London: Bloomsbury, 2000).
2.   Ibid., 39-46.
3.   Ibid., 100.
4.   Ibid., 148. Novick concedes that "there were surprisingly few explicit references to the Holocaust in American Jewish mobilization on behalf of Israel before the war," yet he qualifies this admission with the speculation that "thoughts of a new Holocaust were surely present." No evidence is cited.
5.   Ibid., 176. "In recent years," he adds, "the ADL itself has been the primary catalyst of the attention black hustlers have received – and thus the dispensers of rewards for anti-Semitic trash talk." Ibid., 324, n19. Here he is asking us to believe that Jesse Jackson, Louis Farrakhan and Al Sharpton would have languished in obscurity, but for the paranoid attentions of the ADL. On the ravings of black antisemites, including political spokesmen, rap stars and academics, see Arch Puddington, "Black Anti-Semitism and How It Grows," *Commentary*, April 1994.
6.   Ibid., 133.
7.   Hannah Arendt, *Eichmann in Jerusalem: A Report on the Banality of Evil* (New York: Viking Press, 1963).
8.   *The Holocaust in American Life*, 137.
9.   Ibid., 134-35, 137-38.
10.   Ibid., 149.
11.   Ibid., 160.
12.   Ibid., 149.
13.   Ibid., 92.
14.   Lucy S. Dawidowicz, *The War Against the Jews, 1933-1945* (New York: Holt, Rinehart and Winston, 1975).
15.   *The Holocaust in American Life*, 151-53.
16.   Ibid., 256-57.
17.   See Hannah Arendt, *The Jew As Pariah: Jewish Identity and Politics in the Modern Age* (New York: Grove Press, 1978).

10

Daniel Boyarin and the Herd
of Independent Minds

Menachem Kellner

"One who separates himself from the community, even if he does not commit a transgression but only holds aloof from the congregation of Israel, does not fulfill religious precepts in common with his people, shows himself indifferent when they are in distress, does not observe their fasts, but goes his own way, as if he were one of the gentiles and did not belong to the Jewish people - such a person has no share in the world to come." — Maimonides, Laws of Repentance, *III*

We all trim our sails, consciously or unconsciously, to fit into our reference groups. This common psychological insight is nowhere truer than on college campuses. Academics pride themselves on having independent minds, but it is quite amazing how these independent minds manage to herd together, hunting in packs for all those who do not agree with the reigning orthodoxy of the moment. Even when this is not done consciously, like attracts like, and academic departments all across North America have achieved a remarkable level of internal ideological homogeneity.

It is against this background that we must understand Daniel Boyarin, professor of Talmud and hater of Israel.

Daniel Boyarin's self-involved and self-indulgent "Interrogate My Love"[1] begs for a reply which is equally self-involved and self-indulgent. I shall try to resist the temptation, but a certain amount of self-introduction cannot be avoided. Daniel Boyarin and I should have much in common. Born in 1946, we both grew up in the Shore Area of New Jersey (indeed, I went to day-school in his home town of Asbury Park and, for all I know, we were classmates). As adults, we both became scholars of Judaic studies and we both made aliyah. Indeed, Boyarin writes of himself a sentence which I could write about myself. Like Boyarin, I "occupy an 'orthodox'—or at least quite conventional—form of Jewish identification, belief and practice, but on the other hand, find myself driven to write a history that calls the very terms of that orthodox identity into question" (201). In Boyarin's case the history in question involves the relations between Judaism and Christianity two millennia ago; in my case, it involves the way in which Maimonides' adoption of Aristotelian categories of thought led him to concretize an orthodoxy I take to be at variance with the letter and spirit of rabbinic texts. But, despite all these similarities, Boyarin chose to become a potentially dangerous enemy of the Jews and of the Jewish State while I have been forced, over the last four years, to devote an inordinate amount of time and psychic energy defending the Jews and their state from the likes of Boyarin.

Why bother? Boyarin's early scholarship earned him an enviable reputation as a Talmudist and is likely to stand the test of time. His writing in recent years reflects the dreary trend towards political correctness, "theory," and "cultural studies" which so disfigures American academe and is likely to molder in libraries after the fads change. Why dignify his writings on Israel and Zionism with a reply, when they, too, are likely to sink like lead in the turgid waters poisoned by self-proclaimed progressives?

In order to explain why I bother to write this when I would so prefer to spend my time and energy reading medieval Jewish philosophers and writing about them, I must emulate Boyarin and talk about myself. If anyone had asked me a few years ago if I would accept an invitation to contribute a piece to a collection on Israel and Zionism edited by Edward Alexander, I would have said no, and emphatically at that. I grew up in a household in which it was clear that Jews simply did not do certain things: eat *treyf*, violate the Sabbath, cross picket lines or, God forbid, vote Republican. My late father, a Hungarian-born Orthodox rabbi, was an active Stevenson Democrat and enthusiastic Zionist. He died in the mid-1960s and I remember thinking, while protesting the Vietnam War in the 1970s, that his early death had at least spared him the sight of his son marching against the government of the country he so loved. One last comment about this background, which, perhaps, sums it all up: I wrote my Ph.D. dissertation under the direction of the late Steven Schwarzchild, professor of Judaic studies at Washington University in St Louis, devoted adherent of the philosophy of Hermann Cohen, and radical Jewish anti-Zionist, on "Civil Disobedience in Democracy: A Philosophical Justification." Steven tolerated me as a Zionist and I came to cherish him as a mentor despite our very different views.

Given this background it is no surprise that I gravitated to the moderate left end of the Israeli political spectrum after moving to Israel with my wife and children in 1980. I supported the "two-state" solution, never considered voting for a religious party, and usually found some grouping to the left of the Labor Party to support. There was even a time when members of the Haifa Meretz party sounded me—in my own eyes a garden variety modern Orthodox Jew - out about representing them on the Haifa religious council.

So of course I supported the Oslo accords, and dreamed of the day that I could board a train in Haifa and disembark in Paris. I read Edward Alexander and Ruth Wisse in *Commentary* with irritation. I participated in encounter groups with settler leaders as a leftist. I supported Rabin, z"l, and Peres, of course, disdained Bibi, and rejoiced when Barak defeated him. At Barak's victory celebration my friend, colleague, and fellow Orthodox leftist Avi Ravitzky stood next to the new prime minister on the podium. It seemed as if all my hopes and dreams might be coming true. Would that it had been so!

The Menachem Kellner of six years ago, thus, would have found much in common with Daniel Boyarin and certainly did not expect to be contributing an essay intensely critical of Boyarin to a volume edited by Edward Alexander. What changed? Why I am willing to invest energy in writing about a person whom I now deeply disdain?

First, the so-called "Al Aqsa Intifada" has slowly driven me to the realization that the Palestinian leadership (and so far as one can judge, the Palestinian "street") was using the war, not to reverse the results of 1967, but to reverse the results of 1948. The Palestinians were not seeking to create a Palestinian state next to a Jewish state. The debate is not over where to modify the 1948-1967 armistice line, but whether Israeli Jews will be allowed to stay in the new "state of all its citizens." It does not take much imagination to envision our lives in the "free and democratic" Palestine which is meant to replace Israel.

A second point relates to the world in which I grew up as opposed to the world in which I now live. It now appears that I spent the first half-century of my life in a bubble of time, a bubble unique in the history of the Jews over the last two millennia. Jew hatred, I was convinced, was a thing of the past. I disdained Menachem Begin's constant harping on the Holocaust and his regular attempts to paint the enemies of Israel as Nazi-like Jew-haters. After all, I reasoned, many of these people were convinced that they had good reasons to be our enemies. Their fight against us was over land, over national honor, over self-respect.

Facts on the ground have shown me to be wrong. Political and social forces with which I used to be allied, who call themselves "progressive," have proven themselves over and over again to be viciously and unthinkingly antisemitic. A hatred that I thought had died with Hitler and Stalin, a hatred I always associated with the forces of reaction and stupidity, has proven itself to be very much alive, and has found a home in precisely those precincts which should abhor it. Let me explain.

As a Jew, I strongly believe that I have an obligation to demand of Jews a higher moral standard than I demand of others. That, in a nutshell, is what the ancient prophets of Israel demanded. On the other hand, when non-Jews demand of Jews a higher moral standard than they demand of others, my antennae quiver with the vibrations of antisemitism. During recent years, they have been quivering non-stop. Israel has been subjected to a barrage of criticism (much of it based on the uncritical acceptance of false Palestinian propaganda, the most blatant, but hardly the only example being the Jenin "massacre" of April 2002) by the same people who view with apparent equanimity half a century of Chinese outrages in Tibet, horrific Russian crimes in Chechnya, not to mention the bombings in Israel.

To cite one example. A recent issue of the *London Review of Books* prominently featured an article by my colleague and erstwhile friend Ilan Pappe, calling for sanctions on Israel. The *London Review of Books*, and its sister publication, the *New York Review of Books*, have made the demolition of Israel as a Jewish state into a crusade. Of all the states created in the aftermath of World War II, only Israel must be destroyed. Of all the millions of refugees created in the aftermath of that war (including the miserable survivors of the concentration camps, called in Orwellian fashion, "displaced persons," and the million or so Jews forced to flee from Arab countries), only the Palestinian Arabs have been kept festering in refugee camps (by their Arab brethren and a callow UN) and only they must be allowed to return to the homes from which they fled. I cannot but see that crusade as an example of antisemitism: of all the peoples in the world, only the Jews have no right of self-determination? Further, can one imagine the *LRB* publishing a call by a Palestinian intellectual calling upon Europe to impose sanctions on the Palestinian Authority (a thuggish kleptocracy), or calling for sanctions against Hamas (an organization whose stated aim is the massacre of Israeli Jews and which regularly targets civilians)? Forget about the *LRB* publishing such a call. Can one imagine a Palestinian intellectual willing to make it? Further, by refusing to demand of Palestinian Arabs the same moral standards they demand of Israeli Jews, "progressive" forces appear to me to be treating the former as innately inferior, a people who cannot be held to strict moral standards.

In short, I have been dragged, kicking and screaming, to a number of realizations: Palestinians, by and large, want to see Israel destroyed; antisemitism is alive and well and has found a home, especially in Europe, not just among the unwashed masses, but among the washed and the perfumed.

People like Daniel Boyarin are deeply pained—rightfully so—by the suffering of Palestinians. But sacralizing that suffering, denying Israeli suffering, ignoring the fact that the "Al-Aksa Intifada" was the Palestinian response to Ehud Barak's attempts to make peace, all this gives aid and comfort to people who simply hate Jews, who want to see the Jewish state as such simply destroyed, and who apparently do not care too much what will happen to Israeli Jews after that destruction. The Palestinians declared war on Israel. Let me characterize that war in one sentence: every single Jewish kindergarten in Israel has and needs an armed guard; not a single Palestinian kindergarten has or needs an armed guard. Once again the Palestinians have started a war, lost it (thank God!), and now expect to be rewarded. Like many Israelis who have spent their adult lives calling for the establishment of a Palestinian state, I continue to do so, but now do so out of disgust for the Palestinian national movement, no longer out of sympathy for their national aspirations.

People like Daniel Boyarin are either knaves or fools; either way they are dangerous and cannot be ignored. What do they want? Boyarin is not in the business, at least not in his article "Interrogate My Love," of making concrete proposals. It is clear that he opposes the "fetishizing of borders and boundaries" (204). From this I understand that he supports some sort of binational state West of the River Jordan, a state called with touching naiveté by its Israeli supporters: *medinah shel kol ezraheha*—a state of all its citizens. Such a state, it is envisioned, would ignore the national and or religious identities of its citizens, treating them all alike. It would be neither Jewish nor Arab in national terms, neither Jewish, nor Muslim, nor Christian in religious terms. All citizens of this "United States of Palestine" would be entirely equal, with no particular culture or religion "privileged" or "hegemonic." How anyone in their right mind, be they Daniel Boyarin or Tony Judt, could believe that of all the countries of the Middle East only this mooted "state of all its citizens" would respect the rights of minorities (or of majorities for that matter) is beyond comprehension. People who hold this view are either cynical in the extreme or naïve in the extreme. In the former case they knowingly condemn my family and me to persecution and probable death; in the latter case they insouciantly and casually condemn us to the same fate. Either way they are dangerous people.

Boyarin presents himself as being out of step with his community, as being forced into a painful marginality by a Jewish orthodoxy which "has been redefined as including the unquestioning support for a political entity, the State of Israel, and all its martial adventures" (201). Not only is our poor hero marginalized in this fashion, but even the object of his love, Christianity, disappoints. He writes, he tells us, at a time (2003) "in which many Jews and many powerful Christians (millennial enemies) are suddenly strange bedfellows, collectively engaged in war/wars against Muslims. Ariel Sharon's war of ethnic cleansing against the Palestinians is applauded by fundamentalist Christians and American President George W. Bush's crusade against Iraq is cheered by most Jews in the name of a battle against Muslim terrorists" (201).

Let us look at these sentences. The first thing to strike the reader is Boyarin's apparent emotional distance from the State of Israel. For Boyarin it is a "political entity," not the fulfillment of Jewish national aspirations, not the fulfillment of millennial (not necessarily millenarian!) dreams, not the object of "the hope" of Israel through the generations, not even, one suspects, the "political entity" to which Boyarin and his family moved, presumably out of some sort of Zionist motivation. Just as lapsed Catholics often hate the Church with an unreasoning passion, Daniel Boyarin appears here as a lapsed Zionist, suffering from the same sort of neuroses which afflicts so many lapsed Catholics. Indeed, Boyarin defines himself as a "diasporic rabbinic Jew," apparently unaffected by the dreams of Zion of his "beloved rabbis" (who, I suspect, would happily dispense with his love).

I agree with Boyarin that Jews and evangelical Christians are strange bedfellows; politics as is well known makes for strange bedfellows, and the politics forced upon people by wars of survival even more so. But are we and the Christians strange bedfellows because we are millennial enemies? I find the expression symptomatic of much that is wrong with Daniel Boyarin. For close to two thousand years Christianity and many Christians have been enemies of Judaism and the Jews. But have Judaism and Jews been enemies of the Christians? The implied equivalence distorts the history of the two religions, and trivializes the deaths of so many Jews who were killed by Christians because the former were Jews and the latter Christians. How many Christians were killed by Jews during this period simply for the "sin" of being Christian?

According to Boyarin, Jews and powerful Christians are "collectively engaged in war/wars against Muslims." But, of course, if memory serves, it is Muslims who declared the war, on September 11. Whatever one thinks of the U.S. war against the Saddam Hussein regime in Iraq, it is hard to see it as a war against Muslims, per se. Boyarin further wants to equate America's war in Iraq with Israel's war against the Palestinian Authority. He knows as well as I do that the war between Israel and Palestine is a war of nationalities, not of religions. There are, of course, religious leaders and followers on both sides who paint the war in religious terms, but it hard to see Boyarin's *bête noire*, Ariel Sharon, and someone for whom he apparently has less hatred, Yasser Arafat, as motivated by religious concerns. Apparently, Boyarin the Jew, as opposed to Boyarin the scholar, wants to live in a simple universe, governed by simplistic (and false) equivalences: Sharon = Bush = evangelical Christians = hegemons vs freedom-loving Palestinian Arabs in particular and Muslims in general.

But all this malicious nonsense pales to insignificance next to the following, irresponsible, immoral, and evil sentence: "Ariel Sharon's war of ethnic cleansing against the Palestinians is applauded by fundamentalist Christians and American President George W. Bush's crusade against Iraq is cheered by most Jews in the name of a battle against Muslim terrorists."

Let us unpack this.

Ariel Sharon is the duly elected leader of Israel. If Israel is fighting a war, it is not Sharon's war, but Israel's war. To imply otherwise is to say that Israeli leaders are dictators, not responsible to their electorate, and hence to remove responsibility from that electorate for the actions of their leaders. It also seeks to give the impression that Sharon leads a regime, or clique, or otherwise less than legitimate government.

Ariel Sharon is the prime minister of Israel instead of Ehud Barak because of the actions of one evil man, Yasser Arafat, and his kleptocratic, thuggish henchmen. Were it not for Arafat, Barak would, it is very likely, still be our prime minister, the State of Palestine would already exist or virtually exist and thousands of Israeli Jews and Palestinian Arabs would still be alive, and many thousands of maimed would be whole. To write of "Sharon's war" instead of "Arafat's war" is to distort history and to ally oneself with the aggressor.

What sort of war is Sharon alleged to be waging? A war of "ethnic cleansing." In making this maliciously false and preposterous claim Boyarin shows his true colors, allying himself with the enemies of truth and decency who in this case are also the enemies of Israel. The Oxford English Dictionary defines "ethnic cleansing" as "the purging, by mass expulsion or killing, of one ethnic or religious group by another, esp. from an area of former cohabitation." There is not a single politician in Israel who advocates the purging, by expulsion or killing, of Arabs from Israel proper or the West Bank and Gaza. Even the late Rehavam Ze'evi (murdered in his Jerusalem hotel room by Boyarin's friends), advocate of "transfer," always spoke in terms of a negotiated agreement whereby Palestinian Arabs would relinquish their homes in return for financial incentives. One can think that Ze'evi lived in cloud-cuckoo land, one can deplore the paternalism inherent in the notion that Palestinian Arabs would sell what they consider their patrimony for a mess of pottage, but what one cannot do is ignore the fact that Sharon and the overwhelmingly vast majority of Israeli Jews opposed these ideas as immoral and/or unworkable. By talking of "Sharon's war of ethnic cleansing" Boyarin paints Ariel Sharon in the colors we all associate with Slobodan Milosevic.

Boyarin used to live in Israel. I find it incredible that anyone who knows Israeli society could entertain for a moment the idea that Israel would ever treat innocent human beings like waste products that need to be disposed of. That fantasy is a perverse hallucination with no connection to reality; that should be clear based on Israel's long record of trying to distinguish between innocent civilians and the murderous terrorists who use them as shields.

But, morality aside, can any person moderately in touch with the real world actually believe that even if it wanted to, any Israeli government could actually succeed in expelling hundreds of thousands of Palestinians from their homes? No one who knows Israel at all could take this seriously. Even if half the Jewish population of the country supported such a move (which is very, very far from the case) the other half (myself included) would oppose it so strenuously as to make it impossible to implement. Has Boyarin given any thought to the logistical problems involved? Let us say that all Israeli Jews supported the idea, does he seriously think that it is practically possible? Let us give it some thought—how many trucks would it take? How many soldiers to enforce it? How many police to keep "*yefeh nefesh*" such as me from blocking it?

Boyarin will no doubt reply that I am being too literal, that he uses the expression "ethnic cleansing" as a euphemism for a harsh war of conquest and dispossession. Let us grant him that linguistic sloppiness. The war is certainly harsh, but it certainly was not our idea to start it, and if anyone should be accused of a harsh war of conquest and dispossession it should be the Palestinians, who applaud the murderers of children, and very many of whom quite literally want to drive the Israeli Jews into the sea.

But to accept this is to give Boyarin too much credit. It is to ignore the lessons of Orwell's essay on politics and the English language and of the whole miserable twentieth century. Words kill. Boyarin's irresponsible words will be used by the enemies of his children, of his parents, of his siblings, of his cousins, of his nephews and nieces, of any and all Jews to justify their murder. Boyarin's shameful use of the expression "ethnic cleansing" constitutes a blood libel in the clearest and most non-euphemistic sense of that chilling term. He libels Jews as bloody-minded and bloody-handed killers of Arabs, inviting the bloody murder and maiming of Jews. Were this not a common, every-day occurrence here in Israel (and, one fears, elsewhere as well), were not "progressive" forces around the world singling out every Israeli sin, real and imagined, for instant, blanket condemnation while ignoring the many greater and all-too-real sins committed by Israel's enemies, and by tyrants around the globe, were not these "same" progressive forces not seeking to turn the Jewish state into what individual Jews used to be, a pariah among the nations, one could shake one's head pityingly at Boyarin. Sadly, the world is too dangerous to allow us this languid response.

The sentences just analyzed are not the worst in this shameful article. Boyarin sees his Judaism "morally disintegrating before" his eyes because of the "violent actions taken in the name of defense" at places he calls Nablus (not Shechem), Beteen (not Beth-El) and al-Khalil (not Hebron); his Judaism, he says in the most obscene sentence in this dreadful screed, may be dying in those places, just as many Christians felt that "Christianity died at Auschwitz, Treblinka, and Sobibor" (202). Nablus and Auschwitz; Beth-El and Treblinka; Hebron and Sobibor: what more could any Holocaust denier want?

How can we account for Professor Daniel Boyarin and people like him? It is ludicrous to accuse him of simple (or even complex) antisemitism; it is equally ludicrous in my eyes to dismiss him as a self-hating Jew. He is certainly not stupid; he is not even misinformed about events in the Middle East. Yet this man joins anti-Israel demonstrations (sponsored by apologists for murder), off-handedly accuses Israel of crimes neither contemplated nor committed, and casually compares Israel's efforts at self-defense with the Nazi Holocaust. How can we account for Professor Daniel Boyarin and people like him?

I shall permit myself a schematic presentation of what is admittedly a more complex (if often not very attractive) phenomenon, one that has been traced by far more competent hands than mine. The program of "multiculturalism" has made major contributions towards opening up a curriculum which used to focus on "dead white European males" and in so doing has enriched scholarship and education. But all too often it brought with it a sense of guilt on the part of "living white European males." The equations "Western = bad, non-Western = good," and "Enlightenment values = bad, all others = good," coupled with a pernicious moral relativism, have come to dominate the thinking (actually, I believe, not the thinking, but the gut reactions) of far too many otherwise smart, talented, and widely read people.

Israel takes pride in its Western Enlightenment values; Israel is a functioning democracy, as democracy is defined in the West. Israel is thus part of the "domineering, hegemonic, West"; by definition, according to this reigning orthodoxy, its enemies must be purer.

In such a climate I am not sure it takes a lot of courage to espouse the sorts of views which Boyarin and his friends advocate. In the world of academe, being an apologist for suicide bombers and other terrorist murderers opens many doors. Jewish academics in particular can congratulate themselves on their open-mindedness, on their universal values, and bask in glorious self-congratulation for their "brave" stance against the "fascists" in Israel. Moreover, Boyarin, who is so upset about being marginalized in the Jewish community (even as he seeks to marginalize Israel in the world community), must see the prospect of being marginalized by his academic peers as too painful to bear.

Daniel Boyarin is driven to batter down barriers, most notably between male and female,[2] and between Judaism and Christianity. In this he is a true deconstructonist. The destruction of such barriers, when carried out in the world of ideas, can be fruitful and enlightening. Boyarin, with the reckless irresponsibility so typical of intellectuals, wants to tear down barriers which protect living, breathing human beings from those who seek to murder them. For shame.

There also appears to be a very personal issue here. Boyarin thinks that he is called a *min*, sectarian, monster (in the literal sense of the term, a creature combining the elements of more than one form) by Judaism and Christianity. Lashing out against his perceived tormentors, he identifies with another group excluded, he claims, by the world dominated by Jews and Christians, namely the Muslim fundamentalists in general and Palestinian suicide bombers in particular. In seeking to protect himself from his own mythical monsters, he wants to expose my children to real monsters. For shame.[3]

Notes

1. Daniel Boyarin, "Interrogate My Love," in *Wrestling with Zion: Progressive Jewish-American Responses to the Israeli-Palestinian Conflict,* ed. Tony Kushner and Alisa Solomon (New York: Grove Press, 2003), 198-204. All quotations from Boyarin will be drawn from this essay. A revised version of the essay appeared as a preface to Boyarin's *Border Lines: The Partition of Judaeo-Christianity* (Philadelphia: University of Pennsylvania Press, 2004).
2. Boyarin, never shy, calls himself "oddly gendered" and in much of his recent writing has sought to replace the "muscular" Judaism of Zionism with a feminized Judaism that he finds in rabbinic texts.
3. I would like to thank Jolene S. Kellner and Tyra Lieberman for their very valuable help in improving this essay.

11

Marc Ellis: The Torah as a Suicide Pact

Alan Mittleman

Unlike the other authors considered in this volume, Marc Ellis writes exclusively as a theologian. In this he has achieved a certain celebrity, traveling the world to argue against the legitimacy of Israel and declare the moral vacuity of contemporary Judaism. His jeremiads are based on a presumptive prophetic critique of "state power" and its craven religious legitimation. Ellis sees himself as the last Jew standing, the sole moral voice crying in the wilderness of a people's mass dereliction of conscience. Contemporary Judaism is trapped in a cycle of self-congratulatory "innocence" and delusional, immoral "redemption." The memory of the Holocaust is cynically manipulated by Jewish elites as a moral club with which to silence their opponents, while the wicked enchantment with the State of Israel—born in unforgivable sin against the Palestinians—corrupts the legitimate recollection of the Holocaust. Contemporary Judaism has become a pernicious pseudo-Judaism, a "Constantinian Judaism," as Ellis styles it, feigning victimhood while celebrating a state power and militarization that mimics Nazism.[1] Indeed, in Ellis' portentous prose the Jewish state often sinks to the level of Nazi Germany.[2]

Judaism has reached its end and its last men and women of conscience must go into exile and form a new moral diaspora in which the covenant, first enacted by the prophets, can be reborn. The principal focus of this new, salvific covenant will be—glossing (and rejecting) Emil Fackenheim—a 615th commandment, "Thou shalt not lessen the humanity of Palestinians."[3] Given the gravity of Jewish criminality against that people, no "peace" process (often in quotation marks) can suffice. Reconciliation requires transcending the fundamental flaw of modern Judaism, the State of Israel, which ought to be consigned to the dustbin of history. Precisely what should replace the Jewish state is left unclear although a "state of all its citizens," a secular binational democracy, seems to be the top contender.[4] Every expression of Judaism that does not lead to a radical abnegation of all that the majority of Jews consider constitutive and sane is bankrupt and complicit. Jewish history has reached its end. Persons of conscience should no longer choose to be ensconced in it; they must learn to "practice exile."[5]

That this is theology is undeniable but whether it should be considered Jewish theology is questionable. Ellis himself often questions the Jewish status or character of his work, sometimes calling for a new covenant community of post-Jews and post-Christians, of "exiles," to replace the old, compromised communities. His talk of the end of Jewish history suggests an eschatological anticipation: a new community of "exiles" will inaugurate a new covenant. At other points, he affirms his standing within the Jewish world as it is but insists on marginality, on living at the periphery, as the only morally defensible Jewish option. Although his works are largely repetitive (he says himself that his later books are only footnotes to *Toward a Jewish Theology of Liberation*) there does seem to be a drift away from the belief that his teaching can renew Judaism toward a belief that Judaism and the Jews are incorrigible. In a recent work—which begins with a narration of his nightmare that an Israeli soldier holds a gun to his head and shoots him—his weary disbelief in the possibility of radical Jewish change is palpable.[6] He praises the "courage" of those who, like the late British philosopher Gillian Rose, have converted to Christianity.[7] Although conversion to Christianity as such is not appealing to Ellis insofar as he finds similar problems of moral bankruptcy in it, the radical transgression of boundaries in favor of self-imposed exile has become his *raison d'être*.[8] It may be that he has withdrawn entirely from self-definition as a Jewish theologian by this point. It is not clear. It is likely the case that however much he has given up on the Jewish community he continues to struggle with his relation to the Jewish tradition. If so, then it is appropriate to begin with how Ellis defines that tradition, with what he understands Judaism to be. Ellis' radical and alienated judgments, I hope to show, are formed against a background of a one or at best two dimensional construction of Judaism.

The influences that loom largest in Ellis' thought, the intellectual prisms through which he views Judaism, are Holocaust theology and liberation theology. Much of his work consists of a repudiation of the former, along the lines indicated above, and an articulation of the latter. Other than Holocaust theology, Ellis does not appear to be conversant with older, richer sources of Jewish religious expression. His books are filled with expositions and criticisms of Elie Wiesel, Irving Greenberg, Emil Fackenheim, his teacher, Richard Rubenstein, and other Jewish theologians of the Holocaust but never with references to Bible—except through the lens of Christian liberation theology—or midrash, or Talmud, or medieval thought. The near exclusive focus on the Holocaust renders his approach to Judaism immediately sclerotic.

However different the various Holocaust theologians are in their theoretical approach to the Shoah, Ellis sees in them the common thread of neglect of the alleged Nazi-like behavior of the Jews in founding the State of Israel in 1948 and in maintaining it through constant expansionary war and occupation. With respect to the Holocaust, Ellis does not deny or diminish its enormity. He is, however, a constant critic of the uses to which its memory is put by Jewish theology and the vulgarization of that theology in public discourse and ceremony. The contribution of Holocaust memory to the maintenance of the presumption of Jewish innocence, despite complicity in the alleged crimes of Israel vis-à-vis the Palestinians, renders the memory per se corrupt.[9] The only way for the very memory of the Holocaust once again to acquire moral legitimacy is for it to issue into the embrace of the Palestinians, the confession of sin against them, the request for forgiveness from them, the sharing of the land and polity with them. Only acts of self-abnegating compassion in the present can redeem the memory of or discourse about the Holocaust from invidious politicization. Even these, however, would not be enough for us to atone for our sins.

The issue of the politicization of the Holocaust aside, one senses a deep ambivalence in Ellis as to the meta-political meanings of the Holocaust, as to whether there remains a residuum of truth, a non-political meaning, in Holocaust memory. On the one hand, the Holocaust is emblematic of Jewish history, which Ellis sees as subaltern, a history of genuine victimization and marginality. The Holocaust ought, therefore, to remind Jews of the true character of Judaism and the Jewish past. It ought to be the entryway into solidarity with the victimized and marginal of today, most especially the Palestinians. The Palestinian *nakba* (or Shoah-like catastrophe, i.e., the founding of the State of Israel), in defiance of the will of official Judaism's guardians of memory, must be included in the Holocaust's "liturgy of destruction." In this way, Jews could entertain once again the memory of the Holocaust with a cleaner conscience, redeem their future and identify with their past as a victim people.

On the other hand, the Holocaust seems to be entirely meaningless; an abyss so deep that no theology can explicate or redeem it.[10] This is both because the absence of God seems so total and because Ellis' proposed moral resolution of the Holocaust problematic, the possibility of embracing the Palestinians, of thereby truly finding meaning in the Holocaust experience, is so remote. The Holocaust represents then a caesura in the Jewish past, a barrier that blocks return to previous Jewish culture and experience. Jews cannot appropriate their pre-Auschwitz Judaism, nor can they dwell in the innocent martyrdom of the Holocaust, given their complicity in Israeli crime against another people, nor are they ready to break Auschwitz's "cycle of atrocity" which has led to "violence." In this way, Jews have run out of possibilities and Judaism and Jewish history have come to an end.

One senses here the lingering presence of his undergraduate teacher, Richard Rubenstein, who famously rejected the God of Israel and thereby Judaism as the only honest religious conclusion that one could draw from Auschwitz and, for all intents and purposes, left the Jewish community. Ellis' theological radicalism—however different in effect from Rubenstein's—nonetheless resembles his teacher's in extremity and audacity. Like Rubenstein, Ellis sees the theological resources of pre-Holocaust Judaism as more or less exhausted and no longer available. Like Rubenstein, Ellis is unafraid to pursue truth, as he sees it, wherever it may lead, even if it leads him out of the Jewish community and earns him its disapproval. (What better vindication of one's self-sacrificial fidelity to the truth than the contempt of philistines and chauvinists?) In both cases, there is a cautionary lesson to be drawn from an exclusive focus on the Holocaust. Taken alone, the Holocaust teaches us nothing and leads nowhere. Were Ellis able to draw on richer sources of the Jewish past he might not have painted himself into such a corner.

Still, as a persistent skeptic and inveterate questioner (when he is not strident or fulminating, Ellis seems constantly perplexed and adrift), Ellis cannot decide whether the Holocaust can bear meaning or is resistant to it. As indicated above, Ellis' preferred solution to this dilemma seems to be to subordinate the problem of theological meaning to a practical, moral response: seeking solidarity with the Palestinians, to the extent that this is possible. Visiting them, succoring them, arguing their case, fighting Israel and American Jewry's self-serving distortions and evasions, saying no to the presumptive Jewish acquiescence in the idolatries of state power can alone allow the Jews to live morally in the post-Auschwitz world. Where God was at Auschwitz can no longer be our problem. We must bring God into being now through initiating a post-Israel world; a world in which the Jews embrace their victims, the Palestinians, and share land and life with them: "... God has yet to exist for our time; our image of God is in the making."[11] Breaking the "cycle of atrocity and violence," the blindness to the harm Jews have inflicted on another people caused by their blinding obsession with their own victimhood, will offer a new basis for religious life in a post-Auschwitz, post-Israel world.

Ellis, reminiscent of Shabbtai Zvi, becomes alternately rhapsodic and depressed about this messianic possibility. If it could occur, it would be redemptive, a true moral future. But it is hardly likely that it will occur. Ellis, the religious visionary, seems in tension with Ellis the worldly critic of culture and politics. The best one can do is live truthfully, in anticipation of a coming kingdom as it were. This emphasis on living truth, as Ellis sees it, through pursuing justice, on praxis as the resolution of theological conundrums, derives from the other source of his theological formation, Christian liberation theology.

Liberation theology, which had its heyday in the 1970s and 1980s, has both Protestant and Catholic roots. Ellis has worked tirelessly to import it into Judaism although, with its relative decline among Christians, he too has sounded defeatist notes in the third edition of his *Toward a Jewish Theology of Liberation* (2004). The Vatican, especially in the persons of the current and former Pope, was severe in its criticism of liberation theology and disciplined some of its proponents, both vulgar (for example, Ernesto Cardinal, a priest who was the minister of culture in the Sandinista government in Nicaragua) and academic (for example, Friar Leonardo Boff of Brazil). The cynical reading (which Ellis readily endorses) of this Vatican rejection portrays the Catholic hierarchy as merely corrupt, unwilling to side with the poor and eager to maintain its support and privileged relationship with the power elites of Latin America. Some segments of the Church have "persecuted" the liberation theologians. The murder (or "martyrdom") of Maryknoll sisters in Guatemala is equated, in the often promiscuous way that Ellis uses language, with the "silencing" of the liberation theologians. ("Death to some, hence the increasing number of martyrs, and the silencing of others who have spoken."[12])

An impartial reading of the Vatican's 1984 *Instruction on Certain Aspects of the "Theology of Liberation,"* however, shows that the Church shares liberation theology's commitment to abolish the scandal of poverty. What the Vatican wanted to resist in liberation theology was its too uncritical adoption of Marxist ideology and its concurrence in class warfare. Although various liberation theologians took different stands on Marxism, and meant different things by Marxism, an essentially Marxist perspective informed the whole project.[13] Having experienced the results of Marxist analysis firsthand, the late Pope knew only too well where it led. The Church asserted that all, not only the rich, are guilty of sin and that repentance rather than revolutionary politics is the deepest answer to an evil such as poverty insofar as it is within human power to alleviate it. The Church remembered that it had its own beginnings in a struggle with rigid, Manichean dualisms represented by such heresies as Marcionism and Gnosticism. It is one thing to opt for the relief and dignity of the poor, as the Vatican counseled. It is another, as a matter of theological principle, to demonize the rich. The liberationist legacy of invidious dualism—where the humanity of those who are not-poor (such as affluent American Jews) or not-Palestinian (such as Jewish Israelis) is stiffly dismissed—runs deep in Ellis' own theology.

In addition to the reflexive moral denigration of those who are "empowered," Ellis derives from liberation theology a blinkered reading of the Hebrew Scriptures.[14] The Bible is read from the point of view of the disempowered and in solidarity with them. Much of scripture must therefore be written off as the religious aggrandizing of the rich and powerful. The usable core of scripture, the literary prophets, "grounds critiques of power and innocence and even provides the foundations of the monotheistic faith traditions." The prophets are the "most distinctive Jewish contribution to the world" and the very core of Judaism.[15] All that which is not prophecy, especially the legal traditions of the Torah, appears to be without worth in Ellis' theology. Religion is constantly about the business, then and now, of constraining the prophetic, blunting and diverting it into inimical ritual. Religion gives birth to holy radicalism and then strangles its child. The prophetic voice was and is in conflict with the very traditions that claim the prophets as their own. Those who would practice prophetic critique today can expect a treatment similar to what Jeremiah, if not Jesus, received.

What constitution of Judaism then arises from Ellis' theological orientation? First, Judaism's essential core is a prophetic critique of power and an astringent demand for justice, both within and among peoples. No polity is without sin; no social world lacks its downtrodden poor and overweening rich. Judaism is about the naming, exposing, and overthrowing of these inequities, all of which are occasioned by the always malignant state. Judaism is prophetic, which is to say anomian or antinomian. Although Judaism is not about law—rabbinic Judaism is an oppressive outgrowth of the ritualized stultification of prophetic Judaism—it is, secondly, about community. The covenant, a key biblical trope, engenders a community that means to practice prophetic justice. For some time, it seems, this covenant community was identical with the historic Jewish community. For two millennia, Jews were stateless, powerless, and innocent. As such, they were true heirs of the covenant. Ellis takes the Holocaust, the nadir of Jewish powerlessness and "marginality," as typical of all Jewish history. Jewish covenantalism, however, has come to an end with Jewish "empowerment" in the Israeli state and acquiescence in the status quo in the United States, whose immoral policies in Latin America and the Middle East mock the moral pretensions of those who associate with her. Whatever new covenantal community of exiles from Judaism (and Christianity) might form will lay claim to the biblical heritage of prophecy far more than its degenerate progeny, the Jewish people and the Church, do at present. Indeed, it is only in light of covenantal renewal that God can be said to exist. Although the prospects of such renewal are in no way assured—Ellis often sounds quite pessimistic about its chances—one must endure in the hope and work in love and fidelity. Fidelity, which does not mean faithfulness to the historic covenant of God with the Jews, indicates steadfastness in the way of critique despite bullying from the side of the American Jewish community and Israel. It is *hesed* against the historic *brit*, as it were. True Judaism, if such there be, is sectarian: an exilic, borderless, covenant community-in-formation of dissidents of conscience, the true Children of Light.

Some of these elements are familiar to students of Jewish thought and history. One thinks of the Qumran sectarians, of Paul, of Shabbtai Zvi. From an Orthodox or, broadly speaking, a normative point of view, these were heresies or heretics. From the decidedly secular point of view of the academy, these were all legitimately Jewish expressions of ideas, currents, cultural movements and responses to historical crises. So too, Ellis, by the inclusive standards of modern historicism, is as much a Jewish thinker as Soloveitchik or whomever one prefers. But if any normative criteria are in order, it is questionable whether Ellis can count as a Jewish thinker. He is most definitely a religious thinker but his religiosity is deeply problematic from a mainstream point of view—from what Ellis would refer to as the "center" of the religion. Issues of politics aside, consider the following theological objections.

Ellis professes to write out of concern for the moral future of the Jewish people but it is hard, if not impossible, to square this profession with the absence of *ahavat yisrael* (love for the Jewish people) in his writings. His pervasive critique of Jews, modern Judaism and Jewish thought is unrelieved by any expression of sympathy for the difficulties Jews face. The horrific acts of terrorism perpetrated by Palestinians, especially during the heyday of the second Intifada, to which he refers, in approving solidarity with the Palestinians, as the Al-Aksa Intifada, merit nary a mention in his recent writings while the atrocities alleged to have been committed by Israelis fill pages. Where he does refer to suicide bombers, he blandly includes them in a Palestinian resistance that he considers heroic. (This is also true of his attitude toward Americans. His response to 9/11: "In the wake of September 11, Americans feel a new sense of urgency about security and safety. But few ask how we as Americans contribute to the cycle of violence. Few Jews understand that the terror we feel has been felt by Palestinians for decades."[16]) It is possible to sympathize with the dilemmas Palestinians face, to resist demonizing them or, in the language of classical Judaism, to resist characterizing them as Amalek *and* to criticize them, as well as to show sympathy for Israelis. But such a stance ill accords with the Manicheanism of Ellis. For him, the putatively innocent are always innocent; the Jews, some of whom have blood on their hands, most of whom are fellow travelers, are always guilty. The gestures of sympathy toward Palestinians of the most liberal Jews, for example, the contributors to *Tikkun* magazine, or of the Israeli peace camp are mostly self-serving, tainted. To the extent that they envision the endurance, however reduced geographically, of an Israel alongside a Palestine, they inevitably perpetuate "the cycle of atrocity and violence." To the extent that the "Jewish renewal movement" wants to renew Judaism, it evades the decisive issue. The existence of Israel has consumed and perverted Judaism beyond redemption. Israel is the father of impurities from which all lesser moral deformities flow.

The absence of *ahavat yisrael*, of solidarity with Jews as they are here and now, would not be thought a deficit by Ellis. After all, had Amos, Hosea, or Jeremiah trimmed their sails out of the instincts of identification, they would not have made Judaism's "most distinctive contribution to the world." But Ellis is not Amos, Hosea, or Jeremiah. He does not speak in the name of God nor has God, prophecy being closed, chosen to speak through him. Ellis, like the Christian theologians of whom he is most enamored, is a prophet manqué. The Jewish thinkers who appropriated a prophetic modality for modern Judaism, whether the highly heterodox (Martin Buber) or the traditional (Abraham Joshua Heschel), continued to identify themselves, passionately, with the Jewish people in the here and now. They did not violate Hillel's fundamental rule of Jewish solidarity and seek to "separate themselves from the congregation." Ellis writes from the vantage point of extreme estrangement, as if only the dissidents of conscience, the exiled denizens of the new diaspora, serve God. As if all Jews were not human, both loved and judged by their Creator.

Ellis' attempt to appropriate a prophetic Judaism—mediated by the scholarship of Protestant exegetes such as Walter Brueggeman and the liberation theologians, but never by recourse to the sources themselves—entirely avoids the rabbinic tradition, which is to say, historic Judaism. For the rabbis, prophecy represented an ambivalent inheritance. They accepted the inspiration of the prophets but subordinated it to Moses, whose teaching was definitive. Whenever prophetic revelation contravened Mosaic revelation, as in Ezekiel, the rabbis rejected it. (See, for example, Kimchi's comment on Ezekiel 43:25.) The prophets cannot innovate laws that contradict the rabbinic law (see B. Shabbat 104a). As Jerold Auerbach argued in *From Torah to Constitution*, American Jews designed an Americanized Judaism that was short on rabbinic law and long on Protestant-compatible prophetic moralism.[17] Ellis' Judaism, although diffident toward the bourgeois traditions of American Jewish coalescence, is nonetheless a direct descendant of this project. He has posited an ahistorical, wholly moralized Judaism, entirely focused on social and political critique, against which all other modes of belonging or believing are thought to be hollow shells or worse. Indeed, they are idols. Ellis is the lonely, albeit reluctant prophet in the midst of a nation of idolaters.

The rabbis subordinated prophetic revelation to their own access to the divine. They claimed to absorb and to neutralize prophecy, asserting that a "sage (*hakham*) is preferable to a prophet" (Baba Batra 12a-b). No doubt they feared, and properly so, the antinomian tendencies latent in claims of private revelation and social agitation. Did not his followers ascribe the mantle of prophecy to the man from Nazareth? The revival of prophet-like pretensions in the loosely connected communities of late modernity owes more to Protestantism than to Judaism. Jews should be wary of the easy claims to moral superiority made by tenured radicals who adopt the trappings of prophetic criticism. The moral and political dilemmas of our public life, both Jewish and general, are too complex to be solved by recourse to prophetic passion. It is, following Weber, irresponsible for genuine actors in public life to make their often painful and tragic decisions in foreign or public policy on the basis of black and white imperatives. I am not suggesting—far from it—an amoral utilitarianism as the basis for political decision. That would violate the consciences of the majority of people in democracies such as the U.S. or Israel. But those same majorities, however, understand that religious morality, especially one mediated by the moral absolutes of prophecy, cannot be squared in a simple manner with political decision. Why this lesson—that government is made for men not angels—so fundamental to the political science of American founders such as Madison, is lost on one whose credentials include his impressive self-description as University Professor of American and Jewish Studies at Baylor University is unclear.

Nor was this lesson lost on the biblical and rabbinic sources of Judaism. Ellis writes as if Judaism were always meta-political, never concerned with hard choices and tragic trade-offs in this world. Franz Rosenzweig, whose political theology was shaped by his massive study of Hegel, may be excused for his static, apolitical portrayal of Judaism in the *Star of Redemption*. But Ellis is not Rosenzweig. He sees contemporary Jews and Judaism as knee deep in politics, polluted by politics, and yet he holds up an entirely unrealistic standard for politics—the complete renunciation of national interest—as the only measure of a just politics. The historic Jewish community, marginal and victimized, apparently lived according to this standard. Only with the state, with the return to history, have Jews forfeited their pristine morality for a sinful compromise with the world. Does Ellis not know that Jewish communities lived, until rather recently in European history, under their own laws where they punished their own wrongdoers, sometimes, as in medieval Spain, by execution? Has he ever read, to cite one example, Maimonides' *Hilchot Hovel u'Mazzik* in the *Mishneh Torah* where we learn that a Jewish community is duty bound at any time and any place to execute, by extra-judicial means if necessary, anyone who intends to denounce the community to the gentile authorities? Does he not know that medieval communities taxed, disciplined, and excommunicated their members or engaged in state-like functions, such as prudent foreign policy with non-Jewish overlords or other Jewish communities? Does he not know that Jews were sometimes better off, which is to say, following David Biale, more power-ful than the masses of European peasants?[18] Jews survived in large measure because of their canniness in the sphere of politics, their prudent ability to adapt to different manners of regime and politics, making themselves useful to "the state." Jews survived by being able to puzzle out the dilemmas of the present armed with a subtle and dialectical moral-political tradition. All of this is eviscerated by appeals to prophetic absolutism and ill-informed invocations of a lachrymose and apolitical Jewish history. One of the ill effects of the focus on Holocaust theology, which Ellis repudiates for his own reasons but in whose thrall he nonetheless partially remains, is its presentation of Jews as absolutely powerless. Although true for the period of the Holocaust, it is wrong, as Biale has shown, to generalize this to the whole history of the diaspora. This was, ironically, a penchant of some early Zionist historians, the very thinkers from whom Ellis would most want to distance himself.

Ellis' utter lack of dialectic is what strikes the attentive reader as the most un-Jewish attribute of his writing. Contrast Ellis with the Israeli historian, Benny Morris, whose scholarship is analyzed by Efraim Karsh elsewhere in this book. Ellis relies heavily on Morris and other "new historians" for his account of the birth of Israel and the origins of the Palestinian refugee crisis. Morris' *The Birth of the Palestinian Refugee Problem: 1947-1949* is the best-known example of this revisionist literature. Yet in a remarkable 2004 interview with a reporter after the publication of his new book, Morris *justifies* alleged Israeli tactics during the War of Independence, going so far as to say that if he, Benny Morris, had been in Ben Gurion's shoes, he would have acted even more decisively.

Morris does not revel in war but he recognizes that necessary actions do not always have benign consequences. In political life, especially, right action cannot be governed by pure intentions but by judicious weighing of probable costs and benefits. Such a mentality is native to rabbinic Judaism, however foreign it is to Ellis.

Although Ellis has learned much from Christian liberation theology, he seems not to have absorbed anything from Catholic or Protestant political theology other than the one dimensional revolutionary moralism of the liberationists. Augustine, Aquinas, Luther, Calvin, and closer to home Courtney Murray or Niebuhr have no resonance in his work. In addition to the liberationist analysis, his perspective is shaped by his post-graduate experience of living in a Catholic Worker settlement in New York. The Catholic Worker movement, founded by Dorothy Day, was a lay Catholic renewal movement devoted to living among the urban poor in America, ministering, in a lay capacity, to the needs of impoverished people and engaging in political activism on their behalf. While undeniably valuable, such activity, due to its immediacy, precludes dispassionate theorizing on the causes of poverty, crime, or welfare dependence. So too with Ellis, one looks in vain for a developed political analysis of alternatives to his much maligned "nation-state." True, rampaging nationalism contributed to the debacle of two world wars and to the Nazi pathology. But it is not true that extreme nationalism is a necessary concomitant to the life of nations. Nor is it true that states—which come in more varieties than Ellis' reflexive usage "nation-state" admits—always put their power to malign uses. The Nazis would not have been defeated without the power and sacrifice of the United States, nor would the recent tsunami relief effort have been organized, nor would Ellis have a secure place to write his books without American government by the consent of the governed. This utter lack of appreciation for the positive dimensions of political life is part of the zero-sum mentality of liberation theology: the prosperity or power of some necessarily comes at the expense of the poverty and powerlessness of others. There is no engagement here with the problems of development, of political economy, of credible public and foreign policy options, only outrage, blame and contempt; "prophetic" rather than rational analysis. Nor is there any room for patriotism. American Jews are constantly faulted for their "assimilation" to American power, their becoming part of the "establishment." No trace of patriotism, however critical or sober, is allowed. Once again, Ellis positions himself on the alienated margins. Only there is conscience possible.

How does Ellis reconcile these extreme stances with the covenant, the theological foundation of Jewish community? Covenant plays a crucial role in biblical and Jewish thought. Ellis tries to make covenant foundational to his own thought as well. Covenant has a vertical dimension, signifying the compactual relationship of God with the Jewish people. The concept also has a robust political thrust; its horizontal dimension signifies the manner by which the Jews shaped their polity under God. When Hamilton, in the first Federalist, refers to societies founded through "reflection and choice" he alludes to this manner of founding a polity through agreement between free and equal individuals. The Bible, as the late Daniel Elazar tirelessly insisted, is the great document of political founding on the basis of "reflection and choice."

A covenantal polity, although it is non-hierarchical and non-centralized, does have boundaries, relatively clear markers of who is in and who is out, who is a *ben brit* (a member of the covenantal community), who is a *ger* or *toshav* (resident alien), and who is wholly excluded. Covenantal communities are founded on oaths, often enacted (and reenacted; covenant renewal is periodically required) in ceremonies among freely consenting individuals. Responsibilities are assumed, loyalty pledged, rights secured. These are not grants of a human sovereign, bills of privileges or rights, but human endowments (for man is made in the image of God) that human government, under ultimate divine governance, is intended to protect. Nonetheless, although universal, they are most fully exercised within the liberty of the covenantal community. Determining boundaries, as the Jews did when they renewed the covenant under Ezra during the Persian period (Nehemiah 8-10), is analogous to determining republican citizenship in a cognate political model.

Ellis, by contrast, has a horror of boundaries and, therefore, an entirely open, which is to say incoherent, concept of covenant.

> Though I have become more articulate about the covenant and its place in my life, I question where this covenant comes from. Where does it reside? By what name is it to be called? On Shabbat I find it within the Jewish tradition. When I sit Zen I find the covenant within silence. In Peru among the poor, I experience the covenant when God is called on to empower the people. When I think of the Catholic Worker movement, the covenant is palpable. In pictures I have seen of Jesus in breadlines among the poor, the covenant is invoked with an intensity that is haunting. Do I embrace the Jesus portrayed as a Christian? Or do I embrace the Jesus of the breadlines as a Jew?[19]

For Ellis covenant appears to be a mode of religious and moral experience, shorn of its particularity as solidarity with the Jewish people, service to God, and obedience to the Torah. "Here the answer is less important than the experience. Truth ceases to be a primary objective. Does the covenant propose a truth? Or is it an accompanying inner voice without destination or destiny? Perhaps the destiny is found within the path itself. In the covenant, endings are beginnings."[20] Covenant is an elusive journey of solidarity with a world of suffering peoples, especially with that people whose suffering is caused, entirely it appears, by the Jews. Covenant mediates brokenness and fragmentation, as Ellis identifies with the historical suffering of the Palestinians and others: "The suffering that has brought about the fragmentation I inherit is beyond words. It continues today in many countries and cultures. Still, within the horror, the journey continues. The covenant beckons and fidelity is called for."[21] But fidelity to what precisely? Not, as we have seen, to the historic covenant of identifiable community and specifiable responsibilities as understood by classical Judaism. Ellis excludes such a simplistic reference for the covenant:

> It is precisely in the brokenness that gratitude comes into view. I experience a power that sometimes overwhelms me. Sometimes the power is so subtle that I miss the experience. I often miss the overwhelming and subtle experience of gratitude because I seek to place it within *a framework that no longer exists. I seek to place a reality that is beyond naming into a historical naming*...[22] (Emphasis added)

Ellis has fidelity to a universal struggle in which the Jews, alas, are on the wrong side. His experience of the "covenant" cannot be confined within what Jews have understood the covenant to be. He goes on to valorize the religious insights and lives of various liberation theologians, dissident Jews, Jesus, Buddha, and others, affirming their inclusion in his expansive conception of covenant. "Should I be denied their insights and struggle?" he asks rhetorically. "By denying them I diminish my own sensitivity to others around me. I diminish my own struggle to be faithful."[23]

Perhaps the most dramatic example of this exilic "struggle to be faithful" is Ellis' recounting of a lecture that he gave at Union Theological Seminary in Manhattan on Yom Kippur. Ellis was invited to give a lecture at Union by the black liberation theologian, James Cone. Through a fluke of scheduling, it was slated for Yom Kippur.[24] Ellis' decision to go ahead with the lecture gives rise to an extended reflection on the vapidity and false consciousness of American Jewish observance, the pernicious "deal" cut by liberal Protestantism to pursue dialogue with Jews at the expense of honesty about Israel (as if liberal Protestant bodies, such as the Presbyterian Church USA, have been friends of Israel!), and the moral superiority of his own "public confession" of Jewish sin at Union Seminary vis-à-vis the formal rituals of confession that other Jews are practicing in their synagogues. As Ellis stands at Union, he looks out across the street to the Jewish Theological Seminary, and offers a dismissive analysis of American Jewish rabbinic leadership:

> Trained in the texts of the traditions and the ability to guide congregations largely ignorant of those texts, Jewish seminary students are a bridge between the Jewish tradition and their congregants who are busy pursuing life in a Christian and secular America. In public, outside of the synagogue, the new rabbis, like many of the more experienced ones, act simply to deflect critical public discussion on Israel. They enforce a silence on Christians who want to speak publicly. Dissenting Jews are also silenced. Since critical discussion on the central issues facing Jews is largely absent in the core curriculum of the seminary, how could one expect rabbis to speak intelligently on these issues?[25]

Since Ellis spends Yom Kippur lecturing at a Christian seminary it is unclear how he knows what happens in synagogues. How does he know, for example, that "If Palestinians are mentioned at all on Yom Kippur it is in the framework of terrorism," or that "Yom Kippur sermons often demonized the Palestinians"?

As he observes the Jewish Theological Seminary, he reflects that the rabbinical students, who have fanned out across the country to serve congregations, will give "predictable" sermons: "Few of these future leaders of the Jewish community would risk themselves in speaking the confession that resides at the heart of Jewish life."[26]

That confession, of course, is not the traditional liturgical confession of sins against other human beings and God, but against the Palestinians. Ellis takes it upon himself to make that confession in public:

> As a people, we have never confessed to the Palestinians on Yom Kippur or any other day of the year. In the synagogues, the rabbis are silent. Those who want to voice this confession are not invited to speak. Even if allowed to speak in the synagogue, however, is that enough?... A confession among Jews... is not enough. The confession has to be public, outside of the synagogue, where all can hear, including Palestinians. That is how I thought of my lecture that evening at Union.[27]

Ellis admits that, from the perspective of the Jewish community, his act was a violation of, not exactly Judaism, but of "the Jewishness we embrace in America." Yet, it had to be done. The rituals of Yom Kippur are broken and redolent with false consciousness. They have become "a place of hiding rather than confrontation, a place of safety rather than risk."[28]

After the lecture, one of the Christian participants, a Catholic professor who is actively engaged in Jewish-Christian dialogue, questioned whether Ellis had undermined his message by the public violation of Yom Kippur. She counseled him to remain within the Jewish community.[29] Ellis responds by expatiating on the artificiality of the boundary between Judaism and Christianity, as well as the exhaustion of both of these traditions. Jews, Christians, and others must surmount their traditions and engender a new covenantal solidarity. Judaism has come to a "dead end." "Unable to admit the end, the future is being created without acknowledgement."[30]

> For those who can no longer avert their eyes [from the crisis engendered by Israel— A.M.], what religion and ritual is left for them? If they do not seek another religion and ritual, as if they could in this way avoid the fate of the religions they come from, where do those who travel the diaspora turn? Their particularities have come to a dead end. Does the argument for its core realization [i.e., attempts to renew Judaism or Christianity—A.M.] simply prolong the agony and destination that is clear?[31]

In this sense, the Torah for Marc Ellis has become, with apologies to Justice Jackson, a suicide pact. Ellis' Judaism is an astringent, self-abnegating moralism. It is Paul's curse of the law minus the offer of Christian salvation. Judaism, like Dante's inferno, requires the placard "Abandon all hope, you who enter here." There is a misty anticipation of a radical new birth, an eschatological event, but this will not be a renewal of God's covenant with the Jews. It will be a new covenant of exiles. It will be a new God. Perhaps the old one, like the god of the Gnostics, created too dark and impure a world to be worthy of worship by the children of light.

In what way then can Ellis continue to be considered a Jewish theologian? Why do prominent Jewish theologians commend his work to us in endorsements of the third edition of *Toward a Jewish Theology of Liberation*? Marc Ellis, for reasons known only to himself and his therapist if he has one, has turned from any credible Jewish religious path into the way of a Jewish masochism, brooding on every torment that can afflict the Jewish people while taking no part in its solace and support. He has given himself over to an idée fixe and let it consume his Jewish world. The Torah, we are told by Scripture, is a Torah of life. How odd and sad that a "Jewish theologian" in our day should cling to the Torah of death.

Notes

1.   Marc H. Ellis, *Israel and Palestine Out of the Ashes: The Search for Jewish Identity in the Twenty-First Century* (London: Pluto Press, 2002), 70. The equation of contemporary Judaism with the Christianity of Constantine, in addition to calling attention to the putative unholy marriage of religion and power, also equates Judaism with heresy hunting and state-sponsored religious persecution. Ellis often laments his own and other dissenters' alleged persecution at the hands of mainstream Jewish opinion.

2.   Consider, for example:

> Were the Palestinians [during the first intifada - A.M.] being crushed by soldiers that hate? Was this a Jewish payback for what had happened to us in another place and time? Male assertion where before we were emasculated? These reasons could account for the humiliation that was meted out by the soldiers. Reports abounded of the stripping of Palestinian males in the public view, knocking on the doors to force the elderly to wash away the graffiti of the uprising, searching homes and bodies without dignity or restraint. I met Palestinians who had been tortured by Jewish soldiers. Their physical and psychological scars were visible. Some Palestinians appealed to me, questioned Jewish innocence, and sometimes compared Israelis to Nazis. I could only observe and listen.

> —In Marc H. Ellis, *Practicing Exile: The Religious Odyssey of an American Jew* (Minneapolis: Fortress Press, 2002), 105. Ellis' general approach is to cite, with implicit approval, the writings of others who explicitly compare Israel with Nazi Germany or Israeli behavior with Nazi actions. These others include inter alia William Zuckerman, Noam Chomsky, Roberta Strauss Feuerlicht, Israel Shahak. See especially references to "Nazis; Israelis likened to" in the index of Marc H. Ellis, *Toward a Jewish Theology of Liberation: The Challenge of the Twenty First Century*, third edition (Waco: Baylor University Press, 2004). On the alleged similarity of Israeli medical personnel to Josef Mengele, see the story recounted in Ellis, *Israel and Palestine Out of the Ashes*, 39.

3.   Ellis, *Israel and Palestine Out of the Ashes*, 33-41.
4.   As much as it would have been to everyone's benefit had the State of Israel not come into existence, it does not appear to Ellis that it will soon pass out of existence. Rather, he envisions an eventual transformation of Israel into a new Jewish and Palestinian amalgam that will fit naturally into the region's ancient cycle of invasion, displacement, and indigenization. Thus, a grudging acceptance of the "facts on the ground," despite a moral disapproval of them:

Jews who suggest that the recent settlements that comprise the state of Israel represent a return to the land where the Jewish people originated are not far off, once the cycle of settlers and indigenous people is understood. This is quite different from the claim of some Jews that the land once settled by Jews millennia ago is by right for Jews only. The sin of twentieth century Jewish settlements is less the desire or need for space and some form of autonomy than it is the uprooting and domination of the Palestinians inhabiting the land… Needed here is less the reversal of the last fifty years, an impossibility in any case, and more a vision that sees the recent history of Europe and the Middle East as time-bound and fleeting… The cycle of violence and dislocation should be transformed into the struggle for equal rights within a common political destiny. Here citizenship—the recognition of a place within a democratic social and political culture that is bound to neither ethnic nor religious identity —is crucial.

—In Ellis, *Israel and Palestine Out of the Ashes*, 77. Ellis' endorsement of citizenship identity as a panacea to Jewish nationalism, ethno-religious conflict etc. is in tension with his overall dismissive attitude toward the United States, which one would think is the most successful model for what he advocates.

5.   In his words:

> In the displacement, torture and murder of Palestinians, in the sealing of the borders that makes permanent loss and exclusion, the center of Jewish history has been turned inside out and gutted. A Jew in exile knows this at the deepest level of his being. The attempt to renew that history is a return to a false innocence and redemption contradicted by the details of history. Solidarity with the Palestinian people cannot restore that history as though we can move back in time. Nor can solidarity transcend this history, as though a new social order absolves us of past mistakes. Solidarity recognizes that Jewish history *as we have known and inherited it* is over. Those in exile embody this ending. But they also point toward and embody a new history and identity that one day will come into being.

Ellis, *Practicing Exile*, 35-36 (emphasis in the original). Ellis introduces an eschatological theme. Dissident Jews, such as himself, are a saving remnant, anticipating a new order of justice and peace in time to come.

6.   Ellis professes to have dreamt that he was called before a commission of former Israeli prime ministers, along with such worthies as Hannah Arendt, Judah Magnes, Martin Buber, Gershom Scholem and Albert Einstein, to testify to the moral betrayal of Israel. After his testimony on the need to repent before the Palestinian people, "an Israeli military guard entered the room. He approached and told me that the prime ministers had concluded their deliberations. The guard pulled out his revolver, placed it at my temple, and pulled the trigger." The dream gun, he assures us, was not loaded. As if his imaginary self-insertion in such a company were not enough, Ellis lightly castigates himself: "It was naïve of me to think that Israel would respond differently to my critique than any other nation would. Does moral persuasion override the imperatives of power?" Whatever else one can say about Professor Ellis, he does not seem to suffer from a lack of self-esteem. See Ellis, *Practicing Exile*, 21-22, 27.

7.   Ellis, *Practicing Exile*, 80. "This great philosopher had crossed a boundary that few Jews had the inclination or courage to cross."

8.   Thus:

A tension surfaced between my call for Jewish accountability and the fact that even progressive Jewish voices were caught in a cycle they would not end. When the very presence of Palestinians is offensive, then the dream of Zion is a nightmare. The dreams of Jews within that nightmare can only reflect that sensibility and, in my case, the dream is one of diaspora and exile. I, with other Jews, will find my way among others, until a new path is found. Whether that way will be identifiably Jewish or not is open to question. Still the warnings are clear. The language of Jewish tradition cannot make this transition. Those like myself who attempt this are doomed to failure.

This seems to be the credo of one who has given up on Judaism as it is and holds out little hope for a sufficiently radical renewal. Ellis, *Practicing Exile*, 134.

9.   See, e.g., a typically turgid expression in Ellis, *Israel and Palestine Out of the Ashes*, 56:

If memorialization is defined as the essence of what it means to be Jewish, and if the connection between memorialization and the creation of new victims is central to the contemporary Jewish exile, I fear the gaps between Jewish groups can only widen in the years ahead. Over time, and with the extension of state power, the memory of suffering loses its depth and becomes superficial in its liturgical aspects. By embracing the power of the state to memorialize the victims in America and by shielding Israel from the most obvious scrutiny, the memory of those who suffered is increasingly trivialized. I find it strange that I am sometimes accused of trivializing the Holocaust because of my support of the Palestinians. The opposite is the case. *The trivialization of the memory of the Holocaust victims and the marginalization of the Jewish exile are two aspects of the same process.*" (emphasis in the original)

This passage neatly analogizes the suffering of Jews in the Holocaust and the "marginalization" of Jewish dissidents ("exiles") such as Ellis. The reader can be excused for sensing more than a little trivialization here.

10.   Ellis, *Practicing Exile*, 58:

So, too, with the question of God, like the debate about meaning in suffering. I find the memory of God's presence and the absence of God in the Holocaust an unresolvable problem. Still I find it difficult to see how the next stage of the journey can arise when the memories of suffering and God are used to inflict injury on another people. Militarizing memory and God can only further distance us from the healing and presence that time, confession and reconciliation may offer. I wonder if in carrying the memory of suffering and God into exile, the exile offers the possibility of healing and reconciliation as a way out of a cycle that promises little but pain.

11.   Ellis, *Practicing Exile*, 150.
12.   Ibid., 101
13.   For a critical but sometimes appreciative appraisal of liberation theology, see Michael Novak, *Will it liberate? Questions about Liberation Theology* (Mahwah: Paulist Press, 1986) , 27
14.   While liberation theologians seek to empower the people with whom they identify, Ellis seeks to disempower the Jews. This point was made in an earlier critique of Ellis' use of liberation theology by Erich and Rael Jean Isaac, "A Kaddish for Liberation Theology?", *Conservative Judaism*, Volume, Spring 1993, 56-58.

15. Ellis, *Israel and Palestine: Out of the Ashes*, 12.
16. Ellis, *Practicing Exile*, x.
17. Jerold S. Auerbach, *Rabbis and Lawyers: The Journey from Torah to Constitution* (Bloomington: Indiana University Press, 1990), 66-67. For a useful compendium of rabbinic texts on prophecy that exemplify this ambivalence see Michael Walzer et al, *The Jewish Political Tradition*, (New Haven: Yale University Press, 2000), I, 257-273..
18. David Biale, *Power and Powerlessness in Jewish History* (New York: Schocken Books, 1986).
19. Ellis, *Practicing Exile*, 16-17.
20. Ibid., 17.
21. Ibid.
22. Ibid.
23. Ibid., 19.
24. Ibid., 123.
25. Ibid., 120-21. Ellis is unaware that the Jewish Theological Seminary, which he ignorantly refers to as "Jewish Theological," a locution used by no one, hosts Israeli speakers and visiting scholars from across the political spectrum, sponsors student discussions where perspectives not dissimilar to his own are advocated, etc. His willingness to express unscholarly hyperbolic generalizations is by no means limited to rather minor points such as these. He presents himself as a knowing insider, so as to give his faux-heroic option for exile a presumptive authenticity.
26. Ibid., 123-124.
27. Ibid., 124.
28. Ibid.
29. This recalls the event at Union half a century ago when Will Herberg approached Prof. Reinhold Niebuhr to inquire into conversion to Christianity. Niebuhr counseled Herberg to go across the street to JTS and learn Judaism. The result was happier in Herberg's case than in Ellis'.
30. Ibid., 131.
31. Ibid., 130.

12

Antisemitism-Denial: The Berkeley School

Edward Alexander

"I have to be here. Berkeley is the center of the world-historical spirit."
—*Michael Lerner*[1]

"No, It's Not Antisemitic": Judith Butler vs. Lawrence Summers

Few contemporary literary critics have placed so much emphasis on the power of language as Judith Butler, professor of rhetoric and literature at the University of California at Berkeley. She has insisted that "Language plays an important role in shaping and attuning our common or 'natural' understanding of social and political realities."[2] Invoking Marxist thinkers, she has asserted that critics of "postmodern" style understand "only the word coined by commerce," the "commodified" truisms of the capitalist system.

It is against this background of Butler's intensely political approach to language as well as her general attitude (often complained of by other feminists) that linguistic gestures are an adequate substitute for, if not actually a form of, political action, that we should examine her recent forays into the campus struggles against Israel.

Prior to the autumn of 2003 she was, like many members of Berkeley's "progressive" Jewish community with which she habitually identifies herself, somebody who defined her "Jewishness" (not exactly Judaism) in opposition to the State of Israel. She was mainly a signer of petitions harshly critical of the Jewish state. She was, for example, one of the 3,700 American Jews opposed to "occupation" (Israeli, not Syrian or Chinese or any other) who signed an "Open Letter" urging the American government to cut financial aid to Israel; later she expressed misgiving about signing that particular petition — it "was not nearly strong enough... it did not call for the end of Zionism."[3] In autumn of 2002 she requested honorary membership in the Campus Watch organization's listing of Middle East specialists polemicizing in their classrooms on behalf of radical Islam and against Israel and America. In June 2003, her name could be found on the ubiquitous "Stop the Wall Immediately" petition. The wall, signatories alleged, was "supposed to block 'terrorist attacks' but certainly won't prevent missiles and helicopters from hitting their human target." Suicide bombings, lynchings, pogroms, and roadside shootings were not terrorist attacks but only "terrorist attacks," whereas Israeli response to those so-called "terrorist attacks" injured real human targets.

But deeper currents were also stirring in Butler. She had undertaken some research into the history of Zionism and discovered that there had been "debates among Jews throughout the 19th and early 20th centuries as to whether Zionism ought to become the basis of a state."[4] From this she swiftly concluded that demanding an end to Zionism in 2003, that is, calling for politicide, was no different from taking a debater's position against Zionism fifty years before the state existed.

By August 2003, Butler was belatedly moved to a classic utterance by a speech given at Harvard a year earlier, a speech that touched in her a raw nerve of anger that not even Ariel Sharon's attempts to keep suicide bombers from blowing up Israelis had been able to inflame. Lawrence H. Summers, Harvard's president, delivered to the Harvard community on September 20, 2002 a speech deploring the upsurge of antisemitism in many parts of the globe: he included synagogue bombings, physical assaults on Jews, desecration of Jewish holy places, and (this with special emphasis) denial of the right of "the Jewish state to exist." But his most immediate concern was that "at Harvard and... universities across the country" faculty-initiated petitions were calling "for the University to single out Israel among all nations as the lone country where it is inappropriate for any part of the university's endowment to be invested."[5]

One of the Harvard faculty, Ruth Wisse, described the divestment petition as "corrupt and cowardly" in offering its reasons for calling on the U. S. government to stop military aid and arms sales to Israel and upon universities to divest both from Israel and from American companies selling arms to Israel. "The petition," wrote Wisse, "requires that Israel comply with certain resolutions of the UN—the terms of which it distorts to say what those resolutions do not mean"; she also pointed out that the petition says nothing of the fact that all the Arab states remain in perpetual violation of the entire UN Charter, which is based on the principle of mutual respect for the sovereignty of member states, which are to settle disputes by peaceful means.[6]

Butler had herself signed the same divestment petition at its place of origin, Berkeley, where it had circulated in February 2001. She therefore found Summers' remarks not only wrong but personally "hurtful" since they implicated Judith Butler herself in the newly resurgent campus antisemitism. She could hardly have failed to notice that the Berkeley divestment petition had supplied the impetus for anti-Israel mob violence on her own campus on April 24, 2001, a few weeks after it had been circulated, and for more explicitly anti-Jewish mobs at San Francisco State University in May of the following year. Slander of Israel has provoked physical violence on many campuses, especially those (like Wayne State in Detroit or Concordia in Montreal) with a large Arab presence.

Summers, aware of how ubiquitous in anti-Israel discourse is the straw man called "the defender of Israel who decries any criticism of Israeli policy as antisemitism," went out of his way in his address to separate himself from this (conjectural) figure: "I have always throughout my life been put off by those who... conjured up images of Hitler's Kristallnacht at any disagreement with Israel." Nobody has ever discovered just who these conjurors might be, but if Summers thought he would separate himself from them by this disclaimer he was mistaken.

Despite the large role played in promoting the divestment campaign by people like Noam Chomsky, Summers chivalrously went out of his way to say that "Serious and thoughtful people are advocating and taking actions that are anti-Semitic in their effect if not their intent." To annihilate this distinction between intentional and effective antisemitism is the primary aim of Butler's counterattack. Her strategy is what logicians call the *tu quoque* (i.e., you too, or you're another) argument: Summers' accusations, says Butler, are "a blow against academic freedom, in effect, if not intent." His words have had "a chilling effect on political discourse." No evidence is (or could be) adduced for the allegation. Of one thing we can be sure: the chill did not take hold at Harvard itself, which would soon (in November) play host to Oxford's Tom Paulin, who had urged (in yet another "criticism of Israeli policy") that Jews living in Judea/Samaria "should be shot dead," or at Columbia, where Paulin continued merrily through autumn semester as a visiting professor, or at the *New York Review of Books,* which in October 2003 would publish Professor Tony Judt's "Israel: The Alternative," a call for an end to the state; neither did Summers dampen the fires of Israel-hatred at the *London Review of Books* itself, which in January 2003 published another 133 lines of Paulin doggerel called "On Being Dealt the Anti-Semitic Card," a versified rehearsal of Butler's "No, It's Not Anti-Semitic." If Summers' speech had a chilling effect on antisemitic clarion calls, including incitement to raw murder, one would not want to know what the fully heated versions would sound like.

Butler perfunctorily assented to Summers' recommendation that—as she artfully restated it—"every progressive person ought to challenge anti-semitism vigorously wherever it occurs," but she seemed incapable either of recognizing it in such (to her) mild "public criticisms" as economic warfare against the Jewish state or calls for its dismantling or assaults on Zionism itself or opposing any effort Israel might make to defend her population against suicide bombers. Indeed, she made it clear that she saw no difference between Jews intentionally murdered by suicide bombers (and their sponsors and despatchers) and Arabs accidentally killed by Israeli efforts to repel would-be murderers. She presented herself as offering Jews a salutary warning against crying wolf: "if the charge of anti-semitism is used to defend Israel at all costs, then its power when used against those who do discriminate against Jews—who do violence to synagogues in Europe [synagogues and Passover seders in Israel are not mentioned], wave Nazi flags or support anti-semitic organizations—is radically diluted."

In trying to confute Summers' distinction between intentional and effective antisemitism, Butler calls it wildly improbable that somebody examining the disinvestment petitions signed by herself and her co-conspirators might take them (as hundreds on her own campus already had done), as condoning antisemitism. She therefore poses this conundrum: "We are asked to conjure a listener who attributes an intention to the speaker: so-and-so has made a public statement against the Israeli occupation, and this must mean that so-and-so hates Jews or is willing to fuel those who do." But Summers was perfectly correct in stating that one need not "hate Jews" in order to perform actions or utter words that are "antisemitic in their effect if not their intent."

Let us take a well-known case: when Dickens wrote *Oliver Twist* he harbored no hatred of Jews and had no programmatic or conscious intention to harm them. Indeed, he said of his character Fagin that "he's such an out and outer I don't know what to make of him." The reason for Dickens' puzzlement was that, in an important sense, he did not indeed "make" Fagin, and therefore didn't know what to make *of* him. Fagin was ready-made for Dickens by the collective folklore of Christendom, which had for centuries fixed the Jew in the role of Christ-killer, surrogate of Satan, inheritor of Judas, thief, fence, corrupter of the young; to which list of attributes Butler and her friends would now add "Zionist imperialist and occupier." Has *Oliver Twist* been antisemitic in its effect? Of course—or does Butler think that it is for their interest in Bill Sikes and Nancy and the plight of the homeless in early Victorian England that Arab publishers have long kept cheap paperback translations of the book in print?

Butler also uses the *tu quoque* "argument" in rebutting the charge of selectivity that Summers had made. Why, among all the nations on earth, has Israel alone been singled out for punishment and pariah status by the advocates of disinvestment and academic boycott? Where was their advocacy of disinvestment in China until China withdraws from Tibet, or from Morocco until that country ceases to occupy Western Sahara, or from Zimbabwe until it ceases persecuting its white citizens, or from Egypt until it stops building tunnels for the smuggling of arms to Palestinian killers? Could the singling out of Israel possibly have anything to do with the fact that it is a Jewish country? Despite the inordinate length of her essay, Butler cannot find space to answer this question. Instead, she accuses Summers himself of biased selectivity. "If we say that the case of Israel is different, that any criticism of it is considered as an attack on Israelis, or Jews in general, then we have singled out this political allegiance from all other allegiances that are open to public debate. We have engaged in the most outrageous form of 'effective' censorship..."

Her ultimate use of the *tu quoque* strategy is to make Summers, the critic of antisemitism, himself guilty of what he attacks. Why? Because he assumes that Jews can only be victims, conflates "Jews" with Israel, and writes as if all Jews were a single, undifferentiated group.

Apparently the 1,135 Israelis murdered and the nearly 10,000 mutilated (in a Jewish population of about five million) by Arab terrorists between September 27, 2000 and the time Butler published her essay were not sufficient to meet her stringent requirements for (Jewish) victim status. But if Israelis are not the victims of Palestinian aggression in the latest round of the Arab nations' fifty-six-year-old war to eradicate the Jewish state, why is it that Jewish schools in Tel-Aviv and Jerusalem must be protected by armed guards while Arab schools in Nazareth or Ramallah require no such safeguards? Why is it that getting on a bus in Jerusalem or going to a cafe in Haifa is a form of Russian roulette, a far more dangerous activity than prancing about as a "human shield" for Yasser Arafat?

As for the argument that nothing is antisemitic which does not explicitly target every single Jew in the world, it is jejune. After all, insists Butler, not all Jews are committed to Israel: "Some Jews have a heartfelt investment in corned beef sandwiches." But does she really think that when Josef Pfefferkorn, whose distinction between "good" and "bad" Jews became the paradigm for Jewish self-haters, urged his countrymen (in the 1520s) to "drive the old Jews out [of Germany]" he had himself in mind? When Karl Marx excoriated Jews as "the filthiest of all races," did he really mean to include himself? Do the operators of Nazi websites have trouble making "exceptions" for the writings of Chomsky or Norman Finkelstein? Indeed, Butler's requirement of total inclusiveness would have allowed Hitler himself to say (had he so wished) of his racial policy: "No, it's not antisemitic."

Although Butler's essay is a loose, baggy monster, what it leaves out is even more blatant than what it includes. It omits history altogether, torturing a text and omitting context. Did it never occur to Butler that the divestment effort is the latest installment of the fifty-eight-year-old Arab economic boycott of Israel, one prong in the endless Arab campaign to destroy the Jewish state? Equally egregious is the omission of context that is *de rigueur* among all those who have made the "Palestinian cause" the touchstone of campus progressivism. The "occupation" which they constantly bemoan did not precede and cause Arab hatred and violence; it was Arab hatred and violence that led—in 1967 as in 1993—to the occupation.

But the crucial omission from this essay by somebody who has relentlessly insisted on the political implications of language is—the political implications of the language of the advocates of divestment. Josef Joffe, editor of the German weekly *Der Zeit*, has succinctly defined the linguistic difference between "criticism of Israeli policy" and antisemitism:

Take this statement:

"Demolishing the houses of the families of terrorists is morally wrong because it imputes guilt by association, and politically wrong because it pushes more people into the arms of Hamas." Such a statement is neither anti-Israel nor anti-Semitic; it might even be correct. By contrast, "the Israelis are latter-day Nazis who want to drive the Palestinians from their land in order to realize an imperialist biblical dream" inhabits a very different order of discourse, ascribing evil to an entire collective and, in its equation of Israelis and Nazis, revealing an obsessive need for moral denigration.[7]

The Harvard/MIT divestment petition that Butler champions against Summers was, as noted above, promoted at MIT by Chomsky, for whom the Israeli-Nazi equation is axiomatic; it was promoted at Harvard by Professor Paul Hanson, who called Israel the "pariah" state. Butler was herself one of the "first signatories" of a July 28, 2003 petition that uses the Israeli-Nazi equation beloved of nearly all denigrators of the Zionist enterprise (going back to British official circles in Cairo in 1941) in asserting that "concrete, barbed wire and electronic fortifications whose precedents... belong to the totalitarian tradition" were transforming the Israel "'defense forces'" (again the rhetorical quotation marks) and indeed "Israeli citizens themselves into a people of camp wardens."[8]

And so it would seem that, for Butler, "Language plays an important role in shaping and attuning our... understanding of social and political realities" except when it happens to be the antisemitic language that demonizes Israel as being like unto Gehenna and the pit of Hell.

Making the Case for Jew-Hatred: Martin Jay Explains

"There is a great temptation to explain away the intrinsically incredible by means of liberal rationalizations. In each one of us, there lurks such a liberal, wheedling us with the voice of common sense."—Hannah Arendt

The academic boycotters of Israeli universities and the professorial advocates of suicide bombing of Israeli citizens are in the front lines of the defense of terror, which is the very essence of Palestinian nationalism.[10] But they themselves are supported by a rearguard of fellow travellers, a far more numerous academic group whose defining characteristic is not fanaticism but time-serving timorousness. In the thirties, "fellow travellers" usually referred to the intellectual friends of communism (well analyzed in David Caute's book on the subject[11]), although Hitler competed with Stalin in attracting people from America and Britain who never actually joined the Nazi or Communist parties but served their purposes in the conviction that they were engaged (at a safe distance) in a noble cause. At the moment, as Martin Peretz has pointed out,[12] the favorite cause of peregrinating political tourists is the Palestinian movement; and the reason why fellow-travellers favor this most barbaric of all movements of "national liberation" is that its adversaries are Jews, always a tempting target because of their ridiculously small numbers (currently, 997 out of every 1,000 people in the world are not Jews) and their enormous image (as Christ-killers and agents of Satan).

As a representative example of the academic fellow-traveller in the ongoing campaign to depict Israel as the center of the world's evil and make it ideologically vulnerable to terror, take the case of Martin Jay, a professor of history at University of California, Berkeley and author of books about the Frankfurt school in Germany and "ocularcentric discourse" in France. In the Winter-Spring 2003 issue of *Salmagundi*, a quarterly journal of the social sciences and humanities, Jay argues, in an essay entitled "Ariel Sharon and the Rise of the New Anti-Semitism,"[13] that Jews themselves, primarily Sharon and the "fanatic settlers" (22) but also the American Jews who question the infallibility of the *New York Times* and National Public Radio or protest the antics of tenured guerrillas on the campuses, are "causing" the "new" antisemitism. Jay, unlike such people as Edward Said (of whom he writes with oily sycophancy), does not deny the existence of a resurgent antisemitism, although his examples of its manifestations are vandalized synagogues and cemeteries, "tipping over a tombstone in a graveyard in Marseilles or burning torahs in a temple on Long Island [as] payback for *atrocities* [my emphasis] committed by Israeli settlers" (14); such unpleasant words as stabbings, shootings, murder—all of which have been unleashed against Jews in Europe as well as Israel—are not part of Jay's vocabulary. But his main interest is in proposing that the Jews are themselves the cause of the aggression against them. "The actions of contemporary Jews," Jay alleges, "are somehow connected with the upsurge of anti-Semitism around the globe" (21), and it would be foolish to suppose that "the victims are in no way involved in unleashing the animosities they suffer"(17).

Although Jay's main concern is the (supposedly) "new" antisemitism, his heavy reliance on the thesis and even the title of Albert Lindemann's unsavory and deviously polemical book, *Esau's Tears: Modern Anti-Semitism and the Rise of the Jews* (1998) suggests that he believes political antisemitism, from its inception in the nineteenth century, has been in large part the responsibility of the Jews themselves. Lindemann's book argued not merely that Jews had "social interactions" (a favorite euphemism of Jay's) with their persecutors but were responsible for the hatreds that eventually consumed them in Europe; antisemitism was, wherever and whenever it flared up, a response to Jewish misbehavior. According to Lindemann, the Romanians had been subjected to "mean-spirited denigration" of their country by Jews, and so it was reasonable for Romania's elite to conclude that "making life difficult" for the country's Jewish inhabitants, "legally or otherwise," was a "justifiable policy." His abstruse research into Russian history also revealed to him that whatever antisemitism existed there was "hardly a hatred without palpable or understandable cause." The 1903 Kishinev pogrom, Lindemann grudgingly admitted, did occur but was a relatively minor affair in numbers killed and wounded which the Jews, with typical "hyperbole and mendacity," exaggerated in order to attract sympathy and money; it was a major affair only because it revealed "a rising Jewish combativeness." (As for the *Protocols of the Elders of Zion*, Lindemann apparently never heard of it, for it goes unmentioned in his nearly fifty pages on Russia.) In Germany, Jews (especially the historian Heinrich Graetz), were guilty of a "steady stream of insults and withering criticism... directed at Germans"; by contrast, Hitler (who published *Mein Kampf* in 1925-

27) was a "moderate" on the Jewish question prior to the mid-1930s; besides, "nearly everywhere Hitler looked at the end of the war, there were Jews who corresponded to anti-Semitic imagery." In addition to being degenerate, ugly, dirty, tribalist, racist, crooked, and sexually immoral, the Jews, as depicted by Lindemann, further infuriated their gentile neighbors by speaking Yiddish: "a nasal, whining, and crippled ghetto tongue."[14]

Although Jay is by no means in full agreement with Lindemann's thesis (as he is with that of an even cruder polemic by Paul Breines called *Tough Jews*[15]), he is intensely grateful to this courageous pioneer for breaking a "taboo" (18) on the "difficult question about the Jewish role in causing anti-Semitism," for putting it "on the table" (21). (Readers familiar with this dismal topic will be disappointed to learn that neither Lindemann nor his admirer Jay is able to explain the "Jewish role" in causing the belief, widespread among Christian theologians from St. Augustine through the seventeenth century, that Jewish males menstruate.) This is a remarkable statement to come from a historian. Washington Irving's Rip van Winkle lost touch with history for twenty years while he slept; Jay's dogmatic slumber seems to have lasted thirty-six years, since 1967, when the brief post-World War II relaxation of antisemitism came to an end.

A brief history lesson is in order here. At the end of the Second World War, old-fashioned antisemites grudgingly recognized that the Holocaust had given antisemitism a bad name, that perhaps the time was right for a temporary respite in the ideological war against the Jews. But in 1967 the Jews in Israel had the misfortune to win the war that was unleashed against them by Gamal Nasser, who had proclaimed—in a locution very much akin to Jay's style of reasoning—that "Israel's existence is itself an aggression." After their defeat, the Arabs de-emphasized their ambition to "turn the Mediterranean red with Jewish blood" and instead blamed "the Middle East conflict" on the Jews themselves for denying the Palestinians a state (something that, of course, the Arabs could have given them any time during the nineteen years that they were entirely in control of the disputed territories of "the West Bank"). Since that time, what Jay calls the "difficult question about the Jewish role in causing anti-Semitism" has not only been "on the table"; it has provided a royal feast for such heavy feeders as Alexander Cockburn, Desmond Tutu, Michael Lerner, the aforementioned Said, Patrick Buchanan, Noam Chomsky, most of the Israeli left, and scores (if not hundreds) of other scribblers. Indeed, the *New York Times*, which during World War II did its best to conceal the fact that Jews were being murdered en masse, now admits they are being murdered, but blames them for, in Jay-speak, "unleashing the animosities they suffer."

The particular form given by nearly all these forerunners of Lindemann is, of course, blatant reversal of cause and effect in taking for granted that it is Israeli occupation that leads to Arab hatred and aggression, when every normally attentive sixth-grader knows that it is Arab hatred and aggression that lead (as they have always done from 1967 to 2002) to Israeli occupation. Jay is (characteristically) very fierce not with Lindemann for regurgitating every antisemitic slander dredged up from the bad dreams of Christendom but with Lindemann's "overheated" (18) critics (in *Commentary*, in the *American Historical Review*, in Midstream). In the same manner, his outrage about suicide bombings is not against the bombers or their instructors and financiers but against "American Jewish panic" (23) and "Israeli toughness" (23) in reacting to them and so perpetuating (no cliché is too stale and stupid for Jay) "the spiral of violence" (23).

Just as Jay insinuates some mild criticism of Lindemann, he also "qualifies" every now and then his insistence that the Jews themselves are to blame for antisemitism, but always in a way that only serves to make his core argument all the more gross and flagrant. "Acknowledging this fact [that the Jewish victims are "involved in unleashing" hatred of themselves] is not 'blaming the victim,' an overly simple formula that prevents asking hard and sometimes awkward questions, but rather understanding that social interactions are never as neat as moral oppositions of good and evil" (17). Like most liberals, Jay cannot credit the full evil of the world. "In the case of the Arab war against the Jewish state," Ruth Wisse has observed, "obscuring Arab intentions requires identifying Jews as the cause of the conflict. The notion of Jewish responsibility for Arab rejectionism is almost irresistibly attractive to liberals, because the truth otherwise seems so bleak."[16] Although Jay tries to twist Hannah Arendt's well-known criticism of Sartre's foolish argument that the Jews survived in exile thanks to gentile persecution into an endorsement of his own foolish argument about Jewish *responsibility* for that persecution, he is himself a classic case of what Arendt called the wheedling voice of "common sense" that lurks inside every liberal, explaining away the "intrinsically incredible,"[17] such as the fact that a people would choose to define itself by its dedication to the destruction of another people.

For the benefit of Jay (and others) in bondage to the liberal dogma that "social interactions are never as neat as moral oppositions of good and evil," and at the risk of violating decorum, I should like here to quote from the description by a physicist (Dr. Pekka Sinervo of the University of Toronto) of what happens when a conventional bomb is exploded in a contained space, such as a city bus travelling through downtown Jerusalem: "A person sitting nearby would feel, momentarily, a shock wave slamming into his or her body, with an 'overpressure' of 300,000 pounds. Such a blast would crush the chest, rupture liver, spleen, heart and lungs, melt eyes, pull organs away from surrounding tissue, separate hands from arms and feet from legs. Bodies would fly through the air or be impaled on the jagged edges of crumpled metal and broken glass."[18] These are among the little "animosities," the "social interactions" that Martin Jay says Israelis, including (one assumes) the schoolchildren who usually fill these buses, have brought upon themselves.

.Jay does take note of the suicide bombers, brainwashed teenage Arab versions of the Hitler Youth, by administering a little slap on the wrist to tearful Esau: "To be fair, the Palestinian leadership that encourages or winks at suicide bombers shows no less counter-productive stupidity [than Sharon taking action against suicide bombers]" (23). (The flabby syntax matches the fatuous moral equation.) Thus does Jay's labored distinction between "causation" and "legitimation" (17) or between blaming the Jewish victims and making them responsible for antisemitic aggression, turn out to be a distinction without a difference. *"Tout comprendre,"* as the French say, *"c'est tout pardonner."*

But pointing out Jay's shoddy history, Orwellian logic, and addiction to worn-out clichés about settlements and "occupied territories" does not quite bring us to the quick of this ulcer. Matthew Arnold used to say that there is such a thing as conscience in intellectual affairs. An examination of the tainted character of Jay's documentation, his "evidence," reveals an intellectual conscience almost totally atrophied; for there is hardly a single reference in the essay to recent events in Intifada II (the Oslo War, that is) or the many responses to it that is not unreliable, deceptive, false.

The essay starts with a reference to the "occupation of Jenin" (12), which always lurks in the background of Jay's ominous albeit vague allusions to Sharon's "heavy-handed" policies and actions (23) and "bulldozer mentality" (22). The April 2002 reoccupation of Jenin infuriated both the academic Israel-haters alluded to above (their boycott of Israeli universities and research institutes, mainly a British operation, went into high gear at this point) and their fellow-travellers. As always with Jay, cause and effect are reversed, as if the actions of firefighters were to be blamed for the depredations of arsonists. The Israeli "incursion" into Jenin, for example, is treated by people like Jay as if it had nothing whatever to do with the series of suicide bombings, culminating with the Passover massacre that immediately preceded it. Jenin was reoccupied in April 2002 after the suicide bombing at the Park Hotel in Netanya on Passover evening, March 27.

Jenin was the base of the terrorist infrastructure: most of the bombers were "educated" in Jenin, worked in Jenin, trained in Jenin, or passed through Jenin to be "blessed" before going out to kill Jews. Of some one hundred terrorists who carried out suicide bombings between October 2000 and April 2002, twenty-three were sent directly from Jenin. Prior to the Passover slaughter the supposedly tough Sharon had done little more in response to the almost daily murder of Israeli citizens than make blustery speeches and then turn the other cheek, or bulldoze or bomb empty buildings belonging to the Palestinian Authority. He had seemed far more inclined to the Christian precept "Resist Not Evil" than were the Christian ministers of Europe who were excoriating him for that "bulldozer mentality." (It does not require a powerful imagination to guess how France or Germany or America would deal with a "Jenin" that dispatched murderers to butcher French or German or American citizens on a daily basis. Of one thing we can be sure: there would have been no bulldozers for Mr. Jay to complain of and also no twenty-three dead Israeli soldiers in Jenin, because the terrorist headquarters would have been obliterated by aerial bombing—and there really might have been not fifty dead Palestinians [most of them fighters] in Jenin but the "genocide of thousands," the "Jeningrad" trumpeted by Jay's favorite news media.)

Thirty Jews were killed and 140 injured at the Netanya seder table, a desecration of a holy place as flagrant as any in recent memory. But Jay's compassion is reserved for the victims of *real* "atrocities," such as "the cruel and vindictive destruction of the venerable olive groves under the pretext that they were hiding places for snipers" (24). Pretext? On October 30, 2002, Israel Radio reported that the terrorist who murdered two girls, ages one and fourteen, and also a woman in Hermesh exploited the olive trees that reach up to the community located between Mevo Dotan and Baka al-Gharbiya some six kilometers west of the Green Line in northern Samaria. The trees had indeed provided cover that made it possible for the killer first to reconnoiter the area in advance—as an olive harvester—and then to slip under the fence to do his murderous work.

Jay's congenital inability to report accurately is also apparent in his allusion to Adam Shapiro, offered as an instance of the atrocities visited by American Jews on people whose only sin is "criticism of Israeli policies" (22). He identifies Shapiro as "the idealistic... American Jewish peace activist" (22). Whatever Shapiro is, he is not a peace activist; he was a Yasser Arafat activist. A leader of the International Solidarity Movement founded by his wife, Huwaida Arraf, his "idealism" consisted of offering himself as a human shield (also breakfast companion) for Arafat in Ramallah, in the hope of making it easier for the arch-terrorist to murder Jewish children with impunity. His "criticism of Israeli policies" consisted of celebrating "suicide operations" as "noble" and urging that violence is a necessity of "Palestinian resistance."

One might expect that Jay would do better in reporting on Jewish misdeeds that "cause" the release of untidy emotions in antisemites when these misdeeds occur right under his nose, so to speak. But in fact the most egregious example of deceptive reporting in his essay is his account of an event on his own (Berkeley) campus. It reads as follows: "When literally thousands of emails and withdrawals of substantial alumni donations to the University of California at Berkeley followed the disclosure that a course description for an English class... endorsed the Palestinian position, it becomes abundantly clear how concerted the effort has become to punish dissenters from Sharon's heavy-handed policies" (22-23). And here is the description (not provided by Jay, needless to add) of that course, offered by one Snehal Shingavi:

The Politics and Poetics of Palestinian Resistance:

Since the inception of the intifada in September 2000, Palestinians have been fighting for their right to exist. The brutal Israeli military occupation of Palestine, an occupation that has been ongoing since 1948, has systematically displaced, killed, and maimed millions of Palestinian people. And yet, from under the brutal weight of the occupation, Palestinians have produced their own culture and poetry of resistance. This class will examine the history of the Palestinian resistance... in order to produce an understanding of the Intifada and to develop a coherent political analysis of the situation. This class takes as its starting point the right of Palestinians to fight for their own self-determination. Conservative thinkers are encouraged to seek other sections.

For Jay, this polemical balderdash, reeking of Stalinist pedagogy, a violation of the very idea of a university, and a blatant call for violence against Israelis and destruction of their state, supported by a booklist that covers the whole gamut of political opinion about Palestinian "resistance" from the omnipresent Edward Said (three separate titles) to Norman Finkelstein (discussed earlier in this book) is nothing more than "dissent" from the policies of Sharon (who is not even mentioned in the description). The real culprit in Jay's eyes is not the puffed-up insurrectionary who conceived this obscene travesty of "an English class," but the people who have the temerity to criticize it. And somehow he knows that, in a state where millions of people consider themselves to be "conservative thinkers," all the objectors were Jews.[19]

Coming to the defense of Jews and Israel has never attracted timorous people; and to do so in a place like Berkeley, where mob rule prevented Benjamin Netanyahu (in September 2000) from giving a lecture in the city, and where cadres of Arab and leftist students can shut down campus buildings and disrupt final exams whenever the anti-Israel fit is upon them, may even require a special degree of courage. Jews who assign responsibility for anti-Jewish aggression to Jewish misbehavior not only save themselves from the unpleasant and often dangerous task of coming to the defense of the Jews under attack but also retain the delightful charms of good conscience. Hitler's professors (to borrow the title of Max Weinreich's famous book of 1946)[20] were the first to make antisemitism both academically respectable and complicit in murder. They have now been succeeded by Arafat's professors: not only the boycotters, not only the advocates of suicide bombings, but also the fellow-travellers like Martin Jay.

Notes

1.   Quoted in David Horowitz, *Radical Son* (New York: Simon & Schuster, 1997), 176.
2.   "A 'Bad' Writer Bites Back," *New York Times*, March 20, 1999.
3.   "No, It Isn't Anti-Semitic," *London Review of Books*, August 21, 2003.
4.   Ibid.
5.   The full text of Summers' speech may be found in *Congress Monthly*, September/October 2003.
6.   Ruth Wisse, "How Harvard and MIT Professors Are Planting a Seed of Malevolence," *New York Sun*, May 20, 2002.
7.   Josef Joffe, "The Demons of Europe," *Commentary*, January 2004, 30.
8.   "Israel and Palestine: Stop the Wall Immediately" petition.

9.   Hannah Arendt, *The Origins of Totalitarianism*, 3 vols. (New York: Harcourt, Brace & World,1951), III, 138.

10.   See Edward Alexander, "The Academic Boycott of Israel: Back to 1933?" *Jerusalem Post*, January 3, 2003; "Evil Educators Defend the Indefensible," *Jerusalem Post*, January 10, 2003; and "Suicide Bombing 101," *American Spectator*, June/ July 2001, 28-30.

11.   David Caute, *The Fellow-Travellers: Intellectual Friends of Communism* (New Haven: Yale University Press, 1988).

12.   Martin Peretz, "Traveling With Bad Companions," *Los Angeles Times*, June 23, 2003.

13.   Subsequent page references to Martin Jay's essay will be in parentheses in the text.

14.   Albert Lindemann, *Esau's Tears: Modern Anti-Semitism and the Rise of the Jews* (Cambridge: Cambridge University Press, 1997), 308, 311,291,140-41,496, 554.

15.   Paul Breines, *Tough Jews: Political Fantasies and the Moral Dilemma of American Jewry* (New York: Basic Books, 1990).

16.   Ruth R. Wisse, *If I Am Not for Myself.. The Liberal Betrayal of the Jews* (New York: Free Press, 1992), 138.

17.   Arendt, *Origins of Totalitarianism*, III, 138.

18.   Quoted in Rosie DiManno, "Unlike Victims, Bomber Died without Pain," *Toronto Star*, June19, 2002.

19.   In a well-hidden place, n. 33, Jay acknowledges that "some of the outcry" about the course had to do with its last sentence telling Conservative thinkers to get lost; but he is confident that "the main reason for the response was the content of the course" (p. 28). Another Berkeley faculty member, who teaches in the English department, provided me with the following description of the incident, which may be instructive:

> I don't think that any chairman would dare disallow such a class on political grounds for fear of PC [Political Correctness] extortion. Of course, the crucial point —that such a class has nothing to do with English—doesn't even enter the picture since so many English composition classes have been politicized... that it's hard to imagine an English chair eager to defend the teaching of grammar and logic. Hence, the brazenness of the instructor who wrote that course description: without the statement that conservatives were not welcome (which is discriminatory), the pedagogy and politics of the course would have been unassailable in the current climate. One thing I distinctly remember with regard to the Palestinian composition class incident was that it coincided with a very loud anti-Israel rally—louder than the anti-war demonstration last week.

20.   Max Weinreich, *Hitler's Professor's: The Part of Scholarship in Hitler's Crimes Against the Jewish People* (New York: YIVO, 1946).

13

Jerome Segal and the Stockholm Five: The PLO's Jewish Advisers

Jacob Neusner

I

No country in the world finds its foreign policy subject to so wide a variety of interested parties' negotiation as the State of Israel. Nearly everybody has an opinion on what is to be done. And citizens of other countries besides the State of Israel or one of its enemies do not hesitate to devise plans and proposals for how to resolve long-standing disputes between the State of Israel and its enemies.

Examples are not hard to find. Writing in 2002 in the *Nation*—a magazine which (as every literate American is well aware) glories in its status as the focal point of radical left-wing hatred for the Jewish state—Jerome Segal lays out his shopping list of musts: "Israel must withdraw from all of the Gaza strip, Israel must withdraw from a minimum of 95 percent of the West Bank..." Within evacuated areas, "there must be territorial contiguity for the State of Palestine, with access to Jordan," and Israel must provide for "the full evacuation of Israeli citizens," by means which presumably do not exclude the use of violence. The UN Security Council would run the negotiations and "end the territorial dimension of the conflict: the Council would call upon the two states, at the earliest date, to undertake bilateral negotiations on the remaining issues, including Jerusalem, the Temple Mount, refugees, security arrangements and economic cooperation." Oslo Redivivus, nothing has happened since 1991, the past four years forgotten. Segal states his proposal in a simple phrase, "externally directed separation."[1]

Segal represents a whole phalanx of Golah-Jews writing about what the State of Israel should or should not do to solve its problems. These self-righteous overseas initiatives take place so regularly that tedium has taken over. But we must ask, isn't that bizarre? I cannot point to counterpart writings by Peruvians advising Russia to write off Chechnya, or by Nepalese telling the Turks to give up its Kurdish population to a new Kurdistan. Nor do a great many Danes intervene in Kashmir. Citizens of various countries tend to take positions on issues facing those countries, not on matters involving third- and fourth-parties. But every Jew wants to be king of the Jews and impose peace on the warring parties.

So we must ask, who has persuaded Jews of the Golah that they form part of a people, one people, to the extent that wherever they live they may cast their ballot in the political process of that state that embodies the politics of that people, one people, which is the State of Israel? Asked in that way, the question answers itself: Zionism has created the conception of a Jewish People realized in the nation-State of Israel and accorded psychological citizenship to every one who regards himself as a member of the Jewish People. So it is quite natural for Jewish Americans, exempt from Israeli taxes and service in the Israel Defense Forces, to pass their opinions on Israeli public policy, doing so in the language, "I'm Jewish and I think," or more simply, "Not in my name."

For Israelis this constant Golah-meddling in the politics of the State of Israel cannot claim a welcome. No doubt the contempt expressed in the statement I have heard, "When we in Israel want to hear from the Golah, we just go and rattle their cages a little," cannot convey the last word. But the Talmud has its answer for irrelevant opinion when a given rabbi (or case of law) is cited out of context: "Rabbi So-and-so— *man dekhar shemeh*," "Rabbi So-and-So—who ever mentioned his name?" The meaning is, what's he doing here, and why do we have to contend with irrelevancies? "Not in my name" finds its answer there: *man dekhar shemeh*. What body of ideas, what embodied ideology, has converted Jews all over the world into sometime-citizens of the Jewish state by reason of all-the-time-belonging to the Jewish People, embodied in that state? It is Zionism in its post-1948 formulation, illustrating the law of unintended consequences.

II

The Zionist movement set out to achieve three goals: the (re)definition of the Jews into a political entity, the "territorialization" and empowerment of the Jews, and the normalization of the public policy of the Jews—all three accomplished in the creation of the State of Israel. None debate whether or not Jewry constitutes a political entity, capable of defining and effecting public policy; none can deny that the Jews have and use power; none call into question the proposition that the Jews now are pretty much like other groups of their class. These propositions, moreover, pertain to not only the Jews of the State of Israel, but, in point of fact, also the Jews of Golah in general, and the United States in particular. With the realization of the Zionist theory of Jewry through the State of Israel has come the embodiment of the principal components of that same theory in American Jewry.

That community, after all, does undertake a program of political action. The PACs under Jewish sponsorship, concerned with Near and Middle Eastern matters, as well as those, also under Jewish sponsorship, with strong interests in public policy at home, together constitute a formidable Jewish political presence in Washington and in New York as well. American Jewry comprises not only a religious, cultural, ethnic, and social entity; it is very much a political component in the politics of the American power system. Using power, the Jews are like others of their class, which is to say, distinct subdivisions within the American social system, bearing indicators that point to enduring difference. Just as the State of Israel is like other states, so American Jewry is like other American ethnic and social entities: like others in many ways, different in some, distinct through and through. So the success of Zionism in achieving its goals should be measured, also, in the transformation of the Golah communities into the model and after the likeness of Zionist theory: normal if not territorialized (which, within Zionism, can only take place in the Land of Israel), then, at least, empowered in precisely the categories, mutatis mutandis, in which the State of Israel has empowered Jewry. In its context, American Jewry is as normal, has been as fully normalized and regularized, as the State of Israel is in its context.

That fact renders all the more bizarre the events culminating in the diplomatic coup accomplished a decade and a half ago for the Palestine Liberation Organization by people deeply engaged by the issues of public policy confronting the State of Israel, but in no way empowered or territorialized in such a way as to form part of the normal political class of the State of Israel. When citizens of one state undertake to negotiate with representatives of another (*soi-disant*) state concerning the affairs of a third state, we must regard that action as highly irregular. The reason is that in the affairs of states and nations, third party intervention is deemed an offense and may be construed as an act of not treason or sedition but war. When, for example, in 1938 the French and British negotiated with the Germans about the fate of certain Czech territories, the Czechs deemed that action an intervention and a betrayal. When, again, American citizens such as Jane Fonda flew to Hanoi to lend aid and comfort to North Vietnam in its invasion of America's ally and co-belligerent, South Vietnam, many construed that action as treason and sedition.[2] The two actions are, of course, not comparable, since Chamberlain returned not to Prague but to London, while Fonda came home to California. But the somewhat mixed analogies serve to make the simple point that third party intervention is odd and unusual and memorable.

III

What, then, shall we make of the Stockholm Five,[3] who, nearly twenty years ago, inaugurated the process that led to the Oslo Agreements and hence the second Intifada? No one has improved on their claim to exemplify the meddling Golah-Jews. They provide a perfect illustration of the outcome of "a people, one people," an outcome intended by no-one. There we have the bizarre case of Jewish Americans meeting without authorization or mission, with officials of the Palestine Liberation Organization and negotiating the terms under which the verbal recognition by the PLO could be worded so as to meet the conditions set by the United States for legitimation of the PLO as a public and recognized negotiating partner in Israel's war of survival with its Arab enemies.

Whom did the Stockholm Five represent? And what empowered them to enter into the political process? They were not Israeli citizens, so they could not stand for any political faction in that state, let alone the Foreign Ministry of Israel. They were not American diplomats, so they could not claim to negotiate on behalf of a party to the issue, American recognition of the PLO being what was, and remains, at stake. When Presidents Clinton and Bush spoke of Palestine as a nation, they realized American policy. Then do American or Canadian or British or French Jews—with their opinions on what the state of Israel should or should not do—speak for a deeply concerned party, American Jewry or World Jewry? Their sponsor in the Stockholm case, the late Philip Klutznick, perennial office holder and self-promoter in world Jewish organizations, certainly thought so; he could not, however, be accorded more standing and authority than his money could buy him.[4]

In fact, the self-appointed spokesman of this self-appointed group never hesitated to avow that he did not, in truth, speak for anyone at all:

> ... there are no Israeli leaders acting decisively for the self-interest of their own country. Inside the United States, the American Jewish community is unable to find a strong moral voice, and within the Palestinian world there seems to be a shortage of ideas as to how to move from the present situation to statehood.[5]

Thus Jerome Segal, philosopher, aspiring statesman, and self-declared savior of Israelis, American Jews, Palestinian Arabs, and doubtless anyone else whose earthly conduct falls short of the Olympian heights of his political wisdom. With counsel such as his, who can doubt that humanity is on the verge of universal peace and brotherhood, or that solutions to poverty, hunger and disease will promptly follow?

Stockholm presented the spectacle of citizens of one country negotiating with a second country about the vital—the most vital—concerns of a third country, and that seems to me simply unprecedented in the affairs of states and nations. It is, in an exact sense of the word, abnormal, and it calls into question whether or not the conduct of Jews' public policy has attained that state of normality that the normalization of the Jews' condition by Zionism was meant to accomplish and has, in the main, accomplished. Jane Fonda in Hanoi does not provide our analogy, but Chamberlain in Munich does. The analogy remains inexact, however, since Chamberlain represented a party to the affair and Britain's interests (as he read them) were at stake in Czech possession of the Sudeten territories; but whom did the Stockholm Five represent as counterpart to Chamberlain's speaking for Britain? If it was the State Department and the

United States, then the portfolio was deeply tucked into the attaché cases of the Five, who neither produced their credentials nor had any to make manifest. And that brings us to the simple and inescapable conclusion that, in our own century, there is simply no precedent for what happened in Stockholm, not even in Munich, though the sell-out is, in limited but telling ways, comparable.

Since the State of Israel has achieved for its Jewish population that normalization through territorialization and empowerment that Zionism promised, our attention turns to the situation of American Jewry. For clearly here a sizable component of Jewry has not grasped the fact that those Jews in the State of Israel have attained a normal political life, comparable to the politics of Americans in the United States. And in a nation's normal politics, while foreigners are free to form opinions on what a nation should or should not do—how a nation may or may not solve its problems—it is a simple fact that foreigners are not free to undertake formal negotiations with that nation's enemies (or friends, for that matter). So we must ask ourselves: how do we make sense of the mentality that deemed legitimate the activities of the Stockholm Five?

IV

A case will serve to frame the issue, the case of Jerome M. Segal, quoted at the outset in his 2002 configuration. Nearly two decades ago, he embodied the Golah-Jew who aspired to be King of the Jews. In secular terms, in his 1988 configuration, he was identified by the national media as "a research scholar at the University of Maryland's Institute for Philosophy and Public Policy."[6] Dr. Segal was then a research scholar, working, as a matter of fact, on the Palestinian-Israeli conflict; his counterparts in the Greater Washington area, scholars employed full time in the study of public policy, are numerous. But when we read more closely the record of what Dr. Segal has said and done, we must wonder just how apt is the analogy of a research scholar at all, for, in his case, analysis of a problem and advocacy of a position spill over into something quite different: public engagement in the practice, not merely the studious analysis, of politics.

Not many members of the American Enterprise Institute, the Brookings Institution, or the Heritage Foundation (to name the three most prominent and effective public policy institutions) so interpret their scholarly responsibilities as to transform their careers from analysis to diplomacy. Segal is reported as describing himself in newspapers as "the PLO's Jewish adviser." His advice includes the following stipulation: "Stone-throwing is permitted, but only insofar as it is undertaken symbolically."[7] I wonder how Israelis courageous enough to ride buses or drink coffee in street cafes will respond to the notion that the Palestinian Arabs, who have advanced from stone throwing to suicide bombing, have American Jewish advisers, or what advice they would give these advisers.

The mind boggles, the imagination fails: who can think such things? But Dr. Segal has indulged his political passions to the extent that he drafted a "declaration of Palestinian independence" on behalf of the PLO.[8] I am inclined to think that, among the greater Washington think tanks, his activities in relationship to his scholarship scarcely define the norm.

And that case calls attention to the simple fact that Dr. Segal is a Jew; attains a hearing because he is a Jew; means, because he is a Jew, to gain for himself a hearing in American Jewry and in the State of Israel; speaks not as a scholar but as a Jew, when, for example, he identifies his message as coming from a Jew:

> It might seem odd that a Jew should offer his thoughts on how Palestinians can be successful in the struggle for statehood.... But the struggle for an independent Palestinian State is also the struggle for a humane and safe Israel. Resolution of the Israeli-Palestinian conflict in a way that provides justice for Palestinians is critical for the Jewish tradition. There can be no Judaism without a commitment to justice.[9]

One need not read with inordinate care to find a slippage, a kind of wandering, in those sentences which begin with "a Jew" and end with "Judaism" and "commitment to justice." Clearly, Segal sees himself (and assuredly so do the Stockholm Five) as a Jew by reason of Judaism; obviously, he and they explain, by appeal to their being Jews, why they identify with the State of Israel, profess concern for its welfare, undertake public actions and express deep engagement with its policies. But the connection between their being Jewish and their Judaism, on the one side, and their entering public discourse and even undertaking political activities pertaining to the foreign policy of the State of Israel, on the other, is not self-evident and assuredly is not normal.

The fruitless search for analogies between Dr. Segal's definition of the correct role of the scholar in public policy and the conduct of others in equivalent posts has already alerted us to the odd situation before us. Do American Roman Catholics propose to dictate the foreign policy of such Catholic countries as Mexico, Spain, Italy, or Brazil? Do American Lutherans presume to tell Sweden or Denmark how to conduct their relationships with the USSR? Obviously not. And if we proceed to ask whether American Roman Catholics negotiate with Britain on Spain's claim to Gibraltar, or with Britain on the conflict in Ulster; whether American Presbyterians (with their heavy stake in Korean Protestantism) presume to fly to Pyongyang to talk with North Korea about its relationships with South Korea; whether American Methodists fly about the Pacific working out the relationships between the New Caledonian Kanaks and the South Asian-Indians and French in those same islands; or finally, whether American orthodox Christians address the Turks about what they should do to establish the Turkish Republic of Cyprus in relationship with the Republic of Cyprus—but why go on? The list piles absurdity on absurdity.

Except of course for the absurdity of Stockholm and what it represents: the meddling of Golah-Jews in Israeli public policy. So we must now ask how to reform the mentality of American, and Israeli, Jews so as to normalize and regularize the rules of framing and carrying out public policy, even among the Jews. The answer to the question, framed as I have presented it, is not difficult to discern. We have to accept as normal the fact that outside of the State of Israel there are Jews in various parts of the world, all of them citizens of their own nations, none of them territorialized and empowered within the State of Israel. All of these Jews care deeply for what happens in and to the State of Israel, just as American Roman Catholics of Italian origin are engaged by the affairs of the Church and the Italian state and polity; just as American Roman Catholics of Hispanic origin care deeply about what happens in Mexico and Central America. But caring, for other Americans, ordinarily does not spill over into meddling, and the intense and unrelenting engagement of American Jews in Israeli public policy ordinarily does.

Until Israelis declare their independence of world Jewry, they can expect more Stockholms. For the Golah mentality endows us with vast enjoyment of the role of Jewish martyr to the Jews, and the Christians, for their part, take pleasure in identifying yet another prophet without honor to add to their indictment of us. Child of the Holocaust, Menachem Z. Rosensaft, of the Stockholm Five, surely took much pleasure in displaying his stigmata:

> their shabby treatment of Israelis and diaspora Jews who have had any dealings with the members of the Palestine Liberation Organization... right-wing Israelis and their acolytes in the American Jewish establishment immediately denounced us as 'willing dupes,' renegades and worse... attempts to ostracize anyone who even sits in the same room with members of the PLO... try so hard to delegitimize those of us who recognize the Palestinians' right to both self-determination and a leadership of their own choosing...[10]

And so on. How delicious, how righteous, how wholly on the side of the angels! And, after all, it's free: without cost, without consequence, martyrdom without a cross. To be sure, there is always the danger of subsequent embarrassment: barely two years after his visit to Stockholm, Rosensaft had uncovered a "troubling contradiction" between Arafat's "rhetoric and reality...The PLO's vision of its state thus directly negates Israel's continued existence."[11]

And then there is the case of Rita Hauser, also of the Stockholm Five, now described as "a high-profile New York philanthropist whose former law firm was a registered agent of the Palestinian Authority." By 2003, Ms. Hauser's commitment to the single-handed promotion of Middle East peace had led her to propose and finance an Edward Said Chair in Arab Studies at Columbia University, in honor of the infamous "professor of terror" and long-time member of the PLO's ruling council.[12] If Rita Hauser has experienced even the slightest unease at the disjunction between her Jewish identity and her services to the purveyors of anti-Jewish hatred, she has yet to disclose it to the world.

All of this is made possible by the mentality, shared by Israeli and American Jewry alike, that posits a special relationship between, a special responsibility among, a special and reciprocal claim upon, the one and the other. The alternative is normalization. I do not claim to know all that it may mean. I am absolutely certain about what it must no longer entail.

What then defines normality, and how to normalize what is now a highly irregular relationship? American Jews have got to accept the fact that, living here, not there, they cannot bear the consequences of the policies they advocate; hence, the course of responsibility requires them to frame opinions however they wish, but to work to effect them, if at all, only within the norms of American public life.

That in my view means, first, we speak here at home in terms of our political system and structure, arguing in terms of American interests on behalf of those policies that we deem favorable to the State of Israel. The Zionist Organization of America has done just that for generations now; so too do most of the pro-Israel lobbies in Washington.

Second, where we cannot as foreigners enter into the formation of Israeli policy, we should support what we can when we can, and otherwise, let the Israelis make their own mistakes. For, after all, their political process, democratic and just, must be free to do its work, and will do its work. We who live far off must give up our prophet's cloak, ceasing to leap to condemn the slightest Israeli infringement upon our heightened and selective sensitivity to the requirements of justice. Segal's language here, as he moves from Israeli policy and the Jews, to the religion, Judaism, and his conception of its conception of justice, shows what is at stake.

Third, the Israelis must now recognize that the cost of the special relationship with world Jewry exceeds the benefit. Insisting that they form the center of world Jewry, and proposing to utilize Jews throughout the world in the achievement of their national goals, the Israelis subject the State of Israel to a political dilemma it cannot accommodate: constituencies in not only Holon but also West Hartford. Just as the Israelis have built a normal state, so they have now to rethink the requirements of the normalization of relationships with Jews outside of Israel. No other country in the world today relies on its overseas friends in the way in which Israelis do, and whether the Israelis will continue to wish to do so in the aftermath of the fiasco of the Stockholm Five seems to me a question worth raising.

The plain truth is that normality is the condition that must characterize everyone. The alternative is that special relationship that, in their minds, endows American Jews with a special status and a privileged right of speech.

The choice is between the spectacle of Stockholm, a charade conducted by self-righteous and self-important nonentities, and the drama of a normal state, in full charge of the political processes that, in response to the will of its electorate, frame public policy. The counterpart to the imaginative world of the Stockholm Five is the mentality of Jonathan Pollard, but he paid for his commitment, and for them it was without charge.

For the price was paid not by any *soi-disant* martyrs, who enjoyed only the adulation of the believers, but solely by the State of Israel. That is why, in my view, only by reconsidering precisely how Israel wishes to engage in transactions with its honest and concerned friends throughout the world, above all, the vast majority of world Jewry, can future Stockholms be avoided. And only Israel will determine the shape of future transactions. Zionism demands the normalization of the Jews—even in their relationships to the State of Israel.

Notes

1.   Jerome Segal, "A New Middle East Approach," *Nation*, January 28, 2002.
2.   See, e.g., Henry Mark Holzer and Erika Holzer, *"Aid and Comfort": Jane Fonda in North Vietnam* (Jefferson, NC: McFarland & Company, 2002).
3.   Rita Hauser, American head of the International Center for Peace in the Middle East; Drora Kass, executive director of the Center; Menachem Rosensaft, president of the Labor Zionist Alliance of the U.S.; Stanley Sheinbaum, economist and publisher; Abraham Udovitch, professor of Middle East history at Princeton University. See Elaine Ruth Fletcher, "Arafat Meets With US Jews in Sweden," *Jerusalem Post*, December 7, 1988.
4.   See Philip M. Klutznick, "Palestinians Need a State Too," *Los Angeles Times*, January 10, 1989, where the reader is treated to a paean of self-praise:

> I am proud of the modest help that I have been able to give to the building of modern Israel... I was president of Bnai B'rith International in the 1950s and then the World Jewish Congress in the 1970s, and chairman of the Conference of Presidents of Major American Jewish Organizations also back in the '50s... I have spent a lifetime of effort on behalf of a strong and healthy Israel, world peace, a vibrant United Nations and a future that will allow human spirit and creativity to triumph over our destructive and tribal impulses.

5.   Jerome Segal, "A Radical Plan For Mideast Peace," *Washington Post*, May 22, 1988.
6.   Robert Pear, "Jewish Father for Palestinian State?" *New York Times*, August 24, 1988.
7.   Segal, "A Radical Plan For Mideast Peace."
8.   Joel Brinkley, "Palestinians Press For Declaration of Independence," *New York Times*, August 15, 1988. For a detailed presentation of his idea, see Jerome M. Segal, *Creating the Palestinian State: A Strategy For Peace* (Chicago: Lawrence Hill & Co., 1989).
9.   Pear, "Jewish Father for Palestinian State?" See also Segal, "A Radical Plan For Mideast Peace."
10.   Menachem Z. Rosensaft, "Shamir Won't Make Peace," *New York Times*, February 28, 1989.
11.   Menachem Z. Rosensaft, "PLO Has Made No Concessions," *Jerusalem Post*, August 13, 1990.
12.   Adam Daifallah, "Hauser Helped Fund Professor of Hate: Said Chair at Columbia Also Backed by Saudis," *New York Sun*, July 23, 2003. On Said, see Edward Alexander, "Professor of Terror," *Commentary*, August 1989.

14

Thomas Friedman, Diplomat from Chelm

Martin Krossel

Thomas L. Friedman, a veteran *New York Times* foreign affairs columnist, has long known that Israel is not treated fairly by news organizations in the Western democracies. He admits as much in some anecdotes in *From Beirut to Jerusalem,* his memoir of his first decade of writing about the Middle East. (He was a correspondent for United Press International and the *Times*, first in Lebanon and then in Israel, between 1979 and 1989).

In one such illustration, he discusses a *Boston Globe* editorial written during the Arab uprising that became known as the first Intifada. The paper was commenting on an incident in which four Palestinian youths were buried alive by Israeli soldiers. The youths were quickly dug up before they suffered serious injury and the Israeli reservists were imprisoned for trying to murder the Palestinians. Still, for the *Globe,* the incident "called up the collective memories from the history of the Jewish people... the czarist pogroms, the centuries of homelessness and persecution, the mass graves at Babi Yar, the piled bodies found at Nazi death camps." Friedman comments: "To be sure, Israel's handling of the Palestinian uprising was at times brutal and stupid. But to compare it to the genocide at Babi Yar, where 33,000 Jews were massacred solely for being Jews? To the mass graves of 6 million Jews systematically liquidated by the Nazis? That is too much."[1]

Of course Friedman himself has been highly critical of Israel, and often that criticism goes far beyond the limits of fair comment. How Friedman portrays Israel matters, because his words carry weight in both media and diplomatic circles. Friedman is a media superstar. He has influence in both public discourse and the behavior of politicians and statesmen. He has won three Pulitzer Prizes. *From Beirut to Jerusalem* won him a National Book Award. Undeservedly, the book is considered must reading for students of the Arab-Israeli conflict. For a time, "Tom's Journal" was an occasional feature on "NewsHour with Jim Lehrer" on PBS. And he has been a favorite foreign policy pundit of talk-show hosts as different as Charlie Rose and Don Imus.

In 1990 it was Friedman who is said to have recommended that Secretary of State James Baker publicly declare, with reference to the Arab-Israeli conflict, "Everybody should know, the [White House] telephone number is 1-202-456-1414. When you're serious about peace give us a call." This was universally seen as a public flagellation of Israel. When Friedman suggested that NATO forces replace the Israeli army in the territories that Israel had captured in the 1967 Six Day War, that proposal was taken up in Congress. But his biggest diplomatic coup was the apparent adoption by Saudi Crown Prince Abdullah of an Arab-Israeli "peace plan" originally put forward in his column. (The plan involved Arab states granting Israel "full peace" in return for Israel's "full withdrawal" from the West Bank and Gaza.)

Certainly, part of Friedman's influence stems from his position as a columnist for perhaps the world's most prestigious newspaper. But Friedman is also a facile writer and inventive raconteur. He is the master of the quip and the cute turn of phrase. His description of Crown Prince Abdullah telling him about the Saudi peace plan reads like the script of a Hollywood B-movie. But entertainment value aside, it appears too contrived to have occurred exactly as Friedman described. (As told in his column, Friedman and the Crown Prince almost miraculously discover that they share the same ideas for resolving the Arab-Israeli conflict.) If Friedman fabricated any part of his account, he committed essentially the same offense that forced his *New York Times* colleague Jayson Blair to resign in disgrace.

Michael Wolff, formerly *New York* magazine's media columnist, has attributed Friedman's appeal to his self-portrayal as "the opposite of the sophisticated, world-weary foreign correspondent." Further, "He's naturally anti-analytical. In a sense he's the anti-*Times*. He's evangelical."[2] But journalists aren't supposed to be evangelists. Even when they are paid for their opinions, as Friedman has been since the mid-1990s, their job is to inform and educate—not to propagandize. The truth is that readers rarely learn anything from Friedman's work. He is rarely insightful and often superficial. When he's right, he's either entirely conventional or perfectly obvious. When he's wrong—and that happens often—he has usually ignored essential elements of his story.

Tom Friedman—the journalist—admits to coming to the Middle East with an intense interest in the Arab-Israeli conflict. He has worn that passion on his sleeve throughout his career. You can see it throughout *From Beirut to Jerusalem,* the memoir of his first decade covering the Middle East. Once he made the transition to columnist, his beat was, in theory, the entire world; apparently he had an unlimited expense account to cover it. But, almost obsessively, he returns to the Middle East. Even when he's in another part of the world, he often relates whatever he's writing about back to that part of the world.

As Martin Peretz noted in the *New Republic, From Beirut to Jerusalem* is "a personal melodrama. Its author portrays himself as a crushed Jewish romantic."[3] In the book Friedman describes his own conversion to the Zionist cause. In

1968, when he was fifteen years old, he went to visit his sister, then studying at Tel Aviv University. "I don't know if it was just the shock of the new, or a fascination waiting to be discovered, but something about Israel and the Middle East that grabbed me in both heart and mind... Indeed from the first day I walked through the walled city of the Old Jerusalem, inhaled its spices, and lost myself in the multicolored river of humanity that flowed through its maze of alleyways, I felt at home."

Friedman claims that when he returned to Minnesota his obsession with Israel became "insufferable." In high school he undertook many projects on various aspects of Israeli life—for instance, one on how Israel won the Six Day War, and another on kibbutz life. The first story he wrote for his high school newspaper was a report of a speech at the University of Minnesota by a then-unknown Israeli general: Ariel Sharon. Friedman writes: "high school for me, I am now embarrassed to say, was one big celebration of Israel's victory in the Six Day War."[4] But on his return to the Middle East as a journalist, he claims to have experienced a grand disillusionment. The scales allegedly fell from his eyes when he witnessed the results of Israel's 1982 invasion of Lebanon, and then the impact of Israel's occupation on the Arab residents of the territories captured in 1967.

But there are problems with this story. First, Friedman attended the University of Cairo in the summer of 1974, between his junior and senior year at Brandeis. This was at a time when Egypt had neither made peace with Israel nor recognized the Jewish state's legitimacy. Cairo was hardly a place where a fervent Zionist would be expected to go to study. Furthermore, historian Jerold S. Auerbach maintains that while at Brandeis, Friedman co-steered the Middle East Peace Group, which professed its "concern" for Israel by denouncing American "military and political elites" for supporting the country. Friedman went on to do graduate work at St. Antony's College at Oxford University. As Auerbach also points out, "British academics, like British Foreign Service officers, were hardly renowned for their sympathetic scholarly interpretations of Israel."

Still, Friedman—as a journalist—hardly came to the Middle East as an intellectual neophyte. This makes the superficiality of his analysis even more inexcusable. Auerbach remarks: "Once Friedman reached Israel he was drawn, like a duck to water, to American immigrants, beset by suffocating idealism and guilty moralism, and to Israeli leftists, for whom the world ended when Likud came to power." If you're an Israeli who doesn't believe that Israel should immediately surrender the West Bank and Gaza to a Palestinian state, don't expect Friedman to give you a fair hearing. Denying a voice to people with whom he disagrees gives him the leeway to demonize them and misrepresent their views. Thus for Friedman anyone who opposes an Israeli withdrawal from the territories is encumbered by an irrationality caused by religious fanaticism, by unhealthy obsessions with the Holocaust, or by racist attitudes towards Arabs. (At one point in *From Beirut to Jerusalem*, he even accuses Israelis of wanting to subjugate

Arabs because they are "niggers.") Friedman doesn't want his readers to know that there are serious Israelis with carefully considered objections to unilateral territorial surrender. So he simply ignores them.

Jewish settlers in the West Bank and Gaza are often the target of Friedman's columns. Repeatedly he has likened the settlers to the insurgents attacking American soldiers and civilians in Iraq. In one recent article, Friedman argued that "both movements combine religious messianism and a willingness to sacrifice their followers and others for absolute visions."[5] Subsequently he asserted that Israel and Iraq were in the middle of the same struggle pitting "theocratic, fascist, and messianic forces on one side, claiming to be acting on the will of God, or in the name of the primordial aspirations of 'the nation,' against more moderate, tolerant, democratic majorities."[6]

This comparison was too much for Israeli writer Hillel Halkin, who noted that while the insurgents in Iraq had been using violence to prevent the establishment of a democratic government there, the Jewish settlers in the territories had always obeyed the rules of the democratic system when advancing their agenda. Indeed, the settlers' "great success in fostering their own interest has been due to their enthusiastic participation in the democratic process by voting, lobbying, demonstrating, and grass-root organizing."[7]

In the same column, Friedman suggested that the settler movement would openly rebel against the Sharon government if it went ahead with plans to remove settlers from Gaza. He cited a statement published in an Israeli newspaper in which thirty-four army officers, who were residents of the territories, had declared that they would not obey any orders to remove Jews from these settlements. According to Friedman, this was "an open rebuke of Prime Minister Ariel Sharon's cabinet-approved plan to withdraw all Israeli forces and settlements from Gaza and a small part of the West Bank." Clearly, he wanted to suggest that the majority of the settlers, intoxicated by their fundamentalist brand of Judaism, would defy the authority of their military superiors. Was this so? As Halkin reported: "Over and over the question has come up in internal settler debates of whether it is permissible to oppose violently the enforcement of the law by Israel's army or police, even if this should involve the evacuation of settlers from their homes, and over and over the answer has been 'No.'" Friedman ignored the outcome of these debates. He also chose to ignore the fact that soldiers who refused to remove settlers from their homes would hardly be setting a precedent in their defiance of military orders; officers with left-leaning sentiments had long refused to serve in the territories. Evidently, he believes that only Israeli soldiers who share his political opinions have the right to defy their commanders.

Friedman also failed to notice that while the Iraqi insurgents typically target civilians, Jewish settlers have almost always been the civilian targets of Arab attacks. Concerning the settlers' general abstention from retaliation or revenge attacks, Halkin wrote: "During the past four years of mass Palestinian violence, in the course of which scores of settlers have been murdered on the roads and in their houses, there have been only a few isolated cases of settlers taking the law into their own hands in revenge, and to the best of my knowledge, no Palestinian deaths resulting from them."

Friedman's equation of Jewish settlers with the Iraqi terrorists is one of his many gratuitous cheap shots at Israelis. But it is also emblematic of his disturbing knack of finding superficial comparisons between people and situations with only the most tenuous resemblance. When he moved from Lebanon to Israel he found more similarities than differences—this, in spite of the fact that Israel was and is a liberal democracy, while war-torn Lebanon had, according to Friedman himself, descended into a Hobbesian state of nature in which "every man is enemy to every man."[8] The similarities he claimed to identify were "rooted in the fact that since the late 1960's both nations have been forced to answer anew the most fundamental questions: What kind of state do we want to have—with what boundaries; what system of power sharing; and what values?" He maintained that political paralysis in both Israel and Lebanon prevented each country from resolving these questions.[9]

For Friedman any qualitative moral difference between Israel and Lebanon—indeed between Israel and any of its Arab neighbors—has been further reduced because, in his view, Israel's continued occupation of the territories has made democracy and the rule of law no more than a sham. When he first arrived to report from Israel, he was distressed to find that there was no debate among leading political figures about how to dispose of the territories:

> Outsiders watching a debate in the Israeli parliament, the Knesset, would marvel over what a healthy democracy Israel had, when they saw all the politicians arguing with each other. But in fact all that was going on was that two minority fringes, one on the right, and the other on the left, were shouting at each other across a massive, inert, Labor-Likud functional pragmatic alliance in the middle. It was a chorus of monologues in which everyone was speaking and no one was listening. In America, advertising is most hysterical and competitive between products that are virtually the same, such as dog food or breakfast cereal. The same applied to Labor and Likud. They each pointed to their written platforms and said, "Look how different we are from them," but in daily life they were each selling the same Puppy Chow.[10]

(The Jewishly illiterate Friedman was incapable of recognizing the enormity of a debate over renouncing the Jewish claim to part of the historic land of Israel.) Additionally, Israel treated the Palestinian population in a manner that Friedman regarded as incompatible with the rule of law. As he tells it, the Shin Bet, Israel's security service, "operated like an unseen hand, arresting Palestinians at night, recruiting reformers, tapping phones, beating the living daylights out of Palestinians behind closed doors of interrogation rooms, and it was rumored, even arranging for certain particularly troublesome Palestinians to 'accidentally' blow themselves up while supposedly assembling bombs meant for Israelis." He lamented that the military courts gave all of these practices the semblance of legality, providing "the veneer that enabled the Israelis to get in their revenge on the Palestinians while still feeling clean and civilized."[11]

In Friedman's eyes, all of this showed that Israel routinely conducted itself according to what he was pleased to call the "Hama Rules"—a reference to the city obliterated by the Syrian dictatorship in 1982, with tens of thousands murdered. Employed by Friedman, "Hama Rules" is shorthand for the merciless spilling of blood in pursuit of a political objective. As Martin Peretz observed, "Suggesting that Israel's conduct is equivalent to Syria's and Iraq's is like saying that America's conduct during World War II was equivalent to the conduct of the Nazis. What Friedman has done is to mistake similarities (and not many similarities) for essences."[12]

Perhaps the most egregious example of Friedman's mistaking "similarities for essences" is his portrayal of Palestinian nationalism as a mirror image of Zionism. This portrayal is based on a number of false notions that—either explicitly or implicitly—he imparts to his readers. His starting point is the presumption that a distinctively Palestinian Arab people has existed since time immemorial, and that Israelis were culpable for failing to recognize that fact. "Many Israelis," he wrote, "convinced themselves that there was no such thing as a legitimate Palestinian nation with a legitimate national claim to any part of Palestine. They saw the Palestinians instead as part of an undifferentiated Arab mass stretching from Morocco to Iraq and with no particular cultural, historical, or ethnic identity to the land of Palestine. This myth was one of the oldest and most enduring in Zionist history." Friedman notes with disdain that even Israel's Labor Party accepted this supposed myth, quoting, as evidence, Golda Meir's famous statement about the Palestinians: "They do not exist." But what she actually said was this:

> When was there an independent Palestinian people with a Palestinian state? It was either southern Syria before the First World War, and then it was a Palestine including Jordan. It was not as though there was a Palestinian people in Palestine considering itself as a Palestinian people and we came and threw them out and took their country away from them. They *did not* exist [emphasis added].

In other words, far from denying that a Palestinian people existed at the time of her interview, as Friedman's misquoted sentence suggests, Meir was denying that Palestinian nationalism existed before the creation of Israel—a very different proposition.[13]

In fact, as the eminent historian Bernard Lewis points out, "Until the very end of the Ottoman Empire the great majority of the residents of Palestine, as of neighboring countries, remained loyal subjects of the Ottoman sultan, whom they saw not as the representative of an alien Turkish domination over Arabs... but as the legitimate Muslim sovereign of a Muslim state, in which Arab, Turkish, and other Muslims were equal citizens." Once the Ottoman Empire collapsed, the Arabs resisted the notion that Palestine was a separate political entity. Rather, the residents directed their loyalty to a larger Arab political whole, of which Palestine was only a part. Right up until the time the British withdrew from Palestine to make room for a Jewish state, there was little support among Palestinian Arabs for a separate Palestinian Arab state.[14]

Nor can the Zionists or anyone else be accused of preventing the Arabs living in Palestine from gaining self-determination. In fact, they have had a number of opportunities to form their own state. The first presented itself in 1938 when the Peel Commission recommended that Mandatory Palestine be divided into a Jewish and a Arab state. The territories of the proposed Jewish state were microscopic. Yet the Jews accepted the Peel proposals; it was the Arabs who rejected them.

The Palestinian Arabs had another opportunity for statehood after the United Nations partition resolution in 1947. Again the Jews accepted the proposal; the Arabs rejected it. As soon as Israel declared its independence, five Arab armies attacked it in an attempt to crush the new Jewish state. Had they succeeded, they probably would have divided up the spoils among themselves. Historian Efraim Karsh points out that Transjordan wanted to incorporate much of mandatory Palestine into a greater Syrian empire. Egypt wanted to forestall this by grabbing the southern part of the land. Syria and Lebanon both wanted to annex the Galilee, while Iraq, in Karsh's words, "viewed the 1948 war as a stepping stone in its long-standing ambition to bring the entire Fertile Crescent under its rule." Thus, had the Arabs won the war, a Palestinian Arab state most likely would not have emerged on Israel's ashes.[15] Still, from 1948-67 the Arabs were entirely in control of the so-called "occupied territories," theirs to do with what they liked; yet during all those years it did not occur to them to establish a Palestinian state there, but only to use the territories mainly as a base for attacks on Israel.

The Oslo Accords provided yet another opportunity for Palestinian independence. It is quite evident that, in the absence of the massive explosion of Palestinian terrorism against Israeli Jews, which became known as the second Intifada, Oslo would have led to the creation of an independent Palestinian state. Thus it is clear that the Palestinians are not engaged in a classic nationalist struggle, and their aim is not to secure their own self-determination through statehood.

Nor were the Palestinians fighting to throw off a harsh Israeli occupation. The Arab population was hostile toward Israel long before there was an occupation and hostile toward Jews long before there was an Israel. The Arabs opposed not only the creation of a Jewish state, but also Jewish immigration to the birthplace of Jewish history and culture. The leaders of the Palestinian Arab community, most notably Haj Amin al-Husseini (the Mufti of Jerusalem) spent World War II in Germany, and they collaborated openly with the Nazi effort to destroy the Jews. When Israelis captured the West Bank and Gaza, they found that many of the local schools were inculcating virulent racist antisemitism into their students.[16] Obviously, then, the Arab residents of the West Bank and Gaza hated Israel and Jews long before Israel captured the territories.

A working journalist, like Friedman, who regularly files reports or commentaries about an ongoing conflict, like the Arab-Israeli dispute, cannot retell the whole history of the conflict in every article. But a book author is usually not under the time pressure of an impending deadline, nor subject to the space restrictions of a newspaper or magazine. He therefore has more of an obligation to readers to place any account of contemporary events in their proper historical context. That's why, in *From Beirut to Jerusalem*, the omission of any reference to the violent history of Arab malice toward Jews is so glaring. Indeed, many years of columns and books by Friedman would pass before he would make any mention of topics like the antisemitism of the Arab nations; their absolute opposition to the existence of the Israel or even the presence of Jews in their part of the world; and their use of terror in order to kill as many Jews as possible or to goad Israel into concessions which would make it strategically vulnerable.

Friedman has continually paid too little attention to these topics; he has consistently underestimated their significance for the Arab-Israeli conflict as a whole and he has waited far too long to address them. He barely criticized Arafat until the PLO leader walked out of the Camp David negotiations and launched the second Intifada, a murderous campaign of bombings and suicide attacks targeting Israeli civilians.

Friedman has addressed Arab antisemitism obliquely in a number of columns, usually discussing his own experiences. In one, he recounted that an Arab editor in London asked whether Jews in the American media are "behind the campaign to smear Saudi Arabia and Islam."[17] A few days later he revealed that various people he met in Saudi Arabia told him that the 9/11 hijackers were dispatched by the CIA or the Mossad; that Jews control the American government; and that the hijackers carried out the 9/11 attacks in response to the crimes of Israel.[18] By now, Friedman has spent many years traveling in the Arab world; he has been a student of Middle East politics for even a longer period. It is not plausible that Friedman has just found out about Arab antisemitism. Why, then, has it taken him so long to write about it?

By late 2001, Friedman had concluded that the second intifada had become "a nihilistic pursuit of murderous violence" and had "morphed into Bin Laden II, a Palestinian attempt to eliminate 100 percent of Israel."[19] Again, it seems very late for Friedman to have discovered that the Palestinians were waging a "nihilistic" war against the Israelis. By the time Friedman was ready to characterize Palestinian violence as "nihilistic" the latest round of killing was in its third year, and Israelis had been the victims of Palestinian terrorism for many decades. So why did he choose December 2001 to condemn the Palestinian uprising as being "nihilistic"? Apparently this column had been prompted in part by the release of a poll showing that a large majority of Israelis favored a Palestinian state. Was Friedman then implying that this was the first time that Israelis were willing to support the establishment of a Palestinian Arab state on the western side of the Jordan River? If so, then he was about sixty-four years too late.

In January 2002, Friedman finally came to terms with the fact that Arafat had not accepted Israel's legitimacy. Stephen P. Cohen, a Middle East pundit on whose analysis Friedman frequently relies, had told him that Arafat "wanted a state negotiated with Israel today. And he wanted a state inside Israel that would be brought about by a return of Palestinian refugees and their soaring birthrate tomorrow."[20] Two months later, Friedman was asking: "Have you ever heard Mr. Arafat talk about what sort of education system or economy he would prefer, what sort of constitution he wants? No, because Mr. Arafat is not interested in the content of a Palestinian state, only the contours."[21] By the time Friedman wrote this Arafat had exercised political control over the West Bank and Gaza for a decade. Had Friedman really not noticed that Arafat had done nothing to build a state? That's hard to believe. More plausibly, Friedman, like many other journalists, chose to overlook the fact that the focus of Arafat's plans was not the functioning of a Palestinian state, but the next confrontation with Israel.

No journalist was in a better position to know Arafat than Friedman. After all, he had been covering Arafat since they were both in Lebanon during that country's civil war. Yet Arafat was seemingly able to fool Friedman, as he did many journalists, into believing that he really was a peacemaker. In the post-Oslo edition of *From Beirut to Jerusalem*, Friedman wrote: "By mutually recognizing each other, Arafat and Rabin were in effect saying, 'I recognize your rights to this piece of earth, now let's talk about how much each of us really needs and wants.'"[22]

Some see Friedman's willingness to criticize both Palestinians and Israelis as an indication of his genuine even-handedness, and a sign that he really bears Israel no ill-will. It is true that the post-2000 Friedman is tougher on the Palestinians than the Friedman who wrote *From Beirut to Jerusalem*. Still, he has really only expressed token criticism of the Palestinians in comparison to his relentless assaults on Israelis. And it is Friedman's obsession with his opposition to Israel's presence in the West Bank and Gaza, as well as the presence of Jewish settlements in those territories, that explains why he overlooks Arab misdeeds. Ultimately, it is virtually impossible to argue convincingly that the occupation and the settlements are the main obstacle to the resolution of the Arab-Israeli conflict, when they are considered in the context of the long history of Arab hostility and bigotry.

Friedman now asserts that Israel is "in peril" if it does not withdraw behind the lines that existed before the Six Day War. His argument is—like much of his work—muddled, and it does not support his thesis. He outlines the large geopolitical factors which supposedly require an Israeli withdrawal and the evacuation of the settlements. First, oil revenues have allowed the "Arab-Muslim" world to take "a vacation from globalization," but "there is not enough oil wealth anymore to cushion or employ the huge population growth going on in the region. Every Arab country is going to have to make a wrenching adjustment." An Israeli withdrawal would "strip the worst Arab leaders of an excuse not to reform." So "Israel needs to get out of the way and reduce its nodes with the Arab world as it goes through this unstable and at times humiliating catch-up." Furthermore, Arab media outlets "from *al-Jazeera* to the Internet" are projecting images of Israeli-Palestinian violence to the Arab world, "radicalizing it, and melding in the heads of young Arabs and Muslims the notion that the biggest threat to their future is JIA—Jews, Israel, and America." Still further, the "occupation" is undermining Zionism as a just cause: "if Israel does not relinquish the West Bank and Gaza, the Palestinians will soon outnumber the Jews and Israel will become either an apartheid state or a non-Jewish state."[23]

Reading Friedman, one gets the impression that Israel occupies almost the entire Arab world, instead of a small strip of land along the Mediterranean. If Arabs are really interested in instituting the social and economic reforms that will help them to grow in a globalized world, Israel won't and can't stop them. Moreover, Arab political and media leaders, as well as the ordinary citizenry, have never needed either Israel's presence or the sight on their television sets of Israelis fighting Palestinians in order to hate Jews, Israelis, or Americans. The notion that what has happened in the territories is "radicalizing" the young Arab masses rests on the assumption that the Arab masses were once more moderate and tolerant. Throughout his writing, Friedman has insisted that there does exist within the Arab world a constituency willing to accept both Jewish individuals and a Jewish state. But nowhere does he present convincing evidence for the existence of such a constituency. Indeed, as we have seen, hatred of Jews has been central to Arab culture for almost a century. The Arab hatred of Jews, Israel, and Americans, like any form of prejudice, is not rational and therefore not affected by passing events. In one column, Friedman charged that Iraqis hate Americans because President George W. Bush was "embracing Ariel Sharon so tightly that it's impossible to know where US policy stops and Mr. Sharon's begins." To which the *New York Sun* rightly replied: "It is not either Mr. Bush's or Mr. Sharon's fault that many Arabs—or many Europeans—hate Jews. They were hating Jews long before Mr. Bush, even before Mr. Sharon was born, even before there was a Jewish state."[24]

Consistently, Friedman has asserted that there are Palestinian Arabs in the territories who would be willing to make a lasting peace with Israel once they are given a state of their own. In 1999, he asserted that the majority of the residents of the territories were ready to support this kind of a peace.[25] At that time, he still maintained that Arafat himself sided with that peace-minded Palestinian majority. Indeed, the very use of the term "peace process" by Friedman (and many others) in the context of the Arab-Israeli conflict presumed the existence on the Palestinian Arab side of a constituency willing to be Israel's partner in making peace. But by 2004 Friedman had retreated: "Ideally," he wrote, "the withdrawal should be negotiated along the Clinton plan. But if necessary, it should be done unilaterally."[26] Translation: Israel doesn't really have anyone to negotiate with among the Palestinian Arabs, but it should pull out of the territories anyway.

Friedman has probably believed this all along. He tells the readers of *From Beirut to Jerusalem* that already in 1984 he was distressed that Israel had not pulled out of the territories. At that time it was an undisputed fact that the PLO Covenant (a document which Friedman hardly ever mentions) called for the destruction of Israel. No West Bank leader had declared a willingness to accept Israel's existence. Friedman does not clarify precisely when he would have had Israel withdraw. On the day after the cease-fire ending the Six Day War came into force? No answer is given.

In December 1988, Arafat reluctantly made a series of ambiguous statements, in which he seemed to acknowledge Israel's right to exist. It was widely understood that he made these statements, not to promote reconciliation with Israel, but to gain diplomatic recognition from the United States. In his account of this incident in *From Beirut to Jerusalem*, Friedman wrote: "Arafat wanted to end the PLO's diplomatic isolation from Washington, and to do so he had to speak words literally dictated by [U.S. Secretary of State] George Schultz. Schultz, in effect, told Arafat: 'Read my lips,' and after several tries Arafat finally read his lips."

Quite naturally, Israelis were unimpressed by Arafat's performance. Even Friedman's only rabbinical guru, the liberal Orthodox Rabbi David Hartman, shared his countrymen's skepticism. "That Arafat is prepared to recognize me is irrelevant," he told Friedman. Hartman elaborated:

> Israelis know that they are fact, they don't need Arafat to tell them. What they need to hear from Arafat and the Palestinians is that they see the Jews in Israel as having coming home, because the deepest impulse that brought Jews back to Israel was their enormous sense of homelessness, of not having a real place in history. Arafat says I'm a fact, but then he calls my government a junta. He says I'm a fact, but an alien implant. He says I'm a fact because I have power, not because I'm home. Until he speaks to Israelis in terms of how they see themselves, it will be as though he hasn't even spoken to them at all.[27]

Yet, inexplicably, just a few pages after Friedman has demonstrated that Arafat held out the possibility of recognizing Israel for purely cynical reasons, he begins a long passage with the question: "When might the Israelis be ready to hear Arafat's message?" Then he remarks: "I am convinced that one day Yasir Arafat is going to stand up and sing 'Hatikva,' the Israeli national anthem in Hebrew. When he does, some Israelis are going to shake their heads and say, 'Geez,' we'd love to talk to you but you sang the national anthem in the wrong key. Come back when you can sing it right."[28] Not only did Arafat never sing "Hatikva," he never came close to fulfilling Rabbi Hartman's conditions for Israelis to pay attention to him. Still, only a few years later, when Arafat vaguely offered Israelis "peace" at Oslo, Israel accepted and gave him land in return. Israelis, on the whole, proved themselves to be much more accommodating and flexible than Friedman predicted.

But it is the inherent contradictions in Friedman's account of Arafat's supposed recognition of Israel in 1988 that make that account noteworthy. Friedman recognizes that Arafat was posturing in order to get into the good graces of the United States. Nevertheless, he castigates Israel for not responding to this disingenuous offer. These contradictory themes permeate all of Friedman's writings. On one hand, he acknowledges that the Palestinians can't or won't offer Israel genuine peace. On the other, he is angered by Israel's refusal to trade "land for peace." In other words, Friedman condemns Israelis for turning down an offer that was never made. He uses this doubletalk to conceal the fact that he believes, not in "land for peace," but in "land for no peace."

Friedman has always maintained that Israel overestimated the security risks associated with leaving the territories. In some of the most odious passages of his book, he decries the centrality of the Holocaust in the consciousness of every Israeli—even though the Holocaust is outside the historical experience of many Jewish Israelis, particularly the Sephardim from Asia and North Africa. "Today—unfortunately—the teaching of the Holocaust is an essential part of Israeli high school education," he writes. Furthermore, "all Israeli youngsters are not only taken to Yad Vashem but also go by the hundreds on field trips to Poland, where they visit firsthand the death camps... The subliminal message is that these camps are what the State of Israel is all about." These observations are surpassed only by Friedman's characterization of Israel as "Yad Vashem with an air force." He accuses Israel's leading politicians of co-opting Jewish suffering in the Holocaust to further their own political agendas. "Israeli leaders, such as Golda Meir, Menachem Begin, and Yitzhak Shamir, instead of fighting against this 'Holocausting' of the Israeli psyche, actually encourage it," turning Israel into "a modern-day Warsaw Ghetto aligned against the world."[29] Given the murderous fanaticism of Arab intentions towards the Jews, the centrality of Jew-hatred in the Palestinians' national "identity," and the degree of international support for the Palestinian "cause," such analogies may not be as inappropriate as Friedman thinks.

Arguing against the second Bush administration's abrogation of the Anti-Ballistic Missile Treaty, Friedman asserted: "What the Russians fear is a total Star Wars umbrella that might make the United States invulnerable to missile attack and thus able to strike Russia without fear of retaliation."[30] Thus Friedman expects his readers to believe that Russia has a more realistic fear of the United States than Israel has of a prospective Palestinian state. This is absurd. During the seventy years that the United States and the Soviet Union were ideological rivals, including the forty years that they were bitter Cold War adversaries, the Americans never tried to attack the Soviets. In fact, often during the Cold War the Americans made no more than token responses to blatant acts of Soviet aggression. Yet, even though the collapse of Soviet communism eliminated this ideological rivalry between the U.S. and the USSR, Friedman expects us to believe that the Russians still have a reasonable fear of an American attack. In marked contrast, one could legitimately argue that neither the Palestinian Authority nor any Arab state—including Egypt and Jordan—has abandoned the goal of eventually destroying the Jewish state. Yet Friedman simply dismisses the notion that Israel could face a genuine threat after withdrawing from the territories.

The Oslo "peace process" was effectively a laboratory for Friedman's ideas on how to solve the Arab-Israeli conflict. Very early on, his counterpart at the *Washington Post*, columnist Charles Krauthammer, recognized that the defining characteristic of Oslo was not land for peace but land for nothing. But Friedman did not want his readers to understand this. The collapse of Oslo into vicious Arab violence marked the failure of the experiment; territorial concessions only increased the number and ferocity of Arab attacks on Israelis. Yet Friedman learned very little from the demise of Oslo. His obsession with occupation and settlements prevented him from seeing that the Oslo "peace process" would end in Arab violence, and it prevented him from seeing that only Israel's military presence in the territories made it possible to smother the second intifada.

Friedman did acknowledge that, because of the second Intifada, "No Israeli in his right mind would trust Yasir Arafat, who has used suicide bombers when it suited his purposes, not to do the same thing if he got the West Bank back and some of his people started demanding Tel Aviv."[31] His solution is to hand the West Bank and Gaza to U.S. and NATO troops, with a new UN mandate. But Israel's experience with entrusting its security to others has been bitter. The most egregious example was the failure of the United States and the rest of the international community to break the naval blockade that Egypt imposed on Israel in 1967. Had the world done so, there would have been no Six Day War and no ongoing controversy over the ultimate disposition of the territories. Since 1967, Europeans especially have become much more hostile to Israel. All but two of NATO's members are European. Could Israelis be expected to turn over part of the responsibility for their survival to such a force? Certainly, the international community seems to have no desire to run the kind of intrusive occupation that would produce a Palestinian leadership and populace favoring coexistence with Israelis. In such circumstances, is it wrong for Israel to maintain its presence in the territories?

By demanding the destruction of settlements, Friedman shows he is the extremist who advocates "ethnic cleansing"—of his fellow Jews. He insists that the central issue in the conflict is the Palestinian demand for statehood, but ordinary states are expected to protect ethnic minorities living within their borders. Friedman champions the exemption of a future Palestinian state from norms to which all other states are held. Middle East analyst Daniel Pipes has noted that the evacuation of thousands of law-abiding Jews from their homes in Gaza is "unprecedented for a democracy." Were Friedman to have his way, Arabs would be able to live throughout the two states, but Jews would not.

Some very ugly themes are scattered in Friedman's writings: Israel stands in the way of Arab reform and globalization; Israel's actions interfere with America's

War on Terror; Iraqis hate Americans because Bush's foreign policy is indistinguishable from Sharon's, indeed Sharon has George Bush "under house arrest in the Oval Office"; the Jewish state is nothing but a schizophrenic Holocaust museum—"Yad Vashem with an air force." The animating principle in this noxious worldview is that the Jews, and not their enemies, are to blame for the hatred and violence directed against them. One cannot but suspect that Friedman's commitment to these ideas is bound up with his monomaniacal insistence that Israeli occupation and settlements, rather than decades of Arab aggression against the Jewish people, are the main obstacles to peace in the Middle East.

Notes

1.   Thomas L. Friedman, *From Beirut to Jerusalem (Updated With a New Chapter)* (New York: Anchor Books, 1995), 432.
2.   Michael Wolff, "Peace Pipe," *New York Magazine*, March 18, 2002.
3.   Martin Peretz, "Field of Dreams," *New Republic,* September 4, 1989.
4.   *From Beirut to Jerusalem*, 4-5.
5.   "Tyranny of the Minorities," *New York Times*, May 16, 2004.
6.   "Remapping the Middle East, Maybe," *New York Times*, January 9, 2005.
7.   "Friedman Falls on His Head," *New York Sun*, May 19, 2004.
8.   *From Beirut to Jerusalem*, 29.
9.   Ibid., 252.
10.   Ibid., 268.
11.   Ibid., 354.
12.   Peretz, "Field of Dreams."
13.   *From Beirut to Jerusalem*, 141-2; Golda Meir, Interview, *Sunday Times* (UK), June 15, 1969, *Washington Post*, June 16, 1969.
14.   Bernard Lewis, "The Palestinians and the PLO," *Commentary,* January 1975.
15.   Efraim Karsh, "Arafat Lives," *Commentary,* January 2005.
16.   Bernard Lewis, *Semites and Anti-Semites: An Inquiry Into Conflict and Prejudice* (New York: W.W. Norton, 1999), pp. 219-20
17.   "Blunt Question, Blunt Answer," *New York Times*, February 10, 2002.
18.   "A Traveler to Saudi Arabia," *New York Times*, February 24, 2002.
19.   "The Intifada is Over," *New York Times*, December 5, 2001.
20.   "Dead Man Walking," *New York Times*, January 30, 2002.
21.   "Suicidal Lies," *New York Times*, March, 31, 2002.
22.   *From Beirut to Jerusalem*, 554.
23.   "War of Ideas: Part 4," *New York Times*, January 18, 2004.
24.   Editorial, "Sticks and Stones," *New York Sun*, October 25, 2004.
25.   "Who Are We," *New York Times*, March 6, 1999.
26.   "War of Ideas: Part 4."
27.   *From Beirut to Jerusalem*, 404-5.
28.   Ibid., 408
29.   Ibid., 280-1.
30.   "Pay Attention," *New York Times,* November 30, 2001.
31.   "The Hard Truth," *New York Times*, April 3, 2002.

15

Investigating Seymour Hersh

Rael Jean Isaac

Character assassination. A simplistic moral universe in which the U.S. is the villain and Israel the only country yet more villainous. Anonymous sources that cannot be checked. Dark charges based on a crazy patchwork of suppositions. Far-out conspiracy theories. Con men as sources. Reputable sources misquoted. These constitute the decades-long modus operandi of Seymour Hersh, the man now serving as star investigative reporter of the *New Yorker*.

That modus operandi is clearly in evidence in Hersh's only book-length assault on Israel, *The Samson Option* (about Israel's nuclear deterrent), published in 1991. Typically for Hersh, he even gets the Biblical account wrong. Explaining the book's title, Hersh writes that "Samson, according to the Bible, had been captured after a bloody fight."[1] What the Bible records—as any literate person knows—is that Samson became helpless after Delilah seduced him into telling her that the secret of his strength lay in his long hair, and she summoned one of the Philistines to cut it off as he slept in her arms.

Anyone who had followed Hersh's career as a 1960s style "Movement" journalist would have expected Hersh to take up cudgels against Israel sooner or later. His books and articles are permeated by the theme of America-the-enemy; indeed *The Samson Option* was his first book without that theme. Here the U.S. government is the innocent, deceived victim of Israel and the nefarious Jewish lobby. It took Israel to purify (however briefly) America by contrast.

Although the reader would never guess it from the book, with its tone of awestruck disclosure, there had been a series of books about Israel's development of a nuclear capability. Hersh himself cites four books in English (mention of them is buried in the footnotes) specifically devoted to the subject.[2] What Hersh offers that is "new" is his sinister interpretation of supposed behind-the-scenes American-Jewish machinations and a series of sensational revelations about the actions of Israeli leaders, all of them false, the fantasies of his source, a delusional con man, served up as fact.

Hersh's thesis is that Israel, impelled by the megalomania of its leaders, built an atomic bomb facility at Dimona, deceiving the United States until the wicked deed was done. Part of the deception, according to Hersh, was self-deception: American political leaders did not dare face up to what their intelligence agencies had uncovered for fear of the Jews. Jewish fund-raisers, says Hersh, warned political candidates in no uncertain terms that they were finished if they did not toe the line. American presidents, including John F. Kennedy, were resentful, but helpless in the face of what Hersh describes as the message of the Jewish lobby: "We're ready to pay your bills if you'll let us have control of your Middle East policy."[3]

Any intelligence (or other) official who tried to alert his superiors to Israel's secret development of a nuclear arsenal, Hersh alleges, was fired or (if lucky) demoted or set back in his career. And so bureaucrats soon got the message – keep quiet or you will be ruined.[4]

In dark suggestions more appropriate to the antisemitic Liberty Lobby than an American Jewish journalist, Hersh implies sinister motivations on the part of Jewish Americans in high places. For example, Hersh goes on for pages assailing Admiral Lewis Strauss, chairman of the Atomic Energy Commission in the 1950s, as a closet practitioner of "dual loyalty." Hersh writes that Strauss was a life-long opponent of Zionism[5] and an adamant opponent of nuclear proliferation.[6] On what basis then is Strauss accused of secretly forwarding Israel's nuclear ambitions? Hersh claims that Strauss ignored his responsibility to tell John McCone, his successor at the Atomic Energy Commission, of what he knew about the existence of the Dimona reactor. He writes that "Strauss's [Jewish] background and his strong feelings about the Holocaust cannot be disregarded in analyzing why he did not tell anyone—especially John McCone—about Dimona."[7] In reality, what explains Strauss's "silence" is the simple fact that there was nothing to tell. Strauss left the AEC in 1958. As Yuval Ne'eman, the distinguished physicist, government adviser and former Israeli cabinet minister, told this writer, construction at Dimona did not begin until 1960—in 1958, says Ne'eman, Dimona was no more than "a gleam in somebody's eye."[8]

Other "evidence?" "The strongest evidence," according to Hersh, for Strauss' "sympathy for the Israeli nuclear weapons program" was that in 1966 Strauss recommended Ernst David Bergmann as a two-month visiting fellow at Princeton's Institute for Advanced Studies.[9] But this reveals nothing. Bergmann, an outstanding scientist, was chairman of Israel's Atomic Energy Commission in the 1950s, and he and Strauss would have come to know each other, as Hersh himself admits, at the conferences on peaceful use of the atom. Does Hersh have any more "proof" of Strauss's dual loyalty? Yes, says Hersh, Atomic Energy Commission official Myron Kratzer found out, after Strauss had left the Commission, that he "followed the tradition of fasting during Yom Kippur."[10] In Hersh's Elders of Zion mentality, that clinches it!

But what Hersh's book offers that is new are the fabrications of Ari Ben Menashe, a notorious tale-spinner who recently, in a scenario beyond the imagination of the most far-out screenwriter, served as chief witness in Robert

Mugabe's farcical treason trial of the leader of the chief opposition party in Zimbabwe.[11] Ben Menashe first achieved worldwide notoriety with his claim to have been with the first George Bush (then running for vice president on the Reagan ticket) in Paris in October 1980 arranging for Iran to hold the hostages until after the presidential elections—this on dates when Secret Service logs show Bush engaged in a large number of appearances in the United States, one of them before the Zionist Organization of America.[12] Hersh swallows whole both Ben Menashe's bogus credentials and wild allegations.

Hersh tells us that Ben Menashe "served more than ten years in the External Relations Department of the Israeli Defense Force, one of the most sensitive offices in Israel's intelligence community" and left the ministry in 1987 "to work directly for Prime Minister Yitzhak Shamir as an adviser on intelligence affairs."[13] Ben Menashe's ties to Shamir, says Hersh, were also familial: his father had served with Shamir "in the fervently anti-British Stern gang before the 1948 War of Independence."[14] All this is pure hokum. Iraqi-born Ben Menashe served as a low-level translator for the Mossad, Israel's intelligence service, was judged delusional, denied a security clearance, and resigned.[15]

Ben Menashe's revelations, breathlessly recounted by Hersh, are of a piece with his biography: made up out of whole cloth. According to Ben Menashe, Begin, who became prime minister in 1977, had "strongly endorsed" existing plans to target Soviet cities and "gave orders to target more Soviet cities."[16] Hersh also cites Ben Menashe as his source for the claim that Prime Minister Shamir personally authorized purloined U.S. intelligence obtained through Jonathan Pollard to be "sanitized, retyped and turned over to Soviet intelligence officials"[17] as part of Israel's ongoing exchange of intelligence with the Soviets on U.S. weapons systems.[18] (How this squares with Ben Menashe's claim that Israel was using its stolen U.S. intelligence to target the Soviet Union, which, writes Hersh, "was always Israel's primary nuclear target,"[19] is not explained.) By Hersh's account, Ben Menashe was a key player throughout. He was assigned in 1980 to a small "working group" within Israeli intelligence to get around the arms embargo to Iran.[20] He was sent to London to get hold of the Vanunu photographs (taken inside the Dimona reactor) so they could be checked for authenticity in Israel and the damage done by their publication minimized.[21] He was privy to supposed nuclear weapons collaboration with South Africa. ("[Ezer] Weizman came back, Ben Menashe recalled, "and said 'We've promised these guys nuclear warheads'... Begin responded by saying, in effect, 'Yes. Do it.'")[22]

It is ironic, given the emphasis the book places on alleged U.S. self-deception concerning the Israeli bomb, that Hersh deluded himself on the bona fides of Ari Ben Menashe. And Hersh was not merely guilty of failing to check on the credibility of a source making charges he himself calls "hard to believe." (One of Ben Menashe's claims—that Israel had planted nuclear mines along the Golan Heights[23]—was too much even for a sycophantic reviewer in the *New*

York Times who pointed out that such mines, if used at the start of hostilities, would mean "going nuclear" when conventional resistance was still possible, while if overrun without being detonated, they would be a gift to the enemy.[24]) Writer Steven Emerson reports that Hersh refused to look at evidence urged upon him of Ben Menashe's mendacity. Nor did the proffered evidence come from a suspicious source, that is, for Hersh one friendly to Israel. It came from the chief investigative reporter for the London *Sunday Times'* "Insight" team, Peter Hounam, who had broken the Vanunu story, complete with photographs, on the Dimona reactor. Hounam warned Hersh not to rely on Ben Menashe, offering to let Hersh go through his personal files on the Vanunu affair which showed that Ben Menashe's claims did not hold up. Hersh was not interested.[25]

Another illustration of Hersh's propensity to be conned followed the book's publication. Hersh, stung by challenges to Ben Menashe's credibility, claimed to have confirming documents from a "private detective" on supposed logs of telephone calls supporting Ben Menashe's claim that Robert Maxwell had worked closely with the Mossad. Five days later, as Emerson tells it, "the *Sunday Times* revealed that the 'private detective' was actually a well-known British hoaxer, Joe Flynn, who admitted that he had deceived Hersh in exchange for money. 'I am a conman,' Mr. Flynn told the *Times*." What is of special interest, as Emerson shows, is that Hersh, before realizing it was a con, said he had acquired the documentation, when he had no such thing, for the promised phone logs did not exist.[26]

As this claim by Hersh illustrates, he is more than a passive victim of his own gullibility. In *The Samson Option* he says that "Ben Menashe's account might seem almost too startling to be believed, had it not been subsequently amplified by a second Israeli, who cannot be named."[27] Hersh has a pattern of claiming to have "independently corroborated" material that defies corroboration. Working on a book on John F. Kennedy several years later, Hersh fell for a stash of phony documents peddled by one Lawrence S. Cusack who claimed to have papers that included a contract in which Marilyn Monroe promised to keep silent about her affair with Kennedy for $600,000, as well as documents linking Kennedy directly to mobster Sam Giancana.[28] In Cusack's trial for defrauding "investors" in the documents, Hersh wound up on the stand, where he was asked to explain a letter he had sent to Cusack claiming he had "independently confirmed some of the most interesting materials in the papers." An embarrassed Hersh testified: "Here is where I absolutely misstated things."[29]

Hersh's charges that Maxwell and Nicholas Davies, then foreign editor of London's *Daily Mirror*, had spied for Israel precipitated an in-depth investigation by *Newsweek* into assorted Ben Menashe claims. Not surprisingly the magazine's reporters found his credibility was zero.[30] And *Newsweek* only investigated Ben Menashe's more plausible allegations. Among the less plausible, which had not even made it into Hersh's book, Ben Menashe claimed he had been Israel's top spy, a commander of the Entebbe operation, planted a homing device in the Iraqi nuclear reactor at Osirak and declined an offer to become head of the Mossad.[31] Little wonder that John Barry, lead author of the *Newsweek* article, would tell CNN "If you were talking about the American civil war, he would tell you he was the guy who planned Lee's campaign."[32] (Eventually Hersh himself would admit that Ben Menashe "lies like people breathe.")[33]

Even when Hersh cites reputable sources, what he writes cannot be trusted. Hersh cites Yuval Ne'eman as having told him that in the Yom Kippur War of 1973, Israel went on nuclear alert twice.[34] This writer interviewed Ne'eman, who said he had indeed spoken to Hersh and told him, based on public sources, that the United States—not Israel—went on nuclear alert twice.[35]

Hersh cannot be bothered to get the most readily available facts straight. Chronicling Begin's evil deeds as an underground leader (Hersh has something insulting to say in introducing each Israeli leader—even, as in the case of General Rafael Eitan, if it is only that his socks smell!),[36] Hersh describes the Irgun's bombing of the King David Hotel and says the British responded a week later by hanging three suspected Irgun terrorists.[37] In fact, the three Jews were hanged a year later for their role in the daring assault on the Acre fortress, which freed a large number of Irgun prisoners.

According to Hersh, the famed U.S. airlift to Israel during the Yom Kippur war of 1973 was only undertaken because Israel blackmailed President Nixon, threatening to use its atomic arsenal if supplies were not sent immediately. Veteran foreign correspondent Russ Braley, a friend of Nixon, wrote to ask if what Hersh wrote was accurate. In a letter dated January 22, 1992 Nixon replied: "The story has no foundation whatever."[38] (Nixon added: "I have refused to read any of Seymour Hersh's books or articles because I consider him to be totally unreliable.")

What makes Hersh's allegation that Israel engaged in nuclear blackmail more interesting than his other false claims is that, were it true, Hersh would have destroyed his thesis—that Israel was both immoral and foolish to create a nuclear capability. For were Hersh correct, the Israeli leaders who insisted on producing an Israel; bomb would, in this one incident, have proved they made the right decision. In the crunch, Israel's atomic arsenal had shown its effectiveness. Without having to employ it, Israel's leaders had been able to use its existence to save their country.

Why does this not occur to Hersh? The answer is that he never for a moment considers Israel's point of view. Hersh has written a book about Israel's development of a nuclear deterrent without asking himself why Israel might need or want it. Hersh conveys no sense that Israel throughout its history has confronted Arab states seeking to destroy it. He never points out that Israel was not even permitted to buy conventional arms from the United States throughout the 1950s. Hersh does not have to bother his head about how Israel is to survive, since it is by no means clear to him that Israel deserves to survive. When he first describes Israel as a "pariah" state, he uses quotation marks.[39] Later he drops the quotation marks.[40]

If Hersh conveys no sense of Israel's dilemma, neither does he provide any context on nonproliferation. Israel was not the only country outside the great power club developing nuclear weapons. Given his theme that the U.S. should have "done something" about Israel, Hersh should have something to say about the U.S. posture on Pakistan and India's development of a nuclear arsenal. But Hersh is not interested. Indeed, so obsessed is he with Israeli misdeeds that he only refers to Iraq's nuclear bomb program in order to condemn Israel. His reaction to the Israeli bombing of Iraq's Osirak reactor in 1981, which mercifully ensured that Saddam Hussein would not have his finger on a nuclear trigger a decade later in the first Gulf War, is to complain of Israel's "abuse" of U.S. photographic intelligence and the "misuse" of U.S. F-16s in the raid.[41]

Why is Hersh so hostile that he can only see Israel as malign without motive? To understand this, one must look at Hersh's evolution as a journalist of the 1960s "Movement." Under the influence of assorted Marxist and Trotskyite groupings, the Movement increasingly came to interpret Zionism as the product of Western racism, colonialism, and imperialism. To attack Israel was to attack what was worst about the United States.

Hersh was part of a group of young journalists whose perspectives were shaped by the Institute for Policy Studies, the radical left (and radically anti-Israel) think tank, founded in 1963, which served as ideological center of the Movement. It was IPS which indirectly propelled Hersh to stardom, for he first achieved fame freelancing for Dispatch News Service, an IPS spinoff founded to disseminate anti-Vietnam war stories to the mainstream press. A source called with a tip, and Hersh broke the story that the army was in process of court-martialing Lt. William Calley (whom Hersh interviewed) for the shooting of civilians in what became known as the My Lai massacre.[42] Typically, Hersh insisted My Lai was not an isolated incident: the true villain, he wrote, was "the Army as an institution."[43]

The My Lai story turned Hersh overnight into what A.M. Rosenthal, then *New York Times* managing editor, called "the hottest piece of journalistic property in the United States."[44] The *Times* hired him and he remained there from 1972 to 1979. He wrote a series of stories attacking the CIA for covert actions abroad and for illegal spying on domestic groups (the material, which had been assembled by the CIA itself and turned over to the congressional committee with oversight of the CIA, was leaked to Hersh by CIA head William Colby.)[45] In the anti-establishment atmosphere of the period, Hersh's stories had a major impact, playing an important role in launching congressional investigations by both houses of Congress into the CIA. The upshot of the "reforms" Congress enacted was to seriously compromise our intelligence capabilities, setting up a firewall between the FBI and CIA, the price being paid on 9/11. It is significant that Rosenthal would say that a number of Hersh's stories would not have been publishable under the standards he demanded of *Times* reporters a few years later.[46]

In 1979 Hersh left the *Times* to work on an anti-Kissinger book *The Price of Power* (published in 1983). There are hints of the themes that would dominate *The Samson Option*: according to Hersh, foreign services officers, recognizing that those who reported critically on Israeli policy in State Department cables ran the risk of being labeled antisemitic, were forced into self-censorship.[47] (Given the long domination of the State Department by highly partisan Arabists, this verges on the comical.) Kissinger himself is treated as part of the Israel lobby, a notion, as international affairs expert Michael Ledeen observed wryly, "that has not previously occurred to anyone involved in the Arab-Israeli conflict."[48]

Hersh followed up his anti-Kissinger screed with a book in which he managed to get the entire story wrong. The thesis of his 1986 *The Target is Destroyed*, on the Soviet downing of Korean civilian airliner KAL 007, is that the Soviet pilot made an honest mistake, confusing the Boeing 747 with the RC-135, a U.S. reconnaissance aircraft, and the U.S. "rushed to judgment" because "strong hostility to communism had led them to misread the intelligence." The "real story," said Hersh, was the "politically corrupt" use of intelligence by the U.S.[49] In 1991 *Izvestiya* took advantage of its new freedom to revisit the fate of KAL 007. It interviewed Lt. Col. Gennadi Osipovich, the Soviet fighter pilot who shot down the plane; he indignantly rejected the suggestion that he had mistaken the plane for an RC-135 and described how he had been fortified with vodka before going on Soviet state television to recite, on order, a wholly false account.[50]

Hersh had received an official invitation to do his research on KAL 007 in the Soviet Union and reports being taken aback when Deputy Foreign Minister George Kornienko told him his "assignment" was to find that the plane was on a CIA spy mission.[51] Hersh did not oblige his hosts on this point but what is worth noting is that the Soviets deemed Hersh so sympathetic a journalist that they thought him amenable to such an outright order. Presumably they were influenced in their judgment in part by the series of articles Hersh had written for the *New York Times* in 1979 on conditions in Vietnam, this at a time when vast numbers of "boat people" were braving death on the open seas in their desperation to escape. Hersh, one of a few selected American journalists the Communists permitted entry, exhibited not a shred of the critical zeal with which he challenged U.S. government claims. Instead he gushed Vietnamese propaganda—no claim of his hosts was too absurd for Hersh to parrot.[52]

In recent years, the *New Yorker*, for decades open to Hersh, has served as his exclusive platform. This has been a wonderful period for Hersh given that, especially since 9/11, he has been able to combine all his obsessions into one story line: an inept, morally odious American government works in tandem with (sometimes in opposition to) evil Israel while a tiny cabal of Jewish neocons

(Hersh tirelessly cites the trio of Perle-Wolfowitz-Feith) manipulate policy. Hersh marvels: "How did they do it? How did eight or nine neo-conservatives... get their way? How did they redirect the government and rearrange long-standing American priorities with so much ease? How did they overcome the bureaucracy, intimidate the press, mislead the Congress, and dominate the military?"[53] Although he avoids the term "Jewish cabal," Hersh is clearly treading in the steps of the more explicit Patrick Buchanan, for he knows that his reader/listener will supply what is missing. On the radio show *Democracy Now*, reports *The American Enterprise* (April/May 2005), Hersh declared that the U.S. had "been taken over basically by a cult; eight or nine neo-conservatives have somehow grabbed the government."

Hersh finds a perfect target in Richard Perle, one of his neocon leadership trio. Perle embodies the attitudes Hersh finds most offensive—friendship for Israel and a belief that the United States is a force for good in the world. In a March 17, 2003 article Hersh assails Perle, who then headed the unpaid Defense Policy Board (which meets several times a year to advise the Pentagon on strategic issues) for alleged ethics violations. The only substantive fact Hersh offers is that in the runup to the Iraq war, Perle met with two Saudi businessmen to discuss Iraq. One was Adnan Kashoggi, the longtime arms dealer and middleman, who arranged the luncheon meeting at the request of the other, Iraqi-born Harb Saleh al-Zuhair, who claimed to have come from Iraq with a negotiating offer from Saddam. All three agree that the only topic discussed was Iraq. On this frail stick Hersh builds a huge speculative edifice, concluding confidently that Perle's "real" motive was to obtain investment in a venture capital company and that his views on Iraq were a product of his business interests.[54] In the subsequent furor, Hersh succeeded in his aim – Perle resigned as chairman of the Defense Policy Board.

In a number of essays Hersh emphasizes "close, and largely unacknowledged, cooperation with Israel"[55] in everything from supposed joint U.S.-Israel contingency plans to take over Pakistan's nuclear arsenal to conducting the war in Iraq to what Hersh maintains is the upcoming war with Iran. Hersh writes that no one wants to talk about this because it's "incendiary."[56] Given that such claims of secret joint actions are impossible to disprove, the only effect of making these claims, as Hersh well knows, is to strain relations between the U.S. and Muslim states. Indeed, an alarmed President Musharraf in his first meeting with President Bush brought up Hersh's article and was told by Bush "Seymour Hersh is a liar."[57]

According to Hersh, Israel is also working with the U.S. to "develop and refine potential nuclear, chemical-weapons and missile targets inside Iran."[58] Hersh made headlines with this piece, entitled "The Coming Wars," that claimed super-secret U.S. reconnaissance missions in Iran, conducted together with Pakistan, were laying the groundwork for destroying Iran's nuclear facilities and invading the country.[59] Of course, if true, Hersh was endangering the lives of the

American commandos on these missions, especially since he names the areas in which they are operating.

In other articles Hersh forgets his close cooperation thesis and portrays Israel as a wild card, deliberately undermining U.S. policy. In "Plan B," Hersh tells us Israel has poured money into a "potentially reckless move that could create even more chaos and violence," sending her "intelligence and military operatives" to train Kurdish commando units and run "covert operations in Kurdish areas of Iran and Syria."[60] Hersh, pro forma, quotes the Israeli embassy spokesman: "The story is simply untrue and the relevant governments know it's untrue."[61] Hersh's own sources are the usual anonymous assortment of "high-level" this and that with whom he peppers his books and articles. So has Israel sent commandos to Kurdistan? The reader has no way of knowing.

Still, common sense makes it obvious that much of what Hersh writes is balderdash. He warns that Israel may "unleash" the Kurds on Sunni and Shiite militias, splitting Iraq apart, that Kurds are being "programmed" to fight in Syria, Turkey and Iran, and that an independent Kurdistan could become "an Israeli land-based aircraft carrier" on Iran's border.[62] But even if Israel had training personnel on the ground, the notion that Israel can "program" the Kurds to do its bidding or turn Kurdistan into an Israeli military base is silly: the notoriously independent Kurds will act in accordance with what they deem to be their own best interests. Indulging yet another fantasy, Hersh credits Israel's supposed presence in Kurdistan with alienating Turkey from Israel, producing "a major regional shift, a new alliance among Iran, Syria and Turkey."[63] It is true that the Turkish-Israel relationship has been strained for several years, but the reason lies elsewhere—in the rise to power, for the first time since Ataturk's campaign of secularization, of an Islamic party in Turkey.

When Hersh's articles are criticized for their reliance on anonymous sources, *New Yorker* editor David Remnick counters that the magazine's army of fact-checkers carefully ascertain that each statement is true. But there are a number of reasons why fact-checking Hersh is a ludicrous exercise. One is that the lowly fact-checker will be extremely reluctant to challenge the magazine's star reporter; if he angers Hersh, he knows who will be fired. Even more important, Hersh generally cites only a single source for his major "disclosures." Let us say the fact-checker is given the name and phone number of this source. He can speak to someone but ultimately is in no better position than Hersh's reader to know if the supposed "former high intelligence official" or "government consultant" or "retired CIA official" has the credentials he claims or has provided accurate information or interpretation (much of what Hersh offers is a web of sinister interpretation built on very few facts). The stubborn reality is that statements by people guaranteed anonymity require especially careful vetting because anonymity is an invitation to angry bureaucrats to take revenge on superiors or rival bureaucracies or to spin their own far-out theories as fact. It is Hersh who should be carefully checking and evaluating the reliability of his sources, but his record indicates that he does no such thing. Under these circumstances, fact-checkers are useful only in giving Hersh—and the *New Yorker* —cover.

Conde Nast, the *New Yorker*'s publisher, would do better to save the hundreds of thousands of dollars that Remnick says he spends on fact-checkers. Case in point: Michael Rubin, formerly with the Pentagon, now a fellow at the American Enterprise Institute, describes what happened when the *New Yorker* ostensibly fact-checked a Hersh piece that recycled antisemitic canards about the Department of Defense's Office of Special Plans that had earlier been purveyed by the far-out Lyndon LaRouche organization. Rubin reports that the *New Yorker* fact-checker duly called the Office of Special Plans (where Rubin then worked) with a number of "inquiries," that the office responded immediately and made a great number of corrections, including on matters of simple fact. But, notes Rubin, none of the corrections were incorporated into the article.[64] And where were the fact-checkers when Hersh, in 2001, wrote of a raid on Taliban leader Mullah Omar's compound in which sixteen AC-130 planes were used? The Air Force only has twenty-one of these large, heavily armed planes and they are not flown in groups. When John Miller, writing for *National Review*, asked Hersh if sixteen of them would lead a small special-forces operation, Hersh replied that he may have "misheard."[65] Where were the fact-checkers when Hersh gave the price tag of a predator drone as $40 million when in fact it costs $2.5 million?[66] The list is endless.

For all its emptiness, the *New Yorker*'s facade of fact-checking provides Hersh with a teflon coat. In a *New York Magazine* article of April 18, 2005, "Sy Hersh Says It's Okay to Lie (Just Not in Print)," Chris Suellentrop provides what would seem to be a devastating exposé of Hersh. He reveals that on the lecture circuit Hersh, by his own admission, is cavalier about mere "facts," changing "events, dates and places" (the core elements of journalism). Suellentrop shows that Hersh's idea of giving his audience its money's worth (up to $15,000 a performance on college campuses) is to lob an incendiary charge (never mind the absence of any evidence for its validity). Suellentrop provides a number of such on-the-road "scoops": Zarqawi is likely a composite figure or a propaganda creation of the U.S. government or the insurgency itself; an American platoon killed thirty-six Iraqi guards; the U.S. government has video of young boys (who had been arrested with their mothers) being sodomized at Abu Ghraib and the worst "is the soundtrack of the boys shrieking." Suellentrop points out that blogger-believers quickly disseminate Hersh's wildest charges through cyberspace, where they rapidly assume the status of facts.

Hersh spins further fantasies to Suellentrop, suggesting the process by which he converts the imaginary into the real. Hersh starts out hypothetically: "You're a soldier on a patrol... and you see people running, and you open fire, okay?... Maybe they were bad guys, but then they run into a soccer game. You're a bunch of young kids. And so maybe you pull the bodies together and you drop

RPGs and you take some photographs about it because you're gonna be investigated." By now in the swing of things, Hersh shifts to "reality." He claims he obtained photographs of the incident but didn't write the story because his own sense of responsibility precluded it: "Because then six, eight, ten American kids who did nothing but panic, and did what anybody would, would get in trouble."

But what is most astonishing is that Suellentrop winds up portraying Hersh as a great journalist nonetheless: he decides there are two Hershes, the lecturer who spins yarns, and the writer upon whose every word we can rely. But why should Suellentrop assume someone so reckless with the spoken word to be scrupulous with the written word? It turns out that Suellentrop puts his belief in the *New Yorker*: he assures us that Hersh's articles "are fact-checked tight as a drum." Suellentrop should be sophisticated enough to know the weaknesses of fact-checking. But then it turns out that for Suellentrop what counts is the higher truth purveyed by Hersh. This is how he concludes his article: "Yet a more careful Hersh may not be what the world needs at this moment. Former *Washington Post* reporter Scott Armstrong puts it this way: "Say Hersh writes a story about how an elephant knocked someone down in a dark room. 'If it was a camel or three cows, what difference does it make? It was dark, and it wasn't supposed to be there.' And nobody else had yet described it. Sometimes, says Knight-Ridder reporter Warrren Strobel, 'it's worth it for him to be wrong.'"[67]

Why does Suellentrop back off from his own devastating exposé? One can only speculate that he may not want to take on frontally an icon of the left. Which leaves the question: What is the secret of Hersh's enormous success? Why, rather than being banished to supermarket tabloids, has Hersh attained what *People* magazine, in a fawning piece, called "a kind of mythic status as a journalist"?[68]

Perhaps the answer is that Hersh has an uncanny sense of what a significant sector of the reading public—an affluent progressive intelligentsia (a great many of them Jewish) that prides itself on reading the *New York Times*, the *New Yorker* and the *New York Review of Books*—wants to hear. Hersh knows how to flatter the intellectual pretensions of these people. He caters to their sense of superiority as intellectual insiders with sophisticated-sounding revelations about the source of the neo-con takeover in Straussian political theory at the University of Chicago.[69] They don't want to hear that a bunch of hillbillies behaved outrageously at Abu Ghraib prison; they want to be told the "real story," that the responsibility goes to the top, to George Bush and Donald Rumsfeld. This helps them to validate the hatred and contempt they already feel for these leaders.

Hersh's anti-Israel animus does not discredit him among this set of "progressive" Jewish readers. While few may call themselves anti-Zionist, and indeed many may say they support the pristine Labor Zionism of a bygone era when the kibbutz symbolized the Zionist enterprise, they are alienated from today's

Israel. Many would probably blame the "settlements," as Alvin Rosenfeld points out in these pages, but the real problem with Israel for these Jews is that the ideological left opposes the state and they feel themselves part of the left. That Jews like Hersh—and so many other Jews in the journalistic and intellectual elite—are hostile to Israel is comforting, for it indicates that to share the perspective of the left is not to espouse antisemitism but some variant of "prophetic" Judaism.

What Hersh offers his public is a high-class version of the paranoid politics typified in the (once popular) conspiracy theory that fluoride was being used to poison the water. Hersh's audience would have the greatest contempt for "low-class" conspiracy theories of this sort. They consider themselves connoisseurs of all that is finest, such as the expensive merchandise advertised in the *New Yorker*. But they fall head over heels for junk journalism that spins tales of sinister cabals in high places, nefarious secret missions, any and every conceivable evil deed by top government officials. The writing itself may be convoluted, contradictory, incoherent—as Michael Ledeen has noted, Hersh cannot even write a logically consistent paragraph.[70] It may be painfully obvious to a reader less sophisticated than those subscribing to the *New Yorker* that Hersh has never heard of standards of evidence, is incapable of real policy analysis, and is helpless to understand complicated issues. None of this matters.

But if it is not hard to understand Hersh's appeal, what accounts for the standing other journalists have given him? (It must be admitted that without their backing, his trendy audience would melt away.) This is the real issue, not Hersh himself, but the way his profession views him. Hersh has won over a dozen major journalism awards, including the Pulitzer Prize, the National Book Critics Circle Award, four George Polk awards and last year's National Magazine Award. How could such dreadful stuff be so well rewarded? The answer would seem to be that Hersh's long history of hewing to a simplistic unwavering political line—the United States and Israel are the world's chief malefactors—resonates with a journalistic elite still moored in, or nostalgic for, the good old days of 1960s radicalism.

Notes

1.   Seymour Hersh, *The Samson Option: Israel's Nuclear Policy and American Foreign Policy* (New York: Random House, 1991), 137.
2.   Ibid., 323. The books Hersh cites are *Israel and Nuclear Weapons* by Fuad Jabber, 1971; *Israel's Nuclear Arsenal* by Peter Pry, 1982, *Israeli Nuclear Deterrence* by Shai Feldman, 1982 and *Dimona: The Third Temple?* by Mark Gaffney, 1989.
3.   *The Samson Option*, 97.
4.   Ibid., 168, 239-40.
5.   Ibid., 88.
6.   Ibid., 83.
7.   Ibid., 89.
8.   Interview of Yuval Ne'eman by Rael Jean Isaac, February 8, 1992.
9.   *The Samson Option,* 86.
10.   Ibid., 89.

11.   Ben Menashe eventually settled in Canada where he went into partnership with former U.S. businessman Alexander Henri Legault, who had repeatedly been indicted on fraud charges in the U.S. After a corporation they established to sell commodities failed, the pair reconstituted themselves as a political consultancy with the confidence-inspiring name of Dickens and Madsen Inc. Further details of Ben Menashe's exploits can be found in Rael Jean Isaac, "Africa's Saddam," *American Spectator* (June/July 2003), 50-51.

12.   *Newsweek*, November 4, 1991, 38.

13.   *The Samson Option*, 260.

14.   Ibid., 297-98.

15.   Steven Emerson, "The Man Behind the 'October Surprise' Lie," *Wall Street Journal*, November 27, 1991.

16.   *The Samson Option*, 260.

17.   Ibid., 286.

18.   Ibid., 298.

19.   Ibid., 139.

20.   Ibid., 309.

21.   Ibid., 312.

22.   Ibid., 276.

23.   Ibid., 312.

24.   Lawrence Freedman, "What Do They Have and When Did We Know It?" *New York Times Book Review*, November 17, 1991.

25.   Emerson, "Man Behind the 'October Surprise' Lie."

26.   Ibid.

27.   *The Samson Option*, 299.

28.   Hersh had pulled down a huge contract with ABC for a Kennedy documentary based on the documents; it fell apart when ABC concluded they were phony. Journalist John Miller has observed that Hersh came up "with desperate rationalizations for skeptics who wondered why documents containing Zip codes were dated before zip codes even existed."— Rael Jean Isaac, "The Cult of Seymour Hersh," *American Spectator* (July/August 2004), 19.

29.   *New York Times*, May 3, 1999. Comically, in one of his letters to Cusack, quoted in the *Times* article, Hersh wrote: "We got along so well at that dinner Tuesday night because, I like to think, we are all what we seem to be."

30.   *Newsweek*, November 4, 1991, 36-38. Maxwell and Davies sued but Maxwell died the following month, an apparent suicide, and his reputation was shattered amidst revelations of his extensive financial misconduct. The Mirror Group decided to get out of the action on any basis it could, paying Hersh undisclosed damages and his legal costs. It was a clear win for Hersh. *New York Times*, August 19, 1994.

31.   Emerson, "Man Behind the 'October Surprise' Lie."

32.   Ibid.

33.   John J. Miller, "Sly Sy," *National Review*, December 3, 2001, 33.

34.   *The Samson Option,* 233.

35.   Interview of Yuval Ne'eman by Rael Jean Isaac, Feb. 8, 1992.

36.   *The Samson Option,* 288-89.

37.   Ibid., 259.

38.   Letter from Richard M. Nixon to Russ Braley of January 22, 1992.

39.   *The Samson Option,* 264.

40.   Ibid., 274.

41.   Ibid., 12-13.

42.   Russ Braley, *Bad News: The Foreign Policy of the New York Times* (Chicago: Regnery Gateway, 1984), 340.

43.   Seymour Hersh, *Cover-Up: The Army's Secret Investigation of the Massacre at My Lai 4* (New York: Random House, 1972), 267.
44.   *Bad News,* 340.
45.   Ibid., 534.
46.   Joseph C. Goulden, *Fit to Print: A.M. Rosenthal and His Times* (Fort Lee: Lyle Stuart, 1988), 192.
47.   Seymour Hersh, *The Price of Power: Kissinger in the Nixon White House* (New York: Summit Books, 1983), 224.
48.   Michael Ledeen, "Getting Kissinger," *Commentary* (September 1983), 77.
49.   Seymour Hersh, *"The Target is Destroyed": What Really Happened to Flight 007 and What America Knew About It,* (New York: Random House, 1986), 103.
50.   John Barron, "KAL 007: The Hidden Story," *Reader's Digest,* November 1991, 73.
51.   *"The Target is Destroyed",* 190-91.
52.   The *New York Times* ran the series of six articles in August 1979.
53.   Seymour Hersh, *Chain of Command: The Road from 9/11 to Abu Ghraib* (New York: HarperCollins, 2004), 362.
54.   Seymour Hersh, "Lunch with the Chairman: Why Was Richard Perle Meeting with Adnan Kashoggi?" *New Yorker,* March 17, 2003, 76-80. In the first heat of anger Perle threatened to sue, calling Hersh the "closest thing American journalism has to a terrorist." He did not sue, probably wisely, given the difficulty a public figure has in prevailing under U.S. libel law. But the failure to sue was treated by both Remnick and Hersh as proof of the accuracy of Hersh's charges. See *Chain of Command,* xvii.
55.   Seymour Hersh, "The Coming Wars: What the Pentagon Can Now Do in Secret," *New Yorker,* January 24&31, 2005, 43.
56.   Seymour Hersh, "Moving Targets: A Vietnam Style Mission in Iraq," *New Yorker,* December 15, 2003, 48.
57.   Musharraf's question and Bush's reply, from Bob Woodward's book *Bush at War,* are quoted proudly by *New Yorker* editor David Remnick in his introduction to Hersh's *Chain of Command* (xix). Perversely, Remnick seems to take any testimony from government leaders regarding Hersh's falsehoods as tributes to his accuracy and integrity.
58.   Seymour Hersh, "The Coming Wars," 43.
59.   Ibid., 42-43. Actually, as Michael Ledeen points out, the article is not about American foreign policy at all, but "an overwritten and hyperventilated assault on Secretary Rumsfeld, for, according to Hersh, crushing the CIA in the interagency battles over control of intelligence operations," a claim which Ledeen says, like much else in the piece, is ridiculous. ("The Hersh File: Sy Gets it Wrong, Again," http://www.nationalreview.com, January 21, 2005).
60.   Seymour Hersh, "Plan B: As June 30th Approaches Israel Looks to the Kurds," *New Yorker,* June 28, 2004, 65.
61.   Ibid., 55.
62.   Ibid., 65.
63.   Ibid., 55.
64.   Michael Rubin, "Web of Conspiracies," *National Review Online,* May 18, 2004. While Rubin shows that Hersh bases himself on LaRouche-disseminated material here, in his attack on Perle "Lunch with the Chairman" Hersh accuses the Defense Policy Board of receiving a briefing from Rand Corporation analyst Laurent Murawiec, who was a former editor of La Rouche's *Executive Intelligence Review*: Hersh describes LaRouche as a "conspiracy theorist and felon." (78-79).
65.   John Miller, "Sly Sy," 32-33.

66. Max Boot, "Digging into Seymour Hersh," *Los Angeles Times*, January 27, 2005.
67. Chris Suellentrop, "Sy Hersh Says It's Okay to Lie (Just Not in Print)," *New York Magazine*, April 18, 2005, 40, 42.
68. Montgomery Brower, "Reporter Seymour Hersh Unravels the Tragic Mystery of Flight 007," *People Magazine*, October 15, 1986, 58.
69. *Chain of Command*, 219-20.
70. Michael Ledeen, "The Hersh File."

16

Benny Morris and the Myths
of Post-Zionist History

Efraim Karsh

The collapse and dispersion of Palestine's Arab society during the 1948 war is one of the most charged issues in the politics and historiography of the Arab-Israeli conflict. Initially, Palestinians blamed the Arab world for having promised military support that never materialized.[1] Arab host states in turn regarded the Palestinians as having shamefully deserted their homeland. With the passage of time and the dimming of historical memory, the story of the 1948 war was gradually rewritten with Israel rather than the Arab states and the extremist and shortsighted Palestinian leadership becoming the main if not only culprit of the Palestinian dispersion. This false narrative received a major boost in the late 1980s with the rise of several left-leaning Israeli academics and journalists calling themselves the New Historians, who sought to question and revise understanding of the Arab-Israeli conflict.[2] Ostensibly basing their research on recently declassified documents from the British Mandate period and the first years of Israeli independence, they systematically redrew the history of Zionism, turning upside down the saga of Israel's struggle for survival. Among the new historians, none has been more visible or more influential than Benny Morris, a professor at Ben-Gurion University in Beersheba, whose 1987 book, *The Birth of the Palestinian Refugee Problem 1947-1949*, became the New Historians' definitive work.

Prominent Palestinian politicians such as Mahmoud Abbas (Abu Mazen) and Hanan Ashrawi cited the "findings" of the New Historians to support extreme Palestinian territorial and political claims. Academics lauded Morris for using newly available documents to expose the allegedly immoral circumstances of Israel's creation. With frequent media exposure, the New Historians had an impact on mainstream Israeli opinion, which became increasingly receptive to the notion that both the blame for and the solution to the Arab-Israeli conflict lay disproportionately with Israel's own actions.

Such plaudits, however, were undeserved. Far from unearthing new facts or offering a novel interpretation of the Palestinian exodus, *The Birth* recycled the standard Arab narrative of the conflict. Morris portrayed the Palestinians as the hapless victims of unprovoked Jewish aggression. Israel's very creation became the "original sin" underlying the perpetuation of the Arab-Israeli conflict. Had there been an academic foundation to Morris's revisionism, such acclaim may have been warranted. But rather than incorporate new Israeli source material, Morris did little more than rehash old historiography. While laying blame for the Palestinian refugee crisis on the actions of the Israeli Defense Forces and its pre-state precursor, the Haganah, Morris failed to consult the millions of declassified documents in their archives, even as other historians used them in painstaking research.[3]

Once this fact was publicly exposed,[4] Morris conceded that he had "no access to the materials in the IDFA [Israel Defense Forces Archive] or Haganah archive and precious little to firsthand military materials deposited elsewhere."[5] Yet instead of acknowledging the implications of this omission for his conclusions, Morris sought to use this "major methodological flaw" as the rationale for a new edition of *The Birth*, which he claimed would include new sourcematerial.[6]

Dishonest Revisionism

Readers will be disappointed if they hope to find evidence of renewed intellectual honesty in this new edition, published in 2004 as *The Birth of the Palestinian Refugee Problem Revisited*.[7] Morris continues to ignore archival evidence both of relentless Arab rejection of Jewish statehood and of demonstrated commitment to Israel's destruction. Available Arabic sources little utilized by Morris include not only official documents but also religious incitement and numerous statements by politicians, intellectuals, and journalists.

While Morris perfunctorily acknowledges Palestinian and Arab culpability for the 1948 war,[8] *The Birth... Revisited* continues to portray Israeli actions as the main trigger of the Palestinian exodus. Morris explains,

> this is not a history of the 1948 war or a history of what the Arabs did to the Jews but a history of how and why the Palestinian refugee problem came about. In this context, what Jews did to Arabs, including massacres, played a role; what Arabs did to Jews was barely relevant.[9]

It is doubtful whether Morris believes his own assertion. In his writings and interviews over the past few years, he acknowledged that in war the activities of one belligerent affect all others. "From the moment the Yishuv [the pre-1948 Jewish community in Palestine] was attacked by the Palestinians and afterward by the Arab states, there was no choice but to expel the Palestinian population," he argued in January 2004.[10] Four months later he put the same idea in somewhat blunter terms: "When an armed thug tries to murder you in your home, you have every right to defend yourself, even by throwing him out."[11]

Not only does Morris miss the opportunity to reconcile his evolving positions regarding Arab and Palestinian culpability for the origin and perpetuation of the refugee problem, but he also intensifies efforts to give academic respectability to the Arab indictment of Zionism as "a colonizing and expansionist ideology and movement... intent on politically, or even physically, dispossessing and supplanting the Arabs."[12] In the original version of *The Birth*, Morris traced this alleged intention to the late 1930s and 1940s, claiming that Zionist leaders had despaired of achieving a Jewish majority in Palestine through mass immigration and had instead come to view the expulsion or "transfer" of the Arab population as the best means "to establish a Jewish state without an Arab minority, or with as small an Arab minority as possible."[13]

In reality, the archives show that, far from despairing of mass immigration, Zionist leaders in the 1930s worried about the country's short-term absorptive capacity should millions of Jews enter Palestine. In an implicit acknowledgment of their inaccuracy, Morris has removed some of *The Birth*'s most inaccurate or distorted quotations about transfer. (The most egregious of these was the distortion of an October 1937 letter from David Ben-Gurion to his son. Morris cited the letter as saying, "We must expel Arabs and take their places," when Ben-Gurion actually said, "We do not wish and do not need to expel Arabs and take their place.")[14] Nevertheless, he reverts to the problematic technique of relying on a small number of Zionist statements either taken out of context or simply misrepresented. In *The Birth... Revisited*, Morris takes his initial claim further by attempting to prove, in a new chapter trumpeted as one of the book's chief innovations, that "the displacement of Arabs from Palestine or from areas of Palestine that would become the Jewish State was inherent in Zionist ideology" and could be traced back to the father of political Zionism, Theodor Herzl.[15]

Distorting Herzl

Consider, for example, Morris's charge that Herzl wished to dispossess Palestinian Arabs because of his fear that the Jewish state would lack viability if it were to contain a large Arab minority. Morris bases this assertion only upon a truncated paragraph from Herzl's June 12, 1895 diary entry, which had already been a feature of Palestinian propaganda for decades.[16] But this entry was not enough to support such a claim. Below is the complete text, with the passages omitted by Morris in italics:

> *When we occupy the land, we shall bring immediate benefits to the state that receives us.* We must expropriate gently *the private property on the estates assigned to us.* We shall try to spirit the penniless population across the border by procuring employment for it in the transit countries, while denying it any employment in our country. *The property owners will come over to our side.* Both the process of expropriation and the removal of the poor must be carried out discreetly and circumspectly... *It goes without saying that we shall respectfully tolerate persons of other faiths and protect their property, their honor, and their freedom with the harshest means of coercion. This is another area in which we shall set the entire world a wonderful example... Should there be many such immovable owners in individual areas [who would not sell their prop-*

erty to us], we shall simply leave them there and develop our commerce in the direction of other areas which belong to us.[17]

By omitting the opening sentence, Morris hides the fact that Herzl viewed Jewish settlement as beneficial to the indigenous population and that he did not conceive of the new Jewish entity as comprising this country in its entirety. This is further underscored by Herzl's confinement of the envisaged expropriation of private property to "the estates assigned to us"—another fact omitted by Morris. Any discussion of relocation was clearly limited to the specific lands assigned to the Jews, rather than to the entire territory. Had Herzl envisaged the mass expulsion of population, as claimed by Morris, there would have been no need to discuss its position in the Jewish entity. Morris further ignored context. There was no trace of a belief in transfer in either Herzl's famous political treatise, *The Jewish State* (1896), or his 1902 Zionist novel, *Altneuland* (*Old-New Land*).[18] Nor for that matter is there any allusion to "transfer" in Herzl's public writings, his private correspondence, his speeches, or his political and diplomatic discussions. Morris simply discards the canon of Herzl's lifework in favor of a single, isolated comment.

Most importantly, Herzl's diary entry makes no mention of either Arabs or Palestine, and for good reason. A careful reading of Herzl's diary entries for June 1895 reveals that, at the time, he did not consider Palestine to be the future site of Jewish resettlement but rather South America.[19] "I am assuming that we shall go to Argentina," Herzl recorded in his diary on June 13. In his view, South America "would have a lot in its favor on account of its distance from militarized and seedy Europe.... If we are in South America, the establishment of our State will not come to Europe's notice for a considerable period of time."[20] Indeed, Herzl's diary entries during the same month illustrate that he conceived all political and diplomatic activities for the creation of the future Jewish state, including the question of the land and its settlement, in the Latin American context. "Should we go to South America," Herzl wrote on June 9, "our first state treaties will have to be with South American republics. We shall grant them loans in return for territorial privileges and guarantees." Four days later he wrote, "Through us and with us, an unprecedented commercial prosperity will come to South America."[21]

In short, Morris based his arguments on a red herring. He not only parsed a quotation to distort its original meaning, but he ignored the context, which had nothing to do with Palestine or Arabs.

Misrepresenting the Early Zionists

Morris applies similar distortions to other early Zionist leaders. He repeatedly takes isolated and unrepresentative assertions out of context while omitting the often overwhelming evidence that undercut his thesis. For example, Morris takes an extraordinary approach to Ze'ev (Vladimir) Jabotinsky, the founding father of the branch of Zionism that was the forerunner of today's

Likud party. While Morris cites a number of statements showing Jabotinsky's public rejection of transfer—for example, his testimony before the 1936 Peel Commission, which investigated the roots of the Arab uprising—he, nevertheless, makes the unsubstantiated assertion that Jabotinsky "generally supported transfer."[22] Just as with his treatment of Herzl, Morris's conclusions fly in the face of the historical record. In 1934, for example, Jabotinsky's Revisionist Party prepared a draft constitution for Jewish Palestine that put the Arab minority on an equal footing with its Jewish counterpart "throughout all sectors of the country's public life." The two communities were to share the state's duties, both military and civil service, and enjoy its prerogatives. Jabotinsky proposed that Hebrew and Arabic should enjoy equal rights and that "in every cabinet where the prime minister is a Jew, the vice-premiership shall be offered to an Arab and vice versa."[23]

Morris also twists the historical record to indict Arthur Ruppin, who headed the Zionist Organization's Palestine office. Morris's condemnation of Ruppin revolves around the latter's sole suggestion at a 1911 meeting of "'a limited population transfer' of peasants to Syria."[24] Again, Morris cites selectively in order to make his comment appear to be something it was not. The original document shows that Ruppin was not discussing Palestine's Arab population as a whole but rather those Arabs squatting on land purchased by Jews. Far from becoming policy, Ruppin's limited proposal was rejected. Morris further makes no mention of Ruppin's comments two years later at the eleventh Zionist congress, where he stated, "It is, of course, useless to content ourselves with merely assuring the Arabs that we are coming into the country as their friends. We must prove this by our deeds."[25]

Morris's treatment of Ruppin shows shoddy scholarship. Part of the problem is that Morris neglected to examine the original document. He, instead, points readers to his own book, *Righteous Victims*, which in turn cited the polemical book, *Expulsion of the Palestinians: The Concept of Transfer in Zionist Political Thought, 1882-1948*,[26] by the London-based Palestinian academic, Nur Masalha. Masalha worked from Walter Laqueur's *A History of Zionism* (1972), which itself was based on an earlier study by the Israeli scholar Paul Alsberg, once chief archivist of Israel's State Archives. The inaccuracy developed with Morris's trust of Masalha, who dismissed the historical context. As Laqueur explained in his original work:

> [T]he idea of a population transfer was never official Zionist policy. Ben-Gurion emphatically rejected it, saying that even if the Jews were given the right to evict the Arabs, they would not make use of it. Most thought at that time that there would be sufficient room in Palestine for both Jews and Arabs following the industrialization of the country and the introduction of intensive methods of agriculture. Since no one before 1914 expected the disintegration of the Turkish Empire... the question of political autonomy did not figure in their thoughts. They were genuinely aggrieved that the Arabs were not more grateful for the economic benefits that they had come to enjoy as the result of Jewish immigration and settlement.[27]

Morris also butchers Chaim Weizmann's record by claiming that Weizmann "suggested to British Colonial Secretary Lord Passfield that a solution to Palestine's problems might lie across the Jordan: Palestine's troublesome Arabs could be transferred over the river."[28] In fact, it was Passfield, not Weizmann, who made this suggestion. As Weizmann recounted:

> Lord Passfield agreed with the force of the argument; at the same time he said one had to stabilize conditions in the country. He didn't think it was an insuperable difficulty, and there could be no question of conceding anything to the Arabs which was against the spirit of the Mandate, and the report did not concede anything. Possibly, he said, Transjordan might be a way out.[29]

Morris repeats the same distortion with regard to a January 1941 conversation between Weizmann and Ivan Maiskii, the Soviet ambassador in London, by claiming that Weizmann initiated talk of a transfer when the opposite was true.[30] "The British are hardly likely to agree to this," Weizmann told Maiskii. "And if they don't agree, what happens next?"[31]

In July 1937, the Peel Commission recommended partition of Palestine into two states: a Jewish state to comprise 15 percent of the territory west of the Jordan River and an Arab state, to be united with Transjordan, itself carved from eastern Palestine in 1921. To prevent friction between the two communities, the commission suggested "a transfer of land and, as far as possible, an exchange of population" between the Jewish and the Arab states. The idea was not to transfer either community outside the bounds of Palestine but rather to the territories of the respective Arab and Jewish states, nor even to transfer the Jewish state's entire Arab population.[32] Here is how Morris related Weizmann's reaction to the report:

> After seeing a copy of the Peel Commission Report, Weizmann met Colonial Secretary William Ormsby-Gore, in secret, on 19 July 1937, and wholeheartedly endorsed the transfer recommendation: "I said," Weizmann reported, "that the whole success of the [partition] scheme depended on whether the Government... [carried] out this recommendation." Ormsby-Gore "agreed that once the Galilee was given to the Jews... the position would be very difficult without transfer."[33]

But, when Morris's omissions are restored, Weizmann's reaction was actually quite different. Again, text removed by Morris is included in italics.

> I said that the whole success of the scheme depended on whether the Government *genuinely did or did not wish to carry* out this recommendation; *the transfer could be carried out only by the British Government, and not by the Jews. I explained the reasons why we considered this proposal of such importance. Mr. Ormsby-Gore said that he was proposing to set up a committee for the twofold purpose (a) of finding land for the transferees (they hoped to find land in Transjordan, and possibly also in the Negev), and (b) of arranging the actual terms of the transfer...* He agreed that once [the] Galilee was given to the Jews, *and not the Negev*, the position would be very difficult without transfer.[34]

By twisting quotations to fit his thesis, Morris misrepresents Weizmann, who did not meet Ormsby-Gore to express his delight, as Morris implies, but rather to inform the colonial secretary of Jewish apprehensions about the Peel report. As Weizmann related in his report, "I said that I had come to see him to try and clarify a number of points. The Jews were perplexed, and a great many of them were against the partition scheme."[35] While Weizmann was concerned about the British government's intention to carry out the proposed population exchange, Morris rewrote the passage to imply that Weizmann spoke about its actual implementation.

Distorting Ben-Gurion

Perhaps no figure is a greater victim of Morris's distortions than David Ben-Gurion, Israel's founding father and the man who announced the Jewish state's independence. By discrediting Ben-Gurion, Morris seeks to indict Israel's birth. As in the first edition, the base for Morris's assertions that Ben-Gurion was a strong transfer advocate revolves around misreading of the Peel Commission and the subsequent Woodhead Commission.

Morris describes a July 1936 meeting between Ben-Gurion and the high commissioner for Palestine. According to Morris:

> by 1936, the mainstream Zionist leaders were more forthright in their support of transfer. In July, Ben-Gurion, the chairman of the Jewish Agency Executive and de facto leader of the Yishuv, and his deputy, Moshe Shertok (Sharett), the director of the agency's political department, went to the high commissioner to plead the Zionist case on immigration, which the Mandatory was considering suspending: Ben-Gurion asked whether the government would make it possible for Arab cultivators displaced through Jewish land purchase... to be settled in Transjordan. If Transjordan was for the time being a country closed to the Jews, surely it could not be closed to Arabs, also. The high commissioner thought this a good idea.... He asked whether the Jews would be prepared to spend money on the settlement of such Palestinian Arabs in Transjordan. Mr. Ben-Gurion replied that this might be considered.[36]

By linking the issue of Jewish immigration to expulsion of Palestinians, Morris implies a zero-sum relationship between the two. Nothing could be further from the truth. The Zionists in general and Ben-Gurion in particular had since the early twentieth century emphasized that there was sufficient room in Palestine for the two communities. Indeed, the "transfer issue" was not raised at the above meeting at all.

And Morris's first ellipsis in the passage he did quote? He omitted Ben-Gurion's mention of western Palestine, thereby obfuscating the Zionist leader's perception of Transjordan as "eastern Palestine." Such a perception would undercut Morris's thesis that the Zionists sought to expel the Arabs from Palestine.[37]

Further compounding this misrepresentation, Morris takes out of context a Ben-Gurion comment from a November 1, 1936 Jewish Agency Executive meeting. In reporting Ben-Gurion's words, he omits those words present in the original document, represented below in italics:

We will tell [the Peel Commission] that Palestine extends over both banks of the Jordan River, and that we have the right to settle there. But if because of security considerations, the time is not yet ripe for our settlement there (and the government acknowledges our right to do so, albeit not in public), why can't we acquire land there for Arabs, who wish to settle in Transjordan? If it was permissible to move an Arab from the Galilee to Judea, why is it impossible to move an Arab from the Hebron area to Transjordan, which is much closer? *He, Mr. Ben-Gurion, sees no fundamental difference between the eastern and the western parts of Palestine.*

Dr. Hexter: It is clear that any agricultural question in the country is tied to political issues.

Mr. Ben-Gurion: If the government agrees to move the Arabs from place to place, why shouldn't it agree to move peasants to Transjordan? There are vast expenses of land there and we [in western Palestine] are over-crowded.

Rabbi Fishman asks whether the removal of Arabs to Transjordan does not imply an acknowledgement that we have no rights in Transjordan?

Mr. Ben-Gurion: Certainly not. We now want to create concentrated areas of Jewish settlement, and by transferring the land-selling Arab to Transjordan, we can solve the problem of this concentration.[38]

By misrepresenting the original text, Morris seeks to create an impression that Ben-Gurion endeavored to expel the Arabs from Palestine when what he discussed was resettlement within Palestine. After all, the record demonstrates repeatedly that Zionists viewed Transjordan as an integral part of Palestine in accordance with the League of Nations mandate.[39]

Morris repeats the same distortion when describing a later Jewish Agency Executive meeting:

[T]he Jewish Agency Executive—the "government" of the Yishuv—discussed transfer [Morris writes]. On June 7, 1938, proposing Zionist policy guidelines, Ben-Gurion declared: "The Jewish State will discuss with the neighboring Arab states the matter of voluntarily transferring Arab tenant-farmers, laborers, and peasants from the Jewish state to the neighboring Arab states."[40]

Morris creates the impression that Ben-Gurion proposed his policy guidelines in the midst of a discussion of the transfer idea and that these guidelines revolved around that idea. In fact, there was no discussion of transfer at that particular meeting. The agenda included eight items, of which the question of the Arabs in the prospective Jewish state ranked sixth. Of the eighteen packed pages of the meeting's protocol, only four lines referred to the possibility of the voluntary removal of some Arabs who, "of their free will" (*mi-toch retsonam ha-hofshi*), might choose to leave the Jewish state.[41]

Without evidence, Morris speculates that "some executive members may have regarded this [the granting of full equality to the Arab citizens of the prospective Jewish state] as for-the-record lip service and posturing for posterity."[42] But the fact remains that the meeting dealt with the position of the Arab minority in the prospective Jewish state—not their expulsion. Not only was this tolerant vision of Arab-Jewish coexistence inherent in Ben-Gurion's strategic thinking from the 1910s until the 1948 war, but also many of the guidelines presented at this meeting became Israel's established policy toward its Arab minority.

Such selective rendering is reflective of Morris's method. He repeatedly takes a remark out of context and then dismisses the rest of the text as insincere propaganda. Thus, for example, at the November 1, 1936 Jewish Agency Executive meeting, he ignores Ben-Gurion's statement, "We do not deny the right of the Arab inhabitants of the country, and we do not see this right as a hindrance to the realization of Zionism."[43] He likewise dismisses as phony "professions of liberal egalitarianism"[44] Ben-Gurion's assertions, in an October 1941 internal policy paper, that "Jewish immigration and colonization in Palestine on a large scale can be carried out without displacing Arabs," and that "in a Jewish Palestine the position of the Arabs will not be worse than the position of the Jews themselves."[45]

The list of Morris's inaccuracies extends even further, though. In April 1944, the British Labor Party adopted an election platform, which among other positions advocated a transfer of Arabs from Palestine. According to Morris, "the publication of the resolution prompted a debate on May 7 in the Jewish Agency Executive—not so much about the notion of transfer (all were agreed about its merits if not its practicality) as about how the Zionist leadership should react."[46] Reality, however, was quite different. The meeting was not convened in response to the Labor resolution but to hear a political report by Moshe Sharett, then head of the Jewish Agency's political department, upon his return from a working trip to London. This focused on a number of issues that preoccupied the Zionist movement at the time, from the acrimonious working relationship between Ben-Gurion and Weizmann, to the rescue of the remnants of European Jewry, to Jewish immigration to Palestine, to general U.S. and British policy. Labor's election platform occupied a minor place in Sharett's presentation (about two of seventeen pages)—not surprising given Labor's position as an opposition party at the time. There was no debate whatsoever at the May 7 meeting although some participants did express their views.

Again, Morris provides only a truncated rendition of Ben-Gurion's comments, ignoring all that text italicized below:

> *This resolution has three phases: 1) [the creation of] a Jewish state; 2) the expansion of the Jewish state's borders; 3) transfer. The first thing should be received with great satisfaction; at least from a moral point of view, it is very satisfactory. As for the second thing, we will certainly not bemoan it. The third thing [transfer] can be problematic.*
> When I heard about these things *from the newspapers*, I had some difficult thoughts. *This question troubled me last night, and even more so yesterday. I asked myself: "What if I happened to be in London, and they came to ask me whether or not to introduce [the transfer issue], or if after introducing this [clause] they asked me whether or not to leave it in place?" I would like to tell [you] the conclusion I reached,*

and it might not be the correct one. I can't say that I have a feeling of complete certainty. There are pros and cons in this issue. The question is that of weighing one factor against the other, and should we not be able to do something to keep the first two items alone, should we do this [i.e., support the keeping of the transfer issue as well]? And I reached the conclusion that it is better that this thing remains.[47]

By ignoring the most important elements of the Labor resolution, Morris withholds the real gist of Ben-Gurion's reasoning. In contrast to Morris's claim, far from relishing the introduction of transfer into Labor's platform, Ben-Gurion viewed it as an unwarranted impediment that might complicate an otherwise historic platform. Had transfer been proposed on its own, Ben-Gurion would have dismissed it out of hand:

> Were they to ask [me]: "What should be our [i.e. the British Labor's] program?" I would find it inconceivable to tell them transfer. Were they to ask me whether to introduce this [transfer] as well [in addition to the proposal on a Jewish state], I would not have advised them to do so, because talk on the subject might cause harm... But now we are confronted with a fait accompli. It is not the Jews who made or publicized this [proposal] but rather gentiles. Englishmen made this proposal and advertised it.[48]

None of this elaborate reasoning is noted by Morris.

In the end, whatever was said at the Jewish Agency Executive meeting is immaterial simply because the Zionist movement rejected the British Labor Party's transfer recommendation. In the original edition of *The Birth*, Morris concedes that "Ben-Gurion, testifying before UNSCOP [United Nations Special Commission on Palestine] on 8 July 1947, went out of his way to reject the 1945 British Labor Party platform 'International Post-war Settlement' which supported the encouragement of the movement of the Palestine Arabs to the neighbouring countries to make room for Jews."[49] In the revised edition, he ignores this fact altogether in an attempt to create the false impression of Zionist endorsement of the proposal.

Morris's misrepresentation is all the more significant since just months after Ben-Gurion's testimony before the UN Special Commission on Palestine, the Palestinian Arabs launched a war to abort the UN's partition resolution of November 29, 1947. Having falsified Ben-Gurion's actual position, Morris claims that "by 1948, transfer was in the air." While he concedes that "the Yishuv and its military forces did not enter the 1948 war, which was initiated by the Arab side, with a policy or plan of expulsion," he argues that lack of an official policy made little difference, since "thinking about the possibilities of transfer in the 1930s and 1940s had prepared and conditioned hearts and minds for its implementation in the course of 1948."[50] Morris cites no evidence to support this claim nor could he, for there was never any Zionist attempt to inculcate the "transfer" idea in the hearts and minds of Jews. He could find no evidence of any press campaign, radio broadcasts, public rallies, or political gatherings, for none existed.

In contrast to Morris's thesis—and the rhetoric of many Arab politicians at the time—Ben-Gurion told his party members, "In our state there will be non-

Jews as well—and all of them will be equal citizens; equal in everything without any exception; that is: the state will be their state as well."[51] In line with this conception, committees laying the groundwork for the nascent Jewish state discussed in detail the establishment of an Arabic-language press, Arab health care, incorporation of Arab officials into the government, integration of Arabs within the police and the ministry of education, and Arab-Jewish cultural and intellectual interaction. No less importantly, the Haganah's military plan to rebuff an anticipated pan-Arab invasion was itself predicated, in the explicit instructions of Israel Galili, the Haganah's commander-in-chief, on the "acknowledgement of the full rights, needs, and freedom of the Arabs in the Hebrew state without any discrimination, and a desire for coexistence on the basis of mutual freedom and dignity."[52]

Conclusion

The Birth... Revisited is a misnomer. Rather than offer a reassessment of Morris's previous writings on the creation of the Palestinian refugee problem, *The Birth... Revisited* is but a longer replica of its dishonest and shoddy predecessor. To downplay his failure to consult the most important archives in the preparation of *The Birth*, Morris argued that "the new materials... tend to confirm and reinforce the major lines of description and analysis, and the conclusions, in *The Birth*."[53] And so, *The Birth... Revisited* continues the stubborn refusal of Morris to base his arguments and conclusions on archival evidence and the historical record. Far from confirming and reinforcing his arguments, archival documents demonstrate that "the Palestinian refugee problem" was the creation of Palestinian and other Arab leaders, not of the Zionists.

Ironically, Morris's press comments from the time during which he drafted *The Birth... Revisited* again contradict his conclusions, squarely putting the blame for the Palestinian tragedy on "the instinctive rejectionism that runs like a dark thread through Palestinian history."[54] Yet this is not good enough. For the damage done by Morris's written words outweigh his more truthful public assertions. His books have become a staple of the academic curriculum in both Western and Israeli universities. And so the younger generation of students will continue to be inculcated with the lies and distortions on the origin of the Palestinian refugee problem. That Morris admits errors, but continues to print them, raises questions about whether the star New Historian is motivated more by headlines than by truth. Whatever his motives, it is both truth and scholarship which suffer.

Notes

1. Sir J. Troutbeck, "Summary of general impressions gathered during weekend visit to the Gaza district," June 16, 1949, FO 371/75342/E7816, p. 123.
2. Benny Morris, *The Birth of the Palestinian Refugee Problem, 1947-1949* (Cambridge: Cambridge University Press, 1987); Avi Shlaim, *Collusion across the Jordan: King Abdullah, the Zionist Movement, and the Partition of Palestine* (Oxford:

Clarendon Press, 1988); Simha Flapan, *The Birth of Israel: Myths and Reality* (New York: Pantheon, 1987); Ilan Pappe, *The Making of the Arab-Israeli Conflict, 1947-1951* (London: I.B. Tauris, 1992).

3. Among these were Uri Milstein, Shabtai Teveth, Elhannan Orren, Michael Bar-Zohar, Dan Kurzman, Yitzhak Levi, Yuval Arnon-Ohana, and Shmuel Dotan.

4. See, for example, Efraim Karsh, *Fabricating Israeli History: The "New Historians,"* 2nd rev. ed. (London: Cass, 2000), 195-6.

5. Morris, "Revisiting the Palestinian Exodus of 1948," in *The War for Palestine: Rewriting the History of 1948*, ed. Eugene L. Rogan and Avi Shlaim (Cambridge: Cambridge University Press, 2001), 37.

6. Morris, "For the Record," *Guardian*, January 14, 2004.

7. Cambridge: Cambridge University Press, 2004.

8. Morris, *The Birth of the Palestinian Refugee Problem Revisited* (Cambridge: Cambridge University Press, 2004), 7, 588 (hereinafter *The Birth... Revisited*).

9. Ibid., 7.

10. Ari Shavit, "Survival of the Fittest," interview with Benny Morris, *Ha'aretz Weekly Magazine* (Tel Aviv), January 1, 2004.

11. *New Republic*, May 3, 2004.

12. Morris, *Righteous Victims: A History of the Zionist-Arab Conflict, 1881-1999* (New York: Alfred A. Knopf, 1999), 652, 654.

13. Morris, *The Birth*, 24; idem, *1948 and After: Israel and the Palestinians* (Oxford: Clarendon Press, 1994), 17.

14. Morris, *The Birth*, 25.

15. Morris, *The Birth... Revisited*, 5, 60, 588.

16. See, for example, *From Haven to Conquest: Readings in Zionism and the Palestine Problem until 1948*, ed. Walid Khalidi (Washington, DC: Institute for Palestine Studies, 1971), 118-19; David Hirst, *The Gun and the Olive Branch* (London: Futura, 1978), 18; Edward Said, *The Question of Palestine* (New York: Vintage Books, 1979), 13.

17. Morris, *The Birth... Revisited*, 40-1; *The Complete Diaries of Theodor Herzl*, ed Raphael Patai (New York: Herzl Press and Thomas Yoseloff, 1960), I, 88, 90 (hereafter Herzl diaries).

18. Morris, *The Birth... Revisited*, 41.

19. Herzl diaries, 133. Four days earlier, Herzl recorded in his diary, "In Palestine's disfavor is its proximity to Russia and Europe, its lack of room for expansion as well as its climate, which we are no longer accustomed to." He saw only one major advantage in this location: "the mighty legend"—Ibid., 56.

20. Herzl diaries, 69-70, 134.

21. Ibid., 70, 92, 134-5.

22. Morris, *The Birth... Revisited*, 45.

23. Vladimir Jabotinsky, *The Jewish War Front* (London: Allen and Unwin, 1940), 216-17.

24. Morris, *The Birth... Revisited*, p. 41.

25. Walter Laqueur, *A History of Zionism* (New York: MJF Books, 2003; reprint of the original 1972 edition), 230-1.

26. Washington D.C., Institute for Palestine Studies, 1992.

27. Laqueur, *A History of Zionism*, 232.

28. Morris, *The Birth... Revisited*, 44.

29. Chaim Weizmann, "Awaiting the Shaw Report" (report on a conversation with Lord Passfield on March 6, 1930), in *The Letters and Papers of Chaim Weizmann, Series B* (New Brunswick, NJ: Transaction Puublishers, 1983), 591.

30. Morris, *The Birth... Revisited*, 52-3.
31. "Meeting: I.M. Maiskii—Ch. Weizmann (London, 3 February 1941)," in *Documents on Israeli-Soviet Relations, 1941-1953*, part I (London: Frank Cass, 2000), 4-5.
32. Palestine Royal Commission, *Report, Presented by the Secretary of State for the Colonies to Parliament by Command of His Majesty, July 1937*, Cmd. 5479 (London: HMSO, 1937), 291-93 (hereinafter, Peel report).
33. Morris, *The Birth... Revisited*, 62, n. 24.
34. Ibid., 56-7. For the first italicized clause Morris substituted "carried."
35. Chaim Weizmann, "Summary Note of Interview with Mr. Ormsby Gore, Colonial Office, Monday, July 19th, 1937, at 10.45 a.m.," Weizmann Archive, 56.
36. Morris, *The Birth... Revisited*, 45-6.
37. "Note of a Conversation between Mr. D. Ben-Gurion and Mr. M. Shertok and His Excellency the High Commissioner on Thursday, July 9th, 1936, at Government Offices," Central Zionist Archives (CZA), S25/19, pp. 4-5.
38. Morris, *The Birth... Revisited*, 46, compared with "Protocol of the Meeting of the Jewish Agency Executive, held in Jerusalem on Nov. 1, 1936," CZA, S100-20A, pp. 8-9.
39. Peel report, 228, 304.
40. Morris, *The Birth... Revisited*, 49.
41. "Protocol of the Meeting of the Jewish Agency Executive, held in Jerusalem on Jun. 7, 1938," CZA S100/24b, pp. 5970-1 (lines of action 18, 22).
42. Morris, *The Birth... Revisited*, 50.
43. "Protocol of the Meeting of the Jewish Agency Executive, held in Jerusalem on Nov. 1, 1936," CZA, 7.
44. Morris, *The Birth... Revisited*, 63, n. 31.
45. David Ben-Gurion, "Outlines of Zionist Policy—Private and Confidential," Oct. 15, 1941, CZA Z4/14632, p. 15 (iii, iv).
46. Morris, *The Birth... Revisited*, 54.
47. Ibid., 55, compared with "Protocol of the Meeting of the Jewish Agency Executive, held in Jerusalem on May 7, 1944," CZA, S100, p. 10177.
48. "Protocol of the Meeting of the Jewish Agency Executive, May 7, 1944," 10178.
49. Morris, *The Birth*, 28.
50. Morris, *The Birth... Revisited*, 60.
51. David Ben-Gurion, *Ba-ma'araha,* vol. IV, part 2 (Tel Aviv: Misrad Ha'bitahon, 1959), 260.
52. Rama to brigade commanders, "Arabs Residing in the Enclaves," March 24, 1948, Haganah Archives 46/109/5.
53. Morris, "Revisiting the Palestinian Exodus of 1948," 37.
54. Morris, "The Rejection," review of Baruch Kimmerling and Joel S. Migdal, *The Palestinian People: A History,* in *New Republic,* April 21, 2003.

17

New Trends and Old Hatreds: Antisemitism in the Twenty-First Century

Irving Louis Horowitz

"Of all the strange phenomena produced by society certainly one of the most puzzling is self-hatred... Why hate yourself when there are so many willing to do it for you! But the ubiquitousness of self-hatred cannot be denied. And it has shaped the self-awareness of those treated as different perhaps more than they themselves have been aware." —*Sander L. Gilman* (Jewish Self-Hatred)[1]

The greatest difficulty in writing about antisemitism is that appeals to empirical or factual evidence have extremely limited corrective value. Ideologies that have endured for centuries across time and nations are not about to dissolve in the face of citations of actual Jewish achievements, or, for that matter, statistical limits in such achievements. Ideologies dissolve slowly, if at all, over time. Frequent and exaggerated claims to the "end of ideology" and the "end of history" notwithstanding, antisemitic ideologies may change in coloration or emphasis, and even in their capacity to influence actual events on the ground. But such ideologies are unlikely to dissolve under the weight of social research agendas or religious conciliation commissions. To say that is not to reject the need to expose moral rot in a society, or to deny the importance of evidence as a measure of collective worth. It is to say that only an overblown optimist or a supreme egoist could imagine that world historic changes will take place as a result of such efforts.

What I wish to present in these brief remarks is not an empirical treatise on the status of prejudice, but rather a sociology-of-knowledge overview of the status of an embedded ideology as it persists over time and adapts to circumstances, particularly as it encroaches upon Jewish intellectual life.[2] The information presented relates, therefore, to changes in the forms and formations of bias, hatred, prejudice, and visions of the good society. The reason why such a topic is significant is that ideologies, like genuine ideas, have real consequences for actions—they influence not just sentiments but activities intended to enhance individuals and groups at one extreme and to annihilate them at the other. These oft-neglected truisms of classical social theory spring readily to mind as we examine the persistence of antisemitism.

It is best to start with a historical commonplace that parallels our sociological starting point. Antisemitism has deep roots in Western culture. Even as we attempt to define current nuances and innovations, it is best to acknowledge these roots. What we experience today is less innovation than variations on an inherited social malady that refuses to disappear—even as the Holocaust remains a living memory. Within Western culture, antisemitism developed a series of stereotypes, half-truths, and mobilizing fantasies, elevated to the doctrinal level. Antisemitism involves a belief that Jews have inherited theological and social characteristics that stamp them as a race, culture, or people apart. That very apartness itself permits the demagogue or fanatic to treat this people as sub-human, hence deserving of inhuman collective punishment.

The subaltern literature of antisemites endows Jews with an amazing ability to survive because they share a fantastic ability to manage and manipulate world markets, a parallel capacity to place themselves or be placed in positions of influence and authority, and an endowed cultural separateness—something geographical as well as cultural—that encourages clanlike behavior and cunning disregard for the generalized "other." Such literature sees all this as made possible by secret codes that reside in the Tanakh or Hebrew Bible, embellished by numerological arrangements found in the Kabbala. These allegedly reveal how Jews acquire an unnatural advantage over the rest of the human race. This delusion has given rise to the curious belief that antisemitism was the same in the first century as it is in the twenty-first. Arthur Blech in *The Causes of Anti-Semitism* has most recently expressed this idiosyncratic view.[3] However, since the Bible is the source of philosemitic as well as antisemitic beliefs, such arguments that everything antisemitic derives from Jewish belief in "false gods" are little more than a theological exercise in antiquarian sources of error.

What has proved more potent in rationalizing antisemitism is the idea that the Hebrew Scriptures, and Jewish practices, contain beliefs that translate into contempt for other religions that claim to have found salvation, or other nations that are rooted in the mysteries of the soil. The ultimate expression of such a view is the *Protocols of the Learned Elders of Zion*, in which world conquest rather than national survival is seen as the goal of the Jewish people. Through such assumptions, antisemites can justify a policy of isolating, disenfranchising, and delegitimizing the Jews, as an act of self-defense; the hatred of the dominant society becomes an extension and reflection of the secret desire of Jews for separation and apartness.

This collective portrait of the Jewish people has been repeated with such frequency and fervor over the past century that some if not all of these slanders are taken as truths not only by overt enemies of the Jewish people, but by a segment of Jews themselves. Indeed, what antisemites first present as a rationale for isolating and even killing Jews is internalized by a small segment of Jews as a source of survival, even strength! Self-hatred, disguised as elite cleverness, can be found in all classes and in all places. "Birthright" Jews - from world-class chess masters like Bobby Fischer (who sees Jewish conspirators behind every media request for an interview) to world-class servants of Nazism like Otto Weininger (Hitler's favorite Jew—doubtless in part because of his early suicide) and Theodor Lessing (the very opposite of his famed predecessor of the German Enlightenment with the same last name) have had little trouble rationalizing their antisemitism as simple candor; making public what is loudly whispered in private. Indeed, even as Stalin was preparing to execute Jewish professionals and send others into permanent exile, he could count on the support of Jews who were part of the Politburo—Lazar Kaganovich being the prime example.

The Court Jew is that special variety of Jewish self-hater who validates the slanderer as he attempts to curry the favor of masters and rulers in order to survive in a world he sees as inhospitable to Jews as a culture, nation or people— or all three rolled into one. And from that survivalist behavior, the canard emerges that Jews must be not just punished but murdered, because they are uniquely capable of extracting blood from a turnip; and therefore the turnip must be eradicated. The marginalization of the Jew in Europe encouraged conflation of the Court Jew with the self-hating Jew.[4] Such a linkage came to a sharp, but temporary, termination with the Holocaust at one end, and the emergence of Israel as an independent nation born of struggle and battle at the other. This strange phenomenon shows signs of renewed life in the human rights movements, especially as they affect the Middle East situation. For example, identification of Jewish "peace now" ethics with Muslim insistence on the removal of the entire Israeli presence from (at least) the so-called West Bank and the Gaza Strip has elicited broad public support. Secular groups see Jewish Orthodoxy as a stumbling block on the ground to reconciliation. Manifestly left-wing groups envision some Greater Palestine moving beyond religious identification to a wholly secular source of state power. Curiously, the same argument for secularization is rarely articulated for the much larger Muslim-led nations.

Double Standards and the Revival of Nationalism

Let me turn now to new variations on this tangled web of hatred and self-hatred. Far from vanishing, the fusion of Gentile antisemitism with the antisemitism of Jews themselves has become an instrument of choice in this never-ending contention over specifically Jewish or Zionist aspirations.

One of the more curious developments in the first decade of the new millennium is the revival of the canard of the Jewish national homeland as a cause of divided loyalties to the nations of the world in which Jews reside. While there is ample evidence that Jews can accommodate themselves, even enthusiastically, to new homelands (especially when they are lodged in democratic nations), they are still pilloried, and with increasing severity, for lack of patriotism and for private schemes to advance Jewish and Zionist interests. What makes this especially bizarre as a charge is that it takes place at the same time that every other minority is being encouraged to advance its "cultural identity" and national character.

In a nation such as the United States, the hyphenated identity has become normal: from Greek-Americans to African-Americans the expectation of dual loyalties, separate holidays, and special rituals has become commonplace. Indeed, even within this growth of dualism between new and old national identities is a further ethnic distinction. Peoples from Jamaica or the Ukraine residing in the United States have yet a third strong identity to go along with their inherited ethnic and acquired national identifications; and that is regionalism, localism, and at times religious affiliation as such. While multiculturalism as an ideology has been argued widely amongst the intelligentsia and policy-making sectors, its existence as a social and political force can hardly be questioned. But Jewish identity alone is frequently castigated as somehow subversive or disrespectful of the citizen's national patriotic obligations.

While this tendency is still held in check in places like the United States, and to a lesser extent, Canada and Great Britain, in France the trend has been to revive the anti-Dreyfusard spirit, and that of the secular Enlightenment of the late eighteenth century, singling out the Jewish community for special vilification.[5] Articles with the title: "Is There a Future for French Jewry?" indicate that the Jew-as-outsider theme persists as a matter of French domestic no less than foreign policy. As Shmuel Trigano has observed:

> Contrary to much of what is said today about anti-Jewish sentiment in France, its roots are to be found not in any specific Israeli policy with respect to the Palestinians. Rather, they lie deep within the French body politic. For this reason, it is a profound error to argue, as many have, that the problem will be resolved through a solution to the Arab-Israeli conflict, or that any of the conventional methods—such as increased law enforcement or public awareness campaigns—will succeed in defeating it. Indeed, the current outbreak of anti-Semitism in France is little more than a symptom of a far deeper crisis confronting French Jewry.[6]

And that deeper crisis is the capacity of democracy itself to withstand the totalitarian onslaught from abroad and the reactionary traditions from within.

Nationalism as the enemy of Jews is not a phenomenon unique to French history—or for that matter, Jewish existence from South Africa to Romania. Double standards have infected democratic states that in the past held high the idea of toleration and fairness to their Jewish citizens, but now have incorporated the vision of extremist regimes, of both the Left and the Right. What prevents this macabre development from becoming immediately explosive is not any love of Jews within democratic polities, but the emergence of other, more pressing opponents to liberal and open societies. In the present period the Arab Muslim influx into Europe is sufficiently disturbing, indeed deadly, to

Europeans to prevent concentrated attention on the Jewish remnants—for that is what they are fact becoming in a demographic context in which Muslims vastly outnumber Jews in European states by huge majorities.

If Jewish accommodation to democratic societies is taken for granted, Muslim resistance to the culture of democracy is now equally a given. The struggle in France over special clothing requirements of Muslim girls attending public educational institutions has thrown this difference into sharp relief. The grounds of secularism as a consequence of the French Revolution of 1789 have been called into question by demands for unique modes of dress. The French government response was to reiterate its secular character, and cautiously resist such separatist tendencies in public places. But the irony of the situation is that the mass demand to wear headscarves among the Muslim minority was conflated with the very rare appearance in public of Jewish children wearing yarmulkes! Equating the two made a common mode of dress appear to be a requirement of democratic order, obscuring acknowledgment by government officials of a unique problem: Muslim clerical resistance to democratic culture as such.

In a thoughtful essay, David Pryce-Jones concludes that France "has had to come to terms with a growing Arab underclass, one whose resentments and tendencies to violence have been whipped up in no small part by the inflexible hostility displayed by the French state to Jewish self-determination. The pursuit of *une puissance musulmane*, fitting Arabs and Jews into a grand design on French terms, has evidently been an intellectual illusion all along, and highly dangerous to the interests of everyone concerned."[7]

It hardly needs to be added that although the sort of nationalist trend evidenced in France may have "roots" in the French Enlightenment, its consequences have been evident in twentieth-century fascist and communist assaults on Jews as foreign influences and "rootless cosmopolitans." The tactics of the Nazis and the Soviets served as a trap door. Those who opposed this sort of extreme nationalism were immediately perceived as enemies of the dictatorial state, and were fortunate if exile awaited them. At the other end, those Jews who wished only to serve their national and nationalist masters were viewed as intrinsically duplicitous, with ulterior and subversive motives. Those who opposed such raw-boned nationalism lost their privileges, while those who supported such efforts lost their Jewishness—whatever forms that may have taken in an ancestral generation.[8] The children of Enlightenment have taken a fancy to totalitarian visions, demanding complete national identity as the price of citizenship, an identity that excludes ancient traditions of Jewish Orthodoxy and modern tendencies to Zionism alike.[9] This is a critical pivot of early twenty-first-century theorizing. It broadens the base of antisemitism from its nourishment in totalitarian regimes, and conceives a general theory of Jewish "internationalism" as the dangerous enemy of both secular and clerical forms of nationalism. This tendency has also led to schisms between allies, such as the United States and Israel, on how best to cope with the final exodus from Europe into new homelands and new settlements in more hospitable and open Western societies.[10]

The Jewish Question as an American Question

A huge shift has occurred from the twentieth to the twenty-first century in where Jews live. Europe, not just Germany, is now largely emptied of its Jewish population. Indeed, Germany is one of the few European countries that have witnessed a modest return of Jews to live and work. Other than the United Kingdom, France, and—to a much smaller degree—other nations in the European Union, most Jews live in Israel and the United States; perhaps little more than two million still live outside these centers.[11] Nations as far removed from each other as Russia, South Africa, and Argentina have long-run trends toward Jewish depopulation and migration. The unique demographic composition of Jewish communities in Israel and the United States (both countries founded by refugees from European persecution) has allowed others to join anti-Zionism to anti-Americanism—to the disquiet (and in some instances, displeasure) of leaders in both nations. Despite the obvious, both the United States and Israel are reluctant to factor such considerations into policy decisions and recommendations, at least publicly. The ideological brew of New Leftist hatreds in democratic nations and old Rightist tendencies in autocratic nations creates a strong impulse to silence, hardly a potent means to dissolve the new alliances of old political enemies.

The United States has been a forthright and stalwart defender of Israel's right to exist as a nation, and, under its current president, has extended this to its right to defend itself against terrorism and external military threat. But the United States has also sought to play the role of honest broker. It has repeatedly—and, in recent years, insistently—argued the case for a Palestinian state, one freed of Israeli supervision or interference (but also of Arab-generated terrorism), while at home it urges a new Trinitarianism of Christian-Jewish-Muslim brotherhood. The new strategy is part of the idea of spreading democracy abroad by advancing multiculturalism at home.[12] But whatever its tactical advantages, the strategy has not curbed anti-American sentiments abroad, or terrorist assaults on its interests, especially in those parts of Europe with a heavy Arab-Muslim population. Moreover, the blending of anti-Zionism with anti-Americanism has allowed for new allies and friends of antisemitism to be recruited from the oppositional Left and isolationist Right and even the forging of a bizarre marriage between them. The Chomskys and the Finkelsteins are revered by neo-Nazis and by Communists.

It might be argued that the assault on globalization as the latest expression of American empire-building is none other than the classical attack on Zionism as the political expression of Jewish impulses toward world-domination. The conflation of Jewish impulses and American interests makes possible a reconfiguration of Left and Right, or at least a tactical fusion of the two. This is not exactly a new turn. I dealt with it in the 1970s under the guise of "Left-Wing Fascism."[13] Although the cast of characters has changed, the same analytical system keeps appearing, to the chagrin of liberals who would like to move Left and conservatives who would welcome moving Right. Indeed, it has become the essence of the struggle against Jews to see them as a threat that transcends conventional differences in political ideologies or economic doctrines.

From the Politics of Religion to the Religion of Politics

The climate of antisemitism has been transformed by linking Israel as a nation with Judaism as a religion. This has been largely a product of Muslim exclusivist belief that Israel is a thorn in the flesh of the Middle East nourished by a Hebrew religion and culture. Centuries of uneasy co-existence between Muslims and Jews have been displaced by outright animosity. The legion of assaults on Jews and Zionists in Arab Palestine, Muslim Iran, Syria, and even moderate Middle East states exhibits a vituperation that equals and in some cases exceeds the rhetoric of the Nazi era. Arabs, once importers of antisemitic ideology from Europe, are now in the export business: thus the flow of antisemitic caricature that emanates from non-Arab and non-Muslim Cuba (where perhaps there are fewer than 1,000 Jewish souls remaining) matches that of *Der Stürmer*. The demonizing of the Jewish people is now so linked with the very existence of Israel that a sense of alarm, if not outright fear, has gripped Jews worldwide, even those living in European enclaves considered exemplars of democracy. The risks transcend verbal abuse, and include explosions at Jewish centers of culture and Hebrew houses of worship that are reported but go unpunished. The statistics on a rising tide of antisemitism or "Judeophobia" in Europe are impressive; its Arabic sources are equally plain.

At the same time, a noticeable shift has taken place in Christian traditional sources: away from antisemitism and the usual canards about Jews' clannish behavior, greed in economic dealings, and world-domination through media control, to a far more nuanced, and in many instances, positive response to Jewish tradition and religious practices. To be sure, this shift has itself led to a certain unease in Jewish circles that see the threat of proselytization and conversion in this change of attitudes toward Judaism.

Still, whatever the ascribed motives, this shift has been pronounced within the Roman Catholic Church (especially in the papacy of John Paul II) and the Evangelical Churches. Many factors are involved in this change: from a sense that too little was done to oppose, much less prevent, the Holocaust, to a belief that the redemption of mankind must proceed through reconciliation of Jerusalem with Rome or Christendom in general. The influence of joint commissions and committees of Jewish and Christian groups, some religious, others committed to human rights, may not reach deep into the popular culture, but it has affected a stratum of the educated classes, and improved Jewish-Christian relations.

On the other hand, it is also true that movements within some denominations, such as Lutheranism, Presbyterianism, Episcopalianism, and (United) Methodism have taken a sharp turn away from such a conciliatory approach, to a generally critical view of Judaism and an overtly hostile approach to Israel. The politically liberal hierarchies of these churches support a wide range of left-of-center causes, from ordaining homosexual and lesbian ministers to boycotting Israeli goods and services. Although these liberal Protestants make *pro forma* distinctions between Israeli and Jewish elements in their (highly selective) assault on Israel, it strains credulity to assume that ordinary parishioners are capable of making clear-eyed distinctions between nations and cultures when their own church hierarchies appear incapable of doing so.

Add to the mix human rights organizations, ostensibly neutral, that have been increasingly partisan in their Middle East interventions. These range from criticizing United States internment policies of terrorists to assailing the Israeli presence in Gaza (until recently) and the West Bank (while taking virtually no account of the Arab hatred and violence that led to occupation in the first place). These non-governmental organizations, despite a small active membership, have tremendous cachet, and supply the media with orientations as well as ideas. They have managed to separate human rights from human obligations; still more, to define those deserving of reprimand in terms of presumed power. Such organizations posit an inverse relationship between actual power and rights. In such a universe, Israel is seen as a satellite of oppressor nations, especially the United States, and therefore not entitled to the benevolence lavished on the oppressed.

It is not acts committed that merit reprimand from such groups; it is the perpetrators. If actions are defined as efforts at liberation, then even the most hideous—such as suicide bombing and pogroms—are seen as not only legitimate but heroic. When a bus is exploded or other forms of mayhem are committed against Israelis, they are entitled to no more consideration than Americans fighting in Iraq. Both are seen as intruders in the heart of the Middle East. That such victims are Jewish has added expediency: the liquidation of the Jewish people is a continuation of acts performed routinely in the twentieth century. The fact that Jews collectively were targeted from 1933-45 by a group that, like the Palestinian Arabs, built its national identity on Jew-hatred serves to both justify those actions, and make them easier to accept emotionally. Jewish suffering may merit some sympathy, but Jewish militancy is seen almost a contradiction in terms, a betrayal of the stereotype of the conniving, but physically powerless Jew from the shtetl. In this way, the principles of even-handedness and democratic equity are perverted into a Manichean theological tradition, which serves as a battering ram of anti-Americanism and antisemitism alike.

The "New History" of Antisemitism

The sixty-year time frame since the end of World War II and the end of the Holocaust nightmare has had its own natural history: First, there was the disbelief in the magnitude of the murder of the Jews; second, an acknowledgement and appreciation of such depravity, with all of its political and religious implications; third, an airbrushing of the Holocaust as part of a routinization of genocide in the present age, especially massacres of innocents in Rwanda, Cambodia, Serbia; fourth, resentment at the idea of guilt as transmitted from the generation that committed acts of brutality to a generation presumably innocent of such acts; fifth, anger at Jews for seeking monetary and proprietary restitution for harms committed; sixth, and finally, *voilà*, the sneaking suspicion that maybe the Nazis and Communists were right all along in their disdain for, and ultimate assault on, the Jewish people as a nation, a culture, a religion.

This natural history is uniform neither across nations nor amongst peoples, nor does it foreclose on the usual variations on classical themes of antisemitism. But it does convey a progression—better, a regression—that has become the stock-in-trade of the new century. It is a pattern often aided and abetted by Jews themselves, as the essays in this volume abundantly demonstrate. One branch of their operation consists of endless variations on the Israel-Nazi equation and (as corollary to it) the Arab-Jewish equation, a licentiousness that bears witness to the nimbleness of what Cynthia Ozick has called the Arabs' campaign to attach themselves to the mournful coattails of the Jewish history of discrimination, oppression, and murder. This is not a pretty picture—nor an easy one to grasp in its entirety.

Perhaps it is best to have recourse to examples and illustrations, imperfect though they may be. One incident that brought the Jewish divide over Israel to the storm center of recent history began in a relatively obscure corner of Haifa University. A fifty-five-year-old graduate student, one Teddy Katz, claimed to document a massacre of 200 unarmed civilians by the Haganah—the pre-state army of Israel—at a village called Tantura, near Haifa. As Professor Fania Oz-Salzberger - a senior lecturer in that university - pointed out, this charge "to put it plainly is false. Mr. Katz's thesis was based almost entirely on transcriptions of oral interviews he conducted with elderly Palestinian former residents of Tantura, who allegedly witnessed a massacre of their kin by Jewish soldiers... a district court ruled that the empirical evidence was grossly manipulated in the course of transliterating the tapes. Mr. Katz had put words in the mouths of his interviewees that were never uttered." Even after the author of the thesis recanted, a senior lecturer in political science at Haifa, Ilan Pappe, a member of the (Hadash) Communist Party and dedicated propagator of the view that Israel was conceived in "sin," continued to support Katz's flawed scholarship.[14]

Since everything that happens in Israel is viewed through a powerful magnifying glass, a local and relatively trivial matter was soon transformed into an international affair, and the alleged persecution of Pappe by Haifa was used by the British Association of University Teachers (AUT) to justify its decision to boycott the university for alleged collusion with Israeli authorities to white-wash the history of Zionism. (In fact, despite his violation of all ethical standards of academic life, Pappe was neither expelled nor even censured.) The wording of this effort to isolate Israeli academics (Bar Ilan University was also targeted) is extraordinary for its breadth and vituperation. The AUT demands "in the spirit of international solidarity" that scholars worldwide abandon any form of academic and cultural cooperation, collaboration or joint projects with Israeli institutions, suspend all forms of subsidy to them, and withdraw investments already made. (It is worth noting that the impact of antisemitic academic chatter in the United States pales in comparison to the English effort to concoct devices for isolating Israel and punishing normal discourse among academics. Little wonder that in a 2004 poll the British expressed the view that Israel was the main impediment to peace in the Middle East and also the least attractive nation in the region.)

Radical critiques of Israel by its Jewish detractors tend to delegitimize the country and even the Jewish people. Benny Morris, leader of the Israeli "New Historians" and subject of Efraim Karsh's essay in this book, perfunctorily acknowledges Arab culpability for the 1948 war, yet reserves his main shafts for Israeli policy. He continues to portray Israeli proprietary claims as the main trigger of the Palestinian exodus. Morris explains that the essence of his work "is not a history of the 1948 war or a history of what the Arabs did to the Jews but a history of how and why the Palestinian refugee problem came about. In this context, what Jews did to Arabs, including massacres, played a role; what Arabs did to Jews was barely relevant." The conflation of poor theory, liberal condescension towards the Arabs, and revanchist zeal (not to mention widespread European publishing support for such efforts) is transparent.[15]

As long ago as 1936 the Labor Zionist leader Berl Katznelson, as noted earlier in this book, expressed his fear that even in the Land of Israel a Jewish child might catch "the virus of self-hate." But in the volatile current circumstances it was perhaps inevitable that some Jews, in Israel as well as the Diaspora, would hear the siren call of the "new" antisemitism, and be infected by it. This is especially the case for the Jew whose primary allegiance is to secular agencies and institutions. He must at least appear even-handed in criticizing human rights abuses (which isolates him from potential allies in the Middle East) and yet must make appeals to evidence and accuracy (which isolates him from the more fanatical extremes of religious zealots insisting that the world must rid itself of the Jewish nation-state).

Isaac Bashevis Singer once said that amnesia was the only disease from which Jews did not suffer; but Singer was wrong. In 1930, Michael Gold, in the classic novel of urban social protest, wrote of *Jews Without Money*, whereas the pressing concern early in the twenty-first century is Jews without memory, victims of historical amnesia. It is one thing to identify Jewish interests with those of the poor and the downtrodden, as in the proletarian thirties, quite another to identify Jewish interests with those intent on the destruction of the Jewish people and the Israeli state in the new millennium. Jewish participation in the delegitimation of Israel and its rights to national survival betrays solidarity and scholarship alike. The question of antisemitism goes to the heart of the Jewish capacity to survive and thrive. It requires clear-sighted recognition that Jewish interests and "universal" ones are not always in perfect alignment, albeit without succumbing to the delusion harbored by many of Israel's Jewish accusers—that putting an end to the Jewish state will not only save them from blushing but usher in the messianic era of universal peace and plenty.

Notes

1. Sander L. Gilman, *Jewish Self-Hatred: Anti-Semitism and the Hidden Language of the Jews* (Baltimore, MD and London: The Johns Hopkins University Press, 1986).
2. I owe a great personal debt to the pioneering efforts of my late colleague, Werner J. Cahnman. His essays and papers on *Jews and Gentiles: A Historical Sociology of Their Relations*, edited by Judith T. Marcus and Zoltan Tarr (New Brunswick, NJ and London: Transaction Publishers, 2003) are a goldmine of information, insight and theory.
3. Arthur Blech, *The Causes of Anti-Semitism: A Critique of the Bible* (New York: Select Books, 2005).
4. Selma Stern, *The Court Jew: A Contribution to the History of Absolutism in Europe* (New Brunswick, NJ and London: Transaction Publishers, 1984).
5. Arthur Hertzberg, *The French Enlightenment and the Jews* (New York: Columbia University Press, 1990).
6. Shmuel Trigano, "Is There a Future for French Jewry?" *Azure*, Spring 2005, .45-61.
7. David Pryce-Jones, "Jews, Arabs, and French Diplomacy," *Commentary*, May 2005, 27-45.
8. Robert S. Wistrich, *Between Redemption and Perdition: Modern Antisemitism and Jewish Identity* (London: Routledge, 1990).
9. Jacob Katz, *Toward Modernity: The European Jewish Model* (New Brunswick, NJ and London: Transaction Publishers, 1987).
10. Irving Louis Horowitz, "Left-Wing Fascism: An Infantile Disorder," *Society*, May-June 1981, 19-24
11. Sergio della Pergola, "World Jewish Population 2002," in *American Jewish Year Book* ed. David Singer (New York: American Jewish Committee, 2002), 102-04.
12. Fred A. Lazin, *The Struggle for Soviet Jewry in American Politics: Israel versus the American Jewish Establishment* (Lanham, MD: Lexington Books, 2005).
13. Irving Louis Horowitz, "The Context of Policy and the Policy of Context: American Resolve and Israeli Legitimacy. *St. Croix Review,* October 2004, 57-64.
14. Fania Oz-Salzberger, "Israelis Need Not Apply," *Wall Street Journal*, May 8, 2005.
15. The literature of the New Historians varies in quality and degree of vituperation. Its leading lights are Benny Morris, whose work is discussed by Efraim Karsh in this book; second in importance in this enterprise is Avi Shlaim, *Collusion Across the Jordan* (New York: Columbia University Press, 1988). Then there is the aforementioned Ilan Pappe, *The Making of the Arab-Israeli Conflict, 1947-1951* (London: I.B. Tauris, 1992). An early and devastating critique of the new historians is Shabtai Teveth's "Charging Israel with Original Sin," *Commentary*, September 1989.

Contributors

Edward Alexander is professor of English at University of Washington in Seattle. He is the author of numerous books and essays on Victorian literature and Jewish subjects. His most recent publications are: *The Jewish Wars: Reflections By One of the Belligerents* (Southern Illinois University Press), 1996; *Irving Howe—Socialist, Critic, Jew* (Indiana University Press, 1998); *Classical Liberalism and the Jewish Tradition* (Transaction Publishers, 2003); scholarly editions of J. S. Mill's *On Liberty* (Broadview) and *The Subjection of Women* (Transaction); a monograph entitled "Lionel Trilling and Irving Howe: A Literary Friendship," in *New England Review* (Autumn 2004).

Benjamin Balint is associate editor of *Azure*, the quarterly journal of the Shalem Center in Jerusalem. He has contributed articles to *Commentary*, where he was assistant editor, and to the *Weekly Standard*, the *Forward*, the *Jerusalem Post*, *Ha'aretz*, and *Judaism*.

Paul Bogdanor, a writer living in London, England, has written for *Judaism*, the *Jewish Chronicle,* and the *Middle East Quarterly*.

Irving Louis Horowitz is University Professor and Hannah Arendt Distinguished Professor of Sociology and Political Science at Rutgers University.

Rael Jean Isaac has published two books—*Israel Divided* (Johns Hopkins University Press) and *Party and Politics in Israel* (Longman)—and many articles on Israeli politics. Her work has appeared in the *Wall Street Journal*, *American Spectator*, *Politique Internationale*.

Efraim Karsh is head of Mediterranean Studies at King's College, London University, and the author of many books and essays about the Middle East.

Menachem Kellner is Wolfson Professor of Jewish Thought at the University of Haifa. His recent publications include: *Must a Jew Believe Anything?* (1999), *Perush Ralbag le-Shir ha-Shirim* [Hebrew] (2003) and *Maimonides' Book of Love* (2004).

Martin Krossel is a Canadian freelance journalist living in the New York City area. His work has appeared in periodicals in both Canada and the United States.

Alan Mittleman is professor of Jewish Philosophy at the Jewish Theological Seminary and director of its Louis Finkelstein Institute for Religious and Social Studies. He is the author of several books on German Jewish philosophy and the editor of a three volume series on the political engagement of American Jews.

Jacob Neusner is Research Professor of Theology at Bard College, Member of the Institute of Advanced Study, Princeton, and life member of Clare Hall, Cambridge University. He holds nine honorary degrees and fourteen academic medals, and has published many books.

Cynthia Ozick is a novelist and essayist.

Alvin Rosenfeld, professor of English and Jewish Studies at Indiana University, is the author of *A Double Dying: Reflections on Holocaust Literature, Imagining Hitler*, and *Thinking About the Holocaust After Half a Century*. He was named by President George W. Bush to the United States Holocaust Memorial Council in May 2002.

David G. Roskies is the Sol and Evelyn Henkind Professor in Yiddish Literature and Culture at the Jewish Theological Seminary. Among his books are *Against the Apocalypse: Responses to Catastrophe in Modern Jewish Culture* (1984), which won the Ralph Waldo Emerson Prize from Phi Beta Kappa, a companion volume, *The Literature of Destruction* (1989), and *A Bridge of Longing: The Lost Art of Yiddish Storytelling* (1995). His most recent book is *The Jewish Search for a Usable Past* (1999).

Assaf Sagiv is associate editor of *Azure*.

Index

contribute to "new" antisemitism, xvii,
23-24, 33, 43, 70, 85, 105, 116-17, 121-
23, 136, 138, 147-50, 154-55, 196,
234, 239-40, 265
deny antisemitism, xix-xx, 4-6, 10-11,
105, 136, 226, 228
display cowardice, xxiv, 6, 124-25, 206,
216
embrace Christian supersessionism, xxi,
xxiii, 49, 54-56, 70, 183
endorse anti-Jewish violence, xx, 28, 43,
81, 122-23, 145-46, 154-55, 213, 231
equate Israel with Nazis, xviii, xxii, 3,
22, 27-28, 36, 38, 42, 78, 88, 93, 105,
115, 116, 117-18, 135-36, 146, 174,
177, 178, 190n, 200
equate Zionism with apartheid, 22-23, 28-
29, 32n, 80, 122, 125
espouse "prophetic" Judaism, xiii, 21-22,
56, 180-82, 183-84, 214, 244
express utopian fantasies, xxiii, 35, 60-
61, 66, 81-82, 125, 209, 231
find Jewish identity in anti-Zionism, xvii,
21, 29-30, 48, 51-53, 177-90, 243-44
suffer shame, xii, xv, 1-2, 4-5, 20, 65-71,
135
urge erasure of Israel, xxiv, 30-31, 38,
51-52, 60, 65-71, 79-82, 137-38

Jabes, Edmond, 47
Jabotinsky, Vladimir, 80, 137, 252-53
Jackson, Robert, 189
Jay, Martin, xv, 200-06
Jenin, 129, 131, 144, 169, 204-05
Jerusalem, 2, 9, 23, 36, 44, 55, 67, 87, 101,
102, 123, 125, 126, 173, 199, 203, 209,
221, 269
Jewish Theological Seminary, 193n
Joffe, Josef, xxvin, 199-200
Jordan, 41, 82, 84, 85, 91, 95, 118, 119-
20, 129, 141, 143, 209, 224, 225, 230,
254-56
Judaism, xiv, xvi, xviii, xxi, xxii, xxiii, xxiv,
3, 8, 10, 15, 17, 19, 21-22, 29, 34, 35,
39, 43, 48-54, 56, 58, 66, 70, 118, 113-
24, 127, 168, 172, 174, 175, 177-90,
195, 214, 216, 222, 244, 269-70
Judt, Tony, xv, xxiii, xxiv, 27, 65-71, 171,
197

Kafka, Franz, 53
Kaganovich, Lazar, 265
Kaplan, Esther, 30
Karsh, Efraim, 225, 272
Kasher, Asa, 40
Kasrils, Ronnie, 126
Katz, Teddy, 271
Katznelson, Berl, 35, 42, 272
Kaye/Kantrowitz, Melanie, 30
Kazin, Alfred, 18
Kennedy, John F., 236
Khaddoumi, Farouk, 84
Kimchi, David, 184
Kimmerling, Baruch, 38, 42, 115
Klein, Morton, 113n
Klepfisz, Irena, 29, 30
Klutznick, Philip, 212, 217n
Kosinski, Jerzy, 148
Kovel, Joel, 29
Kratzer, Myron, 234
Kraus, Karl, xvii
Krauthammer, Charles, 231
Kushner, Tony, 28

Lander, Brad, 30
Laqueur, Walter, 90, 137, 253
Lassalle, Ferdinand, xvi-xvii
Lebanon, 21, 35, 36, 67, 78, 85-90, 99, 100-
01, 104, 118, 120-21, 125, 127-28, 146,
219, 221, 223, 225, 227
Ledeen, Michael, 239, 244
Leff, Laurel, 13-14
Leibowitz, Yeshayahu, xviii, 22, 36, 43, 115,
125
Lerner, Michael, xii-xiv, xx, 202
Lessing, Theodor, 265
Levi, Primo, 148, 155n
Levin, Kenneth, 25-26
Lewis, Anthony, 35, 36
Lewis, Bernard, 224
Lewy, Guenter, 149
Libya, 98, 101, 129
Lilienthal, Alfred, xxiv
Lindemann, Albert, 201-03
Lippmann, Walter, 15, 20
Lipset, Seymour M., 26-27
Lipstadt, Deborah E., 148
London Review of Books, xix, 4, 170, 197
Luttwak, Edward, xxiv